A

Philip E. Lilienthal

BOOK

The Philip E. Lilienthal imprint
honors special books
in commemoration of a man whose work
at University of California Press from 1954 to 1979
was marked by dedication to young authors
and to high standards in the field of Asian Studies.
Friends, family, authors, and foundations have together
endowed the Lilienthal Fund, which enables UC Press
to publish under this imprint selected books
in a way that reflects the taste and judgment
of a great and beloved editor.

The publisher gratefully acknowledges the generous support of the Philip E. Lilienthal Asian Studies Endowment Fund of the University of California Press Foundation, which was established by a major gift from Sally Lilienthal.

MORAL NATION

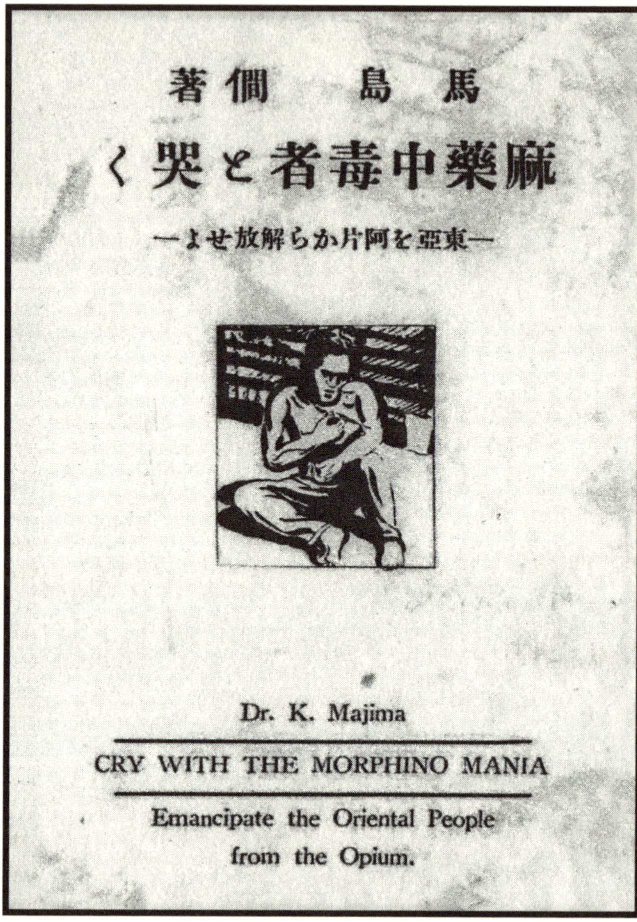

馬島僴著

麻藥中毒者と哭く

—東亞を阿片から解放せよ—

Dr. K. Majima

CRY WITH THE MORPHINO MANIA

Emancipate the Oriental People from the Opium.

Frontispiece. Title page of Majima Kan, *Mayaku chūdokusha to naku*. SOURCE: Majima Kan, *Mayaku chūdokusha to naku: Tō-A wo ahen kara kaikō seyo* (Tokyo: Ajia seisaku kenkyūjo, 1935).

Miriam Kingsberg •

MORAL NATION

Modern Japan and Narcotics in Global History

University of California Press

Berkeley Los Angeles London

University of California Press, one of the most distinguished university presses in the United States, enriches lives around the world by advancing scholarship in the humanities, social sciences, and natural sciences. Its activities are supported by the UC Press Foundation and by philanthropic contributions from individuals and institutions. For more information, visit www.ucpress.edu.

University of California Press
Berkeley and Los Angeles, California

University of California Press, Ltd.
London, England

Library of Congress Cataloging-in-Publication Data

Kingsberg, Miriam, 1981–.
Moral nation : modern Japan and narcotics in global history / Miriam Kingsberg.
pages cm (Asia: Local Studies / Global Themes, 29)
Includes bibliographical references and index.
ISBN 978-0-520-27673-4 (cloth : alk. paper)
ISBN 978-0-520-95748-0 (e-book)
1. Drug abuse—Social aspects—Japan—History. 2. Drug traffic—Japan—History. 3. Japan—Moral conditions. 4. Japan—Civilization—1868– I. Title.
HV5840.J3K56 2013
362.29'30952—dc23 2013031720

Manufactured in the United States of America

21 20 19 18 17 16 15 14
10 9 8 7 6 5 4 3 2 1

In keeping with a commitment to support environmentally responsible and sustainable printing practices, UC Press has printed this book on Natures Natural, a fiber that contains 30% post-consumer waste and meets the minimum requirements of ANSI/NISO Z39.48-1992 (R 1997) (*Permanence of Paper*).

ASIA: LOCAL STUDIES/GLOBAL THEMES

Jeffrey N. Wasserstrom, Kären Wigen, and Hue-Tam Ho Tai, Editors

1. *Bicycle Citizens: The Political World of the Japanese Housewife,* by Robin M. LeBlanc
2. *The Nanjing Massacre in History and Historiography,* edited by Joshua A. Fogel
3. *The Country of Memory: Remaking the Past in Late Socialist Vietnam,* by Hue-Tam Ho Tai
4. *Chinese Femininities/Chinese Masculinities: A Reader,* edited by Susan Brownell and Jeffrey N. Wasserstrom
5. *Chinese Visions of Family and State, 1915–1953,* by Susan L. Glosser
6. *An Artistic Exile: A Life of Feng Zikai (1898–1975),* by Geremie R. Barmé
7. *Mapping Early Modern Japan: Space, Place, and Culture in the Tokugawa Period, 1603–1868,* by Marcia Yonemoto
8. *Republican Beijing: The City and Its Histories,* by Madeleine Yue Dong
9. *Hygienic Modernity: Meanings of Health and Disease in Treaty-Port China,* by Ruth Rogaski

10. *Marrow of the Nation: A History of Sport and Physical Culture in Republican China*, by Andrew D. Morris
11. *Vicarious Language: Gender and Linguistic Modernity in Japan*, by Miyako Inoue
12. *Japan in Print: Information and Nation in the Early Modern Period*, by Mary Elizabeth Berry
13. *Millennial Monsters: Japanese Toys and the Global Imagination*, by Anne Allison
14. *After the Massacre: Commemoration and Consolation in Ha My and My Lai*, by Heonik Kwon
15. *Tears from Iron: Cultural Responses to Famine in Nineteenth-Century China*, by Kathryn Edgerton-Tarpley
16. *Speaking to History: The Story of King Goujian in Twentieth-Century China*, by Paul A. Cohen
17. *A Malleable Map: Geographies of Restoration in Central Japan, 1600–1912*, by Kären Wigen
18. *Coming to Terms with the Nation: Ethnic Classification in Modern China*, by Thomas S. Mullaney
19. *Fabricating Consumers: The Sewing Machine in Modern Japan*, by Andrew Gordon
20. *Recreating Japanese Men*, edited by Sabine Frühstück and Anne Walthall
21. *Selling Women: Prostitution, Markets, and the Household in Early Modern Japan*, by Amy Stanley

22. *Imaging Disaster: Tokyo and the Visual Culture of Japan's Great Earthquake of 1923*, by Gennifer Weisenfeld
23. *Taiko Boom: Japanese Drumming in Place and Motion*, by Shawn Bender
24. *Anyuan: Mining China's Revolutionary Tradition*, by Elizabeth J. Perry
25. *Mabiki: Infanticide and Population Growth in Eastern Japan, 1660–1950*, by Fabian Drixler
26. *The Missionary's Curse and Other Tales from a Chinese Catholic Village*, by Henrietta Harrison
27. *The Nature of the Beasts: Empire and Exhibition at the Tokyo Imperial Zoo*, by Ian Jared Miller
28. *Go Nation: Chinese Masculinities and the Game of Weiqi in China*, by Marc L. Moskowitz
29. *Moral Nation: Modern Japan and Narcotics in Global History*, by Miriam Kingsberg

To my family

CONTENTS

ILLUSTRATIONS

FIGURES

MAP

TABLES

ACKNOWLEDGMENTS

I have long anticipated publicly thanking the people who have made it possible for me to write this book. At Berkeley, where I was fortunate to receive my graduate training, Andrew Barshay supervised this project in its early stages and facilitated my development as an independent researcher. Wen-hsin Yeh made me welcome in the China field; Steve Vogel, in social science. No one is more responsible for teaching me how to think, write, and be in the academic profession than Mary Elizabeth Berry. The critical interlocutor inside my head speaks in her voice.

In Japan, Nakami Tatsuo, Enatsu Yoshiki, Katō Kiyofumi, and Matsushige Mitsuhiro opened many doors for me. During my year in China, Zhang Fuhe and Yamamoto Yū assisted me with archival materials and navigating the research landscape in Beijing, Dalian, and Shenyang. Meg Rithmire became a lifelong friend during many trips around Dongbei, some fruitful, others simply freezing. I am also grateful for her assistance and companionship during my time in Cambridge. A two-year appointment to the Harvard Academy for International and Area Studies allowed me to completely reimagine this project. Jorge Domínguez, Kathleen Hoover, Larry Winnie, and above all Elizabeth McGuire helped me to enjoy as well as endure the process. The Academy also supported a one-day workshop on my manuscript, attended by the late Barbara Brooks, David Courtright, Frank Dikötter, Andy Gordon, Arthur Kleinman, and Bob Tadashi Wakabayashi. I particularly thank David for sharing his expertise in global drug studies, and Bob for saving me from embarrassing errors of language and fact. Frank strongly supported the publication of this book. I was not able to incorporate all his suggestions into the final version, but he, David Ambaras, and an anonymous reviewer at the University of California Press gave me much to consider at the end of my revisions.

Others who read and provided feedback on part or all of the manuscript include Corey Brooks, Céline Dauverd, Harold Kingsberg, Renée Kingsberg, Jie Li, Reo Matsuzaki, Elizabeth McGuire, Janis Mimura, Lisa Onaga, Meg Rithmire, Caroline Shaw, Norman Smith, Emily Wilcox, and Marcia Yonemoto. Fellow panelists at annual meetings of the Alcohol and Drug History Society, American Historical Association, and Association for Asian Studies, and participants in workshops and talks at Berkeley, Boulder, Brandeis, Chicago, Harvard, William and Mary, the University of Warwick, Korea University, Chulalongkorn University, and Waseda University challenged me to articulate and defend my ideas. For their kind interest in my project, I particularly thank Susan Burns, Mark Driscoll, Alexis Dudden, Henrietta Harrison, Chris Hess, Ann Jannetta, Bill Johnston, Sean Lei, Jim Mills, Caroline Reeves, John Schrecker, Franziska Seraphim, Ron Suleski, Julia Thomas, Elise Tipton, Caroline Tsai, Jeff Wasserstrom, and Louise Young.

I am also grateful to librarians and archivists at Berkeley, Boulder, Harvard, the Library of Congress, the National Archives and Records Administration, the National Diet Library of Japan, the University of Tokyo, Waseda University, the Tokyo Metropolitan Library, the Yokohama City Library, Tōyō Bunkō, the Liaoning Provincial Archive, the Dalian City Library, the National Library of China, Academia Sinica, and the British Library. From initial contact through publication, Niels Hooper and Kim Hogeland at the University of California Press have worked hard to realize my vision for this book. Eiko Kimbrough kindly secured the necessary permissions for images in Japan.

My colleagues in the history department at the University of Colorado took on a heavy burden in hiring a new graduate with no publication record or teaching experience. For giving me every chance for a successful career and rich life, I especially thank Céline Dauverd, Susan Kent, Kwangmin Kim, Sungyun Lim, Tim Weston, and John Willis. Above all, Marcia Yonemoto guided me through my first few years as a faculty member and let no opportunity pass to encourage and inspire by example. Friends are happily too numerous to list, but I must name Emily Wilcox, my confidante in all matters academic and personal; and Corey Brooks, a model of intellectual curiosity and human decency.

I owe the largest debt to my family. My parents taught me to read books, take trips, ask questions, and use my imagination. How could I not become a historian? Of everything they have given me, the greatest gifts are my siblings and best friends,

Jess and Harold Kingsberg. I particularly thank my multitalented brother, whose pragmatic assistance included running regressions, generating graphs and tables, and reading multiple drafts of the entire manuscript to banish weak argumentation, sloppy organization, and run-on sentences. My uncle, Warren Gordon, has been a source of unconditional love and support throughout.

The Blakemore-Freeman Foundation enabled me to undertake a year of Japanese language study at the Inter-University Center in Yokohama. Foreign Language and Area Studies academic year and summer awards allowed me to develop proficiency in Chinese at Berkeley and the Inter-University Program in Beijing. The Japan Foundation, Fulbright-IIE, and the Social Science Research Council supported my research at the dissertation stage. Through the SSRC Book Fellowship, I began rethinking my work as a manuscript. I also gratefully acknowledge the assistance of the Association for Asian Studies Northeast Asia and China and Inner Asia Councils, Institute for East Asian Studies (Berkeley), the Center for Asian Studies (Boulder), the Dean's Fund for Excellence (Boulder), and the Department of History (Berkeley and Boulder). A Eugene M. Kayden Research Grant defrayed the costs of production.

Most of chapter 1 appeared in "Abstinent Nation, Addicted Empire: Opium and Japan in the Meiji Period," *Social History of Alcohol and Drugs: An Interdisciplinary Journal* 25 (2011): 88–106. Chapter 7 was published in a slightly different form as "Legitimating Empire, Legitimating Nation: The Scientific Study of Opium Addiction in Japanese Manchuria," *Journal of Japanese Studies* 38, no. 2 (2012): 329–55. Chapter 9 appeared as "Methamphetamine Solution: Drugs and the Reconstruction of Nation in Postwar Japan," *Journal of Asian Studies* 76, no. 1 (Feb. 2013): 141–62. Material from various chapters has also been published in "Status and Smoke: Koreans in Japan's Opium Empire," in *Mobile Subjects: Boundaries and Identities in Modern Korean Diasporas*, edited by Wen-hsin Yeh (Berkeley: Institute for East Asian Studies, 2013), 38–60. I thank the aforementioned venues for permission to reprint my work here.

I take full responsibility for all faults and shortcomings in this book.

Boulder, Colorado
March 2013

MAP 1.

The narcotic empire in 1932. Map created by Lohnes+Wright.

INTRODUCTION · The Moral Nation

One winter day in 1934, an elegantly muffled, elderly Chinese gentleman entered a Japanese police station in Harbin, the northernmost major city in the two-year-old state of Manchukuo. In a gloved hand, he held the long, rusty shackles with which he had chained his son, who trailed behind "as if he were a slave." With tears in his eyes, the father begged the assembled officers to lock up the youth. Laughing at the odd spectacle, the police shook their heads and hustled the pair outside into the snow. A moment later, the son broke free of his parent's grasp, reentered the station, and pleaded for a month or so of jail time "as the sole means of curing him" of his addiction to narcotics.

The British reporter who described the scene could scarcely believe his eyes, professing amazement that "such a horrid thing [drug consumption] is being openly allowed in a country aspiring to a place among the civilized nations of the world."[1] By the time this incident took place, "civilization" had long functioned as the defining justification of nationhood. Initially determined by the great powers of Europe, the criteria of civilization embraced a litany of political, economic, and social customs, practices, and beliefs associated with the moving target of "modernity."[2] Civilization was also a moral condition, and challenges to the legitimacy of the state were moral attacks, implying deficiencies in the values of a national community.[3]

Given its constantly evolving nature, civilization could never be achieved, even by its framers. Crises of legitimacy thus erupted frequently throughout the world during the era of nation building.[4] The response to these convulsions often took the form of a moral crusade: a sudden spike of concern for the welfare of society provoked by a phenomenon seen to represent a collapse in collective values.[5] At the forefront of these movements, "moral entrepreneurs" arose to define and police national norms consonant with civilized statehood. In the late nineteenth and early twentieth centuries, moral entrepreneurs encompassed a steadily widening cohort of socially engaged government officials and professionals, including cultural producers, the media, businessmen (and women), law enforcement, scientists, doctors, and others. By stigmatizing, pathologizing, criminalizing, and finally eliminating "deviants" who threatened to undermine civilization, moral entrepreneurs reestablished the legitimacy of the nation. Although their crusades were inherently temporary, many left behind human and institutional legacies that allowed moral entrepreneurs to repeatedly revive the specter of deviance, buttressing their own status and influence.

Banned consciousness-altering substances, or narcotics, have long incited moral crusades and served as an important site for the assertion of legitimate nationhood.[6] Why have drugs acquired such significance in modern history?[7] Beginning in the sixteenth century, a global "psychoactive revolution" spread not only mind-altering agents but also capitalist practices and mentalities that gave them new meaning. In the early phases of globalization, intercontinental networks produced by commodity markets provided emergent nations with new means of conceptualizing and consolidating their authority. Nongovernment actors, including the professional disciplines, accrued and exercised influence in ways that both challenged and reinforced state building. Collaboration between public and private interests expanded the trade in drugs, generating the revenue that enabled the West to place most of Asia under imperial domination. Empire became an indispensable appendage of the legitimate nation-state.[8]

Narcotics were only one commodity among many within the psychoactive revolution, and globalization more generally. What set drugs apart from sugar, tea, tobacco, pepper, rubber, rice, and other goods that might have served as the focal point of moral crusades?[9] The nations that framed civilization in Western Europe believed that narcotics, alone among these products, produced physiological dependence among the subjects of precisely those states whose legitimacy they wished to deny. Although citizens of the great powers copiously consumed intoxicants, including opium, they nonetheless associated the practice of smoking the drug with "Oriental" populations seen as incapable of self-sovereignty. The Chinese youth in shackles at the Japanese police station in Harbin was the flesh-and-blood embodiment of the enchainment of mind, body, and race at a time when the free nation was defined in opposition to the deeply controversial reality of slavery.[10] Lacking meaningful volition, self-control, and biological fitness, so-called "slaves of the poppy" were thought incapable of political subjectivity, needing a master to govern them or a liberator to save them.[11] Either role offered an ambitious imperial power a pretext for expanding its sovereignty.

In Japan, a non-Western state seeking to avoid colonization at the height of European and American empire building, the ideological resonances of opium virtually predetermined its emergence as a symbol of deviance. During Japan's first century of participation in modern international society, from signing unequal treaties with the great powers in the 1850s through reasserting its independence in the 1950s, the nation experienced three crises of political legitimacy that provoked successively escalating moral crusades against narcotics.

The Sino-Japanese War of 1894–95 ignited the first episode. Japan's military victory, unanticipated by most of the world, overturned a regional balance of power of several millennia, and with it the nation's understanding of its place in the international hierarchy of states. Forty years earlier, the great powers had humiliated and reduced China to semicolonial status following the Opium War, brought on by the Qing government's unsuccessful effort to suppress British drug trafficking. Capitalizing on this negative example, Japan insisted that nineteenth-century trade treaties with the West provide for voluntary export restrictions on narcotics. In the 1890s, scholars, reporters, bureaucrats, judicial authorities, and other elites applied the globally ubiquitous language of social Darwinism to portray opium smoking as the consequence of Sinic racial inferiority and degeneracy, and the cause of China's defeat by Japan. Narcotics, viewed as unhygienic, feudal, inefficient, irrational, ignorant, offensive, vulgar, barbaric, and backward, united in a single issue all conceivable threats to modern civilization and statehood. By asserting its abstinence from opium, Japan sought to "leave" a benighted, politically vulnerable Asia and "enter" the West. In accepting the state to the fraternity of great powers on these terms, Europe and the United States affirmed the rejection of opium as a standard of civilization and upheld Japan's right to participate in framing norms for legitimate nationhood.

The Sino-Japanese War also transformed Japan into a formal empire. The Treaty of Shimonoseki, which restored peace between the two belligerents, shifted sovereignty over the island of Taiwan from China to Japan. In the late nineteenth century, the legitimate nation was an imperial nation, and possession of a new colony undergirded Japan's rising status within international society. Yet Taiwan, with nearly two hundred thousand opium smokers out of a total population of less than three million, threatened the very foundations of Japanese identity. How could a state predicated on abstinence from narcotics administer a colony of drug users? Moral entrepreneurs, including bureaucrats, doctors, journalists, and military officers, sought to formulate a "civilized" response to the Taiwan opium economy. Although some advocated the strict and immediate prohibition of drugs, dissenters feared that forceful and unprecedented state intervention in local customs might provoke popular resistance. A few even suggested the public sale of opium as a potential source of revenue for the financially strapped imperial administration. The establishment of a government monopoly—a feature of narcotics regulation in the European colonies of Southeast Asia—at last achieved consensus as the most enlightened policy. Declaring its commitment to suppressing opium gradually, the state indefinitely delayed the eradication of smoking. In the interim, public drug sales supplied an increasing percentage of the colonial budget, relieving Taiwan's financial dependence on metropolitan Japan. The Western powers applauded this strategy, which implicitly sanctioned their own lucrative opium monopolies as a hallmark of legitimate imperial rule.

Although the enactment of ideologically satisfactory and economically beneficial drug regulation in Taiwan brought Japan's first moral crusade against narcotics to an end by the turn of the twentieth century, the institutional and intellectual legacies of the episode virtually predetermined its recurrence. For moral entrepreneurs, opium represented a "crisis *[kiki]*" in its literal sense of "dangerous opportunity." Their own power and influence rested upon the ability to demonstrate Japan's ongoing need for protection from opium-smoking Others. Their response to the narcotic economy of Taiwan fatefully shaped future drug policy options in the Japanese home islands, the expanding empire, and beyond. In 1905, when Japan established a protectorate over Korea and took control of the Kwantung Leased Territory (KLT) in southern Manchuria, it adopted modified versions of the narcotics regulatory regime in Taiwan, resulting—despite the purported aim of gradual suppression—in the rapid growth of the local opiate market.[12] Within two decades, colonial Korea emerged as the "global capital of morphine," while the KLT port handled the second-highest volume of banned drugs in the world, after Shanghai.[13]

The high imperial age, spanning the period between the end of World War I and Japan's defeat in World War II, witnessed the most protracted, intense moral crusade against narcotics in Japanese history. In contrast to the 1890s, when moral entrepreneurs inflated the importance of a statistically small phenomenon, this second episode was not unjustified by the actual dimensions of the illicit drug economy. Rather, moral entrepreneurs misrepresented a very real crisis as a means of justifying the

Japanese nation and empire in a moment of shifting criteria for political legitimacy. In the wake of World War I, under pressure from increasingly discontented subjects, the great powers determined to prepare their colonies for eventual independence. This liberal ideal gave new purpose to the mission to civilize, the traditional "humanitarian" rationalization of empire as a means of improving the local environment and racial "fitness" of subjects.[14]

In imperial Japan, the goal of preparing colonial populations for self-government prompted the emergence of an ideology of benevolence or benevolent government *(jinsei)*. Benevolence melded traditional neo-Confucian notions of proper relations among status unequals to the display of civilization by civilizing the Other. Fraught with ambiguity and greeted with ambivalence by the Japanese and their subjects, benevolence generally exerted only an indirect impact on policy. As a justification of imperial legitimacy, however, it underwent considerable elaboration in the interwar years. Moral entrepreneurs offered a stereotype of the opium addict as the object of Japan's benevolent quest to liberate subjects from their enslavement to narcotics. The "drug user," a value-neutral consumer of opiates, furnished the basis for imagining the deviant "addict."[15] In the KLT city-state, where narcotics consumption reached globally unprecedented levels, drug users were heterogeneous in their choice of substance, mode of ingestion, and demographic profile. In formulating a politically useful depiction of the addict, however, moral entrepreneurs distorted, deemphasized, or simply disregarded their own data on drug users. The addict they presented was a Chinese opium smoker, whose habit was, tautologically, both the source and the result of racial degeneracy.

Imperial stereotypes of the addict were neither homogenous nor stable over time. Some moral entrepreneurs viewed addicts as virulent and incorrigible deviants fortuitously dispatched by natural selection; others hoped that treatment might save them and their race from the workings of social Darwinism. Many were zealots, more moved by righteous indignation than objective evidence. At the other end of the spectrum, pragmatists sought power and profit by working to reduce the "contagion" of addiction.

The plurality of addict stereotypes reflected the diversity of their creators. By the 1920s, Japan's growing middle class had come to play an important role in framing national morality.[16] Moral entrepreneurs of the interwar era represented much wider social and professional categories than the 1890s elites who claimed the right to determine the hallmarks of civilization by virtue of their high status. Cultural producers, including academics, researchers, travel and fiction writers, filmmakers, and religious leaders, presented the deviant addict to the reading and viewing public. Merchants devised an opium regulatory regime that identified (lucrative) state control of the market with civilized government. Law enforcement at all levels—policing, prosecution, and punishment—meted out benevolent justice to narcotics offenders. Laboratory researchers sought to understand the physiology and pharmacology of drug dependence, legitimizing the Japanese empire through the creation of useful and universal scientific knowledge. Clinical doctors transformed the addict into a medical specimen, inscribing benevolence directly onto the body of the subject through attempted cures.[17]

Notably, moral entrepreneurs also included many imperial subjects, who participated in Japanese nation building to an extent unparalleled in the empires of the West. During the interwar years, the belief that opium consumption caused racial elimination and political collapse was hegemonic even—or especially—among those populations whose capacity for self-sovereignty it denied. Many Chinese, Taiwanese, and Korean leaders admired the Japanese as an abstinent people and sought their cooperation in the struggle against drugs, despite awareness of the imperial stake in the opium traffic. Collectively, a nationally, professionally, and socially diverse cohort of moral entrepreneurs spread the crusade against narcotics into every aspect of public life.

Opium was not only an arena for cross-national collaboration but also a marker of racial differentiation in an empire characterized by a unique sense of ethnic confraternity. Although benevolent government encompassed expectations that colonial subjects would assimilate as Japanese, this ideology was not applied consistently across the empire's possessions or peoples. Benevolence located legitimacy both in differences and the eradication of differences among the Japanese and those they ruled. Between the immobile poles of allegedly abstinent, superior Japanese and addicted, absolutely inferior Chinese, the subjects of the formal colonies—the Taiwanese and Koreans—occupied a peculiar limbo. Opium indexed their status as it changed over time and across space.

In 1931, at the height of the moral crusade against narcotics, the windfalls of the illicit drug economy financed the Japanese military takeover of Manchuria. The following year, the imperial army, rejecting traditional colonialism, organized the region as the nation-state of Manchukuo. Since 1919, the principle of ethnic self-determination had functioned as the defining criterion of nationhood.[18] Given Japan's obvious role in founding the so-called puppet state, Manchukuo, the "Land of the Manchus," could not meet this standard. Like the British reporter who derided Manchukuo's pretensions to civilization, the international community rejected the would-be nation's attempt to feign the norms of political legitimacy. Unable to validate Manchukuo according to global criteria, its creators rejected those criteria—though never completely and always ambivalently. As a substitute justification of statehood, ideologues instead offered the philosophy of the Kingly Way (Japanese, *Ōdō;* Chinese, *Wangdao*). Mobilizing "traditional" East Asian concepts to appeal to imperial audiences, the Kingly Way identified administration by a benevolent sovereign as the ideal form of government. Moral entrepreneurs inserted this new language of legitimacy into their crusade against opium, reformulating the social problem of narcotics from an issue of Chinese racial degeneracy to an imperialist conspiracy on the part of Japan's emerging enemies among the great powers. Meanwhile, the military government organized the public sale of drugs for profit, accumulating the resources to ultimately wage war on Asia and the West. With its political economy, foreign relations, and national morality dependent on opium, Manchukuo was one of the world's first modern narco-states.

The defeat of Japan in 1945 terminated the moral crusade of the high imperial age. For nearly seven years after the end of World War II, the nation, stripped of its empire, was occupied by the United States and its allies. Upon the restoration of self-sovereignty, Japan confronted a new crisis of legitimacy. In the aftermath of the unprecedented experience of rule by a foreign power, the nation faced the challenges of differentiating the present from the past, maintaining the friendship of the United States without becoming an American puppet, and "modernizing" a second time, after the first attempt had failed so catastrophically. Once more, a very real spike in narcotics consumption offered fertile ground for establishing a new identity for the nation. During the "*hiropon* (philopon) age," lasting from about 1952 to 1956, hundreds of thousands of petty entrepreneurs manufactured and sold methamphetamine, while as many as two million Japanese (out of a total population of about ninety million) used the drug regularly.[19]

In contrast to opium in the imperial era, which denoted Otherness, *hiropon* in the 1950s was acknowledged as a "Japanese" issue. The nation's first and only domestic drug crisis precipitated a full-fledged moral panic, mobilizing moral entrepreneurs as well as the broader public in a crusade against methamphetamine. To the Japanese of the mid-1950s, the *hiropon* user was a metaphor for the postwar nation: a powerless victim, a prisoner of anxiety, a bullied inferior, and above all, a deeply flawed, even strange personality. The addict, transformed from the racial Other into the Self, evoked unprecedented popular alarm, attention, and activism. Remodeling drug users into independent citizens provided a measurable index of progress in Japan's attempt to reintegrate into global society as a confident, cooperative, moral nation-state. The stability of this status has prevented the recurrence of a moral crusade against drugs or even the acknowledgment of narcotics as a social problem in the half century since the *hiropon* age, despite the increasing presence and impact of illegal substances in contemporary Japan.

In many ways, the Japanese experience with narcotics, like the Japanese passage through modernity itself, appears highly idiosyncratic. Yet the history of illegal drugs in Japan is much more than a provocative case study of moral crusade in the non-West. At the end of the nineteenth century, opium, a commodity of peculiar significance, served as a site for the articulation and evolution of criteria for legitimate nationhood. Japan, which rejected opium, established abstinence from narcotics as a standard of "civilization." The nation's ensuing acceptance into the ranks of great powers gave civilization credibility as a universal rather than a merely Western value. The determination of global standards for political legitimacy also reinforced the need for strong states that could cultivate "civilized" beliefs, attitudes, and behaviors among their populations. Nation building was therefore a moral activity, even obligation, on the part of every imagined community; and the nation, the pledge of a people to uphold civilization, was the only moral form of collective organization.[20] The history of narcotics in Japan is not simply a domestic or even regional story, but a global account of the emergence of the nation as a moral category in the modern world.

CHAPTER ONE • Moral Crusade in Meiji Japan

"How came any reasonable being," the writer Thomas De Quincey asked in 1821, "to subject himself to such a yoke of misery, voluntarily to incur a captivity so servile, and knowingly fetter himself with such a seven-fold chain?"[1] De Quincey's captor was opium, and his *Confessions of an English Opium-Eater* became a classic of Victorian literature and the forerunner of a new genre, still vibrant today: the addict memoir. The comparison of addiction to slavery, one of the most controversial issues of the nineteenth century, invested opium with particular political significance. In an age that defined sovereignty in opposition to the contemporary reality of unfree labor, dependence of any kind appeared incompatible with nationhood. Given this resonance, opium was a logical moral target during crises of political legitimacy.

De Quincey specifically identified himself as an "English" opium eater because his compatriots typically associated enslavement to drugs with "Orientals," subjects of empire building by Europeans and Americans. Nineteenth-century Japan, taking its cue from Britain's subordination of China in the Opium War of 1839–42, came to view the exclusion of narcotics as a precondition of maintaining independence. But mere rejection of opium was not enough to "leave Asia *[datsu-A]*"—that is, to distinguish a sovereign Japan from a colonizable "Orient." During the crisis of legitimacy caused by the Sino-Japanese War of 1894–95, moral entrepreneurs used positive abstinence from narcotics to signify the civilization of the Japanese nation. Attributing the weakness of the vanquished Qing empire to opium, they sought to sever Japan's attachment to a continent enslaved by narcotics. The acquisition of Taiwan, a spoil of war, transformed the state into an empire akin to the great powers of the West, and provided further opportunities to demonstrate adherence to global norms of nationhood by suppressing the opium market. By the time the moral crusade against narcotics subsided around the turn of the twentieth century, Japan had, in the eyes of many, achieved its goal of "entering the West *[nyū-Ō]*." Perhaps even more importantly, the state won the right to participate in framing the standards of civilization. The moral nation was drug-free.

"LEAVING ASIA"

In the late eighteenth century, China under the Qing dynasty grew rich exporting tea, silk, and ceramics to Great Britain. Facing a steadily worsening trade deficit, the island empire was relieved to discover a latent demand for opium in the Chinese market. The East India Company, which administered South Asia on behalf of the British government, allocated large tracts of colonized territory for poppy cultivation, selling opium to the Qing in exchange for goods desired by consumers in the metropole. By the 1830s, this so-called triangular trade had brought about a balance of exchange unfavorable to China, prompting the state to attempt to ban the drug. Britain's determination to continue the traffic ultimately enmeshed the two empires in the Opium War. Following China's defeat, the Treaty of Nanjing legalized British narcotics exports and conferred other privileges on the victor, including possession of Hong Kong island, extraterritoriality, reparations, and trade concessions.[2]

From the perspective of early nineteenth-century China and Britain, the primary danger of opium was its financial cost to the state. After 1842, rising circulation of the drug in the Qing empire prompted attention to its social impact. Although numerous Britons and Americans earned considerable fortunes selling narcotics in China, in the decade after the Opium War, many Western observers came to consider the business unsavory, associating both traders and consumers with immorality and Otherness. Christian missionaries in China returned home to spread a gospel of horror that specifically emphasized the dangers of smoking opium, an unfamiliar practice that violated Euro-American notions of propriety. Although opium consumption was common throughout the West, the drug was generally ingested orally, in laudanum, patent medicines, or other beverages. The pipe distinguished "Oriental" narcotics use as particularly recreational and degenerate. Long after most Chinese consumers had given up smoking in favor of injecting drugs, stereotypes of dazed, recumbent "yellow" specimens wreathed in fumes continued to furnish evidence of "Oriental deviance" to the Western public.[3]

In the context of rising public opposition to opium trafficking, in 1853 the United States dispatched Commodore Matthew C. Perry to initiate trade and diplomatic relations with Japan, then officially closed to most foreign contact. The following year, the Treaty of Kanagawa opened five Japanese ports and political intercourse between the two states. In a critical follow-up agreement in 1858, the United States pledged to refrain from exporting opium to the archipelago. Despite its seclusion, Japan had received news of the Opium War and had come to view a ban on drugs as a necessary safeguard of sovereignty. The antinarcotics stance of Japanese negotiators, however, would likely have had little impact had America not been willing to voluntarily eschew the traffic. While the Second Opium (Arrow) War of 1856–60 raged between Qing China on one side and Great Britain and France on the other, the United States embraced the opportunity to assert its moral superiority over European rivals. Moreover, in the midst of the Industrial Revolution, some Americans feared that demand for opium might reduce Japan's ability to purchase the manufactured products they wished to export.[4] Most European powers, including Great Britain, Holland, France, and Russia, followed the American example in signing treaties prohibiting their citizens from bringing opium to Japan. China alone did not consent to voluntary export restrictions, on the grounds that the Qing government had itself forfeited such protection by the terms of the Treaty of Nanjing.[5]

Having observed the impact of opium on China's financial solvency and international standing, many Japanese hoped to proscribe it completely. Following the Meiji Restoration of 1868, the new government proclaimed, "Opium is a product that decreases a person's energy and shortens life. . . . [I]t will lead to disaster if it spreads among the public."[6] However, the drug was too deeply embedded in the domestic medical tradition to reject altogether.[7] Legislation in 1870 required doctors and pharmacists to record and report quantities of opium sold as medicine. Following a nationwide survey in 1874–75, the government restricted poppy cultivation to its own permit holders. The newly created Sanitation Bureau took charge of procuring raw opium (mostly from Persia and Turkey), processing it into paste, and distributing the output through a network of offices in Japan's major cities. In the wake of a series of well-publicized violations, the 1880 Criminal Code set forth penalties for the illicit import, manufacture, sale, possession, and use of opium and smoking paraphernalia. Japanese violators faced fines and prison terms. Cases involving Westerners, granted extraterritoriality by the terms of the unequal treaties of the 1850s, were decided in consular courts. The state deported Chinese offenders.[8]

The near exclusion of opium from the home islands made the drug available as a marker of difference between Japan and its neighbors. Establishing Japan as an independent nation-state entailed "leaving Asia": separating the country from an "Orient" defined by backwardness, even barbarity, in the Western mindset, and from China in the domestic conception. In the premodern period, Japanese intellectuals had periodically attempted to distill a native essence from the contributions of Chinese civilization. This effort reached new heights at the end of the nineteenth century. Sinologists were among the first critics of opium as the origin and outcome of China's weakness. Many Japanese scholars who visited the Qing empire in its final decades professed alarm and horror at the impact of the drug on their country's historical cultural mentor. Oka Senjin (1832–1913) spent nearly a year in China in 1884–85. Although initially reverential toward Sinic civilization, Oka became disillusioned when he learned that the prominent Chinese reformer Wang Tao, whom he had long admired, was an opium smoker.[9] Oka abhorred the sight of public smoking in Shanghai and other treaty ports. He gazed in wonder at drug users who lay prone "as though sleeping . . . as though drunk . . . or as though dead." His 1886 travelogue concluded by urging Japan to "secede *[ridatsu]*" from China.[10]

With the exception of a few elites—like Oka, who could afford continental travel—the impressions of most Meiji-era Japanese regarding China were shaped at home by encounters with Qing migrants, either directly or through the media. Following the abrogation of Japan's seclusion policy, Chinese accompanied Westerners as compradors, domestic servants, and translators to treaty ports throughout the archipelago. By the mid-1890s, about five thousand Qing subjects resided in the home islands.[11] As a percentage of all nineteenth-century Chinese emigrants, and by comparison with the number of settlers in the American West, this community was all but insignificant. Nonetheless, Chinese denizens represented the largest "foreigner" population in Japan at the time. As in Europe and the United States, Qing subjects became defined by the unfamiliar practice of opium smoking. "Of all the immoral customs of Chinese migrants, opium smoking and gambling are the most egregious and hardest to correct," lamented one Japanese sinologist.[12]

The nineteenth-century nation demanded a rationally organized population, delineated through the negative labeling and exclusion of the Other as a deviant or social problem *(shakai mondai)*.[13] In the language of social Darwinism, which was introduced to Japan in the late 1870s and achieved near hegemony among the intellectual elite, the prohibition of opium in the home islands demonstrated the "fitness" of the nation and its divergence from a shamed and dependent China.[14] Social Darwinism also supplied various biological metaphors for narcotics. The analogy of poison, an especial preoccupation of nineteenth-century society, dominated early presentations of opium in Japan. The word *chūdoku* (literally, "internal poisoning") emerged as a translation of the Western concept of opium addiction.[15] Oka Senjin attributed Qing China's decline in part to suffering from the disease of smoke poisoning *(endoku)*. "If the poisons of smoking and traditional thought are not wiped out, China will become completely impotent," he warned.[16]

In the late nineteenth century, the steady replacement of the miasma paradigm of disease with germ theory in the new state-led science of public health generated various metaphors involving contagion. For moral entrepreneurs of the 1890s and beyond, contagion *(densen)*, like poison, was associated with impurity, pollution, and the corruption of the body.[17] "The drug evil," bureaucrat Andō Akimichi asserted, "spreads from China like cholera and the plague."[18] In the words of Tazawa Shingo, head of an industrial research institute, opium was a literal vermin *(mushi)*: "In the human body it is said that there are many germs, and in the smoker there is also the germ of opium."[19] According to these writers, opium and the Chinese alike had to be contained for Japan to survive.

A few well-publicized instances of Westerners spreading drugs in Japan also provoked the domestic public. The outrage of these cases, however, derived not from fears of contagion, but rather from the defendant's right to be tried in a consular court and, presumably, escape justice. In the most famous incident, beginning in late 1877, Japanese customs officials apprehended British merchant John Hartley attempting to smuggle fifteen catties of opium into the treaty port of Yokohama. The British authorities put Hartley on trial, but Japanese observers reacted with fury when the judge accepted his defense that the contraband was intended for use as medicine (an exception to the ban). While the verdict was pending, Hartley was arrested a second time for further dealings in opium. In response to the public outcry, the British tried him again. The case ultimately produced no clear judgment for Hartley.[20]

From the Japanese perspective, European and American opium smugglers were merely opportunists taking advantage of a system that could not punish them. By contrast, given Japan's fraught relationship with China, migrant Chinese smokers appeared to pose an acute biological hazard. After several Japanese prostitutes died upon ingesting opium allegedly furnished by Chinese, Japanese foreign minister Mutsu Munemitsu proposed stricter procedures for the suppression of drugs. Among other measures, he authorized police to enter the homes of Chinese denizens without search warrants. This policy resulted in several violent confrontations between Qing migrants and Japanese law enforcement. In the treaty port of Nagasaki in 1883, police killed one individual and wounded five others when a mob attempted to prevent an arrest. The Chinese consulate in Japan protested the incident, but Mutsu's policy remained unchanged.[21]

As tension mounted in the years leading up to the Sino-Japanese War, nascent moral entrepreneurs effectively mobilized the new forum of newspapers to spread public awareness of the threat posed by Chinese opium smokers. Although the first newspaper had appeared in Japan in 1862, at that time few Japanese could read it or understand its purpose. Over the ensuing decades, however, literacy increased thanks to compulsory education, and the circulation of dailies skyrocketed. Spokesmen for the state, Meiji newspapers wooed readers with chauvinistic nationalism and advice on "civilized" behavior.[22] As one collective voice among many in the quest to distinguish a modern Japan from a backward Asia, moral entrepreneurs in the press denounced rising levels of opium cultivation and consumption in the Qing empire, as well as the discovery of drugs handled by migrant Chinese in treaty ports or on British or American ships passing through the home islands on their way to the Americas. Many of the accused were conscripted laborers who had become dependent on narcotics during the long voyage to indentured servitude in the West. Rather than representing these hapless smokers as victims, journalists highlighted their potential to contaminate the drug-free domestic population.[23]

In 1894, the outbreak of the Sino-Japanese War provoked a crisis of legitimacy in Japan. Incipient alarm over opium flared into a full-fledged moral crusade. To moral entrepreneurs, the conflict between Japan and China was nothing less than a challenge to civilization by barbarian soldiers drained by drug use.[24] The Japanese army allegedly forced captured Chinese opium smokers to detoxify and executed drug users among its own troops to prevent them from returning home to spread their habit.[25] Japan's victory, which shocked its opponent and the world, intensified global convictions that opium had sapped the racial fitness and capacity for nationhood of the Chinese people. The great powers at last came to positively differentiate the Japanese from an imagined mass of "Orientals." In the words of one American writer, "the wide-spread prevalence of the opium habit among all classes of the population" was the source of Chinese inferiority, while "the superiority of Japan in energy and progress" derived from abstinence from narcotics.[26]

Also as a result of the war, the rate of Chinese immigration to Japan slowed considerably and permanently. Many long-term merchants repatriated to the mainland, their businesses ruined by nationalist boycotts of Japanese products and their services no longer required by Western traders.[27] Migrants who remained became the object of the "mixed residence debate *[zakkyo mondai]*." Japan's victory allowed the nation to reconsider the terms upon which Chinese would be allowed to settle in the home islands. Policymakers considered banning immigration from the mainland altogether or restricting Chinese to segregated neighborhoods. Opponents of these proposals objected to singling out Qing subjects from other foreigners for particular discrimination.[28] They also cited practical obstacles: given the ethnic and geographic proximity of the Japanese and Chinese, one reporter declared, "it is not possible to hold ourselves a thousand miles apart from the Chinese race." Allowing Qing migrants to live among the domestic population, however, risked spreading "unhygienic, evil customs," including drug use, to "impressionable" Japanese. Moral entrepreneurs viewed the burgeoning population of industrial laborers, so important to the national economy, as particularly vulnerable to contamination. Narcotics, they pointed out, could compromise worker efficiency at the very moment of Japan's economic takeoff. "The Chinese who come to our country to live must be controlled according to our hygiene regulations, and their harmful behavior [using drugs] must be prohibited," one writer concluded.[29]

Data on the criminal prosecution of drug offenses provided moral entrepreneurs with additional ammunition against the opium-smoking Other. Japanese violators of the ban on handling and consuming narcotics were said to be "so few that [they] scarcely . . . entered into the statistics" and were limited to "those who had had a close relation with the Chinese."[30] In fact, however, Chinese offenders were hardly more numerous. In the two decades between 1890 and 1911, police arrested only 338 foreigners of all nationalities for transgressing anti-opium legislation.[31] Given the fraught relationship between narcotics and nationhood, the Japanese judicial system spared no effort in bringing traffickers to justice. The small number of violations suggests that moral entrepreneurs considerably exaggerated the threat of Chinese opium trafficking.

In 1899, the Japanese government resolved the mixed residence debate by enacting stringent controls on the in-migration of Chinese. This policy created a vacuum in the unskilled labor market that was soon filled by Koreans, subjects of a Japanese protectorate from 1905 and a colony from 1910. Over the next decade, Koreans replaced the Chinese as the largest minority population in Japan. As they filled the economic niche the Chinese had vacated, they too came to be stigmatized as narcotics users and a menace to the national body (see chapter 3). In the age of nation building, opium was more than a drug; it was a symbolic marker of difference between the Japanese and the Other, whoever that was.

TABLE 1 Foreigner violations of anti-opium legislation in Japan, 1890–1911

Year	*Violations*
1890	2
1891	1
1892	2
1893	1
1894	11
1895	21
1896	20
1897	12
1898	20
1899	7
1900	13
1901	29
1902	18
1903	13
1904	12
1905	18
1906	18
1907	21
1908	30
1909	31
1910	40
1911	38

SOURCE: *Nihon teikoku tōkei nenkan,* vols. 11–32 (1892–1913).

"ENTERING THE WEST"

In addition to deploying opium to "leave Asia," moral entrepreneurs of the Sino-Japanese War era also sought to "enter the West," or to make Japan part of the international community of sovereign states by demonstrating "civilization and enlightenment *[bunmei kaika].*" The rejection of narcotics not only justified

Japan as a nation, but also normalized abstinence as a criterion of legitimacy in all states.

Framing Japan as a drug-free nation prompted reflection upon how the country had avoided the social and financial catastrophe of large-scale opium use. Moral entrepreneurs tied Japan's evasion of narcotics to nearly every facet of public life. Confident rhetoric notwithstanding, frequent use of the word *nigeru* ("escape") betrayed ongoing uncertainty regarding the superiority and even survival of the Japanese state. Later explanations of abstinence often cited the rational character, pure blood, and developed culture of the Japanese.[32] Simplicity and patriotism, virtues traditionally ascribed to the early modern samurai elite, were generalized to the entire population. In the context of early twentieth-century state efforts to cultivate emperor worship, several moral entrepreneurs also credited the protection of Shintō gods *(kami)*.[33] Imbuing the archipelago with almost magical powers in accordance with religious views of the home islands as the offspring of divinities, Kikuchi Yūji argued that physical isolation had spared the Japanese from the contagion of addiction. Japan's temperate climate, moreover, protected the people from gastroenterological diseases such as cholera, for which opium was a treatment.[34]

Although many moral entrepreneurs commended the prescience of the pre-Meiji government in forbidding opium imports, they generally failed to credit the Western powers for voluntarily renouncing narcotics exports. The drug-free nation was a domestic triumph that set Japan apart from and above its politically weak neighbors. In the words of one sinologist, abstinence "was not due to a foreign reason. That is to say, no matter how favorable external conditions were, Japan was still the only nation [in Asia] to prohibit opium."[35]

The incorporation of abstinence into the national identity was to some extent a self-fulfilling prophecy. Because opium smoking was not a Japanese behavior, narcotics consumers could not be Japanese. An American observer described the public stance toward drug users in the late Meiji period:

> The Japanese to a man fear opium as we fear the cobra or the rattlesnake, and they despise its victims. There has been no moment in the nation's history when the people have wavered in their uncompromising attitude towards the drug and its use, so that an instinctive hatred of it possesses them. . . . [W]oe betide [a Japanese] if he resorts to the seductions of opium."[36]

By the 1930s, the novelist Dazai Osamu, a heavy user of opiates for most of his adult life, believed that his condition permanently "branded him on the forehead as a reject" from the national community. "I presented the figure of a ragged and half-mad derelict. . . . I was the basest, most reptilian young man in Japan," he wrote.[37] Another Japanese youth remembered his years as an addict as a time of worthlessness and hopelessness. Upon regaining his health, he asserted his intention to become a "splendid citizen *[rippa na kokumin]*" and join the national army.[38]

In building a drug-free nation, moral entrepreneurs of the late 1890s skillfully engaged Western understandings of opium, demonstrating civilization through mastery of Euro-American thought. Many late nineteenth-century intellectuals viewed the use of some consciousness-altering agent as fundamental to all peoples. Substances were arranged in a hierarchy pegged to the racial status of their consumers. Representing the essence of the Occident and the Orient, respectively, drink and drugs assumed values reflecting normative rather than scientific criteria.[39] Pursuing dissociation from China and identification with the West, moral entrepreneurs identified Japan as an alcohol- as opposed to opium-consuming nation.

In Europe and the United States, critics of narcotics were isolated voices within a temperance movement that deemed drink the primary agent of social decay. A few moderate reformers even insisted that the soporific effects of opium were more benign than those of alcohol, which produced disorder and rowdiness. One doctor wrote, "That drunkenness and the immoderate use of alcohol are the occasion of greater evils, whether physical or moral, or individual or society, than those attendant on the free use of opium, however indulged in, I should be quite ready to concede." An English missionary in China fretted lest "the beer saloon shall take the place of the abolished opium dens."[40] By contrast, many Japanese viewed rising domestic consumption of alcohol, particularly beer, spirits, and other Western beverages, as a sign of advancing civilization. Only Japan's small temperance movement argued that "the alcohol problem, which is so much deeper and has so much wider an import, should receive more attention than the issue of opium."[41] The anti-alcohol lobby did not, however, depict sake (rice wine) consumption as a form of deviance like narcotics use. As one moral entrepreneur concluded, "There is no comparing opium to sake. If one tries opium once or twice, one descends into addiction and cannot stop oneself from smoking again."[42]

Although narcotics in fin-de-siècle Europe and America were seen as inimical to national values such as liberty, individualism, capitalism, patriotism, and civic engagement, the great powers did not particularly identify themselves as drug-free.[43] It was imperialist interest in China that made the West receptive to abstinence as a signifier of legitimate nationhood. Prior to the Sino-Japanese War, the great powers conducted a form of "treaty port colonialism" that sought economic rather than territorial concessions from China. Japan's victory over the formerly robust Qing dynasty, however, eroded confidence in the ability of the Chinese government to guarantee foreign privileges. Convinced that the conquest of China by any single state would fatally upset the balance of power, the nations of Europe and the United States committed to the Open Door policy, pledging to respect the integrity of the Qing empire while guaranteeing unfettered access to trade for all. The decision not to "carve the Chinese melon" left it available for informal imperialism in the form of so-called spheres of influence. Allowing Japan entry to the club of legitimate states on the grounds of national abstinence helped keep China out, and the ongoing ambiguity of Chinese sovereignty was a source of potential profit for all.

As a result of these considerations, many Westerners came to echo the Japanese in valorizing abstinence from narcotics as an indication of racial superiority. One Spanish missionary wrote, "The morality, the refinement, and the differences of society established on a more enlightened and cultured foundation call out, 'Halt!' against the adoption of the opium vice among Europeans. . . . Our society enjoys diversions of mind and body more agreeable than those of reclining upon the bed of an opium den."[44] The great powers also took unprecedented measures to criminalize narcotics at home. In response to both international and domestic pressures, Food and Drug Acts in Germany (1903 and 1907) and the United States (1906) mandated the full and accurate disclosure of ingredients in pharmaceutical preparations. In 1909, the United States also passed the Smoking Opium Exclusion Act to prevent the spread of a practice identified with Chinese immigrants in the West. Meanwhile, Great Britain updated and strengthened labeling regulations for the protection of consumers with the Poisons and Pharmacy Act of 1908.[45]

By the beginning of the twentieth century, the Japanese had left Asia, but whether they had entered the West remained a subject of debate. The country had Westernized but was not Western; it was an independent civilized state, but its people were not equal representatives of civilization. One British writer compared Japan's embrace of modernity to putting on a garment: despite his approving tone, the analogy made clear his conviction that the transformation was superficial.[46] Joshua Rowntree, a Quaker leader of the anti-opium campaign, believed that "every civilized people in the world would do as the Japanese did" in rejecting opium. Yet he too questioned the degree to which the nation was truly "enlightened": "Japan had only decided to exchange the protection of isolation for the 'protection of mimicry.' It is too soon yet to reach any final conclusions as to the results."[47] To Rowntree, the Japanese were a nation of "mimic men," Asian in race but Euro-American in tastes, opinions, ideologies, and morals—"almost the same but not white."[48]

ABSTINENT NATION, ADDICTED EMPIRE

The Sino-Japanese War established the victor as an empire as well as a nation. By the terms of the Treaty of Shimonoseki, which restored peace in April 1895, Japan acquired the island of Taiwan from China. During negotiations, Li Hongzhang, representing the Qing government, warned his Japanese counterpart Itō Hirobumi, "Formosa will, I think, present immense difficulties in the matter of administration, inasmuch as the people there are deeply addicted to the vicious habit of opium-smoking; and should the island come under Japan's rule, it will cause no small trouble to her."[49] Japan's determination to take possession of Taiwan overwhelmed this appeal to its much-vaunted distaste for narcotics. After much deliberation, the Diet decided to administer the new colony according to the Meiji Constitution, promulgated six years earlier in 1889. As a result, the Taiwanese became Japanese subjects.[50] By law, the "Japanese" were no longer drug-free.

The acquisition of a colony fueled Japan's claims of parity with the imperial powers of the West. The metropole sought to administer Taiwan in a suitably civilized manner, replacing "backward" native customs with modern hygiene, industry, and development. But how could a nation predicated on abstinence rule an empire of addicts? Although moral entrepreneurs spoke of opium as "a matter of national honor before the entire world," initial intervention in island affairs proved both embarrassing and costly.[51] The Japanese takeover of Taiwan ignited sustained and violent opposition, prompting a bloody "pacification" campaign by the imperial army. With the Diet in despair, prime minister Itō Hirobumi solicited the advice of Dr. Gotō Shinpei (1857–1929), a bureaucrat in the Home Ministry.

Though young, Gotō had already built a national reputation due to his rapid progress through the medical ranks and his role in developing public health. His philosophy of "biological colonialism *[seibutsugaku no gensoku]*" called for Japan to acquire an intimate understanding of Taiwanese customs and traditions as the basis for an organic, scientific, and unassailable campaign to modernize the island. In social Darwinist terms, biological colonialism would help the Japanese regime adapt to its environment and transform the Taiwanese from "barbarians" into civilized and enlightened subjects. Gotō's philosophy was thus a humanitarian rationalization of imperialism that cultivated legitimacy for Japanese rule through a display of concern for the welfare of the local population.[52]

At Itō's request, Gotō supervised a thorough survey of the land and customs of Taiwan, including drug use. He counted approximately 170,000 opium smokers, representing over 6 percent of the population.[53] Quantification of the social problem of drug use fed demands for action to contain it, but the ideological entanglement of opium and nationhood in Meiji Japan constrained policy choices. Although metropolitan leaders wished to encourage Japanese migration to Taiwan, the better to subjugate and extract resources from the island, they feared that local opium smokers might lead settlers astray. Immediately upon taking power, the colonial regime, known as the Office of the Governor-General (Taiwan Sōtokufu), declared that any Taiwanese caught supplying drugs to Japanese army troops would be punished with death. The administration subsequently extended this penalty to the sale of narcotics to civilians.[54]

The transplantation of the domestic moral crusade against narcotics to the empire bespoke the ongoing fragility of Japan's identity as a drug-free nation. The belief that the Japanese were biologically or culturally inured to opium existed alongside potent and inexpressible insecurity that abstinence could and would be breached. In his November 1895 "Memorandum on the Formosan Opium Policy" *(Taiwan ahen seido ni kansuru iken sho)*, Gotō Shinpei acknowledged these concerns: "As the Japanese go to the island in large numbers and come in close contact with the natives, and as some of them may contract the evil habit [drug use], it is easy to see that there is a serious danger of it spreading into Japan. . . . Therefore the adoption of suppression measures in Formosa is very urgent." Gotō also pointed out the legal contradiction in severely punishing opium consumption among some imperial subjects (the Japanese), while condoning such behavior among others (the Taiwanese). The obvious way to eliminate this inconsistency and prevent the contagion of smoking to troops and civilian migrants from the home islands was to prohibit opium immediately, absolutely, and without exception *(genkin shugi)*. Yet as colonial administrators had already discovered, zero-tolerance measures were difficult to implement: in Gotō's (likely exaggerated) estimation, enforcement might require as much as two military divisions.[55]

Having established his opposition to opium and explained the inadvisability of an absolute ban, Gotō introduced his solution: gradual suppression *(zenkin shugi)* by means of a government monopoly. The monopoly would dispense falling quantities of opium to licensed individual smokers over a period of time, enabling them to wean themselves off the habit with a minimum of suffering. The monopoly would also provide a temporary source of revenue to the state, allowing Taiwan to become financially independent of Tokyo. In addition to these pragmatic advantages, Gotō highlighted the ideological appeal of gradual suppression. By the mid-1890s, all European colonial administrations in Southeast Asia, including the Dutch East Indies, French Indochina, Portuguese Macau, and British Hong Kong, Singapore, and Malaya, had brought the opium market under state control. Although Gotō believed in creating institutions to suit local conditions rather than adopting metropolitan or Western models wholesale, he nonetheless hoped that, by implementing a policy ubiquitous among the European powers, Japan might demonstrate its ability to meet the norms of colonial rule.

Another moral entrepreneur, Taiwan's chief civil administrator Mizuno Jun, supported Gotō's idea of an opium monopoly. According to Mizuno, Japan had long deplored "the tragic reality of opium poisoning . . . that had ruined the nation of China and its four hundred million people."[56] Japan now had the opportunity to save the Taiwanese from a similar fate. Mizuno suggested proceeding with caution, however: with armed resistance to Japanese rule ongoing, imperial intervention in local customs would likely stimulate violent opposition. He particularly feared inflaming settlers from the Chinese mainland, who might use the prohibition of opium as a cause to muster local support for overthrowing the colonial government. Under these circumstances, gradual rather than immediate suppression of drugs struck him as prudent. In response to critics who feared the interim contagion of opium smoking to Japanese migrants to Taiwan, Mizuno contended that the imperialists were an "active" race, drawn to the stimulant of alcohol and biologically insulated against cravings for the soporific of narcotics. Although some Japanese had been caught trafficking opium, he had learned from military police that these offenders were not using the drug themselves.[57]

Against the consensus of Mizuno and Gotō, some moral entrepreneurs advocated the adoption of immediate suppression measures. Katō Hisayuki of the Home Ministry Sanitation Bureau feared that allowing opium smoking to continue even temporarily would sap the individual and collective racial strength of the Taiwanese. He objected to the proposed monopoly for prioritizing the financial benefit of Japan over the welfare of the colonial subject. Katō called upon his country to "proclaim to the world our government's disinterest in profit" and to "follow the path of humanitarianism and righteousness." In his view, swift suppression of opium would burnish Japan's honor beneath the gaze of the international community. He believed that the abstinent nation-state simply could not accommodate an addicted colony: "Japan and opium are fundamentally incompatible. Wherever the Japanese go, they must get rid of opium."[58]

In early 1897, Ishiguro Tadanori, chief medical inspector for the imperial army in Taiwan, summarized the argument in favor of gradual prohibition in a series of editorials published in the *Yomiuri Shinbun*, a leading newspaper in the Japanese home islands. Ishiguro acknowledged that a strict and immediate ban on opium was ideal. Nonetheless, as a doctor, he opposed sacrificing the health of the opium-smoking minority to protect the abstinent majority from the contagion of narcotics. If the Japanese government cracked down on drug consumption too abruptly, the moral entrepreneur pointed out, many smokers were likely to die from the agony of withdrawal. Instead of exacerbating the local security situation with an unpopular policy, he advocated cultivating the devotion of the Taiwanese to the new government by stretching prohibition over a longer time frame. As an interim measure, Ishiguro suggested restricting the in-migration of mainland Chinese, who might encourage "backsliding" among the Taiwanese. Ishiguro concluded by appealing to Japan's desire to emulate the great powers of the West, which, as Gotō had noted, all maintained opium monopolies in their Southeast Asian colonies.[59]

Ishiguro's editorial primed Japanese readers to accept the temporary continuation of the narcotic economy in Taiwan on pragmatic grounds. It also preempted objections to the creation of a drug monopoly in the home islands. In 1897, the Diet issued new regulations to tighten state control of Japan's domestic market for medical opium. The establishment of a public monopoly over controlled substances in the Japanese archipelago was among the first but by no means only instances in which innovation in the empire brought about change in the metropole. Under the new system, a government monopoly board assumed responsibility for the importation, processing, and distribution of opium to licensed pharmacists, who recorded and reported all consumer sales. Poppies grown domestically underwent inspection by the Tokyo Hygiene Lab; if their morphine content reached a certain level, the state purchased them from cultivators for a fixed price. Crops that failed to meet the requirement were destroyed.[60]

In Taiwan, meanwhile, the Opium Law of 1897 regulated the sourcing and marketing of drugs. By 1901, the Office of the Governor-General had established a formal monopoly bureau to fully realize control over supply. The regime authorized approximately a thousand petty distributors, mostly local elites, to sell the drug on its behalf. This measure secured the support of many Taiwanese power holders for Japanese rule, thus helping to stabilize colonial control. To regulate consumption, the bureau issued permits to all Taiwanese smokers, redeemable at intervals for a fixed, theoretically falling, quantity of drugs. Setting the price of monopoly opium below that of smuggled opium, the authorities furnished smokers with an economic incentive to join the state registry. Applicants for licenses required the approval of a doctor, but beyond an age minimum of twenty, the physical conditions that qualified a patient for a daily ration of drugs were not elaborated. To discourage nonsmokers from taking up the habit, the state issued permits for a limited time only. The Japanese government reported that the law "was received with great joy not only by the old confirmed smokers themselves, but also by the general public."[61] Whether this "great joy" was genuine or only imagined on the part of the colonizers, the regime found compliance satisfactory. Arrests for violations of the Opium Law dwindled from over a thousand in 1901 to barely fifty in 1905.[62]

Moral entrepreneurs applauded the success of their crusade against narcotics. Naitō Konan was a sinologist of some renown when he arrived in Taiwan in the spring of 1897. As the editor of a Japanese-language daily, the *Taiwan nippō* (Taiwan news), he made Japan's progress in extirpating opium a headline issue. Under his direction, the paper regularly published (falling) tallies of smokers, traffickers, and retail establishments in the colony. Naitō believed that the eradication of "shocking" practices like opium use would create a more favorable environment for Japanese settlement in Taiwan. Like Gotō, he upheld Japan's responsibility to gradually civilize the Taiwanese.[63] Naitō depicted the Opium Law as a triumph of Japanese humanitarianism over the looming threat of Taiwanese racial extermination. In his words, "Originally, smoking harmed the people of the Qing empire, and drug use drained the state's strength. Naturally, in our country, narcotics are strictly prohibited. Now the Opium Law will, over a period of many years, save the lives of the Taiwanese from the peril of drugs." Although Naitō had once believed that "the predilection of the natives for opium smoking is stronger than the attraction of the Japanese to alcohol," in early 1898 he debuted a more hopeful stance, observing that drinking establishments had grown more numerous over the past year as the Taiwanese, "in the manner of Japanese," substituted sake for narcotics.[64] Meanwhile, another journalist reported that Japanese settlers were successfully resisting the contagion of drugs: of fifty thousand migrants to the island, only two were confirmed smokers. "When I heard this I could not help feeling proud of my race," he applauded.[65]

Although the Opium Law resolved the controversy over immediate versus gradual suppression, moral entrepreneurs continued to deliberate the issue of medical treatment for smokers. A Taiwanese religious society, the Feiluan Jingbihui (Society of the Flying Phoenix and the Divine Will), grew rapidly after advertising a cure for opium "cravings." Members seeking relief placed a pipe in front of an enshrined deity and requested divine assistance. After this ceremony, they received a quantity of holy water containing incense, ashes, and opium. They were told that their desire for drugs would disappear by the time the water had been completely consumed. By 1901, the Feiluan Jingbihui had established branches throughout Taiwan, attracting adherents among the elite as well as common people. A survey by the Japanese administration in September of that year found that the organization had helped 34,370 individuals to quit smoking, out of a total opium user population of 169,064. These remarkable results led the Office of the Governor-General to fear for the profitability of its new Opium Monopoly Bureau. Denouncing the Feiluan Jingbihui as a religious front for anticolonial mobilization, the government swiftly suppressed it.[66]

Japanese doctors, meanwhile, sought to bring addiction treatment under the purview of the state. Public physicians *(kōi)* experimented with treatments for drug users suffering from withdrawal and overdose. These migrants from the home islands were not technically government employees, but received state subsidies for their work at the district level.[67] In late 1897, they founded a medical society to study the pathology of drug users, among other topics. Already, one public physician claimed, over one hundred opium smokers per day were demanding attention at the new Japanese hospital in Taipei.[68] In 1903, a member of the society published the first Japanese-language research paper on addiction in its journal, the *Taiwan Igakkai zasshi* (Journal of the Taiwan Medical Association, henceforth referred to as the *TIZ*). The author unfavorably compared the height and weight of one hundred Taiwanese opium smokers to a control population of abstinent Japanese. Many of his successors, as well as moral entrepreneurs outside the medical discipline, used this tactic of juxtaposing unhealthy subject bodies with robust Japanese to validate imperialist claims of racial superiority.[69]

Despite initial enthusiasm, interest in the clinical treatment of addiction soon waned.[70] The cure of raging tropical diseases, such as malaria and dengue fever, came to occupy many doctors. Meanwhile, the suppression of the Feiluan Jingbihui and institutionalization of "civilized" drug regulation helped to legitimize Japanese rule over Taiwan, obviating the moral crusade against opium. Moral entrepreneurs began to call attention to the resolution rather than the crisis of narcotics. From a peak of nearly 170,000 licensed users, accounting for 6.3 percent of the population of Taiwan in 1900, the number of smoking permit holders fell below 100,000 in 1910, 50,000 in 1920, and 25,000 in 1930 (0.5 percent of the population, see Table 2).[71]

Accepting Japan's progress against narcotics at face value, reformers in China and the West applauded and even sought to emulate imperial policy. In 1906, the Qing empire adopted a six-year plan for gradual prohibition, declaring its intention to "Cut [opium] off, root and branch. . . . Know the shame of not being like Japan."[72] To reformers in Europe and the Americas, Japan's success in Taiwan offered lessons for both the metropole and the empire. "The Japanese government puts to the blush our Christian administrations by its prohibition of the importation of opium, not only into Japan, *but into Formosa as well,*" wrote one Canadian

TABLE 2 Opium smoking permits in Taiwan, 1897–1938

Year	*Permits*
1897	50,597
1898	95,449
1899	130,962
1900	169,064
1901	157,619
1902	143,492
1903	132,903
1904	137,952
1905	130,476
1906	121,330
1907	113,165
1908	119,991
1909	109,955
1910	98,987
1911	92,975
1912	87,371
1913	82,128
1914	76,995
1915	71,715
1916	66,847
1917	62,317
1918	55,772
1919	52,063
1920	48,012
1921	44,922
1922	42,108
1923	39,463
1924	36,627
1925	33,755
1926	31,434
1927	29,043

TABLE 2 *(continued)*

Year	*Permits*
1928	26,942
1929	24,626
1930	23,237
1931	21,298
1932	19,532
1933	17,820
1934	16,190
1935	14,644
1936	13,278
1937	11,980
1938	10,788

SOURCE: *Taiwan no ahen seido* (Taihoku: Taiwan Sōtokufu keimu-kyoku, 1939), 3–5.

missionary.[73] A reporter for the *London Times* advocated using Japan's antinarcotics campaign as a prototype for alcohol control in Great Britain.[74] Another article about opium suppression appeared in both the *London Times* and the *New York Times* under the headline "Savage Island of Formosa Transformed by Japanese: Wonders Worked in a Few Years with a People That Others Had Failed to Subdue—A Lesson for Other Colonizing Nations."[75] Upon asserting control over the Philippines in 1898, the United States appointed an Episcopalian bishop, Charles H. Brent, to lead a survey of nearby colonies in search of the optimal model of drug regulation. In 1903, the report of the Philippine Commission's Opium Investigation Committee praised Japan:

> What has been done during the past eight years by this quick-witted, enterprising nation for the benefit of the Formosans . . . has resulted in a state of peace such as probably the history of the island has never before known, even temporarily. Not least in the Japanese campaign of progress has been the attempt to grapple with the opium problem and solve it so far as it touches Formosan life.[76]

Through opium, moral entrepreneurs transformed Japan from an indistinguishable part of the "Orient" and the object of Euro-American imperialist designs into a legitimate, even model, nation-state and empire.

CHAPTER TWO · Drug Users in the Epicenter of Consumption

The original draft of the Treaty of Shimonoseki of 1895, by which Japan acquired Taiwan, also gave the empire possession of the Liaodong Peninsula. This fragment of southern Manchuria, organized for administrative purposes as the Kwantung Leased Territory (KLT), was valuable for its harbor, which remained passable in winter.[1] Although Russia, the third power in northeast Asia, was not a party to the treaty, Saint Petersburg nonetheless objected to Japan's ambitions in an area it also aspired to dominate. Together with its allies, Germany and France, the czar's government pressured Japan into returning the 1,300-square-mile peninsula to China in exchange for an augmented indemnity. Three years later, to the rage of Japanese nationalists, Russia itself negotiated a twenty-five-year lease of the KLT. In 1904, competition between the two empires for regional primacy finally erupted in battle. During the Russo-Japanese War of 1904–5, Japan's Kwantung Army invaded and occupied the KLT. When the conflict ended with a tentative victory for Japan, the Treaty of Portsmouth formalized the empire's possession of the leasehold and the South Manchuria Railway Zone (Minami Manshū tetsudō kabushiki kaisha fuzokuchi, hereafter referred to as the SMRZ), a nearly seven-hundred-mile strip of land tracing the railway tracks from the KLT border in the south to the city of Changchun in the north.

The KLT, which Japan retained from 1905 through 1945, was the empire's first and longest-held possession on the Asian mainland. By the 1920s, Dairen, its port and principal city, manifested the world's highest rate of narcotics consumption and second-highest volume of trafficking, after Shanghai.[2] During the crisis of national legitimacy that engulfed the high imperial age, from the end of World War I through the fall of the state in 1945, Dairen naturally emerged as the epicenter of Japan's second moral crusade against opium.

A moral crusade is in part defined by disproportionality. In some moral crusades, disproportionality arises when the sense of crisis exceeds a "rational" assessment of the dimensions of a social problem. In other episodes, agitation may be statistically justifiable, but the issue is understood, represented, and deployed in ways that do not reflect the "facts."[3] Moral entrepreneurs in the KLT, viewing knowledge as a proxy for power, amassed quantitative data to reassure themselves of their control over subjects and the environment.[4] The centerpiece of this project was the *Kantō tōkei sho* (Kwantung statistical gazetteer), a numerical record of the population, economy, and territory of the leasehold, produced annually from 1906 to 1941.[5] The *Kantō tōkei sho* included types of information on narcotics that were not collected anywhere else in the prewar world. Yet no evidence suggests that moral entrepreneurs ever attempted to use this data to understand actual drug consumers in the city-state. Rather, the mere existence of numbers lent an illusion of scientific credibility to the moral crusade against opium.[6]

Performing calculations "against the grain," however, highlights the disproportionality of the very conclusions the data were intended to support. Moral entrepreneurs of the high imperial age, like their 1890s predecessors, tended to stereotype "addicts" as Chinese coolies. Yet "drug users"—value-neutral consumers of narcotics—resisted categorization by nationality, substance of choice, gender, occupation, socioeconomic status, or age. Drug users in the KLT included Japanese, Koreans, Chinese, and Westerners; pipe smokers and refined narcotics injectors; men and women; professionals, laborers, and the unemployed; the elite and the oppressed; and the young, middle-aged, and elderly.

Drug users did not necessarily define themselves as a community or recognize opium consumption as part of their personal identity. What united them was not any demographic variable but their common presence in a city that came into being almost overnight through migration and remained in a state of constant population turnover. In the midst of unceasing transience, Dairen residents were guests in a vast hotel, atomized strangers who asserted agency and individuality by consuming the very commodity that had brought the city into being in the first place.

DEMOGRAPHICS IN THE EPICENTER OF CONSUMPTION

In 1905, when Japan assumed control of the KLT, the city-state had less than four hundred thousand residents, including a mere handful of opium smokers.[7] Only a few years later, both the population and the drug market had expanded considerably. In 1911, the local Japanese administration, the Kwantung Bureau, implemented a public registration policy for opium users based on the Taiwanese model. The licensing system in the leasehold, however, was never as comprehensive or effective as in the formal colony. Because the price of publicly sold opium was no lower than that offered by illegal traffickers, opium users lacked an incentive to buy from the state. Mistrustful of the Japanese administration and reluctant to call attention to their habit, many smokers declined to apply for licenses. Women, whose social roles often kept them out of the public eye, particularly resisted registration. State dealers, moreover, supplied only smoking opium: despite a growing consumer preference for morphine, heroin, and cocaine, the Kwantung Bureau declined to make refined narcotics available for licit purchase. Finally, Chinese alone could buy drugs legally. Maintaining the fiction of imperial abstinence, the registration system excluded large numbers of Japanese as well as Korean and Western opium users.[8]

Drug users registered for smoking permits at their local police station, furnishing their name, age, gender, address, occupation, and daily opium requirement. The law required applicants to submit to a physical examination confirming addiction, but, as one British consul reported, "police officials are prepared, for a small consideration, to grant smokers permits without medical certificates."[9] Although the corruption of KLT law enforcement was legendary, chronic understaffing of sanitation departments also encouraged "shortcuts" in the examination of drug users.[10]

Police initially issued 5,000 smoking permits, representing 1.1 percent of the total Chinese population of the city-state. The number of license holders fell steadily, through attrition, emigration, abandonment of the habit, or recourse to illegally procured drugs, to a mere 2,808 permit holders in 1920.[11] This decline notwithstanding, narcotics consumption increased visibly during the 1910s. In 1918, a KLT official notified the Japanese Foreign Ministry that the city-state contained at least 20,000 drug users.[12] The perceptible gap between the number of licensed and actual opium users prompted the Kwantung Bureau to initiate a second registration campaign in 1923. During the next three years, the government distributed licenses to over 30,000 consumers, representing more than 4 percent of the Chinese population of the leasehold.[13]

Although comparable information on drug consumption in any other early twentieth-century state, territory, or colony is not readily available, the data that do exist highlight the extraordinary extent of opium use in Dairen under Japanese rule. A 1924 study by the United States Narcotics Division counted 106,025 domestic consumers of illegal substances. This figure likely significantly underestimated the

TABLE 3 Registered drug users in the KLT, 1911–1932

Year	Drug users
1911	5,000
1912	2,980
1913	2,998
1914	2,709
1915	2,712
1916	2,779
1917	2,725
1918	2,631
1919	2,799
1920	2,808
1921	5,535
1922	5,364
1923	27,154
1924	29,521
1925	29,172
1926	31,062
1927	31,176
1928	30,854
1929	30,491
1930	30,491
1931	30,673
1932	31,248

SOURCE: Matsubara Nobuyuki, *Kantōshū ahen seido shi* (Dairen: Kantō-chō senbai-kyoku, 1932), 466–67.

actual population of drug users. Allowing for 100 percent underreporting, the United States contained 1.86 drug users per 1,000 inhabitants. In the KLT, if only license holders are counted—a very conservative estimate—the population included over 40 drug users per 1,000 residents in 1924.[14]

Mortality data offers another perspective on the incidence of dependence on narcotics, at least among the subset of drug users whose habit was linked to their

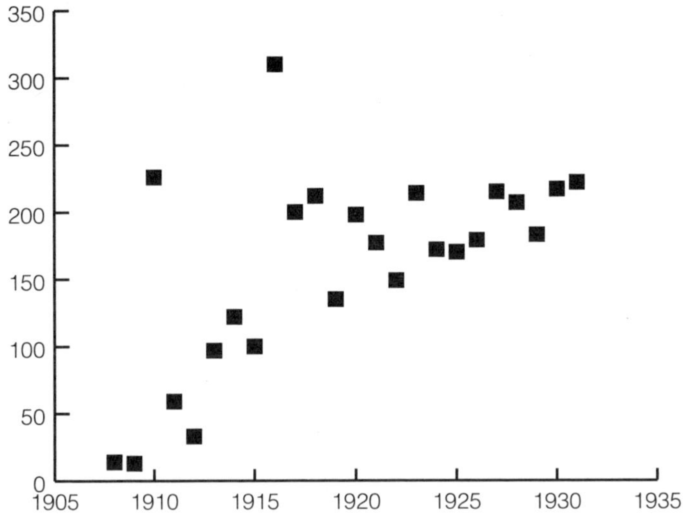

FIGURE 1.
Deaths attributed to addiction in the KLT, 1908–1931

demise. The *Kantō tōkei sho*, which tracked opium addiction as a cause of death in the KLT, provides the only longitudinal perspective on addiction mortality in the prewar world. Due to the stigma attached to drug use, doctors in Japan and the West routinely attributed casualties of dependence on narcotics to proxy conditions.[15]

Between 1908 and 1941, KLT gazetteers recorded 5,011 victims of addiction. Data distinguished between chronic opium dependence *(mansei ahen chūdoku)* and acute overdose *(kyūsei ahen chūdoku)* as a cause of death. This difference is difficult to understand in terms of modern medical science. Some contemporary scholars have contested the very idea that smoking opium is harmful to the body, arguing that moral entrepreneurs of the early twentieth century overdramatized health hazards or mistook the signs of hunger and disease for the ravages of drug use.[16] "Chronic opium dependence" implicated smoking as a contributing factor in mortality. "Acute overdose" likely referred to the more immediately debilitating practice of injecting refined narcotics, or to eating raw opium, a traditional method of suicide among Chinese.

Mortality ascribed to narcotics consumption increased throughout the 1910s and 1920s, peaking at 55.8 per 100,000 population in 1916.[17] The frozen bodies of homeless and impoverished drug users were a common spectacle in Dairen. The child of a Korean migrant family often saw corpses on the streets of the city's Chinese quarter. They were addicts, adults told him with a laugh.[18] Dust-cart drivers recovered their bodies in the early morning and transported them to mass graves. By 1935, four out of every thousand urban residents succumbed annually to addiction and exposure.[19] In terms of the number of individuals affected by narcotics, early twentieth-century Dairen has few contemporary or historical parallels.

Although moral entrepreneurs generally acknowledged opium consumption only among Chinese, drug use was significant—in fact, by some measures more significant—among Japanese migrants to Dairen. In the home islands, the stigma attached to opium use curbed the appeal of the drug. Within the empire, by contrast, the small size and dispersed settlement patterns of the Japanese population allowed many to disregard fundamental cultural taboos. Japanese residents in the KLT included numerous "continental adventurers *[tairiku rōnin]*": the "superfluous men" of modern Japan, "victims without use or function" who came to Manchuria after having been "spat out" by a rigid metropolitan society.[20] During the first quarter century of imperialist penetration of the Asian mainland, continental adventurers constituted the only major group of Japanese migrants not employed by the local administration and its subsidiaries. Many gravitated to narcotics trafficking as a source of quick profits and became dependent on their own products. In the 1930 novel *Busō seru shigai (Militarized Streets)*, Japanese writer Kuroshima Denji depicted the addiction of the *tairiku rōnin* and heroin manufacturer Takezaburō:

> "This time I'll try smoking some myself to see if it's any good." . . . When he said it, neither he nor his wife Osen yet understood the drug's fearsome power.
>
> "Don't be silly. What if you get addicted?" Osen said with a laugh.
>
> "Don't you be so casual about it. There's no way I can go back to Japan!"
>
> And as the product sales gradually improved, his complexion changed to the color of withered pears. The drug had invaded his body cells. He had fallen into the trap.[21]

Continental adventurers also included some Koreans displaced by the Japanese colonization of their homeland in 1910. As a proportion of the total population of the KLT, Koreans never made up more than 0.3 percent of all residents, but contributed nearly 4 percent of addiction-related deaths annually on average from 1912 to 1941.[22]

For Japanese and Chinese, reported deaths from dependence on opium were negligible until 1912. Thereafter, addiction mortality among Japanese rose rapidly. The Chinese population of the KLT was five to seven times larger than the Japanese community, and deaths ascribed to drug dependence were in all years more numerous for Chinese than Japanese. Moreover, the underestimation of addiction fatalities likely disproportionately affected the Chinese, given the relatively greater interest of surveyors in the ruling group. Nonetheless, throughout the 1910s and 1920s, addiction mortality was significantly higher for Japanese than Chinese. Although the moral crusade against opium presented addiction as a particular feature of the Chinese lifestyle, data suggested that the imperialists were more inclined than their subjects to use drugs.[23]

Moral entrepreneurs also distorted the occupational profile of the Dairen drug user community to fit preconceived notions of the "addict" as a Chinese coolie. Three studies provide information on jobs held by registered opium smokers at different moments of Japanese rule over the KLT. In 1927, licensed drug users numbered 31,176. The Kwantung Bureau classified them into fourteen occupational categories. Over 10 percent were farmers, fishermen, and other primary producers. Nearly 40 percent of the sample was composed of low-income tertiary-sector employees: manual laborers, boat crewmen, food industry workers, rickshaw pullers, launderers, and barbers and bathhouse attendants. The remaining drug users were listed as unemployed or in "other" lines of work. The largest single category by far was merchants, who made up 42 percent of the registry.[24] Smoking opium was a traditional courtesy of business among Chinese, who often believed that the drug sharpened their acumen in negotiating.[25]

Another study of 16,715 license holders (54 percent of the total in 1928) found that 86 percent of registrants were between the ages of twenty-five and fifty-five. Drug consumption among KLT Chinese was not predominantly the habit of the rebellious teen or the elderly ill, but the mature adult in his working prime—the prototypical migrant. The survey also drew attention to the high rate of narcotics use among doctors.[26] The "notorious phenomenon of addicted medical men" has appeared in various times and places, but was noteworthy in the KLT even in the context of a global comparison. In Germany, the prewar pharmaceutical manufacturing capital of the world, a 1928 study concluded that about 1 percent of doctors abused banned substances.[27] In Dairen, the best estimate of a corresponding figure is about 3.5 percent.[28] Easy access to narcotics was undoubtedly correlated with the likelihood of use, as in the case of a Korean doctor surnamed Han. After graduating from medical school in 1916, Han set up a practice in Manchuria, where he contracted amoebic dysentery. Treatment with morphine ruined his health and left him unable to work. In 1925, Han attempted to kill himself with a drug overdose, an action that brought his situation to the attention of fellow doctors.[29] Beginning in the mid-1920s, high rates of dependence on opium

TABLE 4 Occupations of registered drug users in the KLT, 1927

Occupation	*Registered drug users*
bathing/barbering	118
teaching/clergy	216
laundry	218
medicine/pharmacy	218
rickshaw pulling	231
finance	258
unemployed	305
fishing	723
other	1,250
hospitality	1,442
farming	2,582
boat crew	2,781
industrial labor	3,356
unskilled labor	4,123
commerce	13,355
Total	31,176

SOURCE: Kantō-chō, "Kantōshū ahen oyobi mayaku seido gaiyō," in Kurahashi Masanao, ed., *Benzoirin fusei yunyū jiken kankei shiryō* (Tokyo: Fuji shuppan, 2003), 104.

among physicians like Han undoubtedly incentivized the medical profession to pursue a cure for addiction (see chapter 8).

In 1935, an international survey team visited Dairen to probe the extent of opium consumption among laborers and its effects on recruitment, efficiency, and welfare. Commissioners estimated the number of drug users at approximately 96,000—just over 11 percent of the population of the KLT and SMRZ, and more than three times the total of registered users. Using data on license holders, the investigation determined that less than 1 percent of farmers and rickshaw pullers, not quite 2 percent of fishermen, and about 4 percent of independent laborers had registered as drug users. By contrast, over 15 percent of unskilled workers held opium-smoking permits.[30] An unknown number of narcotics users declined to apply for licenses from the state; therefore, the actual incidence of opium consumers within each occupation was almost certainly higher than these estimates. Undercounting of narcotics users was especially likely among groups that worked beyond the scrutiny of the Kwantung Bureau. Farmers and fishermen faced less pressure to register than unskilled laborers, who were mostly employed by large public companies. Thus, although opium smoking among these workers was undoubtedly extensive, it may not have been more, or much more, prevalent than among other occupational groups.

In addition to the registration system, addiction treatment clinics collected data on patient occupations. Hospital admissions, like license holders, were subject to various sample biases, and were not necessarily representative of the drug user population as a whole. Of the 693 patients treated for addiction in the state facility in Dairen between 1924 and 1927, 163 were described as coolies, 126 as hired workers, and 78 as factory employees. Together, these groups accounted for over half the patient population—a proportion that nearly matched estimates of unskilled wage earners within the ranks of registered drug users. Tradesmen made up an additional third of the sample. Other patients included opium retailers and pharmacists, Buddhist clergy, and farmers and fishermen.[31] Employees in the primary sector were significantly underrepresented compared to the registration system. The detoxification clinic, situated in the urban heart of Dairen, was likely inconvenient and possibly unknown to rural inhabitants of the KLT.

Hospitals, which provided free room and board, attracted a disproportionate number of disadvantaged patients. By the late 1930s, the unemployed constituted over one-third of clinical admissions.[32] Many checked themselves in voluntarily, but police also rounded up vagrants, especially able-bodied males, for detoxification against their will. In the late 1930s and early 1940s, these cases were discharged directly to work brigades at docks, railways, and factories to overcome a growing labor shortage. Wealthier narcotics consumers often paid bribes to avoid clinical incarceration; a contemporary observer described those who submitted to treatment as "penniless and powerless *[wu qian wu she]*."[33]

Although neither state license holders nor hospital patients were perfectly representative of the Dairen drug user population at large, available information suggests a relatively elevated incidence of opium dependence among low-wage laborers and a generally wide distribution and high rate of narcotics consumption among all major occupational groups. Consumer choices were fundamentally entangled with the interrelated variables of nationality and socioeconomic status. Broadly speaking, the practice of smoking opium dwindled to a small number of Chinese elites. Refined drugs, administered by hypodermic syringe, became popular among Japanese migrants and lower-class Chinese.

Prior to the establishment of imperial rule, smoking opium was the only narcotic available to the population of Dairen. Over the next forty years, the city thrived as a gateway and manufacturing center for refined drugs (alkaloids), including morphine, heroin, and cocaine. Addiction clinic admissions reflected the dramatic increase in the use of refined narcotics relative to smoking opium. In 1925, 83 percent of the total patient population of 528 sought treatment for dependence on smoking opium. The remaining 17 percent were morphine users. A decade later, this ratio was nearly reversed: only 36 percent of the 680 patients treated in 1935 were opium smokers. The majority (61 percent) identified as morphine addicts; the remaining 18 cases sought help for dependence on other refined substances, including cocaine.[34]

Economic factors undergirded the rising consumption of morphine and heroin relative to smoking opium. Smugglers favored processed over raw opium because it was less bulky to ship and had a higher value by weight. As the supply of refined narcotics rose, price dropped. In the 1920s, Dairen entrepreneurs learned to manufacture alkaloids, reducing the need to import pharmaceuticals from Europe. By the end of the 1920s, a syringe of morphine cost less than one-fifth the price of a pipe of smoking opium. A Japanese travel writer reported, “Opium is comparatively expensive and hard for those living hand-to-mouth to afford. Therefore, many prefer the cheaper alternative of morphine, heroin, cocaine, or some other drug. From the middle class down they mostly inject alkaloids.”[35]

Refined narcotics also became popular among workers in the commercial, financial, medical, and pharmaceutical sectors. Time-consuming smoking rituals did not suit a professional lifestyle. A longtime Japanese resident in China explained, “The tempo of the times has speeded up to a gallop; the era of opium was sluggish and slow, and simpler than now, when people use many different types of drugs.”[36] Alkaloids were discreet as well as fast. Italian journalist and spy Amleto Vespa reported, “In many streets the Japanese and Korean dealers have established a very simple and effective system. The morphine, cocaine or heroin addict does not have to enter the place if he is poor. He simply knocks at the door, a small peephole opens, through which he thrusts his bare arm and hand with twenty cents in it. The owner of the joint takes the money and gives the victim a shot in the arm.”[37]

In addition to the ease with which refined narcotics could be obtained and consumed, they also exerted a certain appeal as “modern” drugs. Although vigorously condemned for their physiological impact, alkaloids never acquired the stigma of backwardness attached to smoking opium. On the contrary, they represented the very output of modernity itself. As one Japanese pharmacologist observed, “Smoking opium in primitive fashion or taking it internally was the only method of taking drugs known to those who indulged . . . in olden times, but modern science has introduced morphine."[38] Heroin, first marketed in 1898 in Europe, was an even newer and more alluring product.

Modes of ingesting refined narcotics included smoking (unadulterated or mixed with tobacco), snorting off the back of the hand or from between the palms, rubbing on mucous membranes (particularly the genitals), and injecting subcutaneously, intravenously, or aurally (a practice associated with sexual pleasure).[39] Like opium alkaloids, the syringe reflected a modern sensibility. From its origins in the mid-nineteenth-century West, the hypodermic needle came into widespread use in Japan and China in the 1890s. Uniting the cachet of science with the "needle lore" of traditional medicine, the syringe rapidly became ubiquitous among doctors and laypersons alike. At the end of World War II, one observer reported, "The hypodermic needle is on sale throughout [Japan], in enormous quantities, and is as commonly used as the towel or soap and water."[40] The Chinese mainland was also "flooded" with injection paraphernalia. By the late 1920s, however, needles had come to seem less benign to many Chinese, who associated them with Japan's penetration of the anthropomorphized body of the nation.[41]

Many eventual users of refined narcotics first became habituated to smoking opium. As the social and economic costs of this practice rose, they replaced the pipe with the syringe.[42] Other users simply gave up the habit, rather than adapting to a different drug, means of ingestion, and supply network. Smoking opium was a cultural as well as physiological agent, with a ritual significance that was not easily transferred to other products. In nineteenth-century China, opium "extensified"—that is, metamorphosed from a luxury into an ordinary consumer good available to all ranks of society. This process was reversed in Japanese-occupied Manchuria, where smoking opium became reassociated with elite Chinese in traditional occupations, including Buddhist monks and nuns, classical scholars, women of leisure, and demobilized bannermen.[43] These groups were relatively insulated from critiques of the opium pipe as an artifact of backwardness, and had the time and social context within which to maintain long-standing customs.

With their contrasting modes of use, cultural connotations, and physiological effects, smoking opium and refined narcotics served different purposes, and different populations, in Dairen under Japanese rule. Consumer choices also displayed noteworthy gender patterns. In the Chinese cultural sphere, opium traditionally functioned as an aphrodisiac for men in search of extramarital pleasure. The anonymous author of the eighteenth-century novel *Courtesans and Opium: Romantic Illusions of the Fool of Yangzhou* described the experience: "No sooner has a playboy arrived at the door of a brothel, whether or not he is an addict, whether or not he has smoked before—than a lamp will be lit and a prostitute summoned to lie opposite and roast the opium for him. The addicts go without saying, but even someone who is not addicted will take the opportunity to enjoy a chat and a few laughs with the prostitute and perhaps prolong his visit."[44]

For women, by contrast, drugs were not generally sex aids. An attendant might join her customer in smoking a pipe but did so only at his invitation. Narcotics use often interrupted menses in women and served sex workers as a crude form of birth control. Drugs also relieved exhaustion and pain from sexually transmitted diseases such as syphilis and gonorrhea. Surveying the pleasure districts of urban Manchuria in 1929, sociologist Bingham Dai concluded that most women had little agency in their relationship with narcotics:

> The "flowers" or girl waiters are usually mortgaged to the opium dens for $100.00 or more, all depending on their looks. The girl can be free only after she has paid off this money. She does this in two ways. The first is to wait on opium smokers; for this service she receives one-fourth of the income, that is, ten from every forty cents, which is the price of a single dose of opium. The second is to serve as prostitutes; in that case, she shares the income with her boss. It is a long time before such a girl can gain her freedom.[45]

Some "girl waiters" may have used their employment as a stepping-stone to wealth and influence, perhaps as the concubine of a rich patron. Most, however, could not escape stigmatization as a moral pollutant. In the view of society, even attendants who did not provide sexual services to customers transgressed gender norms by initiating intimate contact with strange men.[46] When the state of Manchukuo banned women from working in opium retail establishments in 1932, many were forced underground, and their vulnerable position deteriorated further.[47]

In addition to empirical observation, moral entrepreneurs used surveys to confirm the prevalence of opium consumption among prostitutes. A 1939 police investigation of 1,600 members of the so-called flower and willow world *(karyūkai)* reported an addiction rate of nearly 10 percent. Other studies concluded that narcotics consumption was virtually universal among sex workers.[48] In 1939, a Japanese-educated Chinese gynecologist undertook the sole known study of female drug users in Manchuria. His sample included 100 female narcotics consumers: 49 opium smokers, 27 heroin users, and 24 morphine injectors. Even though the group was not necessarily representative of the larger population, the relatively high proportion of smokers suggests that women may have been more inclined than men to use opium as opposed to refined narcotics. Smoking opium was a logical drug of choice both for prostitutes, who were expected to sell pipes to male customers, and housewives, who enjoyed the private surroundings and time flexibility needed for ritual consumption. The gynecologist did not collect any information on the social position or occupation of his subjects, but he did calculate the average age of first-time drug use at 19.6. By comparison, male narcotics consumers tended to begin smoking or injecting later in life, most frequently between the ages of 30 and 50. The doctor hypothesized that young females often turned to opium to relieve suffering induced by lingering traditional customs, including footbinding and early sexual activity and reproduction associated with child marriage. Eighty percent of his subjects reported abdominal distress and other symptoms of ill health.[49]

Although fellow scientists deemed the paper fascinating and cited it frequently, this research did not inspire any follow-up studies.[50] Though significant, gender was secondary to nationality in demographics of drug users. Both male and female Japanese migrants to Manchuria were more affected by narcotics than Chinese. As a contributing factor in mortality, opium consumption was most salient among Japanese men, followed by Japanese women, Chinese men, and finally Chinese women.[51]

UNDERSTANDING MOTIVATION IN THE "ADDICT" AND THE "DRUG USER"

In the absence of testimony by drug users themselves, individual reasons for consuming narcotics cannot be known. The epidemiological question of why so many people used opium in Dairen, however, has prompted considerable speculation, both by early twentieth-century moral entrepreneurs and by contemporary scholars.

During the moral crusade of the high imperial age, researchers sought to classify the motivation *(shiyō mokuteki)* of drug users in the KLT in much the same way that they indexed demographic characteristics. Between 1924 and 1927, Dr. Kuroi Tadaichi surveyed nearly 1,500 patients at an addiction treatment clinic in Dairen. Kuroi found that 86 percent of his subjects had "ignorantly" begun using narcotics to relieve pain, particularly of the limbs, lungs, and abdomen. "The Chinese have no idea how [addiction] is scientifically possible, and the facts cannot be easily explained to them," commented a fellow doctor.[52] The remainder of Kuroi's sample was described as "recreational *[goraku* or *kōsai]*" users, who gave no thought to the destruction of their own bodies—or worse, of society and the nation. Kuroi and subsequent investigators did not record the process by which they evaluated patients, nor did they describe the categories they developed to present their results. They allowed only one motive per drug user.[53]

Kuroi, like most moral entrepreneurs, located the drive to consume narcotics in the degeneracy of the individual. By contrast, European and American researchers of the prewar period addressed drug use as a collective phenomenon and generally sought explanations in the environment. They hypothesized that poverty and degradation predisposed many unskilled workers to seek relief in opium. Following a 1935 visit to Dairen, the International Labor Office concluded,

> The social and hygienic conditions under which a great part of the working classes in the Far East live are of so low a standard that these classes of people strive to find some form of diversion permitting them to forget at least for some moments the hardships of life. Their intellectual development is low, housing conditions are primitive and overcrowding general. The working man in the East tends to remain in his own sphere of life on a low level, he has no conception of the amenities of life, which, in any case, he cannot afford.[54]

Migrant laborers typically left their homes on the plains of north China for a two- or three-year stint in Manchuria. They often tried to save travel fare by walking as much as possible of the distance to their port of departure. After a crowded and choppy voyage on a vessel one foreign observer compared to a nineteenth-century slave ship, they arrived in Dairen and began looking for work.[55] For many migrants, the city was merely the first stop on a longer journey north to employment in coal and iron mines. Others took jobs in the port, unloading freight and shifting enormous wheels of soybean cake from railway boxcars to outbound ships. To cut costs, many Japanese enterprises used human labor rather than technology to move heavy loads. "At Anshan coolies carry 80 *kin;* at Fushun, 100 *kin;* and at the port of Dairen, 150 *kin* [about 200 pounds]!" boasted one company.[56]

The imperial regime viewed the Chinese manual laborer as an asset to be exploited, discarded, and replaced. Serious injury and even death on the job were frequent, the result of inadequate training, accidents, floggings, and other abuses. In 1910, the Dairen docks employed approximately 12,000 Chinese; 1,349 were wounded and 4 lost their lives during workdays that averaged over 11 hours. Some migrants, suffering from psychological disorders, harmed or killed themselves. Laborers also fell victim to diseases, including trachoma, gastroenteritis, syphilis, scabies, ear infections, typhus, typhoid fever, and the plague. Even as the state adopted conscription and other drastic measures to address the growing labor shortage, it made little effort to improve working conditions.[57]

The majority of Chinese migrants lived in employee dormitories that offered little comfort, privacy, or sanitation. In Dairen, more than 16,000 laborers squeezed into a space of 12,000 *tsubo* (approximately 2.4 square meters per person). Dormitory residents had access to only a limited array of goods and services sold at inflated prices in the company store. They spent up to 60 percent of their wages on food, yet remained inadequately nourished on coarse and cold meals, particularly after the onset of wartime shortages in the 1940s. In three winter months in 1943, 3,520 laborers died of starvation and disease in a single barrack.[58] Earnings were so low that although remitting money home was a primary motivation for migration, many workers had nothing left over after meeting their own requirements for survival. Some even found themselves in need of support from their families. One migrant, surnamed Huang, wrote to his parents in 1940, "The scarcity of food is truly dire. I am anxious about it every day. I wanted to tell you as quickly as possible, but also feel bad worrying you. I know well the difficulties you are facing at home, but would it be possible to send me even a little food? Every day my stomach is empty. I constantly long for home, but won't be able to return for another four months. . . . If [sending food] isn't possible, money would be fine too."[59]

Historians cite experiences such as Huang's in explaining the high incidence of drug dependence in Dairen and beyond in the early twentieth century.[60] The characterization of workers as miserable, passive victims seeking withdrawal through self-intoxication is challenged, however, by evidence of active efforts to improve conditions in the docks, factories, and railways of the KLT. Hundreds of strikes, mobilizing over one hundred thousand participants, wracked the city-state under imperial rule.[61] Labor disputes were not anti-Japan per se—in fact, nearly five thousand Japanese participated in these actions during the forty years of imperial rule. The mostly poor and illiterate Chinese migrant worker population could not hope to challenge the might of the empire and its local representatives. In any case, the Japanese may have seemed no more brutal or exploitative than the Westerners or warlords under whom they suffered in their native provinces. For most laborers, a sense of obligation to family and home was paramount. They did not intend to settle in the KLT and were not invested in its government.[62] Rather than political change, demonstrations generally sought limited practical benefits, such as shorter workdays, longer rest periods, higher wages, better food and shelter, and compensation for injury or death on the job. When their demands were not met, laborers engaged in acts of passive and active sabotage: taking extended breaks, deliberately wasting time during unsupervised periods, absconding, destroying tools, and setting fire to strategic assets. During the 1920s, several top cadres of the Chinese Communist Party, including Liu Shaoqi, Mao Zedong's future second-in-command, came to Dairen to guide its active labor movement.[63]

The energy of worker protests in the KLT belies the depiction of narcotics consumers as passive subjects who could at most react to conditions imposed upon them. When laborers chose to use drugs, they did so not only to reject the world around them but also to seek a better one by exercising agency over the one factor they could control: their own bodies. For some, drug use was a "weapon of the weak" or an "act of quiet resistance" against the labor regimen that oppressed them.[64] For others, narcotics were a means of increasing efficiency on the job, the better to maximize earnings. The belief that opium use stimulated health, longevity, and productivity was well documented among unskilled workers throughout East and Southeast Asia.[65] In the case of laborers in Japanese Manchuria, private and political interests converged, as the hard work of the individual invigorated the exploiting empire.

The ascription of drug use to the wretched lifestyle of the laborer also fails to account for narcotics consumption among other groups. Explanations of addiction that emphasize occupation or other collective factors, such as nationality, age, socioeconomic status, and gender, do not reflect the heterogeneity of opium users. What united this population was not any demographic characteristic but its common immersion in the urban environment of Dairen. It was within this city, during the forty years of Japanese occupation, that rates of drug use reached a globally unprecedented peak. Addiction is a "disease of civilization" or "developmental disease"—that is, an illness provoked or exacerbated rather than eradicated by modern "progress."[66] Japanese rule over Dairen expanded the supply of opium, making drug consumption possible. By itself, however, supply does not create or explain demand. How did the urban environment make narcotics attractive as well as accessible?

Dairen was a city of migrants. Between 1906 and 1937, the number of inhabitants grew nearly fourteenfold, from 38,896 to 531,989. Each year, Dairen added, on average, 9 percent of its population, although the rate of growth naturally declined as the number of residents increased. Yet, although this pace of urban aggrandizement was extreme, explosive growth characterized many cities around the world in the early twentieth century. It was the constant shifting of the human composition of the city that set Dairen apart as a unique topography of demographic disconnectedness. Data on the comings and goings by ship of urban residents during the first two decades of Japanese rule reveal a population in constant flux. Between 1909

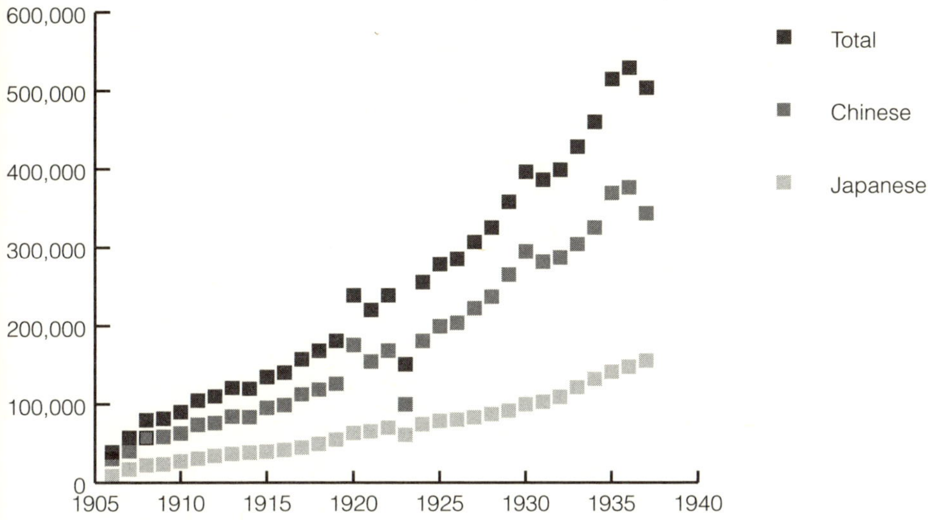

FIGURE 2.
Population of Dairen by nationality, 1906–1937

and 1937, nearly ten million individuals docked in Dairen, while over five million departed. Demographic turnover—the number of people who arrived or left each year as a percentage of the base population—overwhelmed the city, averaging nearly 200 percent annually, and reaching almost 300 percent in some years.[67]

Data on demographic turnover does not distinguish between short-term travel and lengthier settlement. During the early years of Japanese rule, when narcotics consumption came to permeate the urban social fabric, Dairen attracted few tourists. By the 1930s, however, continental travel had become fashionable among middle- and upper-class Japanese. In 1939, over one hundred thousand metropolitan tourists descended upon the city.[68] For many visitors, the local narcotic culture was part of the draw. Bingham Dai wrote, "Naturally the opium dens in Dairen have become a most fascinating place not only to young people living in that locality but also to thousands of travelers passing in and out of this principal port of South Manchuria."[69] Japanese sojourners wrote dramatically of narcotic indulgences followed by carnal ecstasy. As one observer reported, some found themselves subsequently unable to leave: "There are guests who try opium, become addicted, and can't make themselves quit. Even their doctors cease to worry about them; abandoned, they obtain morphine and carry around injection paraphernalia to satisfy their craving for alkaloids. They extend their trip indefinitely. In the end, after several decades of use, drugs wear out the body, and finally the addict wastes away to skin and bone; his strength is dissipated in wandering the streets, and he ends up dead on the side of the road."[70]

Chinese tourists also flocked to Dairen to sample local vice. Zhou Jue, who lived north of the KLT border, lost interest in visiting opium retail establishments in his home province when female attendants were banned. In the red-light districts of Japanese-administered areas, however, "waitresses" remained standard. Zhou vividly recalled an evening of carousing with a friend, during which he witnessed two patrons come to blows over a prostitute.[71]

Although Dairen's reputation for pleasure undoubtedly stimulated tourism, the impact of travelers on urban life was necessarily limited. At the peak of the "Manchuria boom," hotel guests constituted only about one-seventh of total disembarkations at the port. It was short-term settlers, not tourists, who gave Dairen its atmosphere of transience. In most cities in Japan and China, migrants generally arrived with the intention of staying, and leaving almost always represented some kind of economic or moral failure. In Dairen, by contrast, impermanence was a way of life. Very few inhabitants of the KLT were native to the area or wished to spend their lives there. Japanese and Korean migrants included many government employees and adventurers who hoped to make their fortune in Manchuria and return quickly from continental exile. Japan's historical ambivalence toward urbanism climaxed in Dairen, where all the iniquities traditionally ascribed to city life appeared to flourish.[72] For Chinese migrants, temporarily quitting the native village was "dismal but unavoidable"; permanently settling in Manchuria was an acknowledgment of defeat. Of nearly sixteen thousand laborers employed on the Dairen docks in 1933, less than 1 percent had been born in the KLT.[73]

Constant in- and out-migration thwarted the formation of stable social networks. Newcomers naturally had few interpersonal ties, those preparing to leave lacked incentives to participate in community life, and even long-term residents were incessantly jarred by the comings and goings of others. The Japanese novelist Endō Shūsaku (1923–1996), who spent much of his early childhood in Dairen, evokes this atmosphere in his autobiographical short story *Jinsei (Life)*. Over the course of the tale, the young narrator's sense of alienation grows as various characters pass in and out of his world. When four soldiers are garrisoned in his home for a few nights, he attempts to forge a bond with the youngest by offering him a prized harmonica. The soldier, however, abruptly rejects the gift and the human connection. The family's Japanese housekeeper, who returns to her native village, is the next character to abandon the child. With an adult's insight, the narrator deduces, "The more she bragged about it, the more I came to feel that she had idealized the home she had been forced to leave for some reason, and that the very act of idealization had become a kind of reason for living in her mind." Her replacement, a kind Chinese houseboy, also disappears, fired by the narrator's mother for stealing a ring actually taken by her son. Endō himself left Dairen at the age of ten following his parents' divorce.[74]

Migration patterns specific to nationality and gender underline the correlation of demographic turnover with lethal drug use. Chinese women, whose annual turnover averaged 7.8 percent in 1912–25, had a relatively low rate of addiction mortality (0.12 per 1,000 population). Japanese men, with an annual population turnover averaging 168 percent during the same period, had an addiction mortality rate over six times higher, at 0.76 per 1,000. Japanese women and Chinese men fell between these extremes.[75] Although correlation is not causality, the covariation of population turnover and addiction mortality is nonetheless suggestive of a strong sense of urban alienation expressed in narcotics consumption.

Migrants used the city and were used by it. Urban development demanded, depleted, and discarded trained specialists and unskilled laborers alike. The city they produced immersed all residents in an inescapable spatial anomie. Japan sought to fashion Dairen into a showcase of civilization for local, imperial, and international audiences—a consummately "modern" city.[76] Early twentieth-century global ideals of modernity subordinated individuals, with their mortal imperfections, to a rigid set of standards achieved through mechanical technology. In the completed urban utopia, no organic development was necessary or even possible. Subjects were spectators, not participants; guests, not inhabitants.[77]

It was no accident that the structure which came to symbolize Dairen was a hotel. In 1914, the South Manchuria Railway Company opened the Yamato Hotel, a magnificent edifice located in the very center of the city. The four-story building was constructed of stone, a material typically reserved for the most imposing monumental architecture. Its Renaissance style, with Ionic columns and arched first-story windows, epitomized the triumph of contemporary enlightenment over medieval ignorance—the perfect metaphor for Japan's conquest of backward, antiquated China.[78] In front of the hotel, a statue of the first imperial governor of the KLT proclaimed Japanese authority over the leasehold. Inside, the SMR spared no expense in offering the most luxurious and modern accommodations. Each of the hotel's hundred single and double rooms and suites contained its own electric clock, telephone, and private bath with hot and cold running water. Elevator operators and other employees spoke English. The 1930 *Terry's Guide to the Japanese Empire*

FIGURE 3.
Yamato Hotel, Dairen.
SOURCE: South Manchuria Railway Company, *Second Report on Progress in Manchuria to 1930* (Dairen: South Manchuria Railway Company, 1931), 134.

rhapsodized that "travelers will find the Yamato Hotel vastly superior to, and infinitely more comfortable than, any others in the country. . . . [T]he rooms, service, and food are good. . . . [It is] strikingly palatial in nature, and in size and appointments . . . remind[s] the traveler of the best American hotels."[79]

From a financial perspective, the Yamato Hotel was a near-complete loss.[80] But money hardly mattered: the institution existed for public service rather than profit, reaping its rewards in the rave reviews of visitors. Its image appeared in gazetteers, periodicals, journals, newspapers, and even in the memoirs of local Japanese residents who never spent the night there.[81] The Yamato Hotel was not only the most recognizable structure in the city but also the most familiar representation of the city.[82] It was a metonym for Dairen: a self-conscious spectacle for sojourners, a temporary lodging for travelers passing in the night, an alien landscape of unaccustomed amenities. Often described as the most modern city in China and Japan, Dairen gave all its residents, irrespective of national origin, astonishment and awe in place of comfort and familiarity.[83] Opium enabled subjects to mediate the terms of their encounter with urban space—fortifying them for the stage, tranquilizing the frenetic and unbearable, cushioning the loss of the known and safe, replacing traditional social bonds with relationships forged in the drug market. Narcotics consumption was a rare opportunity to exercise autonomy through the privilege of choice. It was at once an attempt to strike out against forces beyond personal control, to withdraw from an unendurable world, to accept complicity in one's own disenfranchisement, and to assert the self in an environment in which the individual was not valued. Drug consumption was an "attempt by modern people to become subjects as well as objects of modernization, to get a grip on the modern world and make themselves at home in it."[84] It was a challenge faced throughout the early twentieth-century world, and nowhere more than in Dairen and the KLT.

CHAPTER THREE • Cultural Producers and the Japanese Empire

At the end of World War I, the great powers, including Japan, came together to re-envision the global order. Delegates at the 1919 Paris Peace Conference were forced to acknowledge rising calls for self-determination among their colonial subjects. In response, they evolved a new justification for empire: grooming colonies for (eventual) independence. Although the sincerity of this aspiration was both variable and questionable, the interwar years nonetheless witnessed sweeping transformations in imperialist ideologies throughout the world.[1] Europeans and Americans gradually distanced themselves from the traditional "mission to civilize," a late nineteenth-century "humanitarian" justification of imperial rule that cloaked economic and political motives for colonization in an alleged moral quest to "uplift" the "backward" peoples of the non-West.[2] In the Japanese empire, meanwhile, the goal of preparing subjects for self-rule inspired the ideology of benevolence or benevolent government *(jinsei)*.

Benevolence merged traditional notions of proper relations among persons and groups of unequal status with an intense determination to reinforce the civilization of the nation by civilizing the empire. The concept of benevolence originated in the writings of the Chinese sage Confucius (551–479 B.C.E.) and served as the philosophical bedrock of Japan's early modern state (1600–1868). Following the Meiji Restoration of 1868, the ideology served to articulate the duties of the modern subject within the nascent emperor-centered polity. In theory, benevolence functioned as the animating principle of all human bonds that involved a discrepancy in social standing. Status was both an indication and an outcome of superior morality. Ideally, within each relationship, the higher party determined and pursued the welfare of the lower party. The only obligation of the latter was to submit, loyally and lovingly, as a son to a father, a wife to a husband, a younger brother to an older brother, and—most important—a subject to a ruler.

During the interwar period, a renewed moral crusade against opium provided the context for the development and implementation of benevolent government as an ideological justification of empire. Moral entrepreneurs used opium both to outline the hierarchical relations among imperial subjects within which benevolence could take place and to depict the "addict" as the object of the mission to civilize.[3] In the cultural realm, sinologists and China experts, researchers, travel and fiction writers, and Christian reformers played a leading though far from exclusive role in producing, popularizing, and propagandizing images of the addict as a debased Chinese slave that a humanitarian Japan was compelled to help.

In contrast to the 1890s, when the moral crusade against opium was largely confined to elites, during the high imperial age moral entrepreneurs and their target audiences represented a much wider cross section of society. The interwar years witnessed the flowering of political consciousness in the middle class, a direct result of earlier efforts to cultivate a modern citizenry. The moral crusade against opium offered cultural producers considerable opportunity to turn the disciplinary apparatus of the state to personal and professional advantage. Moral entrepreneurs also came to include some Taiwanese and Koreans, colonial subjects who sought to modernize their homelands by espousing the "universal" values of civilization set forth by Japan and the West. Given the number and diversity of moral entrepreneurs involved in the production of culture, stereotypes of the addict in the Japanese-language media of the 1920s were ubiquitous but far from uniform or even wholly negative. Collectively, however, they served to distort, exaggerate, and transmogrify the drug user as an embodied justification of imperial rule by Japan.

STATE SINOLOGISTS

In 1898, the Japanese Foreign Ministry merged two study societies to form the Tō-A Dōbunkai (East Asia Common Culture Association). In the context of increasing rivalry between Japan and Russia over China, the organization aimed to gather politically useful information about the Asian mainland. It also sought to nurture progressive reform in the Qing empire and cultivate domestic interest in Sinic affairs. Rejecting calls for Japan to distance itself from Asia, the sixty founding members of the association countered that the "common culture and common race *[dōbun dōshu]*" of the Japanese and Chinese morally impelled the former to understand and protect the Qing empire from Russia and the West.[4]

In 1901, the Tō-A Dōbunkai established the Tō-A Dōbun Shoin, a school to train Japanese students in the study of China.[5] The capstone of this four-year educational experience was the "grand tour *[dai ryokō]*," during which aspiring graduates collected data on some aspect of politics, education, culture, society, or economic life at a field site. By the 1920s, the grand tour had evolved into a fixed-term undertaking of two to six months, carried out in small groups and funded by the Foreign Ministry. Japanese students, unaccustomed to the spectacle of drug consumption at home, marveled at the extent of opium use in China. One commented, "The Chinese cannot seem to give up smoking opium. In the countryside, they do it in public. On the boat from Guangdong to Macau, we saw them smoking completely unselfconsciously. In Shanghai, refined narcotics are very popular, and there are also a lot of illicit traffickers. Most of those addicted appear to be coolies, who, without opium, aren't capable of working."[6]

Like the late nineteenth-century sinologist Oka Senjin, students depicted drug use as an agent of racial and national destruction. After observing a smoking ritual, one lamented, "Three thousand years of history notwithstanding, China's national strength is waning. Opium has already taken a toll on the vitality of the country."[7] In contrast to late-Meiji moral entrepreneurs, who sought to distance Japan from China, the post-1919 generation viewed Japanese abstinence from narcotics as a reason to become more involved in mainland affairs. In the words of one student, "Our country does not grow opium or manufacture alkaloids. Therefore, we should not hesitate to exercise moral courage [against drugs]."[8] Many graduates of Tō-A Dōbun Shōin brought these convictions to careers in public service. By the late 1920s, the Japanese government in Manchuria employed almost a quarter of the school's degree holders.[9]

In addition to the Tō-A Dōbun Shōin, the Tō-A Dōbunkai also founded a medical missionary organization known as the Dōjinkai (Universal Benevolence Association). In its statement of purpose, the Dōjinkai called for the dissemination of Japanese benevolence across Asia in the form of modern scientific (i.e., Western) medicine. Among Dōjinkai members were two-time prime minister Ōkuma Shigenobu, foreign minister Uchida Kōsai, Prince Konoe Atsumarō and his son Konoe Fumimarō, and Kitasato Shibasaburō, an internationally renowned bacteriologist. The organization also included high-profile antinarcotics crusaders such as Gotō Shinpei, KLT civil governor Hayashi Gonsuke, and Kaku Sagatarō, the director of the Opium Monopoly Bureau and civil governor of Taiwan.

Immediately upon its founding, the Dōjinkai built several small medical stations in the KLT. The organization subsequently established clinics throughout Manchuria, China, and the Japanese empire. Journals knit these institutions together, bringing Japanese medicine to Chinese doctors and transmitting mainland knowledge to domestic physicians. By incorporating non-Japanese contributors into its literary community, the Dōjinkai presented the social problem of narcotics as an opportunity for empire-wide collaboration. Journal editors selected opium addiction as one of eight designated fields of emphasis, devoting two special issues to the topic.[10]

One of the most prolific moral entrepreneurs to publish in Dōjinkai journals was Dr. Sakai Yoshio, a professor of physiology at the Tokyo Imperial University Medical College. Sakai viewed addiction as a dark curse over Manchuria and East Asia. During a 1935 tour of Japanese missionary hospitals in north China and Manchukuo, he gave speeches enumerating the characteristics of the prototypical addict: an unclean body, home, and attire; unsanitary eating habits; and a lifestyle devoid of "even a scrap of morality." Fearing that these traits might spread to Japan, Sakai urgently appealed to his fellow citizens to protect their "beautiful custom *[ryōfū bizoku]*" of abstinence from opium. Otherwise, he warned, within a decade the Japanese would become "merely a herd of animals, like the Chinese."[11]

In Sakai's view, extinction threatened the Chinese both as a race and as individuals. To illustrate the latter process, the doctor diagrammed the addict's "descent into hell." Following Sigmund Freud, whose work captured the interest of doctors worldwide in the 1930s, Sakai divided the addict psyche into three components: life and death instinct *(sei no honnō* and *shi no honnō)*, morality *(dokusei)*, and reason *(risei)*. The first phase of extinction witnessed the disintegration of morality and reason in the addict. The second phase erased the life instinct, leaving only the death instinct.[12] Unchecked, this process would lead to the elimination of the Chinese people, according to the principles of social Darwinism. Hope lay in salvation by Japan, with its benevolent tradition of "loving its enemies."[13] "The mission of the great Japanese empire is to lead the nations of East Asia, extirpate the evil custom of opium smoking, and sincerely protect and promote the prosperity of the yellow race," concluded Sakai.[14]

THE SOUTH MANCHURIA RAILWAY COMPANY RESEARCH BUREAU

The Tō-A Dōbunkai was a model for one of the most famous and prolific research institutions of imperial Japan: the South Manchuria Railway Company Research

Bureau (Mantetsu chōsabu). The Research Bureau was the brainchild of colonial administrator and 1890s moral entrepreneur Gotō Shinpei. After his initial posting in Taiwan, Gotō became the first president of the railway (henceforth referred to as the SMR) in 1906. Although he remained in this office for less than two years, he had an enduring influence on his successors and Japanese policy in Manchuria. Under Gotō's leadership, Japan pioneered a form of imperialism by railway, with the SMR taking on a political role often compared to the British East India Company. SMR concerns ultimately came to encompass transportation and freight traffic, manufacturing and industry, coal and mineral mines, oil plants, libraries, hospitals, hotels, shipping, and local public works. These enterprises collectively formed the backbone of the imperial economy in Manchuria, employing hundreds of thousands of workers.[15]

Drawing on his experiences in Taiwan, Gotō believed that any attempt to civilize the Chinese should emanate from an understanding of the local environment and customs. Designated the "eyes and ears" of the imperial regime, the Research Bureau generated thousands of papers on the human and natural world.[16] Based in Dairen, the staff numbered more than three hundred at peak strength and employed over two thousand gifted social and physical scientists during its nearly forty-year lifespan. Many researchers had unsuccessfully applied for academic posts in Japan, where competition was keen and hiring criteria nontransparent. Others, mainly left-leaning university graduates, sought freedom from tightening censorship in the home islands, where they faced imprisonment and pressure to convert to right-wing ideological orthodoxy *(tenkō)*. In Manchuria, by contrast, SMR researchers worked on behalf of, yet independently from, the imperial government and even the railway company. In a postwar memoir, Itō Takeo, a Research Bureau employee from 1920 to 1945, recalled the intellectual freedom of his first decade in Dairen: "If the SMR found fault with my attitude and my activities, it is interesting that they never interfered."[17]

As Marxist scholars, many Research Bureau associates were interested in the impact of opium on the proletariat, represented by the "coolie" (Japanese, *kuri;* Chinese, *kuli*). The global stereotype of the coolie emerged from depictions of migrant laborers in the American West and the European empires in China and Southeast Asia. To the great powers, the coolie was simply "Oriental," but in the imperial Japanese mindset, he was explicitly Chinese. Like most moral entrepreneurs, Research Bureau scholars associated the coolie (literally "pain and power") with dirt, disease, depravity, and deviance.[18] In the capacity of a laborer, the coolie evoked the sympathy of a Marxist; as a Chinese, he confronted the disdain of an imperialist. The coolie, like the addict, was tantamount to a slave, and the convergence of these stereotypes reinforced consensus among the great powers regarding Chinese unfitness for independent nationhood.[19]

A common field site for SMR investigations of the coolie was the Dairen labor barracks of Hekizansō (Chinese, Pishanzhuang), built by the Japanese entrepreneur Aioi Yoshitarō in 1911. During the imperial age, Hekizansō provided temporary and, in some cases, permanent lodging to hundreds of thousands of Dairen dockworkers. Aioi claimed that benevolence had inspired him to establish the so-called Green Mountain Villa, but the concentration of labor also increased managerial efficiency by shortening commuting time, reducing turnover and escapes, and centralizing job training. At the height of annual occupancy, from December to April, the complex typically housed more than sixteen thousand migrants, a majority of the laborers in the port.[20] Hekizansō was in many ways a "total institution" in which all activities of daily life—labor, leisure, and sleep—revolved around meeting production goals. Deindividuated inmates were constantly together but isolated from the rest of society. Their moral worth was indexed by the extent to which they internalized the goals of their overseers.[21]

Aioi presented Hekizansō as a modern social welfare facility that furnished laborers with an economical and superior standard of living, including running water, sewage, and electricity. Maintenance "took adequate care of hygiene," thoroughly disinfecting the barracks twice yearly and providing free weekly baths and bimonthly haircuts. Brick quarters were said to constitute a luxury beyond the imagination of most Chinese, at home or on other work sites: "At Hekizansō, the mud house that is all one can hope for in Shantung [the province of origin of most migrants] is turned into brick buildings."[22] Hekizansō was widely advertised as a Dairen tourist attraction. Seen from a viewing platform at the top of a nearby hill, the barracks made a spectacle of laborers as compliant objects of Japanese benevolence.[23] From the inside, however, SMR investigators deemed Hekizansō less than satisfactory. Many denounced the capitalist exploitation of coolies, who were treated "worse than oxen and horses." Researchers also blamed laborers themselves for their poverty, citing their love of "immoral" recreations such as gambling, drinking, and taking drugs.[24] Derogatory stereotypes of migrants, inmates of the total institution, helped to maintain the power hierarchy upon which it depended.[25]

In the early 1920s, Itō Takeo observed a "flourishing business" in opium in Hekizansō and other dormitories. "Agoniz[ing] in an effort to understand what was going on," Itō ultimately attributed the proliferation of narcotics among coolies to "undisguised colonial control"—not by Japan, but by Chinese coolie bosses (Chinese, *batou;* Japanese, *hatō*).[26] The coolie boss served as the chief agent of unskilled worker recruitment, management, and drug distribution in early twentieth-century Dairen and Manchuria. At the lowest level, a "small boss" assembled a group of up to ten workers through hometown contacts. Successively higher coolie bosses agglomerated these manpower units and negotiated with SMR foremen to hire the entire operation. A "big boss" might be responsible for as many as one hundred laborers. In exchange for a cut of worker earnings, the coolie boss provided travel expenses, interpretation skills, wage advances, remission services, protection and security, insurance against illness and accidents, meals, entertainment, and other benefits.[27] Coolie bosses conveniently freed Japanese directors from time-consuming administrative burdens such as paying wages daily.[28] The SMR and other corporations employing large numbers of unskilled laborers accordingly granted bosses enormous discretion over their ranks. On average, bosses were little better off than those working under them, but even the slight differential of power gave them an incentive to support the status quo. In effect, Japanese companies co-opted many potential labor movement leaders into their own ranks.

In procuring and distributing drugs, coolie bosses capitalized on a preexisting hierarchy to tighten their own control. Research Bureau associates frequently accused bosses of encouraging addiction by forcing workers to accept narcotics in lieu of wages. According to one survey, only 4 percent of migrant laborers had used opium before arriving in the KLT.[29] As for the rest, wrote one moral entrepreneur, "Ignorant coolies don't know any better than to consider this kind of exploitation natural."[30] Drug dependence deepened the subordination of laborers, as migrants who needed regular access to narcotics were less likely to abscond from employment, leaving the recruiter to replace them at his own expense. In this way, bosses transferred their own oppression onto their underlings.

Aioi personally disliked the "semifeudal" practices of coolie bosses, which he viewed as antithetical to modern, rationalized management. Nonetheless, for the sake of convenience he adopted the system, claiming that it suited the Chinese "racial psychology" and family structure.[31] SMR Research Bureau associates also resoundingly condemned "tyranny" in the labor market. Ironically, their left-wing denunciation of the coolie boss, which diverted attention from the larger issues of corporate exploitation of workers and state responsibility for the proliferation of illegal drugs, actually served to align their writings with more orthodox critiques of opium. Shifting blame for narcotics consumption onto a Chinese target, Marxist scholars suggested that only Japanese benevolence could liberate the laborer from double enslavement to feudal overseers and opium addiction.

CHINA EXPERTS

In addition to rising numbers of Japanese who traveled to the Asian mainland in the 1920s, many gleaned impressions of China indirectly, by reading about the experiences of others. Visitors to Dairen and Manchuria during the high imperial age included a number of Japan's most renowned literati, such as Tanizaki Jun'ichirō, Akutagawa Ryūnosuke, Yokomitsu Riichi, and Muramatsu Shōfū. Many authors of continental travelogues virulently condemned the Chinese. They used the terms *minzoku* (race-nation) and *bunka* (culture) interchangeably to frame differences between the Japanese and their continental neighbors.[32] A subset of travel writers, "China experts *[Shina tsū]*" were distinctive in their tendency to disaggregate these concepts. Although few China experts defended the Chinese people, they admired Sinic civilization. For them, benevolence reflected a love of Chinese culture, rather than disdain for the Chinese race.

Yosano Akiko (1878–1942), the most famous female poet of prewar Japan, is not generally grouped with China experts, because most of her work was inspired by domestic experiences. However, her monthlong visit to Manchuria in the spring of 1928 at the invitation of the SMR resulted in the publication of a diary, *Man-Mō yūki* (Travels in Manchuria and Mongolia), which was both erudite and detailed in discussing Chinese literature, history, and geography. Akiko's account is particularly interesting given the paucity of female voices among prewar cultural producers. Although she was no crusader, her impressions of opium users largely dovetailed with stereotypes offered by interwar moral entrepreneurs.

Akiko found China magnificent. "The beautiful, gentle scenery that was reflected in the fresh verdure of the willow trees extended as far as our field of vision—a picturesque scene such as cannot be found in Japan," she rhapsodized over one landscape.[33] The Chinese, by contrast, mostly impinged upon her consciousness as coolies and addicts. In one south Manchurian city, a Japanese guide informed Akiko, "scarcely anything of importance remained of the ancient architecture worth seeing." Instead, he escorted her to a courtroom, a prison, and an opium "den." Reporting on the latter, Akiko exaggerated the alien and offensive customs of the Chinese as a means of demonstrating their collective unfitness for self-rule:

> This opium den was a run-down house, not the sort of place frequented by persons of wealth. In the center of the room was an earthen floor, and several customers were lying prostrate on their sides on bed matting to the left and right as they smoked opium. . . . Already completely intoxicated, they were adrift in a land of dreams, sleeping with their faces turned upward. With the

flame from a hand-held lantern, an assistant enabled those customers half awake and half in a daze to smoke from the large pipe bowl half full of opium the color of refined dark sugar. Not a single customer there seemed to notice us looking at them. Perhaps they were lost at the peak of their pleasurable dreams, but to those of us looking it was a wretched, horrific sight.[34]

In this passage, Akiko, the narrator, describes Chinese drug users in terms that the Japanese reading public had come to expect. No common bond of humanity united the Japanese observer with the Chinese addicts; to Akiko, they presented a spectacle of Otherness and unfitness, already drifting out of existence. They were objectified by her gaze and powerless to return it.

Akiko did not acknowledge the support of the SMR for her journey, but the railway's sponsorship undoubtedly defined what she saw and how she saw it. Although disturbed by Japanese militarism in Manchuria and the imperial tendency to "belittle" the Chinese, she generally upheld the racial rationale of empire.[35] During her few interactions with Chinese elites, Akiko assumed a position of benevolence, evaluating the attire and demeanor of her hosts for evidence of civilization and graciously accepting unfamiliar courtesies. The deference she received may have represented the nature of the "friendship" she longed for between China and Japan. During her trip, Akiko regarded the rise of nationalism among the Chinese as a positive development, if not carried far enough to threaten her country's dominance of the mainland. Upon her return to Japan, however, she became more supportive of imperial expansion, encouraging bravery and sacrifice among Japanese troops and civilians.[36]

Distaste for the Chinese people and respect for Chinese civilization also characterized the works of two of the most prolific male China experts of the period: Gotō Asatarō (1881–1945) and Inoue Kōbai (1881–1949). Gotō (no relation to Gotō Shinpei), a scholar of linguistics, visited China for fieldwork over twenty times between the late 1910s and his assassination by right-wing nationalists in the closing days of World War II. He embraced the persona of the eccentric sinophile, adopting traditional Chinese attire, grooming practices, and domestic architecture. Gotō wrote thirty-one books on Chinese customs, including wedding and funeral practices, eating and drinking, economic life, toilet behavior, and drug consumption. His audience included not only the Japanese of the home islands but also metropolitan settlers throughout the empire.[37]

Gotō's insistent definition of opium smoking as a cultural practice rather than a racial attribute infused his work with noteworthy sympathy and respect for the Chinese. In a number of books on traditional customs, he ignored the issue of narcotics altogether.[38] He also directly countered stereotypes of degeneracy, pleading with his Japanese readers to suspend their "criminal view *[han'aku shi]*" of opium and users.[39] The addict in Gotō's depiction was not the economically destitute coolie that Yosano Akiko saw, but a high-class gentleman, a figure to which his readership might more easily relate. Gotō lovingly described the lavish furnishings and decor of a wealthy Chinese acquaintance's private smoking room and the expensive paraphernalia used to prepare opium for consumption. Seeking pleasure in drugs, he suggested, was not a sign of immorality but a way of participating in tradition.

However, Gotō was hardly an uncritical observer of narcotics. Although tolerant of elite smoking, he viewed morphine and heroin injecting among the poor as evidence of deviance. In Gotō's definition, an addict was "someone who has lost his livelihood through dependence on drugs and become a beggar."[40] "It is public knowledge that narcotics are poisoning the Chinese nation," he wrote. But based on his observation of China's failing anti-opium movement, he was not convinced that the state alone could eradicate addiction.[41] Gotō did not propose any specific assistance from Japan to China, but declared his belief in benevolence according to the Tō-A Dōbunkai doctrine of "common culture, common race." "When we Japanese examine China, it's not at all like looking at a foreign country," he wrote.[42] Whereas earlier moral entrepreneurs had sought to distinguish Japan from the "Orient," Gotō reminded his readers of their ties to Asia.[43]

Gotō's contemporary and fellow China expert, Inoue Kōbai, maintained a similarly complicated relationship to China and the Chinese. Born in Tokyo, Inoue became familiar with China as a youth through his parents' business exporting weapons from Japan to the Asian mainland. Upon his father's death from alcoholism at the age of thirty-eight, Inoue invested his inheritance in a Chinese restaurant. He befriended a Chinese noodle shop owner surnamed Chen, who consistently attracted a larger clientele. Chen later admitted, however, that most of "his" customers were simply passing through the door on their way to an opium "den" upstairs. Chen told Inoue that the manager fought constantly with his Japanese wife, and that the couple's daughter had run away from home. Inoue wondered how opium could cause such familial dysfunction.

"Is it like tobacco?" he asked.

"No, it's different," Chen replied shortly.

"Is it like sake?" Inoue persisted.

"No, not a bit," Chen repeated.

"Does it make you drunk and drowsy?" Inoue wondered.

"No, not that," Chen said finally.

"I didn't understand his answers, so I said I was going upstairs to see for myself. Chen and I went together. That was my first experience with opium," Inoue recalled laconically.[44]

Inoue's restaurant failed, and in the fall of 1913 he sought a fresh start in Shanghai. Six years in China furnished the material for *Shina fūzoku* (Chinese customs), a self-published compendium of iniquities associated with mainland life, including womanizing, gambling, drinking, and smoking opium. Addiction, Inoue argued, degraded both the individual and the nation. "What a dark influence opium has cast over this country [China]," he concluded. "The state is approaching the endpoint of its life. Whatever will happen?"[45]

In late 1921, Inoue left Shanghai for Nanjing. He married a Chinese woman who was ashamed of his Japanese nationality and refused to acknowledge him in public, even locking him in his room when guests visited their home. Her dependence on drugs eventually became apparent even to her distant, alcoholic husband, who wrote of her as "the slave of opium *[ahen no dorei]*," condemned to "serving the devil until she dies."[46] Inoue's 1930 *Sake, ahen, majan* (Sake, opium, mahjong) was a world-weary first-person narration of the vices that flourished in his household. Yet his attitude toward Chinese culture was not wholly negative. In 1932, he published the first Japanese translation of the collected writings of Lu Xun (1881–1936), one of the most revered authors of modern China. The work sold widely, although Lu resented the association with a "popular" writer.[47]

In 1939, Inoue presented a paper on the custom of smoking in China at a Tokyo forum on political, economic, social, and cultural issues in the Japanese empire and beyond. Inoue attributed opium consumption to the egotism and irresponsibility of the Chinese: "Naturally, they do not know how to curb their lusts. . . . [U]pon slipping into a state of addiction, the addict veers from hell to ecstasy at the whim of opium, that merciless drug."[48] Despite—or perhaps owing to—Inoue's relatively deep relationship with China and personal experience of addiction, when discussing narcotics with Japanese colleagues he assumed the position of an observer rather than a participant. He also stopped short of advocating a specific political position for Japan—except through his own life story. To the Japanese Inoue, opium epitomized the consequences of his nation's fascinating, revolting, addictive, and ultimately destructive involvement with China.[49]

FICTION WRITERS

During the high imperial age, fiction writers of diverse genres and stylistic orientations used opium to index Japan's changing status, aspirations, and self-perceptions as the nation left and returned to Asia. Early moral entrepreneurs in the literary realm deployed the trope of abstinence from narcotics to identify Japan with the West, particularly Great Britain, the global hegemon of the day. Subsequent writers, pursuing a stronger justification of imperialism, framed the opium addict as a metaphor for a sick Asia seeking Japanese benevolence.

The defining text of the addiction genre in both Japanese and Western fiction was Thomas De Quincey's 1821 *Confessions of an English Opium-Eater.*[50] *Confessions* narrates the author's relationship with laudanum, a beverage of opium and alcohol that transports him to ecstasy, provokes him with vivid hallucinations, and incites the despair of unbreakable bondage. In early twentieth-century Japan, the popularity of the "I-novel" *(shishōsetsu* or *watakushi shōsetsu)* primed writers and readers alike for the confessional mode of the opium eater.[51] The first Japanese translation, by Tsuji Jun (1884–1944), appeared in 1918. Tsuji's work sold so well that it was reprinted twice and inspired several competing versions.[52] Excerpts of *Confessions* also appeared in a Dōjinkai journal in 1930.[53] When Japanese readers demanded access to the English-language original, two prominent publishing houses issued the text with annotations to facilitate comprehension of unfamiliar proper nouns and terminology.[54]

The 1918 novella *Shimon (The Fingerprint),* by Satō Haruo (1892–1964), represents perhaps the most direct reflection of De Quincey's influence on Japanese fiction. The narrator, "Satō," even acknowledges the contribution of "his friend Tsuji" in making available a Japanese-language version of *Confessions* (although Satō the author was proficient in English). Satō Haruo was a human link among Tsuji and many early twentieth-century cultural producers who commented on drugs, including Yosano Akiko, Inoue Kōbai, Akutagawa Ryūnosuke, and Tanizaki Jun'ichirō.[55] In 1932, Satō helped organize the "Tsuji Jun fan club" to support the translator during his hospitalization for alcohol-induced psychosis. Like De Quincey, Tsuji was an addict for most of his life.[56]

In *The Fingerprint,* Satō the author places Japan in the position of Great Britain vis-à-vis the "Orient" through the figures of two protagonists, both of whom embody aspects of De Quincey's persona. Satō the narrator is a Tokyo painter whose boyhood friend, R.N., has returned from a long sojourn abroad to tell an incredible tale. While in London, R.N. meets a sailor who takes him to smoke opium in the East End. R.N.'s description of his visit to the "den" establishes him as "British": despite his Japanese nationality, he encounters the "Orient" without the slightest sense of self-awareness as an Asian. He does, however, succumb to the "Oriental vice" of addiction.[57] Realizing his condition, R.N. decides to force himself to detoxify by returning to his home country, which, as the sailor observes, "has no opium dens." R.N.'s sea voyage home takes him through the British Orient, including Cairo, Singapore, Hong Kong, and Shanghai. Despite his intention to renounce narcotics, in each port of call he inevitably indulges. Finally he arrives in Nagasaki, the site of the most publicized opium-related crimes of the Meiji period. There, in his native city, R.N. settles into a life of addiction.

After months of oblivion, R.N. unexpectedly appears at Satō's Tokyo home to beg for shelter while overcoming his dependence on drugs. One day during his convalescence, the two friends see a movie together. R.N. becomes perturbed at one frame, a blown-up image of a fingerprint. He subsequently delves into dactylography, his obsession with the topic replacing his passion for opium. Months later, he requests that Satō accompany him on a mysterious trip back to Nagasaki. Still not understanding his friend's motives, the narrator agrees. The pair experience Nagasaki almost as a Western city. Their rickshaw puller speaks English, they drink black tea, and R.N. rents a house built of brick, an atypical construction material in Japan. As he later reveals to his companion, the dwelling was formerly an opium den, in which he awoke one morning beside the bleeding corpse of a foreigner. Next to the body, R.N. found a watch with a fingerprint, his only clue to the identity of the killer. After seeing the image of the very same fingerprint in the movie he attended with Satō, R.N. realized that the American actor, William Wilson, was the murderer. Reflecting the World War I context in which Satō wrote the story, Wilson is also a German spy.

R.N. is a self-conscious acolyte of De Quincey, his appearance, movements, and hallucinations reflecting those of the author of *Confessions*. He insists upon speaking in English, which the narrator speculates he may have found "appropriate . . . for this kind of tale." Transcribing his friend's story, Satō settles for Japanese but intersperses English punctuation and phrases to convey his own sense of strangeness to the reader.[58] The encounter with R.N. places the narrator in a pseudodrugged state from which he never recovers.[59] Following his friend from their shared home in Tokyo, R.N.'s private opium retreat, to the haunted den in Nagasaki, Satō chronicles the contagion of intoxication: "In any case, [R.N.] was crazy. . . . If this continued for another ten days, I myself would become like him, there was no doubt."[60] Satō's transformation culminates in his transcription of R.N.'s hallucinations following the latter's death from illness. "Was it not likely the case that R.N. collected these things according to the example of De Quincey's *Confessions of an English Opium-Eater?*" the narrator wonders.[61] By translating R.N.'s writings into Japanese, Satō appropriates them, just as his first-person narration (under the author's own surname) allows him to take R.N.'s testimony as his own "confession." His final, dubious disclaimer of madness cements the reader's impression that he has become as disoriented as an addict: "I am not in the least bit mad. I say this to my wife and to my readers. To tell the truth, I have recently come to think that R.N. was not mad either."[62]

Satō's concluding words recall the similarly unconvincing declaration of Edgar Allan Poe's antihero in the 1843 short story "The Tell-Tale Heart," which cites memory as evidence of sanity: "TRUE! nervous, very, very dreadfully nervous I had been and am; but why WILL you say that I am mad? Hearken! and observe how healthily, how calmly, I can tell you the whole story."[63] Poe (1809–49), an American writer whose works are often identified with the addiction genre, became known to the Japanese literary community in the 1890s. His widely translated poems and short stories greatly influenced authors of detective fiction *(tantei shōsetsu)*, a form of popular literature often identified with the "erotic grotesque nonsense" culture of the late 1920s and 1930s.[64]

Steeped in the lurid and abnormal, detective fiction frequently deployed drugs and poisons in general, and opium in particular, to set mood and drive plot. The 1930 novel *Ahen fujin* (Madame Opium), by Ōshita Udaru (1896–1966), shares many characteristics with *The Fingerprint*, but situates addiction within a Chinese world that threatens Japan, rather than a British culture that the author seeks to appropriate. The title character of the work, the femme fatale Madame Yoshimachi, uses narcotics to subdue and control the men around her. Her first appearance, in a dark, shabby fifth-floor office in Marunouchi, the government district in downtown Tokyo, suggests the penetration of Chinese vice to the very heart of the Japanese polity. An old man, badly dressed and carrying an umbrella against the afternoon drizzle, knocks at the door of the China Trading Company. When a "yellow-skinned Chinese" surnamed Chen appears, the old man, identified as Tsukata, immediately asks for Madame. Chen informs him that she has not yet arrived. In response to Tsukata's begging, he can only reply helplessly, "But she comes and goes as she pleases. It's useless to summon her."[65]

Finally, her domination established, Madame Yoshimachi arrives at the office. A beautiful woman in her late twenties, her given name, Satomi, means "the beauty of the [Japanese] natal village," but she is attired in Chinese-style clothing. From a gilded box in her handbag, she offers Tsukata a quantity of "tobacco" with "a slightly different appearance from the regular thing."[66] As he smokes, he metamorphoses from a tremulous old man with sallow skin and labored breath to a youth of no more than twenty-five years of age. Addiction to opium has prematurely withered him. In exchange for a week's supply of the drug, he agrees to spy for Madame Yoshimachi. The femme fatale then turns her attention to Chen, pressing opium upon him as well before taking her departure.[67]

Madame Yoshimachi's interaction with Tsukata and Chen is purely a business transaction, but in the next scene, she uses drugs to subdue a more intimate male acquaintance, the Japanese artist Tsumashita. The two meet in a Chinese-style room with green dragon wallpaper, illuminated only by an opium lamp. Even before the act of smoking, they have entered "a land of sweet dreams."[68] As they sit in semi-darkness, Madame Yoshimachi asks Tsumashita why he has ceased to care for her. Tsumashita curses her as a "poison woman *[dokufu]*." He fears the fate of Tsukata, a former university student who has degenerated to the ultimate extreme of opium addiction. Madame Yoshimachi argues with him but is unable to sway him with words. Switching strategies, she begins to prepare opium for smoking. Under his silent gaze, she inhales, intoxication suffusing her features with a wild beauty. "It's good," she says softly, encouraging him. Against the combined temptation of the woman and the opium, Tsumashita is powerless. He sweats, he denounces her, and finally he seizes the pipe from her hand and begins the long descent into addiction.[69]

The early twentieth-century West inscribed submissiveness, domesticity, piety, and sexual purity into its vision of ideal womanhood. Imperial Japan developed a corresponding image of feminine perfection, embodied by the phrase "good wife, wise mother *[ryōsai kenbō]*."[70] In (male-authored) literature and beyond, addicted women transgressed the gender norms of their day. By stepping outside their prescribed role as moral exemplars, they threatened to lead innocent men astray and undermine the paternalistic foundations of decent society. The characterization of Madame Yoshimachi as a "poison woman" explicitly places her within an imagined category of criminal females in modern Japan. Writers subjected the appearance of the poison woman to minute scrutiny, but gave little consideration to her thoughts and motives. Scarcely an individual in her own right, she embodied society's darkest fears.[71] In Ōshita's novel, Madame Yoshimachi's use of opium for personal pleasure and to subjugate men not only violates society's expectations for her sex but also blurs the boundary between Japanese and Chinese, as she, a Japanese woman, moves from the China Trading Company to a stereotyped den, wearing Chinese clothes and interacting with Chinese characters. Through Madame Yoshimachi, Ōshita suggests that deviation from the female norm does not terminate simply in sexual misconduct. Rather, it imperils the very survival of the race-nation by transforming wives and mothers, guardians of domestic (home and national) tranquility and bearers of the next generation, from superior Japanese to inferior Chinese.

In the face of Madame Yoshimachi's corruption, Japanese men are helpless. Unlike the femme fatale, whose power feeds on opium, male victims are emasculated by drugs, transformed from independent agents into cringing objects of scorn. In the novel, Tsukata is the primary representative of this metamorphosis: having exhausted his stash of narcotics, the youth collapses in a seedy Chinese theater in the throes of withdrawal. Summoned to the scene of his demise, police initially believe he has suffered an epileptic fit, but the discovery of his opium pipe exposes his addiction. Tsukata's death, reported in the newspaper the following day, is said to be "piteous *[kawaisō]*," the result of a weak character and undisciplined nature.[72] As a Japanese male, he is deplorable but not evil; as the dupe of a woman and a Chinese, he is not responsible for his actions. His death is a cautionary tale for his nation.

Just as opium pervaded detective fiction, a genre usually set in the Japanese metropole, it also came to play an important role in the literature of the empire. In 1928, a monthlong sojourn in China inspired the writer Yokomitsu Riichi's first and most famous novel, *Shanhai (Shanghai)*. In *Shanghai*, as in *Madame Opium*, narcotics signify Chinese corruption and degeneracy. Addicts, who appear frequently on the seamy streets of the title city, are dehumanized through their association with arthropods. In one scene, the Japanese exile Sanki sits in a bar observing a Chinese man smoking a pipe. His gaze travels from the sizzling ball of opium to the sickening display of an insect gorging itself on food scraps.[73] Oryū, the opium-addicted Japanese manager of a Turkish bathhouse that Sanki frequents, is defined by the tattoo of a spider on her back. Oryū herself is a spider, destroying the virginal Japanese orphan Osugi, one of her employees, in a jealous rage over Sanki. The revelation of Sanki's attraction to Osugi prompts Oryū to fire the girl, leaving her with nowhere to go. Raped by Sanki's friend and fellow expatriate, Kōya, Osugi descends into despair and prostitution. Kōya feels some guilt at her fate, but rather than taking responsibility himself, he blames Oryū, cursing her as a "poison woman" as he strokes her tattoo.[74]

But the shape of Oryū's spider, with its mandibles encircling her torso, indicates that she is also its prey. Oryū, a Japanese woman, is at the sexual service of Qian, a Chinese businessman, and is addicted to opium. Oryū embodies a fear commonly expressed in Western literature: the drugging and seduction of a woman by a foreign male.[75] Nonetheless, Oryū, like her sister "poison woman" Madame Yoshimachi, is able to use narcotics to gain the upper hand over Japanese manhood. In a pivotal scene, she facilitates a business meeting between Qian and Kōya. During their discussion of the lumber market, the latter delivers a lecture on Japan's mission to unite and rule East Asia. Qian ends the conversation by summoning Oryū to prepare his opium pipe. Refusing an offer to partake, Kōya is compelled to watch as the two smoke before him, "their eyes slitted like entranced insects."[76] Oryū's degradation not only represents a breach of the sexual monopoly of Japanese men over Japanese women, but also threatens Kōya, who is drawn into the ritual of opium consumption by his gaze. The prone, sprawling bodies before him render Kōya's imperialist beliefs both erotic and grotesque; his forced viewing of the depraved lovers is a form of political and sexual remuneration to Qian and Oryū.

Like *Shanghai,* the 1930 novel *Busō seru shigai (Militarized Streets)* is set entirely in mainland China. This work, by the proletarian writer Kuroshima Denji (1898–1943), depicts the savage exploitation of Chinese laborers, including women and children, at a Japanese match factory in the treaty port of Qingdao. The Japanese supervisor, Kantarō, belongs to a family of heroin producers; his father, Takezaburō, is an addict. In the opening scene, Kantarō is asked by his Japanese boss, "What are you, Chinese? Or are you Japanese?" As the narrator explains, "Kantarō's father, after all, had unfortunately become an addict. The Japanese did not care if you sold heroin. However, to smoke it like the Chinese was unacceptable."[77] The father's dependence on drugs is inimical to his bloodline.

Caught in the act of manufacturing heroin and thrown in detention, Takezaburō cuts off his toe to gain medical release and access to drugs. Arriving at the hospital with narcotics for his father, Kantarō witnesses a scene that again challenges his national identity: a young, handsome Chinese doctor bandaging the moaning addict's foot. "At first glance," Kantarō thinks, "the doctor gave the impression of being Japanese."[78] Conditioned by imperial ideology, he interprets the interaction before him in racial terms. His Japanese father is made Chinese by his drug addiction; the Chinese physician becomes Japanese through his position of authority and display of benevolence.

By describing this situation in the voice of Kantarō, the author preserves a position of implicit criticism for himself. Of all moral entrepreneurs who engaged with opium in fiction, Kuroshima perhaps came closest to rejecting or at least calling into question the conflation of drugs and race—and, by extension, the legitimacy of Japanese imperialism. Recognizing the subversiveness of the work, censors banned it immediately following publication.[79]

Outside the home islands, some cultural producers attempted the even more radical task of reappropriating opium for the Japanese. The Japan-born Dadaist Anzai Fuyue (1898–1965) migrated to Dairen in 1920 to take a job with the SMR, but was soon forced by illness to give up working. Upon his recovery in 1924, he created a literary journal with another local avant-garde writer. Anzai's first work, the prose poem "Gunkan Mari" (The warship Mari), was published in 1929. The poem begins, "I am the captain of a warship. A figure, the slim and vivid shape of a giraffe, splits aimlessly into the image of a beautiful woman. On the Moroccan leather divan of my quarters, in a world of no night and no day, I destroy myself in a gloomy obsession with opium."[80] In contrast to Satō Haruo, Ōshita Udaru, Yokomitsu Riichi, and Kuroshima Denji, moral entrepreneurs who situated narcotics consumption within a foreign identity, Anzai's addict "I" is a Japanese soldier. Like the Romanticists of nineteenth-century Europe or colonial elites of early twentieth-century Indochina, among whom personal consumption of opium was often an inspiration for literary production, the poet reclaimed the drug as a source of creativity for himself.[81] At the epicenter of the imperial narcotic economy, Anzai transgressed not only the conventions of traditional poetry but also, far more dangerously, the political orthodoxy that opium was "Chinese."

CHRISTIANS

The moral crusade against opium, a generally secular affair, took on explicitly religious dimensions in the work of Christian reformers. Although Christianity was proscribed during Japan's early modern era, following the termination of national seclusion in the 1850s, European and American missionaries won many converts, particularly among former elites. The rise of emperor-centered nationalism in the Meiji period interrupted but did not halt the spread of Western religion: by 1941 the number of Japanese Christians stood at approximately 433,000, or about 0.5 percent of the total population.[82]

Many new converts, particularly Protestants, deplored the human cost of modernization and development. A number became activists for social causes, including fair treatment of labor, women's suffrage, global disarmament, temperance, and the criminalization of prostitution.[83] The moral crusade against opium was a natural addition to their agenda. In 1924, seventy members of the Japanese chapter of the National Christian Council (NCC), a transnational religious fellowship, resolved to cooperate with counterparts on the Asian mainland in seeking an end to the illicit sale of drugs.[84] The following year the organization hosted a visit by Dr. R. Y. Lo, the vice president of the China chapter and a leader of the anti-opium movement. Addressing his audience in English, Lo declared, "Foreigners sometimes say, 'Set your house in order,' but how can China set her house in order if she is no longer the mistress of the house without the power to set her own time, or to prevent the smuggling of opium, which is ruining the morale of the country?" He implored his listeners to encourage the Japanese government to crack down on drug smuggling by continental adventurers in China.[85]

One former trafficker sat in the audience. Kikuchi Yūji was born in Japan around 1884 but spent most of his youth in central China, where he supported himself and his family by selling narcotics. During this protracted period of exposure to opium, Kikuchi himself became addicted. A Japanese Protestant missionary to China converted Kikuchi and helped him recover. Following his return to Japan, Kikuchi vowed to use his experiences to help others. From the mid-1920s until his death in 1931, he was known as one of Japan's most vocal moral entrepreneurs.

In 1925, Kikuchi urged the NCC, "Japanese are especially fitted to deal with the opium problem because Japanese do not smoke opium and are free from its injury."[86] He claimed that Japan was obligated by morality, humanitarianism, and national honor to help "late-developing countries *[kōshinkoku]*" avert the tragedy of extermination by drugs: "We Japanese so easily avoid any discussions of opium, but with regard to the social problem of narcotics, the greatest tragedy ever to strike East Asia, I think it is essential and only proper for us to participate in relief. It is my firm belief that we, the most advanced nation in the region, must help repair the damage caused by drugs."[87] This responsibility was particularly pressing in the "beloved" colonies, where narcotics consumption was a "fundamental social defect" to which the Japanese had closed their eyes. To summon a sense of urgency, Kikuchi compared the home islands to a house in the midst of a raging inferno, believing itself safe even as neighboring dwellings were consumed.[88] In the 1870s, Fukuzawa Yukichi, the leading public intellectual of his generation, had deployed the metaphor of fire to incite Japan to flee Asia.[89] A half century later, Kikuchi invoked the same specter to induce Japan to assume accountability for Asia. He denounced Japan's opium ravages on the mainland as "a policy of convenience tantamount to poisoning the Chinese."[90] Yet he also excused his government's tacit permission of illegal dealing by continental adventurers, claiming that the Foreign Ministry was handicapped by a lack of policy guidelines and noncooperation from the Home Ministry. The sheer scale of the problem, moreover, defied solution. Perhaps remembering his own past, the former trafficker contended that Japanese were unable to compete economically with the Chinese, and resorted to the narcotics trade due to financial necessity and the negative example set by many Westerners in China.[91]

Although Kikuchi's willingness to discuss drug dealing by Japanese nationals was unusual among moral entrepreneurs, his depiction of the addict was more orthodox. Unlike the community-minded Japanese, Kikuchi alleged, the Chinese "have no social morals whatsoever, no trust and no principles." Individuals looked out only for themselves, according to the Chinese maxim *Ziji bao ziji* ("Everyone protects their own"). Extreme alienation rendered society as a whole unable to recognize the difference between "customs" and "morals." Like Gotō Asatarō, Kikuchi regarded the Chinese as inveterate seekers of pleasure and self-gratification. He promoted Christian conversion as a means of cultivating a sense of personal rectitude and social conscience. Spiritual growth, he stressed, would naturally lead drug users to eschew narcotics consumption.[92]

Kikuchi's exhortations and example inspired many fellow Protestants, including Namae Takayuki (1867–1957), a government bureaucrat often remembered today as Japan's "Father of Social Welfare." By 1928, when he met Kikuchi, Namae had already enjoyed a long and distinguished career in the Home Ministry as an advocate of temperance, public housing, antiprostitution legislation, and female education. Together, he and Kikuchi, supported by other distinguished NCC members, including an American Quaker and a Diet representative, founded Japan's first antidrug organization, the Association for the Prevention of Opium Evils in Japan (Nihon ahen haidoku hōshi kai). In its mission statement, the group proposed to establish detoxification clinics and cooperate with international organizations in fighting the narcotics traffic.[93]

In 1929, the Foreign Ministry supported Namae and Kikuchi on a mission to the Asian mainland to learn more about the social problem of opium. In various treaty ports, the two spoke with drug users, leaders of antinarcotics associations, and other reformers. Namae subsequently proceeded alone to Manchuria to investigate various social welfare institutions, including addiction treatment clinics. Meanwhile, Kikuchi journeyed to Qingdao, the leading city of a former German concession occupied by Japan during World War I, to speak at a celebration of National Anti-Opium Day *(Jinyan ri)*. His address, reprinted in a Chinese national newspaper, advocated Sino-Japanese cooperation predicated upon the principle of "common culture, common race" as a solution to the social problem of opium. Standing alongside Yan Yunhang, a prominent Chinese Protestant antinarcotics activist, Kikuchi declared, "The Japanese and Chinese are descended from the same yellow ancestors; we two nations are brothers. . . . Can we not strengthen the ties of friendship between us?"[94]

During his time in Qingdao, Kikuchi also attempted to establish a clinic for treating addiction. He raised funds to cover start-up costs, but the project ultimately failed due to weaknesses in long-term strategic planning and money management.[95] Returning to Japan in despair and poverty, Kikuchi committed suicide.[96] His legacy of moral entrepreneurship, however, lived on in Namae, who succeeded in opening a hospital for drug users in Japan in 1934 (see chapter 8). Other Christians also joined Kikuchi's moral crusade against opium. By the early 1930s, Japanese Protestant missionaries had opened 103 addiction treatment clinics in China. They participated in local anti-opium initiatives and contributed to Chinese-language publications, spreading the ideology of benevolence among its intended recipients.[97] Like Kikuchi, their stance on opium was critical enough to appeal to a mainland audience, and orthodox enough to be compatible with the imperialist belief that drugs were a moral problem.

COLONIAL SUBJECTS

The elaboration of the Chinese addict as the object of Japanese benevolence also affected imperial subjects in Taiwan and Korea. In both colonies, narcotics use had become a visible social phenomenon by the end of World War I. Monopoly bureau profits in Taiwan increased each year for two decades following the passage of the Opium Law. Initially favorable international publicity regarding colonial drug control soon degenerated into skepticism. In the words of one British consul, "It is certain that stringent measures are taken to prevent Japanese from acquiring or indulging in the habit. Foreign observers are of the opinion that the same energy is not shown in dealing with Formosans."[98] While the number of licensed smokers decreased throughout the 1920s, estimates of the actual number of opium users ranged as high as one hundred thousand, or four times the registered population.[99] Moreover, combined annual consumption of morphine, heroin, and cocaine reached 0.1 grams per capita by 1929.[100]

In Korea, opium consumption was minimal prior to the twentieth century but increased swiftly following the imposition of Japanese rule. Within a year of the establishment of the imperial protectorate in 1905, one Japanese pharmacist in Seoul observed, "Narcotics were ubiquitous. Red packages contained cocaine; white, morphine. The Koreans already had their own syringes."[101] Upon annexing Korea in 1910, Japan created a public opium monopoly modeled on the Taiwan system. During the next decade, state licensing of tens of thousands of pharmacists, coupled with the illegal dealings of continental adventurers, substantially expanded the market for drugs. In 1922, gazetteers attributed 1.7 percent of all deaths of Koreans in Korea (nearly seven thousand persons) to drug addiction.[102] A British consul cabled the Foreign Office, "There seems to be a considerable amount of illicit use of the drug [morphine] among the Koreans. One of the American doctors at the

Severance Hospital tells me that he thinks it is fairly prevalent, particularly in the south. I discovered in the autumn that a small lane leading to a side gate of this consulate-general is a rendezvous of morphine injectors and their clients, and as they took no notice of the police I was obliged to complain to the police to prevent them from gathering there."[103] Only a few years later, Kikuchi Yūji estimated the Korean addict population at one hundred thousand.[104] The colonial government profited from this vast market by creating a public monopoly over alkaloids, registering thousands of users of refined narcotics.[105]

As in China, the vibrant opium economy in the formal colonies prompted a moral crusade in the context of the post–World War I crisis of imperial legitimacy. During the interwar years, the great powers viewed the existence of a pecking order of nations and peoples as a natural, even scientific fact.[106] In the haphazardly assembled Japanese empire, moral entrepreneurs offered opium as a means of delineating the hierarchy necessary for benevolent government. Between the allegedly addicted and absolutely inferior Chinese and the abstinent, superior Japanese, the Taiwanese and Koreans occupied an intermediate and unstable position in which narcotics consumption stereotypes reinforced or even stood in for racial difference.

In the years after 1919, many imperialists acknowledged the unique potential of the subjects of the formal colonies to "become the same [as the Japanese] *[dōka]*." Although *dōka* is often translated as "assimilation," this rendering overlooks important differences between the two processes. Proponents of *dōka* believed that colonial subjects, as "brother races," were capable not only of adopting the civilized values of the imperialists but also of becoming an indistinguishable part of the Japanese ethno-nation. *Dōka* was a totalizing agenda that rejected the possibility that the metamorphosis of colonial subjects into Japanese might in turn change the meaning of being Japanese. By contrast, "assimilation" generally permits the most "desirable" characteristics of the target group to exert some impact on "mainstream" society.[107]

Within the moral crusade against opium, the assertion of abstinence distinguished the Japanese, together with Taiwanese and Koreans in the process of becoming Japanese, from the incorrigible Chinese. Taiwan and Korea, like Japan, became sanitized spaces subject to contamination from a mainland culture of addiction. The empire developed quarantine procedures for prospective Chinese migrants to Taiwan, requiring labor procurers to detain them overnight before departure to ferret out drug users.[108] In Korea, the colonial government reported that narcotics consumption was rare among Koreans but not infrequent among Chinese denizens. However, "because Korea is contiguous with that opium nation *[ahen kuni]*, China, naturally the custom of opium smoking has spread here."[109]

In the literary realm, depictions of opium addicts in Taiwan and Korea reflected the metamorphosis of colonial subjects from racial inferiors to (almost) Japanese. In Yokomitsu Riichi's 1927 short story *Aoi taii (The Pale Captain)*, the Japanese narrator, an adult male stranded in Korea following the death of his father, repeatedly encounters a group of disabled morphine injectors on a rubbish heap. At the climax of the story, he paws through the pile of garbage and discovers a body. Turning it over, he finds that one of the Koreans, relieved of his addiction by death, has assumed his own face. The Japanese narrator and Korean morphine user are indistinguishable.[110] Conversely, in *Chin fujin* (Madame Chen), the award-winning 1940 novel by the Taiwan-reared Japanese writer Shōji Sōichi (1906–1961), the deepening drug addiction of the patriarch transforms him from Taiwanese into Chinese, much to the horror of his progressivist son: "His loose, old-fashioned, Chinese-style clothes especially attracted attention. His face had the yellow color of a sick person, and his hair, white like the wool of a mountain sheep, was pale and lusterless. His eyes were cloudy and his mouth was slack. Opium had done this to him."[111]

Doctors also deployed opium as a marker of racial difference among imperial subjects. Sakai Yoshio's 1940 study of narcotics users in Nanjing listed fourteen causes of drug dependence among Chinese, including "recreational" motives such as curiosity, the pursuit of pleasure, and the deliberate addiction of wastrel heirs who might otherwise squander family wealth on women, jewels, and other frivolities.[112] By contrast, physicians ascribed narcotics consumption among Koreans and Taiwanese to the "legitimate" quest for relief from pain. One Pyongyang clinic attributed the addiction of over six hundred patients to self-medication of physiological and nervous disorders.[113] Doctors at the government medical college of Korea correlated spikes in the incidence of addiction in the colony to outbreaks of cholera, for which opium was often administered as a treatment. They even compared the custom of smoking as a prophylactic for gastrointestinal disorders to the consumption of tobacco as a defense against plague in the eighteenth-century West.[114] In the eyes of moral entrepreneurs, Taiwanese and Korean drug users were tragic rather than deviant. As potential "Japanese," they deserved pity; by contrast, their Chinese counterparts were perceived as irredeemable and evoked only contempt.

At the pinnacle of the colonial elite, many Taiwanese doctors joined Japanese moral entrepreneurs in denouncing addicts on racial grounds. Tu Tsungming (*pinyin*, Du Congming; Japanese, Do Sōmei) was the first Taiwanese to earn a doctorate in medicine from a Japanese university. Tu (1893–1986) subsequently spent two and a half years studying in the United States. In 1926, he represented Japan at the World Conference on Narcotic Education in Philadelphia. The meeting aspired to develop and share antidrug curricula with the goal of "liberat[ing] more millions of human beings—many times over—than were emancipated by Abraham Lincoln." Over eighteen thousand individuals received invitations for the event, and more than five thousand attended.[115] Tu gave a presentation entitled "Opium in Formosa," during which he sang a popular tune cautioning juveniles against the "enslavement" of addiction:

Opium Smoker! The wretched fellow!
Face like brass, all pinched and yellow,
Pitiful! His body shrunk;
Weak and stumbling, lean and bony,
Wrinkled skin and features stony.
Gone are honor, strength and money,
Up in smoke, in ashes sunk!
Poor, deluded Opium Smoker!
Living dead, a wheezing croaker,
Health and wealth, house, home and life
Through your pipe they have been flying
Like a dream. Folks laugh, when dying
You leave nothing but a crying
Penniless and lonely wife.[116]

Like Tu, Lü Heruo (1914–50), a leader of the Taiwanese literary community, viewed the opium smoker as a human obstruction to modern development and progress, and the embodiment of political subjugation. Lü was critical of Japanese rule but in many ways represented the ideal subject in the imperial mind: a modern, educated elite who wrote in the language of the colonizer. In his ironically titled short story *Gōka heian* (Family peace), the main character, Father Fan, is a lifelong opium smoker whose addiction steadily degrades his clan. Reckless drug consumption erodes the affection between the patriarch and his wife. The couple's clever second son longs to attend middle school and university, but his mother cannot afford the fees. By the time the children are grown, Fan's addiction has left him penniless and dependent upon the support of a relative. At the end of the story, his benefactor loses patience with the addict. The sparseness of dialogue in the story magnifies the impact of his rebuke: "How is it that you don't yet understand the horror of opium smoking? It's because you're a complete bastard *[kusemono]*. . . . Open your eyes to what has happened to you, or you'll be better off dead."[117] Lü's unsympathetic depiction of Fan showcases the author's conviction that addiction was inimical to attaining racial parity with the Japanese—a precondition for pursuing the more subversive goals of political equality and even independence.

Outside their homelands, colonial subjects found themselves indexed by opium to a very different status. Up to four million Koreans—more than 10 percent of the total population of the peninsula—went into exile following annexation in 1910. Some refused to live under Japanese rule; others were dispossessed of their ancestral fields by the imperial government's comprehensive land reform policy. About two million sought economic opportunity in Japan proper, where they supplied cheap, unskilled labor in an age of industrialization and war mobilization. They replaced the Chinese as the largest ethnic minority, and also greatly outnumbered the resident Taiwanese population of about thirty thousand.[118]

Loathed for creating competition in the lower reaches of the labor market, Korean denizens of the Japanese domestic imagination were lazy, unclean, irrational, and immoral, frittering away their wages on drugs and gambling. In 1926, the Chosen Rōdō Kumiai (Association of Korean Laborers) formed a committee to investigate rising narcotics use among migrants to Osaka. Surveyors counted 1,030 Korean morphine consumers in the city. All except three had begun using drugs after arriving in Japan.[119] Typical was the case of a young laborer identified by his initials, K.K. Born on a farm in Korea, at the age of twenty-eight K.K. came to Japan to live in a dormitory and work as a day laborer. Two years later, struck by a gastroenterological disorder, he followed the advice of a friend to self-medicate with opiates. Over the next few years, his financial situation, already precarious, deteriorated further as he developed an addiction to morphine, heroin, and cocaine. "I came to Japan with so much hope, but my life here got off track," K.K. mourned.[120] Among women migrants, drug use was often linked to prostitution. K.J., a traditional entertainer *(gi-saeng)*, married a patron at the age of seventeen. Within three years, her husband had become dependent on morphine and unable to earn a living. She supported him through sex work, eventually accompanying a Japanese military client to Tokyo. In her new household, she started using narcotics herself.[121]

Rather than viewing Korean migrants to the metropole as candidates for transformation into Japanese, moral entrepreneurs stigmatized them as narcotics pushers and addicts. In the near absence of the Chinese Other, theories of motivation differentiated rather than aligned Korean and Japanese drug users. Of the patients under his care in a Tokyo clinic, Dr. Sakai Yoshio reported, "Japanese addicts had contracted the habit as the result of ordinary illnesses and usually followed their own doctor's instructions as regards the methods of injecting the narcotic drugs. Many of the Koreans admitted that they had been tempted by their fellow-countrymen to resort to drugs, which they usually injected by intravenous methods without taking any antiseptic precautions."[122] Sakai also reported a significantly higher rate of relapse among Korean addicts. Some patients returned for treatment as many as five times, a fact that "confirmed" Korean incorrigibility.[123]

Moral entrepreneurs charged dissolute Korean addicts with contaminating the abstinent and superior race-nation of Japan. Newspapers reported cases like that of a Korean laborer discovered injecting morphine beneath the guardrail of a south Tokyo train station. Pressed to reveal his supplier, the man led police to the home of three fellow Koreans, including a former ginseng merchant who had lost his job. In a closet, police found twenty-two five-gram packages of refined narcotics with a total value of about four hundred yen. The trio was later discovered to have earned the sensational amount of over nine hundred thousand yen dealing drugs in the Japanese capital.[124] In another incident, a group of about fifteen Korean morphine users, led by a middle-aged secondhand goods dealer, "rampaged" through the streets of downtown Tokyo in search of items that could be stolen to exchange for drugs.[125] Such scandals received more coverage in the press than their incidence warranted. In the nearly two decades between 1920 and 1937, fewer than four hundred foreigners, including only a handful of Koreans, stood trial for violating anti-opium legislation in Japan.[126]

The nearly two million Koreans who migrated to Manchuria under Japanese occupation came to occupy a very different position in the imperial racial hierarchy.[127] Unlike Koreans who remained at home to undergo a demeaning process of *dōka*, migrants in the empire automatically enjoyed the rights and privileges of Japanese citizens. Moreover, they filled a politically useful niche. The Japanese in Manchuria, unwilling to come into close contact with their allegedly addicted and inferior Chinese subjects, cast Koreans in the role of an "intermediate elite" fit to carry out orders on behalf of the imperial regime. As such, Korean migrants functioned as a critical liaison between the Japanese and the Chinese, filling the ranks of police, military attaches, camp followers, and low-wage tertiary employees.[128] Up to 90 percent of the approximately 600,000 Koreans who settled in Manchurian cities supported themselves in the illegal drug trade, an easily learned and lucrative occupation for destitute and unskilled migrants.[129] One reporter estimated that Koreans operated 1,500 of the 1,800 retail opium establishments in

Harbin, including 39 out of 40 shops on a single street.[130] According to police, the majority of these traffickers lived with families. In all cases in which the ages of their children were recorded, birth predated migration to Manchuria, suggesting that many Korean dealers arrived as spouses and parents rather than single adventurers.[131] Selling drugs was not a solely male affair. The penniless Baek Hongyong, a wife and mother of two, found work as a mule for a Chinese dealer and eventually built her own opium empire, coordinating a fleet of Korean distributors and Chinese customers.[132]

Positioned between the allegedly superior Japanese and inferior Chinese, Koreans were ideal middlemen in the profitable Manchurian opium market. Some dealers capitalized on this status to situate themselves more securely within the ranks of the imperialists. Baek invested some of her income in a restaurant, where she entertained powerful Japanese clients. She boasted of having "more money than our whole family could have possibly spent in a lifetime. Money bulged from every crack, hole, and panel. It was under our bed, above our heads, and in our bedding."[133] In the coal mining town of Fushun, Kim Taegun attracted a Japanese wife whose ties to the imperial military enhanced the success of his opium retail business.[134] Korean migrants to Harbin in the mid-1920s were said to earn several hundred yen per day dealing drugs, allowing even those who arrived in a state of poverty to achieve economic stability and, in some cases, riches.[135]

Many dealers were also users. Moral entrepreneurs generally discussed Korean opium consumers in Manchuria in the same pitying terms as their Japanese counterparts. A Dairen tabloid article on "the terrifying damage of heroin and the spread of addicts throughout Manchuria" asserted that 20 percent of migrant Japanese and Koreans had become narcotics users. Rather than condemning these individuals in the moral language typically used to denounce the Chinese, the reporter deemed the situation "deplorable *[kanashimubeki]*."[136]

In an empire characterized by an unrivaled degree of ethnocultural similarity, ruled by policymakers who aspired to raise consciousness of confraternity yet higher, opium was a more useful signifier of race than race itself. Moral entrepreneurs represented the Chinese addict as an object of benevolence, the legitimating ideology of empire. Yet the image of the addict reverberated far beyond Japan's territorial possessions and political aspirations in China. The identification of the Chinese as absolute inferiors fundamentally affected the status of the Taiwanese and Koreans, subjects of Japan's formal colonies. The alleged ability to relinquish opium distinguished these populations from the Chinese and suggested their potential to join the abstinent and superior Japanese race-nation. At the same time, as the case of migrant Koreans demonstrates, stereotypes of addicts also established the limits of *dōka*, by maintaining boundaries between imperialists and subjects in the home islands. Racial status in the high imperial age was neither fixed nor secure, but dependent on both time and place and expressed through the moral crusade against opium.

CHAPTER FOUR · Cultural Producers and Manchukuo

On September 18, 1931, Japanese army officers detonated a bomb on the tracks of the South Manchuria Railway. The explosion furnished a pretext for provoking armed conflict with the troops of Zhang Xueliang, the Chinese warlord then in control of northeast China. Within months of this clash, remembered as the Mukden Incident, Japan's Kwantung Army had overrun Zhang's domain and proclaimed the establishment of the state of Manchukuo.[1]

By administering Manchukuo as a nation rather than a colony, the Kwantung Army and its allies hoped to enjoy a free hand in the region rather than to share power with civilian bureaucrats in Tokyo. The decision also reflected the declining global legitimacy of imperialism as a political system.[2] In the wake of World War I, the principle of ethnic self-determination achieved hegemony as the ideological foundation of the legitimate nation-state, in principle if not in practice. Japan accordingly argued that the "Land of the Manchus" was "the result of a spontaneous movement according to the wish of the inhabitants of the country," fulfilling the nationalist aspirations of the Manchu people.[3]

To investigate this claim, the League of Nations, an international organization established by the Treaty of Versailles in 1919 to peacefully resolve disputes among sovereign states, convened the Lytton Commission. In its report to the league, the commission dismissed Manchu self-determination as a Japanese pretense and recommended against recognizing the independence of Manchukuo. Speaking for a shocked and enraged Japan, Dr. Sakai Yoshio sneered that "notoriously deceptive"

Chinese addicts had deployed an arsenal of "tricks and charms" to dupe Lytton and his associates.[4] When the League of Nations voted to deny statehood to Manchukuo, the Japanese delegation staged a dramatic walkout. Within a month, to the general approval of the domestic public, Japan withdrew from the league.

Following this incident, many Japanese accepted the impossibility of legitimizing Manchukuo according to global criteria. Replacing Western political ideals with reconceptualized East Asian traditions, ideologues proposed the Kingly Way (Japanese, *Ōdō;* Chinese, *Wangdao*) as an alternative justification of nationhood. During the 1930s, moral entrepreneurs folded the rhetoric of the Kingly Way into the ongoing moral crusade against narcotics. In their argument, only Wangdao rule, which could be achieved solely through an independent Manchukuo, might save the local population of unfit Chinese addicts from social Darwinist extermination.

In discarding a globally acceptable justification of nationhood in favor of legitimacy staked on alleged Asian "tradition," moral entrepreneurs alienated China and the Western powers. Transnational cooperation and sympathy in the struggle against drugs evaporated, and the favorable international publicity that had sporadically greeted moral entrepreneurs in the early imperial age was replaced with the charge that Japan was engaged in an attempt to "drug the Chinese into submission *[duhua* or *du-Hua zhengce]*." Yet this rift took place within a more fundamental ideological continuity. Although the Kingly Way explicitly rejected the West, it nonetheless retained the tendency to seek validation through Euro-American norms. The establishment of Manchukuo marked a rupture in Japan's manner of engagement with the outside world, but an underlying consensus regarding the nature of "civilization" could not and would not be eroded.

NEW RHETORIC TO JUSTIFY A NATION

To develop the ideology of the Kingly Way in conformity with political needs, the Kwantung Army appointed the eminent scholar Yano Jin'ichi (1872–1970). Yano, a professor emeritus of East Asian history at Kyoto Imperial University, was not the first philosopher to grapple with Wangdao in modern times, but he was among the most prominent and influential.[5] In Yano's formulation, the Kingly Way was nothing more or less than rule by a benevolent sovereign. In Manchukuo, this role was filled by Pu Yi, the deposed last emperor of China's Qing dynasty and a symbol of tradition summoned to represent the modern ideal of self-determination for the Manchus. "The ruler bears responsibility only to Heaven. . . . [T]he people are always to be governed, taught, and guided," Yano wrote. Subjects were invariably peaceful, obedient, and deferential, trusting their ruler to develop the riches of the realm for the benefit of all. On the precise form and mechanisms of administration, Yano and his intellectual collaborators were almost silent—conveniently so for an army that had no intention of respecting the authority of Pu Yi and his opium-smoking empress. Instead, Yano extolled the Kingly Way as both the means and the end of Manchukuo sovereignty. He looked forward to a time when "the most peaceful and best-ruled society [would] appear and there [would] be no need for laws and punishments."[6] Within a year of the state's founding, schoolchildren learned, "When the will of the people is followed and good government established, the self-sufficiency of the people is ensured, everyone is safe, work is enjoyable, there is no discrimination against the various races; and people help each other, keep faith with the world, turn their energies toward peace, and are steeped in friendship. There is no doubt that Manchukuo is a paradise *[rakudo]*!"[7]

In Wangdao, Yano declared, "To extend benevolence is the most important thing."[8] Yano used the familiar term *jinsei* to describe two ties: the fraternal relationship of Japan to Manchukuo and the domestic responsibilities of ruler and ruled. In this sense, his notion of benevolence departed from that of colonial policymakers in Taiwan and Korea, who stressed the unitary bond between Japan and the imperial subject. In the 1930s, benevolence, which had once justified Japanese empire building, was distanced from the mission to civilize. Instead, it came to sanction a political relationship that was explicitly distinguished from imperialism: the "brotherly" guidance of Manchukuo by Japan.

The ideology of Pan-Asianism *[han-Ajia shugi, dai-Ajia shugi,* or *Ajia shugi]* informed relations between the two nations. Pan-Asianism purported to unite the polities of an imagined "East" against the implicit Other of the "West." The ideal of Pan-Asianism was not limited to Japanese thinkers of the 1930s, but the variant that became dominant among the leaders of Manchukuo emphasized Japan's salvation of its continental neighbors from domination by the great powers.[9] Japanese Pan-Asianism was grounded in a novel historical methodology called *Tōyōshi* (Oriental history). *Tōyōshi* substituted the philology of late nineteenth-century sinologists such as Oka Senjin with the positivism of post-Enlightenment Western historical writing. Academics such as Yano, Naitō Konan, and Shiratori Kurakichi (1865–1942), a German-trained professor of history at Tokyo Imperial University, spread *Tōyōshi* through Japanese academia in the 1930s and early 1940s.

Writing the history of China, Japan's historical model, afforded scholars the opportunity to reposition Japan at the center of Eastern civilization. China was no longer "Chūgoku," the Middle Kingdom. Instead, it was "Shina," a toponym derived from the Western pronunciation of "China." Unlike Chūgoku, Shina was an object of Japanese benevolence, and often disrespect or disdain. Shina, Shiratori hypothesized, had failed to coalesce into a modern nation beneath the burden of Confucian social institutions and customs such as opium smoking. In Japan, by contrast, Confucianism had taken a more progressive turn, facilitating state cohesion. In a breathtaking leap, Shiratori posited Japan's ability to meet global criteria for legitimate nationhood as evidence that the empire had followed the true intentions of the ancient classics and was "fit" to supervise the implementation of Wangdao rule in the East.[10] Even as Japan turned its back on the values it had so assiduously cultivated a generation earlier, it could not express its own superiority without reference to earlier standards of civilization.

The fiction of Manchukuo self-determination demanded an ideology of "harmony among the five races *[gozoku kyōwa]*" said to form the population.[11] "Harmony" was not equality. The Japanese, their presence in Manchuria naturalized by inclusion as a "native" ethnic group, retained their preeminent position. Japanese schoolchildren learned in civics class that "as the leading race, we must not lose sight of our imperial responsibility" to encourage progress among "uncivilized races."[12] As in the past, moral entrepreneurs targeted opium use as a symptom of backwardness and a pall over "the light of the spirit in which our State was founded."[13] Reorienting the moral crusade against opium around the axis of Wangdao, cultural producers deployed narcotics both to distinguish between superior and inferior races and to bring them together in a harmonious national body. The majority Han population, formerly categorized as Chinese *(Shinajin)*, was reclassified as "Manchurians *[Manshūjin]*" or "Manchukuoans *[Manshūkokujin]*." Although the Manchukuoans were not seen as candidates for *dōka* in the same way as colonial Koreans and Taiwanese, the changed political status of their homeland nonetheless caused them to advance a rung on the hierarchy of races in the Japanese empire. Manchukuoans, like the subjects of Japan's formal imperial possessions, became prone to contamination by opium from the absolutely inferior Chinese.[14]

Narcotics not only created and shuffled racial categories but also provided an opportunity for cooperation among their constituents. Moral entrepreneurs viewed collaboration against drugs as evidence of "racial unity [Japanese *daidō*, Chinese *datong*]" in the Manchukuo state. As one gazetteer declared, "The secret of racial unity lies in the sharing by different races of their respective difficulties and pains. The suppression of the opium-smoking habit which calls for the highest form of sharing can be regarded therefore as the first step taken towards the establishment of real racial unity." The crusade against opium affirmed Japanese superiority even as it legitimized

Manchukuo through a display of ethnic accord: "Opium smoking cannot be eliminated unless proper collective counter-measures are taken by a group of different but harmonious races. If the Manchurian race, long a slave to opium-smoking, can free itself from its shackles with the assistance and co-operation of the Japanese race, unfurling as it does the banner of racial harmony, then the Manchus would naturally appreciate and feel grateful for the efforts of the Japanese made in the spirit of racial harmony."[15]

The Concordia Association (Japanese, Kyōwakai; Chinese, Xiehehui) functioned as the instrument of harmony among the five races. In contrast to partisanship in the West (or Japan), which moral entrepreneurs presented as a source of wrangling and discord, the Kyōwakai, founded in 1932 as the only legal party in Manchukuo, purported to cultivate a "spirit of unanimity."[16] Inclusiveness was key: all adult males were encouraged to join, and by 1943, membership totaled over 4 million out of a total population of approximately 40 million. Close to 90 percent of members, or 3.7 million, were Chinese (representing about one-tenth of the Han population of Manchukuo). Nearly 350,000 Japanese formed the second-largest national group within the organization, and 35 percent of all Japanese in the state. Almost 200,000 Koreans (about 15 percent of Manchukuo's Korean population) and tens of thousands of Mongolians, Russians, and others also joined the Kyōwakai.[17]

Commanding a budget of nearly ten million yen per year by the 1940s, the Kyōwakai aspired to indoctrinate subjects in the Kingly Way, mediate between the government and the people, "conciliate" the five races, train male youth as paramilitaries, and improve public welfare, particularly through the eradication of opium. The Kyōwakai established addiction clinics to treat drug users and offered public education programs encouraging abstinence. To reach illiterate and isolated communities, the organization hired actors to perform in antidrug plays, singing folksongs like the following:

> Opium first came from a foreign land
> And now kills people.
> Before they are summoned to the underworld,
> Smokers light lamps to warm the raw paste.
> One, they waste their spirit; two, their resources;
> Three, they cannot afford food and drink;
> Four, their clothing is too thin for winter;
> Five, they shiver in their small beds;
> Six, no family can help them;
> Seven, no doors are open to them;
> Eight, they breathe their last.[18]

In a twist of irony, eight, a lucky number in Chinese cosmology, represented the final stage of the drug user's decline.

Moral entrepreneurs also crusaded against opium in Kyōwakai publications. Like the journals of the Dōjinkai, these periodicals served a Japanese and Chinese readership, and welcomed contributions from writers representing each of the five races.[19] One Chinese author celebrated the founding of Manchukuo as a "restoration [Chinese *weixin;* Japanese, *ishin*]" that had ended China's "dark ages" through an enlightened opium policy facilitating racial harmony.[20] Another submission, attributed to the Chinese journalist Chen Yingbin, criticized opium smokers in Manchukuo for lacking a progressive consciousness. Chen blamed the "unscientific and traditionalistic" philosophy of Daoism for the prevalence of the "backward" habit of drug use. In his words, "Among my friends, many are Daoists. They all smoke opium now, and I think if we don't eradicate Daoism by the roots, even if we can extirpate opium, it will simply come back again."[21] Whether Chen Yingbin was a real person, or whether the Kyōwakai believed its readership might be more receptive to his message if presented under a Chinese pen name, is unknown.

ATTACKING ALTERNATIVES TO A MORAL MANCHUKUO

Offering little theoretical substance of its own, Wangdao justified the hegemony of Japan over East Asia by systematically delegitimizing contending authorities as examples of "unrighteous rule [Chinese, *Badao;* Japanese, *Hadō*]." Wangdao and Badao were mutually constitutive opposites: while Wangdao was legitimate, moral, and benevolent, Badao was false, insincere, and coercive. Manchukuo followed the doctrine of the Kingly Way; all political alternatives offered only chaos and corruption.

Having carved the nation of Manchukuo from Chinese territory, the Kwantung Army was particularly eager to depict China as a Badao state. Baba Shachi, a moral entrepreneur in the Manchukuo government, alleged that China's ongoing impotence in the face of the social problem of drugs derived from the failure of the nation at both the government and popular level. According to Baba, the Nationalist Party (Guomindang), which had unified China in the late 1920s after decades of political fragmentation, did not understand how to build effective educational, sanitary, and cultural institutions to cultivate anti-opium attitudes among the people. Moreover, the officials responsible for drug policy prioritized personal gain over public interest. The Chinese people shared the blame for their suffering: they were ignorant of modern medical alternatives to opium, had a strong innate tendency toward pleasure seeking, and most damagingly, lacked national consciousness.[22]

Baba attributed widespread narcotics consumption to the legacy of warlord rule. The warlords themselves were known drug users: Zhang Zuolin (1875–1928), who controlled Manchuria from 1916–1928, smoked opium; his son and successor Zhang Xueliang (1901–2001) became dependent on heroin. At the time of Xueliang's accession to power, Kikuchi Yūji wrote, "Zhang graduated from a mission school, and when he first emerged into the world, he played tennis and all sorts of new-style sports, and for a Chinese was very cultured and modern. But one day he began to smoke opium . . . and unfortunately, he reverted to a real Chinese."[23] In mid-1931, Xueliang sought treatment at a Beijing hospital for his condition, which had worsened due to a bout of typhus. It was during his absence that the Kwantung Army instigated the Mukden Incident and seized control of Manchuria.[24]

Moral entrepreneurs represented the Zhangs as Oriental despots, corrupted by their own power and unfit to rule.[25] In the eighteenth and nineteenth centuries, European Orientalists ranging from the French Enlightenment philosopher Baron de Montesquieu to the English utilitarian James Stuart Mill ascribed the alleged poverty, debasement, and immorality of the Chinese and Indians to "enchainment" and oppression by native sovereigns.[26] Following the establishment of Manchukuo, Japanese cultural producers disseminated similar stereotypes of a weak and primitive people suffering from extended subjugation to tyranny and opium alike:

> During the period preceding the advent of Manchoukuo, many government authorities were slaves to the drug habit. . . . Such a situation naturally resulted in the utter demoralization and the corruption of state machinery. . . . Soon the whole political structure became honeycombed with graft, bribery, extortion, and underhanded connivance. State policies failed to be carried out, peace and order changed to chaos and insecurity. The example of the rulers of the State served to influence the public mind to a tremendous extent. Opium-smokers arose, some in sheer imitation of the life led by the higher officials. Culture, national pride and spirit all deteriorated.[27]

In addition to presenting opium as a personal vice of the Zhangs, moral entrepreneurs described the drug as a financial prop of warlord despotism. In 1927, Zhang Zuolin implemented a series of measures to regulate and tax opium cultivation, distribution, and consumption. Although this policy did not differ dramatically from the monopolies maintained by the Japanese and European imperial governments, Zhang lacked the legitimating cloak of a civilizing mission. Under his version of gradual suppression, dealers sprang up "like bamboo after rain."[28] Cultural producers likened the proliferation of drugs in warlord-administered Manchuria to "the notorious American underground world during the days of [alcohol] prohibition."[29] One moral entrepreneur dismissed Zhang's eradication policy as "nothing more than stuffing his pockets."[30]

Left-wing Japanese scholars joined the denunciation of warlord government. Tanaka Tadao, a researcher at a public think tank in the mid-1930s, portrayed drugs as a primitive source of capital and a medium of exchange for warlords, landlords, guilds, bandits, and other alleged oppressors of the Chinese people.[31] Tanaka argued that the use of opium as currency hindered China's progress through Marx's stages of development and imperiled its capacity for self-rule in the age of imperialism. He pitied downtrodden villagers taxed beyond their means on a noxious crop. In a similar vein, the SMR Research Bureau described Zhang's rule as "half-feudal, half-colonial *[han hōken han shokuminchiteki]*" and expected that government according to the Kingly Way would free the people from their collective enslavement to opium.[32] Like their colleagues of one generation earlier, leftists carved out an intellectual niche within the dominant ideology of the day, despite the explicitly anticommunist stance of Wangdao.

Moral entrepreneurs of the 1930s also castigated the great powers as examples of unrighteous rule. Opium, which had once enabled Japan to "enter the West" through the common criterion of abstinence, came to function as a marker of distinction between the rapacious empire building of Europe and America, and Japan, the benevolent heir of the Kingly Way and leader of an alternative modern civilization. Rather than deploying opium to distinguish between Japan and China, moral entrepreneurs used the assertion of mutual victimization at the hands of drug-dealing white imperialists to assemble a Pan-Asian justification of rule. The study of the Opium War, fought between Great Britain and China in 1839–42, experienced a boom in Japanese academic and popular culture as a textbook example of the bullying of the East by the great powers.[33] During the moral crusade of the 1890s, cultural producers writing on the conflict had often presented the Chinese more negatively than the British. In the years leading up to the establishment of Manchukuo, by contrast, moral entrepreneurs decisively denounced the imperialist ravages of the West against a comprehensively imagined Asia.

In 1929, a Tokyo theater staged the first showing of *Ahen sensō* (The Opium War), a drama by playwright and author Ema Shū (1889–1975). The work, which inspired several imitations, depicts the encounter between Charles Elliot, the British superintendent of trade and consul of the south China port of Canton (Guangzhou) in 1839, and Lin Zexu, the Chinese commissioner of imports.[34] In the opening scene of the piece, Elliot and MacDonald, a Protestant missionary, consider the problem of landing a shipment of opium on the mainland in defiance of Qing law. Ema's dialogue establishes the evil intentions of the British, who are amused rather than concerned by the addiction of the Chinese:

MACDONALD: My goodness! I used to deeply object to opium smuggling, but now I can't help but be grateful for it. *(He laughs.)*

ELLIOT: Mr. MacDonald, do you remember when we spoke a year ago, and I said, half in jest, "Your Bible, my opium—I wonder which will subjugate China first?"

MACDONALD: Yes, I remember. It was your opinion that the two would work together, though back then I was very opposed to the idea.

ELLIOT: That's right, and I haven't changed my mind. In one hand, the Bible; in the other, opium. In this way, we'll advance the grand purpose of our nation *[kokkateki na dai mokuteki]*. Mr. MacDonald, isn't it perfect? Through your martyr-like bravery, the Chinese will become drunk on belief in the boundless love of Deus, and opium will no less soundly lull them into closing their eyes.[35]

Although the British are the chief villains of the play, Ema also emphasizes the degradation of the Chinese, enslaved by narcotics. The third scene begins with an exchange between two opium addicts (simply called A and B) in the throes of withdrawal. "Unemployed Laborer A" finally interrupts their plaintive wheezing: "You opium addicts, crazy bastards, shut up!"[36] The group is subsequently diverted by the appearance of MacDonald, who delivers a defense of imperialism: "We British all live as Christians, and from childhood, we're brought up to love others. Loving others, and loving other countries, is a deeply rooted custom. Precisely for this reason, we've extended our rule to Africa and India, and have now come to faraway China to save it, like a brother." Overwhelmed by the hypocrisy of this statement, the unemployed laborers chase MacDonald off the stage.[37] The opium addicts, however, remain slumped in a daze. They are the closing image of the play: having at last obtained and smoked the drug, they "slept aware of nothing, as though nothing had changed."[38]

Ema was a member of the proletarian writers movement that flourished in 1920s Japan and a committed leftist who opposed militarism and formal imperialism.

FIGURE 4.
Frontispiece, Ushikubo Ainoshin, *Ahen ka*.
SOURCE: Ushikubo Ainoshin, *Ahen ka: Eikoku Tōyō shinryaku shi* (Tokyo: Akatsuki shoin, 1933). Courtesy of the National Diet Library of Japan.

Nonetheless, he supported a less direct form of Japanese control over Asia, in which his country might "champion" China and India against the West.[39] His depiction of the Opium War upheld the racial biases of his age and was by no means incompatible with right-wing ideological orthodoxy. The Chinese characters in *Ahen sensō* mostly lacked names, identities, and even the villainous agency of the British. Audiences might easily interpret the final tableau of impotent addicts as a mute plea for Japanese benevolence.

Beyond the theatrical realm, university professor Ushikubo Ainoshin's *Ahen ka: Eikoku Tōyō shinryaku shi* (The opium crisis: A history of England's invasion of the Orient) offered a scholarly account of Qing China's victimization by the great powers. Ushikubo claimed his purpose in writing the book, which summarized thirty years of research for a nonacademic audience, was to help Japanese readers understand a once familiar and now "strange" China. He also used the history of the nineteenth century to express his own political position. Blaming China's catastrophic encounter with narcotics on the great powers of the West, he suggested that Japan "reconstruct the peace of East Asia and assume leadership in fostering harmony among the various races of the world." With the "friendly support *[yūrinteki enjo]*" of China and Manchukuo, the empire might supplant the corrupt influence of the great powers and protect the emerging unity of Asia.[40]

Six years after the publication of Ushikubo's book, the centennial of the Opium War in 1939 greatly stimulated the production of works on the conflict. With Japan locked in an undeclared all-out military offensive against China from 1937, moral entrepreneurs commemorated the anniversary to reframe a bitter and bloody contemporary war as a humanitarian solution to century-old problems. Following the outbreak of armed conflict between Japan and the Allied powers in 1941, cultural producers came to depict the history of the Opium War as the latest phase in a long history of European and American crimes against the East. Only unity among Asians, moral entrepreneurs argued, could end the legacy of exploitation and enslavement.

One of the most prominent and influential centennial histories of the Opium War, Yano Jin'ichi's *Ahen sensō to Honkon* (The Opium War and Hong Kong), presented the clash as a case study of the alleged Western tendency to rule by military force—in contrast to the Kingly Way of governing by virtue. Like Ema, Yano highlighted the hypocrisy of the British, who "trammeled national law, morality, and humanitarianism to sell opium in China, while strictly banning the drug at home." Yano condemned this legacy for contemporary East Asia. "In my opinion," he declared, "England's greatest crime against China was the illegal seizure of concessions in Hong Kong and Shanghai, where anti-Japanese resistance leaders are today given sanctuary." These contemporary "reactionaries" obstructed Pan-Asian unity and Japan's quest to rescue Asia from Badao.[41]

Takeuchi Chūji's 1939 *Ahen sensō to Eikoku no tai-Shi shinryaku* (The Opium War and Britain's invasion of China) likewise sought to incite Pan-Asian fervor against the West by highlighting the "hell" of drugs and war in the nineteenth century: "The history of the past three hundred years is a tale of global domination by whites *[hakujin]*, but now we, the Asian race *[Ajiya minzoku]*, are once again beginning to rise. We Asians have a glorious past, and today we come together with one head and one body, and great pride, determined to smash the cunning British empire, crush the white devils, take back the Asian continent for ourselves, and press forward in creating a great new civilization."[42]

Takeuchi's depiction reveals a critical shift in Japan's national identification: turning away from Great Britain, the Western power it had so fervently emulated only a generation earlier, the empire aligned itself with the formerly spurned China. In contrast to earlier writers, Takeuchi did not emphasize Japan's fortune in avoiding the political and social catastrophe of opium, nor the abstinence of the Japanese people as a source of racial superiority. Instead, he suggested the confraternity of the imperialists and their Chinese subjects. Allegations of mutual victimization at the hands of "white devil" drug dealers facilitated the imagination of an Asian race encapsulated in a common political community.[43] By this reasoning, the Japanese military offensive against China in the late 1930s was nothing more than a brotherly attempt to restore the Chinese to their rightful place within a Pan-Asian polity.

Both Yano and Takeuchi wrote the word *Ajiya* (Asia) in katakana, Japan's alphabet for transliterating foreign concepts. Ironically, they expressed an active Asian identity in terminology borrowed from the English language. In later texts, by contrast, *Asia* was often transcribed in characters (亞細亜) that served as the basis for a new conceptualization of opium itself. In Chinese, the drug was most commonly called *yapian* (鴉片) in an attempt to reproduce the phonetic pronunciation of *opium*. Sometimes, however, it was referred to as *yangyan* (洋煙), or "Western smoke." In Japanese, opium was typically rendered *ahen* (阿片). Beginning in the 1930s, instead of the semantically empty character *a* (阿), some writers substituted the phonetically identical ideograph (亞) that indicated Asia. Combined with the second character, *hen*, meaning "to settle" or "to dispose of," the new rendering (亜片) implied an active East taking charge of opium and its political future. In this way, moral entrepreneurs reclaimed Western smoke for Asia.

Popular writers joined historians in deploying the Opium War as an incitement to Pan-Asian unity. In 1942, the novelist Osaragi Jirō (1897–1973), best known for his historical fiction and several postwar works, published the first installment of a projected literary trilogy set in 1840s China. Osaragi knew well the propagandistic implications of chronicling the Opium War. A critic of the authoritarian politics of his day, he aspired to present "a just and impartial depiction of the Chinese and British that doesn't make people laugh."[44] Nonetheless, his work followed political orthodoxy (and disregarded historical fact) in representing Japan as China's champion, carrying on a long tradition of protecting its people from the imperialism of the great powers and their own degeneracy, expressed through addiction to opium. In an ahistorical encounter in a Chinese restaurant in Nagasaki, the Qing trade commissioner denounces narcotics to a skeptical Japanese companion. The latter's doubts are vindicated when a young male servant sets a smoking apparatus before them. The Chinese, who has been speaking in Japanese, reverts to his native tongue to praise the opium: "It's good, it's good." Narcotics are figuratively and linguistically

Chinese. The Japanese remains alert to protect his fellow diner, who soon succumbs to a drugged stupor.[45]

In the final, desperate years of empire, moral entrepreneurs also used the lessons of the Opium War to encourage colonial subjects, the targets of nearly fifty years of *dōka*, to unite with Japan against the Allies. Ōhara Masatoshi's 1944 *Ahen sensō* (The Opium War) sought to inflame the Taiwanese, recently allowed to serve in the Japanese army, against the white devils. He exhorted, "As we colored races *[yūshoku jinrui]* read this book, our fighting spirit will be roused. Our hearts cherish an unquenchable and overpowering determination to completely destroy the villainous Americans and British, and to make them taste ten- or even one-hundredfold the great misery and suffering that we have been forced to bear!"[46] In Ōhara's work, opium allowed the Taiwanese, formerly so carefully distinguished from the Chinese, to draw inspiration from the history of China in a Pan-Asian struggle against the West.

Beyond print media, the Opium War also inspired two major films. *Ahen sensō (The Opium War)* was filmed in 1942 and screened in Japanese theaters in early 1943. Influenced by the historical scholarship of Ushikubo Ainoshin and Yano Jin'ichi, producer Matsuzaki Keiji and screenwriter Oguni Hideo collaborated on a heavily politicized interpretation of the encounter between Lin Zexu and Charles Elliot.[47] Their script sought to justify Japan's 1938 invasion and occupation of Guangzhou, the setting of many Opium War battles, by presenting it as the fulfillment of a long-ago promise to rescue East Asia from Western imperialism. In the final scene, a Japanese fishing boat sails into Hong Kong harbor. The crew sing, "We are long-time friends, we fishermen with topknots; the sound of the traditional drum *[taiko]* encourages us; the big fish call to us: 'Come on! Come on! Bring us forth!'" As a British warship slinks away in the background, the narrator concludes, "Although China was powerless [to extirpate opium], a century later, our Japan is benevolently taking up the task!"[48] Rather than depicting the Opium War as a tragedy, the script ends on a note of hope that Japan will reclaim Asia for Asians.

The director of the film, Makino Masahiro, disliked and chose to excise this overtly political and ahistorical conclusion. Nonetheless, his film, which substituted Hollywood-style dance numbers for images of combat, allowed Japanese viewers to dismiss Chinese resistance as mere show, a trick that would ultimately fail rather than a serious military challenge. In the end, Makino's attempt to subordinate propaganda to entertainment won little favor with critics. Whereas reviewers acknowledged the value of spectacle in providing Japanese audiences with an onscreen escape from life amid the unpleasant realities of total war, they contended that poor technical execution, including strange camera angles and the overuse of cranes, ruined the effect. They also objected to the obvious influence of Hollywood. "If Makino was determined to make a blockbuster, he shouldn't have copied it from the enemy Americans," one cinema journal contended.[49]

Feminine and childish rather than threatening or disgusting, the Chinese characters in *The Opium War* were easily imagined as ideal subjects of Japan's Pan-Asian empire. Many viewers, however, attacked the representation of the British in the film.[50] The depiction of Westerners in wartime Japanese cinema generally lacked the hostility that typified Hollywood's portrayal of enemy "Japs." Japanese actors in the role of Englishmen conveyed dignity and refinement—certainly more so than those playing Chinese opium smokers and coolies. In the opening minutes of the film, the character of Charles Elliot arrives in Canton. As he proceeds from the harbor to the inner recesses of Lin Zexu's mansion, he encounters three narcotics addicts: a half-dressed, writhing beggar supported between two gendarmes, an unselfconscious inebriate stumbling along a corridor, and a recumbent Qing official puffing intermittently and drowsily on a pipe. Despite the producers' attempt to cultivate sympathy for China, stereotyped scenes of Chinese intoxication and degeneracy betrayed Japan's ongoing distaste for fellow Asians and identification with the British, mighty masters of an island empire.[51]

Offering mixed messages and condemned by critics, *The Opium War* performed poorly at the metropolitan box office (though audiences in Japanese-occupied Hong Kong and the Philippines were more forgiving).[52] As publicity for the film subsided, its producers, together with the official cinema company of Manchukuo, pressured a Shanghai film studio into collaborating on a second movie on the subject. At least part of the rousing success of the Chinese-language *Wan shi liu fang (Eternal Fame)* in China, Manchukuo, and Japan derived from the popularity of supporting actress Ri Kōran. Ri was born in Manchuria in 1920 to Japanese parents who named her Yamaguchi Yoshiko, but was subsequently adopted by a Chinese family and given the name Li Xianglan. Fluent in both Japanese and Chinese, she became known as Ri Kōran (the Japanese pronunciation of Li Xianglan) upon becoming an actress. Ri was a performer not only onscreen but in her personal life as well. Assuming the identity of a Chinese, she "exuded authenticity" as an idealized metropolitan anthropomorphization of the mainland: feminine, beautiful, and longing for Japan. Cast as the embodiment of Pan-Asian unity, she also achieved considerable renown in Korea, Taiwan, and Japanese-occupied Southeast Asia.[53]

Ri carried the subplot of *Eternal Fame,* playing the love interest of a young, opium-addicted friend of Commissioner Lin. The representation of China by a male actor and Japan by the female Ri Kōran inverted the wartime cinematic convention of a Japanese man saving and winning the allegiance and affection of a Chinese woman. The ambiguity of Ri's nationality, however, complicated any straightforward interpretation of their relationship. To those who were aware of her Japanese birth, Ri may have simply represented Japan rescuing China from the depredations of opium. But whether they knew Ri's true nationality or not, audiences in both Japan and China were supposed to believe she was Chinese. Perhaps as a result of this tension, the Chinese director reserved the most overtly political song in the film for an unequivocally Chinese actress, Chen Yunshang, in the role of Lin Zexu's sweetheart. Attempting to persuade her mother to desist smoking, Chen lilts, "The Western barbarians have conspired against our country, imported opium to try to seduce us, and killed people without using swords. . . . It's a tragedy the way the nation is being destroyed." By contrast, Ri's signature ballad, one of the most popular songs of its day, is a purely personal plea to the addict object of her affections: "Opium is your real sweetheart; you should abandon her and truly love me!"[54]

Eternal Fame was, as noted writer and intellectual Chan Airin (Eileen Chang) observed, the first Chinese-language film to depict opium smoking onscreen.[55] The shocking opening scene takes place in a den, in which female attendants flutter among recumbent male customers, offering them pipes as they recline against satin cushions. Close-up shots of the luxurious surroundings emphasize the degeneracy of the consumers, while wide camera angles fill the screen with patrons, demonstrating the extent of Chinese drug use. The film is, however, ultimately a story of China's triumph over narcotics. In contrast to *The Opium War*, which elides all depictions of battle, *Eternal Fame* shows the Chinese overcoming the British in combat—a spectacle modeled on an actual engagement in 1841. In the movie, following the outbreak of war with Britain, Chen Yunshang's character leads Chinese troops in an ambush of the invading Westerners, driving them back at the cost of her own life. Lin Zexu delivers her eulogy, which includes a stirring call for the Chinese to resist imperialism.

The intentions of its Japanese production company notwithstanding, the complexity of the script and staging of *Eternal Fame* allowed both supporters and opponents of imperialism to draw inspiration from the film. The battle scene appealed to Japanese audiences as a representation of Asia's triumph over the West, while the female gender of the military commander transported the victory of the Chinese from possibility to fantasy. At the same time, soldiers and guerillas of the Korean Communist Party in Manchuria, locked in a war of resistance against Japan, understood *Eternal Fame* as a rousing tale of triumph over imperialism.[56] Chinese civilian audiences responded to the depiction of traditional Confucian virtues such as loyalty, chastity, and single-mindedness—all attributes of the sacred and eternal nation, powerfully and conventionally embodied by Chen.[57]

Like viewers, the studios and cast responsible for *Eternal Fame* found ways to reconcile the movie to a diverse assortment of political loyalties. Despite the proliferation of regulations seeking to transform film into a state mouthpiece in the late 1930s and early 1940s, cinema offered a myriad of artistic and technical means of exploiting the slippage between what was shown and what was seen, subtly subverting ideological orthodoxy.[58] Though pressured to demonstrate loyalty to Japan, the Chinese film studio, director, and screenwriter created a melodrama that deliberately emphasized the romantic and entertaining over the political and propagandistic. With the exception of Ri Kōran, all the cast members were Chinese, and many sympathized with the imperial resistance movement. When a Japanese battleship docked in Shanghai during production, military commanders summoned Chen Yunshang, one of the leading actresses of her day, to greet the invaders. Fearing she might be labeled a "traitor to the Han race *[Hanjian]*," the star refused to appear. Eventually, however, she was pressured into compliance, with the promise that the media would not use her image. The following day, however, local newspapers published photographs of Chen offering flowers to naval officers.[59] Like the Manchukuo state, the onscreen heroine of China was a Japanese puppet in real life.

CRUSADING BEFORE THE WORLD

Throughout the prewar period, China and Japan shared many assumptions about drugs. Influenced by the West, moral entrepreneurs of both nations viewed opium as a source of racial and cultural unfitness. They accepted that earning recognition as an independent state and equal player in the social Darwinist arena of international relations required liberation from the biological bondage of opium addiction. To many Chinese reformers, narcotics were the defining social issue of the interwar years, the most palpable threat to national survival.[60] "The horror of the opium drug is simply unrivaled. It enslaves the smoker and murders him at the same time," declared R. Y. Lo.[61] In propounding an image of the addict consonant with Western and Japanese stereotypes, Lo and fellow reformers of the post-1919 generation implicitly accepted the "fact" of China's backwardness. The addict, who "smirched the honor of the nation," became the object of a domestic civilizing mission that sought to preempt foreign aggression through racial hygiene.[62]

Even as Japanese imperialism on the Asian continent caused relations with China to deteriorate in the late 1920s, many Chinese continued to express admiration for the successful self-defense of the home islands against drugs. A journal editor wrote in 1927, "Much can be done by the education of children and enlightenment of the masses in order to form a public opinion which is aware of the manner that China has handicapped herself by opium smoking. In this respect the example of Japan as a non-smoking Eastern country may be cited."[63] Wang King Ky, China's ambassador to Belgium and a history professor at Peking University, reported, "It has generally been felt that many Chinese may well take a leaf from the history of opium and drug suppression in Japan."[64]

Following the Mukden Incident of 1931, however, political differences increasingly estranged former collaborators. Many Chinese believed that Manchukuo was nothing more than a vast narco-state in which the Japanese military sought to "drug the population into submission *[duhua* or *du-Hua zhengce]*" in preparation for further territorial expansion. "Since Japan invaded the Northeast," one journalist contended, "it has enacted four policies: drugging the people, promoting prostitution, turning a blind eye to gambling, and encouraging opium smoking."[65] The Kingly Way of Manchukuo further alienated many Chinese by replacing an allegedly universal standard for legitimate nationhood with a Japanese frame of reference that decisively denied the independence of China. A patriotic association in Guangzhou warned, "The things [the Japanese] say about 'common culture, common race' and mutual prosperity are just sweet words to fool us!" The promotion of drug consumption throughout mainland Asia "is the first step of their conspiracy to hold our lives in their hands. Afterward, Japan has other plans, which it will forcefully implement against our territory and people. We will become like the [colonized] Koreans, who would be better off dead *[sheng bu ru si]*."[66]

With the nation under ideological and military attack, Chinese nationalists sought to regain the initiative in the campaign against drugs—often by repeating the language of Japanese moral entrepreneurs. One communist writer demanded of his countrymen, "Do we hear of opium being consumed in the various great powers? Do the newly constructed revolutionary nations [of the Soviet Union] have drug users? All addicts belong to weak races *[ruoxiao minzu]*, of which the Chinese are the worst." He denounced addicts as "vermin *[chong]*" destroying themselves, their families, society, and the state.[67] Many Chinese literati of Manchukuo, including the self-exiled Northeast Writers' Group, also linked narcotics use to racial degeneracy, national disintegration, and other evils.[68] Lin Yutang, who dedicated his massive 1939 novel *Moment in Peking* to "the brave soldiers of China who are laying down their lives that our children and grandchildren shall be free men and women," attributed the prevalence of drug consumption to Chinese biological weakness as well as Japanese imperialism. Poya, a young male character, becomes addicted to heroin after smoking a Japanese "cigarette." Significantly, however, Poya is the son of a low-class, opium-smoking bond servant who used drugs to seduce and corrupt the eldest son of a noble house. "Remember your mother and you will surely get over [your addiction]," his uncle advises him. But Poya does not seem to recognize the danger of his heritage.[69]

By contrast, some Chinese remained convinced of the need for Sino-Japanese collaboration against opium. In a 1935 letter to the Dōbunkai, Xu Daolin, a Chinese professor of history, argued, "Japan is an Asian race-nation, therefore it understands the particularities of the East Asian psyche, and especially the feelings, values, and morals of the Chinese." Xu blamed the West for China's twentieth-century disintegration, and promoted Pan-Asian unity as the nation's most logical strategy for survival. Yet, unlike moral entrepreneurs in Manchukuo, Xu insisted on the fact of Chinese nationhood. He warned the Dōbunkai that the invasion of the Northeast had "grievously injured the self-respect" of the Chinese and that the crime of imperial opium trafficking on the mainland would not soon be forgotten.[70]

While Pan-Asianism and the Kingly Way attracted some Chinese adherents like Xu, European and American observers resoundingly denounced the ideology as propaganda. One British consul wrote in 1932, "It is extremely doubtful whether many people in Japan, or for that matter in Manchuria, had even heard of [Wangdao] before September 1931, but since the establishment of Manchukuo it has become, one might almost say, a catchword. It forms, in fact, a most convenient doctrine for the present rulers of Manchukuo." Four years later, he informed the Foreign Office, "The nature of [the Kingly Way] remains sufficiently vague for it to be urged in justification of almost any step favored by the Kwantung Army." By 1938, the consul had grown entirely cynical, dismissing Wangdao as "layers of high-sounding phrases which have to be stripped away before we come to the bed-rock of actual fact."[71] On the verge of Japan's war with the West, moral entrepreneurs worked unsuccessfully to disseminate a more positive impression of the Kingly Way. In 1938, the Manchukuo Publicity Bureau invited a group of American students to tour the country. The state bombarded the group with evidence of its commitment to ending addiction, informing students, "The Manchoukuo opium problem has been made the target of adverse and ridiculous criticisms in foreign newspaper reports but such criticisms are attributed to lack of proper understanding of the true significance of Manchoukuo's opium [policy]."[72]

Some Westerners, like Chinese, favored a conspiracy interpretation of Japan's narcotics operations on the Asian mainland. Mark Gayn, a Russian-born journalist for the *China Press,* the most openly anti-Japanese English-language newspaper in Shanghai, reported, "The drug traffic . . . emerged as a sinister plot for mass poisoning, an integral part of Japan's design for aggression." The passionately pro-Chinese Gayn delighted in rumors of rising narcotics consumption by Japanese, particularly soldiers: "The Army was ready to poison millions of Chinese, but it feared the pollution of the master race. Japan was playing with fire, however, and she was getting burned. From Dairen, Tientsin, and Nanjing, and from my friends in Shanghai, came hints of growing addiction among the Japanese civilians and soldiers alike. . . . [I]t was good to hear that in Nanking alone one soldier in fifty was a hospitalized addict. The 'superior race' was beginning to pay for its crimes."[73]

The Italian Amleto Vespa was similarly gratified by the spread of opium consumption among the Japanese, who were "caught in their own trap, so to speak."[74] A reporter for the *Japan Chronicle,* one of the most widely circulating English-language newspapers in Japan, concluded, "There is no inherent moral quality that prevents Japanese from becoming addicts. Opportunity is all that is needed, and we are seeing today the results of past years when little trouble was taken because there was no visible addiction."[75] Japan, now severed from the West, was no longer viewed as an abstinent nation on a par with the similarly drug-free great powers. Rather, European and American writers routinely called attention to narcotics consumption among the Japanese as a way to distance and dehumanize the enemy.

Even at the height of war, however, the allegation that Japan was encouraging addiction with the intention of taking over Asia and the world remained controversial. Though sympathetic to China, Frederick Merrill of the Institute of Pacific Relations, an international research organization, concluded in 1942, "There is, at present, no proof for the assertion that Japan and its army are actively encouraging addiction, even though widespread addiction has occurred in the wake of the invasion and occupation."[76] Merrill's defense of Japan hinged on the impossibility of proving intent—an argument that was also cited in the decision not to prosecute narcotics policymakers as war criminals at the International Military Tribunal for the Far East in 1945–48.[77] Other writers dismissed allegations against the empire on pragmatic grounds. British professor F. C. Jones reasoned, "The charge that the Japanese higher authorities deliberately spread the use of drugs in order to render the Chinese population more docile may be held unproven—after all they needed Chinese laborers in their factories and drug addicts do not make even moderately good workers." Jones nonetheless held the Japanese morally culpable for the social problem of opium: "They did not exercise effective control over their underlings and camp followers, whether Japanese, Korean, or Chinese, and consequently their evil record in the matter of opium, and in the even more vicious morphine and heroin traffic, both in Manchuria and in China generally, stands in glaring contrast to their glib professions of concern for the welfare and improvement of the peoples whom their armies subjugated."[78] To Jones, the question of whether addiction in China resulted from a conspiracy or an accident of policy scarcely mattered. Japan did not meet its own standards for legitimate nationhood in Manchukuo—and this failure alone sufficed to condemn the state.

CHAPTER FIVE · Merchants

During the interwar years, the KLT was an especially important theater for Japan's moral crusade against narcotics. Not only was the city-state the epicenter of the global opium economy, but it also suffered from a particular problem of political legitimacy. In contrast to the formal colonies of Taiwan and Korea, which Japan theoretically held in perpetuity, the Kwantung was a leased territory, originally scheduled for return to China in 1923.[1] A strong, unified administration like the Office of the Governor-General in Taiwan was not suitable. Instead, Japan split authority among four "heads," or branches of government: the Foreign Ministry, represented by local consulates; the SMR; the Kwantung Army; and the Kwantung Bureau (Kantō Totokufu/Kantō-chō). In fact, the Kwantung Army and the Kwantung Bureau were structurally intertwined, with the latter projecting a civilian front for military control.

Responsibility for regulating the narcotics market devolved upon the Kwantung Bureau. Under its direction, merchants built and staffed lawful institutions to obtain and distribute opium in the city-state and beyond. Merchants were entrepreneurs of morality as well as the market, using the legitimating rhetoric of benevolence to justify economic policies that served their interests and those of the military. Drawing on the example of Taiwan, merchants identified gradual suppression with civilized government. Delaying the implementation of an absolute ban, they channeled revenue from the legal narcotics market to the Kwantung Army and the Kwantung Bureau, buttressing the power of these authorities vis-à-vis the SMR and Foreign

Ministry. In part due to rivalry among the four heads, narcotics policy evolved with utmost slowness in the KLT. The protracted process of bringing the drug market under state control damaged Japan's reputation for benevolent government but allowed the army to covertly amass the financial resources needed to fund its invasion of Manchuria in 1931. The following year, the military swept aside its civilian competitors and established the nation-state of Manchukuo.

As the de facto power in Manchukuo, the Kwantung Army consolidated control of the legal opium market. Within months, the authorities assembled a drug monopoly to finance administration and demonstrate civilization and legitimacy. By the mid-1930s, however, the European empires in Southeast Asia had come to acknowledge the hypocrisy of gradual suppression, which allowed the state to profit from the drug market while continually delaying its eradication on questionable humanitarian grounds. Unable to validate the lucrative narcotics control measures they wished to implement according to global norms, moral entrepreneurs of Manchukuo sought to legitimize their new monopoly through appeals to the Kingly Way. Beneath the shield of Wangdao, merchants, including many former continental adventurers, succored the licit narcotics market for personal and state profit. Growing demand for drugs necessitated fresh supplies of poppies, but the domestically restive and politically isolated pariah state of Manchukuo could depend on neither local production nor international trade. The Kwantung Army accordingly used the revenues of public opium sales to expand into new areas of cultivation. In the late 1930s and early 1940s, the Japanese military invaded much of Inner Mongolia, China, and Southeast Asia, and established collaborationist or puppet governments supported by legal drug markets. The effort to legitimate Manchukuo as a civilized nation ultimately produced an autarkic narco-state that waged war on the world.

THE MARKET BEFORE MORALITY

Between 1898 and 1904, the Russian administration of the KLT taxed but did not attempt to suppress opium.[2] Upon acquiring the leasehold, Japanese policymakers sought to repeat the early successes of the antinarcotics campaign in Taiwan on the Asian mainland. Although the creation of an opium monopoly in Japan's first colony had normalized this institution as a hallmark of civilized imperial rule, the empire's relatively weak claim to the KLT complicated the replication of the Taiwan model. The city-state was a fixed-term lease, not a formal colony subject to absolute and theoretically permanent Japanese sovereignty. China, backed by the West, refused to countenance the establishment of a strong centralized administration over an explicitly noncolonial zone. Japan accordingly divided political authority among the Japanese Foreign Ministry, represented by local consular offices; the South Manchuria Railway Company; the Kwantung Army; and the Kwantung Bureau. Tokyo did not, however, fully clarify the scope of authority of each institution, leading to significant competition and even obstructionism among them.[3]

The Kwantung Bureau (Kantō Totokufu, or Office of the Governor-General) assumed power in September 1906. Headed by a ranking general and based in Ryōjun (Port Arthur) alongside the Kwantung Army, the Kwantung Bureau provided a civilian front for military domination of the leasehold. Its duties included defending the KLT, overseeing the SMR, meting out justice, and formulating narcotics policy. At the beginning of the twentieth century, the small population of local Chinese—less than four hundred thousand in the KLT and barely thirty thousand in Dairen proper—did not consume enough opium to justify the expense of creating a monopoly.[4] The Kwantung Bureau therefore adopted a form of subcontracting known as revenue farming, investing private individuals with the right to collect taxes in exchange for periodic remittances. First practiced in early modern Europe, revenue farming had a long history in South and Southeast Asia, where colonial rulers were strong enough to levy taxes but depended upon local Chinese elites to collect them. As governments grew more efficient and effective, they sought to reclaim the middleman's cut and curtail the influence of the Chinese by replacing farms with state monopolies. By the turn of the twentieth century, the great powers deemed revenue farming "an archaic 'medieval' form of tax collection."[5]

Although Japan understood the disadvantages of revenue farming, the KLT lacked adequate bureaucratic infrastructure to experiment with alternatives. In 1906, the Kwantung Bureau sold the right to collect taxes on opium to Shen Zhongguo, a local Chinese merchant. Born in 1878, Shen learned about business as an apprentice in a commercial house. During the Russo-Japanese War, he spied for Japan's Kwantung Army, winning the favor of General Nogi Maresuke, one of the most important military leaders of the Meiji period. Following the Japanese takeover of the KLT, the general rewarded Shen's service to the empire with the first opium farm.[6] Shen's relationship with the Kwantung Army established an enduring financial connection between drug merchants and the military. His franchise, however, failed to turn a profit. The local Chinese business community, dominated by natives of Shandong Province, regarded the native-born Shen as an outsider and refused to cooperate with him.

In 1907, the Kwantung Bureau awarded a second revenue farm to Ishimoto Kantarō, a Japanese adventurer. Nationality notwithstanding, Ishimoto was in many ways a mirror image of Shen. Born in 1868, he prepared to attend university as a youth but instead migrated to Shanghai, where he studied Chinese and English. In the early 1890s, Ishimoto attempted a succession of careers, including mining, teaching the Chinese language, managing a slaughterhouse, and raising dairy cows. Like Shen, Ishimoto founded his career on military contacts developed during Japan's imperialist wars. Upon the outbreak of the Sino-Japanese War in 1894, he offered his services as a Chinese-speaking aide to General Nogi. After the conflict, Nogi obtained a job for him in the Taiwan opium administration. In 1905, when the general was dispatched to the KLT to lead an army against Russia, Ishimoto again accompanied him as an interpreter. He subsequently remained in the leasehold as a translator for the Kwantung Bureau. Based on his experiences in Taiwan, Ishimoto advocated the creation of a government monopoly over opium. However, Nogi, who had opposed gradual suppression during his tenure as governor-general of the colony, instead awarded a revenue farm to Shen. With the support of Gotō Shinpei, who relocated from Taiwan to the KLT in 1906 to assume the presidency of the SMR, Ishimoto obtained the second license to tax opium.[7]

Backed by the Kwantung Army, Ishimoto almost single-handedly transformed Dairen into the premier drug depot of the early twentieth-century world.[8] Within a year, he had opened 262 retail shops. He invested early profits in extending operations beyond the KLT into northeast Asia. By 1912, over 90 percent of the so-called Opium King's business took place outside the leasehold. He also became involved in refined narcotics trafficking. Morphine and heroin, which had not been available in the city-state prior to the advent of Japanese control, emerged as a cheap alternative to smoking opium. The Kwantung Bureau profited from this traffic by imposing taxes on alkaloids in 1909.[9]

Owing to the growth of the narcotic economy, Ishimoto's reported annual income increased almost sevenfold between 1907 and 1914. He built a lavish hilltop residence and filled it with art, expensive furniture, and other treasures.[10] The development of the opium market by one of its agents also enriched the military. During the 1910s, opium did not appear as an official source of revenue in the KLT budget. Taxes on drugs thus furnished a convenient slush fund for the covert strengthening of the army.[11]

Outside the KLT, however, international opinion opposed the revenue farm. In 1906, the government of China announced a plan to eradicate the domestic narcotics market within ten years. Great Britain pledged to support this campaign by voluntarily terminating opium exports to the Qing empire. The United States, prompted by missionaries, moralists, and a desire to play a greater role in Asian affairs, also encouraged cooperation against the drug trade. In 1909, President Theodore Roosevelt convened the Shanghai Opium Commission, a meeting of all the imperial powers in Southeast Asia (including Japan), to discuss the suppression of smuggling. The event allowed the colonial states to compare strategies of drug control and was significant in producing a common view of narcotics as a global moral problem.[12] In the view of the conference president, Bishop Charles H. Brent, ending the opium traffic was an ethical imperative on a par with the abolition of slavery in the nineteenth-century American South. Echoing this rhetoric, Japan's delegate, Nonami Shizuo, compared his government's commitment to extirpating narcotics to "the resolve of Lincoln . . . against slavery."[13]

Representatives at Shanghai agreed to enact and enforce legislation in their home countries restricting the production, manufacture, distribution, and trade of narcotics. They also promised to crack down on smoking in their leased territories, concessions, and settlements in China. Although the Shanghai resolutions were voluntary, they were subsequently formalized in the binding Hague Convention of 1912. Participating nations agreed that this protocol, which upheld gradual suppression, would come into effect when ratified by all signatories—a process that took nearly a decade.

Following the Shanghai meeting, Tokyo pressured the KLT to align its antinarcotics legislation with global norms. In 1911, the Kwantung Bureau announced plans to suppress drug consumption over the next three years. The administration restricted participation in the opium market to designated individuals and firms, imposing fines and prison terms on unlicensed suppliers. Certificates issued for the licit importation of drugs recorded the quantity, national origin (mainly Persia and Turkey), purchasing agent, and shipping route. Local merchants distributed legal opium to registered consumers. In the two decades following the enactment of these laws, the number of licensed retailers in the KLT ranged from 94 to 114. They remitted a fixed fee per customer and 20 percent of total receipts in taxes to the Kwantung Bureau.[14]

The 1911 regulations provided a façade of compliance with international drug controls while allowing the narcotics market to thrive under Ishimoto's direction. The Opium King was not particularly concerned about moral issues raised by delegates in Shanghai and The Hague. "Generating revenue and eliminating Chinese with one strategy is like killing two birds with one stone," he was said to have declared.[15] Other imperial administrators viewed Japan's opium policy less cynically. When the three-year grace period expired in 1914, Ōuchi Ushinosuke, the chief civil bureaucrat in the leasehold, took advantage of the opportunity to abolish

Ishimoto's revenue farm. Under his direction, the Kwantung Bureau implemented a more "civilized" opium policy that resembled a monopoly system but distanced Japan from the appearance of involvement in the drug market. The state transferred Ishimoto's distribution rights to the Hongji Shantang (Japanese, Kōsai Zendō), a Chinese charity organization with a long history and wide geographic scope in late imperial China. The first Dairen branch of the Hongji Shantang opened in 1909. Although the association claimed to be the city's sole relief agency operated for and by Chinese, it received significant subsidies, including its premises, from the Kwantung Bureau. The authorization of the Hongji Shantang as the sole legal importer and purveyor of opium in the KLT supplemented this official assistance for a price: the semblance of Chinese management of the narcotic economy. To meet its new responsibilities, the association split into two branches. A philanthropic division supervised customary charitable activities: caring for orphans, the elderly, and the dependents of migrant laborers, as well as educating children and providing wet nurses for abandoned babies, free medical services, and financial assistance to individuals and families in crisis. The smoking division, staffed by Japanese appointed by the state, imported and distributed opium and made regular payments to the Kwantung Bureau.[16]

With the exception of taxes, all proceeds from drugs were supposed to fund the relief activities of the Hongji Shantang. However, within a year of the establishment of the system, an undercover investigator expressed "some doubt" regarding the actual disposal of revenues.[17] The prime beneficiary of the Hongji Shantang enterprise was Zhang Benzheng, a Chinese magnate whose career closely paralleled those of Shen Zhongguo and Ishimoto Kantarō. Born in 1865 to impoverished emigrant parents from Shandong, Zhang left school at sixteen and experimented with farming and odd jobs before opening a general store. During the Sino-Japanese War of 1894–95, he ingratiated himself with the Japanese army as a spy and procurer of military supplies. He later established a shipping company with operations in the major ports of China and Japan, which transported munitions and materiel for the Japanese army during the Russo-Japanese War and World War I. By 1920, he owned twenty-three ships, and his company had diversified into banking, currency speculation, oil, and other ventures. Zhang also invested in the local real estate market, acquiring land and more than 1,800 houses and buildings in Dairen. As his stature grew, he became a prominent representative of the local Chinese community, serving on business and government boards and self-defense and morality societies. He was also a noted philanthropist, offering loans to disaster-stricken farmers and acting as the headmaster of a girls' school.[18] Zhang maintained a cozy relationship with the military, funneling a percentage of the proceeds from opium sales to the Kwantung Army. Under the management of "the most Chinese member of the Japanese ruling elite," the profits of the legal drug trade in the KLT soared, outstripping those of Taiwan in the late 1910s.[19]

The transfer of tax farming rights from Ishimotō Kantarō to Zhang Benzheng failed to disrupt the upward mobility of the Opium King, who parlayed his success in the narcotics market into social and political connections. Diversifying his investments into industries ranging from beer production to mining to real estate, Ishimoto continued to build his personal fortune. He served two consecutive terms as Dairen's first mayor, earning the nickname of *genrō* (elder statesman), a term used to describe the venerable oligarchs of the Meiji period. As mayor, Ishimoto built a school for girls, established a newspaper, earmarked land for parks throughout the city, and donated funds for a library and public housing units.[20] He also paid for a paved boulevard linking Dairen and Ryōjun. Popularly referred to as *Ahen dōro* (Opium street) and deemed "the most charming drive in Manchuria," the road was twenty-two miles long and thirty feet wide. It was finished in 1924 for a total cost of 1.35 million yen.[21] A friend of Ishimoto's granddaughter speculated in her memoirs that this gift represented the Opium King's atonement to the city for the drug market he had created. In 1933, Ishimoto died of tuberculosis in the Dairen SMR Hospital, where hundreds of narcotics users had received treatment for addiction.[22]

MORAL ENTREPRENEURS IN THE INTERWAR NARCOTIC ECONOMY

Between 1914 and 1918, the great powers, preoccupied with World War I, paid little attention to the drug trade. In the global reckoning that followed, however, Japan's flourishing narcotics operations in Dairen provoked condemnation and challenges to the legitimacy of the imperial government from around the world. Moral entrepreneurs in the KLT and throughout the empire responded by justifying the state sale of drugs as a hallmark of benevolent rule. Throughout the 1920s, merchants concealed the profit motive beneath the mission to civilize, preventing any real change in imperial opium suppression policy.

Narcotics emerged as the target of a moral crusade barely a month after the armistice. On December 19, 1918, two leading English-language newspapers in Asia published an exposé of Japanese drug trafficking in the KLT and China. The *New York Times* subsequently ran the story under the headline "Charge That Japan Aids Opium Trade." According to the reporter, "Japanese military domination would forbid . . . any interference in a traffic in which the Japanese authorities were interested either officially or unofficially. In Dalny [Dairen], the highest civic dignity [the mayoralty] has been conferred upon the chief dealer in morphia and opium [Ishimoto]."[23] During the following months, newspapers from the *Malaya Tribune* to the *Liverpool Echo* indicted Japan for failing to enforce gradual suppression.[24] Reporters also criticized the "backward" KLT opium farm, now the sole remaining institution of its kind in the world. Yet despite global censure, the Kwantung Bureau resisted reform, arguing that the revenues of the Hongji Shantang supplied half the leasehold's budget and enabled the government to provide basic services.

The Japanese Foreign Ministry, however, could not withstand international disapproval of imperial narcotics policy. Affirming Japan's intention to uphold global standards for drug regulation, representatives at the Paris Peace Conference of 1919 collaborated in founding the Committee on the Traffic in Opium and Other Dangerous Drugs, also known as the Opium Advisory Committee (OAC). This League of Nations subcommittee collected information and advised governments on policies regarding the cultivation, manufacture, and distribution of opiates, cocaine, marijuana, and other ingestible substances considered physiologically harmful.

Politicians in the Japanese metropole also intervened to reform KLT management of the opium economy according to the norms of civilized government. Partly to facilitate this goal, Japan's prime minister, Hara Kei, restructured the Kwantung Bureau. The institution maintained its judicial and legislative powers and jurisdiction over the SMR but was formally dissociated from the Kwantung Army. Influenced by post–World War I liberalism, Hara intended the change to reduce the role of the military in civilian affairs. Instead, the army capitalized on its release from mundane administrative responsibilities to accumulate resources and influence. At the level of the rank and file, troops who had few official duties to occupy their time became more involved in opium trafficking, generating revenue that ultimately supported expansionism.[25]

Although Hara appears to have sincerely wished to eliminate the KLT opium economy, representatives in the metropolitan Diet refused to shoulder the financial burden of compensating the leasehold for lost revenue. Merchants within the restructured Kwantung Bureau also objected to meaningful change. Fujiwara Tetsutarō, a minister of finance, spent two months investigating opium regulatory regimes throughout East Asia. He concluded that antinarcotics policy in the leasehold was at least as stringent as that in British Hong Kong, Portuguese Macau, and the Chinese and Western administrations in Beijing and various treaty ports.

Fujiwara concluded that tightening the prohibition of opium in the KLT would actually violate imperial Japan's mission to civilize the Chinese, and risked increasing local crime. He also doubted the practicality of absolute suppression, given the thriving drug economy of neighboring China.[26]

Ultimately, the Kwantung Bureau succeeded in preventing all but the most superficial adjustments to local narcotics policy. In 1920, merchants renewed their commitment to the benevolent—and lucrative—strategy of gradual prohibition, pledging to end the drug market within five years. The smoking department *(kaienbu)* of the Hongji Shantang was renamed the "pharmaceutical division" *(yakkyoku)* to suggest that the opium it sold was intended for legitimate "medical" use. With the aid of a grant of three million yen, for which Hara Kei directly petitioned the Diet, the government established the Opium Monopoly Bureau (Ahen senbaikyoku) as a supervisory board for the Hongji Shantang. Koga Renzō, a former classmate of Hara's selected to oversee the bureau, promised that the monopoly would gradually put itself out of business as registered drug users died or abandoned smoking.

Far from inspiring any real effort to suppress narcotics, the ideology of benevolence served to whitewash the profits of moral entrepreneurs. Less than two years after the 1920 reforms, an episode that became notorious as the "opium incident *[ahen jiken]*" exposed the corruption of the new system. Koga and his protégé, Nakano Arimitsu, secretly offered their cronies permits to import and distribute opium, pocketing the sale fee and taxes. Holders of these licenses enjoyed the right to purchase opium at the below-market rate available to the Hongji Shantang. One buyer, Kajii Sakari, was a continental adventurer posing as a merchant and journalist, a common professional cover for spying and involvement in the vice industries. Kajii delivered much of the revenue from his franchise to expansionist elements within the Kwantung Army. Obata Teijirō, an employee of the smoking division of the Hongji Shantang, also purchased a license from Koga and Nakano. In just over sixteen months, he imported opium worth over seven hundred thousand yen. Obata channeled his profits into the electoral campaigns of candidates representing the Seiyūkai, the metropolitan political party of Hara Kei. In addition to large-scale traffickers like Kajii and Obata, a fleet of petty dealers, both Japanese and Chinese, also acquired licenses from Nakano.[27]

Early in 1921, a captain of the SMR police who had poor relations with Koga, Nakano, and the Kwantung Bureau discovered this racket. He communicated the matter to a member of the Kenseikai, the rival party of the Seiyūkai. In February, the Kenseikai representative, seeking to gain political advantage by embarrassing the Seiyūkai, brought the scam to the attention of the Diet. Before the assembled company, he emphasized the contradiction between the Kwantung Bureau's alleged commitment to the suppression of drugs in accordance with the norms of civilized rule and the connivance of its officials in the narcotics traffic. That very day, police arrested Nakano, Koga, Obata, and several others. In March, Tokyo ordered the case brought to trial. The court named Nakano as the principal defendant and indicted Koga, Obata, Kajii, and six others. For their actual crime of embezzling from the state, the perpetrators of the opium incident became scapegoats for the hypocrisy of gradual suppression. In August, the court sentenced Nakano to sixteen months in jail. The judge also ordered him to make restitution of over one hundred thousand yen—a large amount but far below what he had received in bribes and kickbacks. Kajii received one year in prison; Koga, six months. The court exonerated six defendants of guilt in the affair. The magnitude of the graft, the prominence of the accused, and the international publicity the case had generated rendered this stunning leniency unacceptable to the Japanese government. Under orders from the metropole, the KLT's chief prosecutor appealed for a retrial. Several months later, the court reconvened to sentence Nakano to three years in prison, Koga and Kajii to two years each, and Obata to one year. The judge also raised Nakano's fine and levied substantial penalties on several other defendants.[28]

The outcome of the case generated a range of reactions. One Japanese observer denounced the verdict as "a complete and unfortunate miscarriage of justice" in which the defendants were sacrificed to please Chinese and Western critics of imperial opium policy.[29] Far from expressing satisfaction with the outcome, however, foreign diplomats derided the punishment of Koga and Nakano as absurdly inadequate. In the opinion of the American consul, "It would seem that the two officials particularly got off very lightly, considering the gravity of their offenses. It is difficult to understand how such leniency can be reconciled with the Government's announced purpose of taking drastic measures against official corruption."[30]

Although the Hongji Shantang withstood the scandal of the opium incident, Japan's 1921 ratification of the Hague Convention, nine years after it was drafted, demanded action to bring KLT drug regulation policy into compliance with international law. In 1924, the Kwantung Bureau promulgated the KLT Opium Law *(Kantōshū ahen rei)*. This legislation reaffirmed many existing principles of narcotics control: prohibition of unlicensed handling of raw and refined opium; restriction of drug importing and manufacturing to license holders; distribution of controlled substances by doctors, dentists, veterinarians, pharmacists, and other medical professionals; and imposition of fines and prison sentences on violators. The edict also renewed the regime's intention to eradicate opiate trafficking and consumption within three years.[31] "Like all laws in Japan relating to opium and morphia, they are excellent," a Chinese anti-opium association declared on the subject of the regulations. "But will they be enforced?"[32] As feared, the three-year grace period passed without any discernible slowdown in the Dairen drug market.

Only months after the enactment of the Opium Law, the OAC held two conferences in Geneva to discuss the international traffic. At these meetings, which took place in the winter of 1924–25, European participants praised Japan's opium monopoly in Taiwan for having reduced drug consumption. In the words of Edouard Daladier, the minister of the Colonies of France, "Japan was a great and noble Empire, not only in view of its civilisation, but because it had taken a foremost part in the efforts made to improve the general level of civilisation throughout the world."[33] The Americans and Chinese, by contrast, questioned the "benevolence" of state monopolies. The eradication of opium smoking in the Philippines, an American colony since 1898, furnished the United States, again represented by Bishop Brent, with moral high ground from which to critique the Japanese and Europeans in East and Southeast Asia.[34] Journalist Ellen N. La Motte, who covered the Geneva Conferences for the reading public of New York City, deemed gradual suppression hypocritical. "It appears to be only the subject peoples, whose well-being has become the White Man's burden, who receive the blessings of this peculiar form of altruism," she observed.[35] China, which forbore to implement an opium monopoly for another decade, also denounced the institution as a disguise for state rent seeking at the expense of local welfare. Chu Chao-Hsin, an economics professor at Peking University, pointed out, "The furnishing of opium to smokers was not an act of benevolence, but one which did harm to the individuals in particular, and to the community in general."[36]

The American and Chinese representatives failed to persuade Japan and the European colonial powers to abandon their lucrative opium monopolies. Disgusted, they withdrew from the conference. Following their departure, the remaining nations affirmed state control of the drug market as a hallmark of civilized imperial rule and deferred the termination of government monopolies by at least five years. The delegates also collectively resolved "that the farm system, where it is still in operation, should be abolished and that the opium business should be made a Government monopoly and kept entirely in the hands of the Government."[37] This declaration constituted a direct attack on the KLT, where the Hongji Shantang remained the sole opium farm in the world.

Embarrassed by the accusation of backwardness, Japan's representatives in Geneva pleaded with officials and bureaucrats at home to align KLT drug policy with global standards. If Taiwan was a model of narcotics prohibition for the world, the Kwantung endangered the legitimacy of the Japanese empire by lagging behind international norms. Delegate Nonami Shizuo, who had attended the Shanghai Commission in 1909 on behalf of Japan and personally surveyed the drug administrations of the Western colonies and treaty ports in Southeast Asia and China in the early 1920s, urged his nation to "bring a halt to its perverse behavior regarding opium, revitalize China's four hundred million people, and take responsibility for the restoration of East Asia."[38] In addition to proposing the establishment of a monopoly over refined narcotics as well as opium, Nonami suggested building clinics for drug users and facilities to train doctors and farmers in addiction treatment and crop substitution strategies, respectively. Anticipating the Pan-Asian ideology of the 1930s, he called attention to the moral responsibility of Japan, "the only strong country in East Asia," to protect its neighbors. "The whites will not guard the interests of the yellow people," he warned.[39]

In 1928, the Kwantung Bureau finally caved to international and metropolitan pressure and consolidated its authority over the drug market. The Hongji Shantang transferred its legal trading and distribution rights to the new Opium Monopoly Bureau, freshly capitalized and installed in a costly new building.[40] The initial performance of the monopoly disappointed the administration. Offering smoking opium only to drug users at a price above street value, the system gave consumers little incentive to register. Traffickers competed successfully with legal sales. Moreover, although the assertion of government control over the KLT narcotics market brought local regulations in line with global standards for enlightened rule, the Kwantung Bureau soon came under fire for failing to enforce its own laws. Chinese observers dismissed the monopoly as "but a camouflage": "What is the use, one may ask, of registering addicts if anybody can smoke and buy any quantity of opium he desires from these opium dens? . . . The monopoly, as it is, exists for no other purpose than for the sake of revenue."[41] Western diplomats also found fault with the KLT monopoly, which, in their words, fulfilled "the letter rather than the spirit of Geneva."[42] By the late 1920s, profits from the opium monopolies in the European colonies of Southeast Asia had fallen considerably from their peak only a few years earlier. New commitment to the suppression of narcotics on the part of the great powers gave rise to unsettling attacks on the morality of imperial Japan, where the drug market continued to thrive.[43]

In 1929, as the five-year grace period agreed upon at Geneva drew to a close, the OAC appointed a commission to survey progress toward gradual suppression in the imperial possessions of Great Britain, France, Portugal, the Netherlands, and Japan.

The committee also proposed visiting China but was deterred by Generalissimo Chiang Kai-shek, who feared that exposing the extent of the narcotic economy might suggest the nation's unfitness for self-rule and the deficiencies of his own leadership. In the months preceding the OAC's arrival in the KLT in March 1930, the British consul of Dairen observed, "There are signs . . . of more diligent attempts on the part of the Japanese Government to deal with the traffic, but these measures have been probably no more than the Government's reaction to the impending visit of the Commission of Investigation appointed by the League—and past experience has shown such zeal to be ephemeral." Two days before the visit, the Kwantung Bureau plastered the city with antismoking posters. Upon the departure of the party, the propaganda disappeared, and the consul reiterated his suspicion that "however much the authorities of the territory may outwardly have professed to be willing to permit an investigation of altered conditions, everything pointed to the fact that the ground had been prepared beforehand."[44]

A few months later, in a similar episode, an Indian representative on the OAC accused the KLT Opium Monopoly Bureau of manufacturing and exporting cocaine to the South Asian subcontinent in distinctive packages labeled "Fujitsuru."[45] In response, a Japanese delegate invited the British raj to send a police inspector, J. Slattery, to investigate narcotics production in the leasehold. Although Japanese patrolmen expressed curiosity about Slattery's work in India, the inspector complained that they offered no information in return.[46] The American consul in Dairen suspected, however, that the Kwantung Bureau had authorized a crackdown on trafficking for Slattery's benefit.[47]

In 1931, Andō Akimichi, a finance bureaucrat in the KLT and the author of a study of the global narcotic economy, published a translation of American delegate John Palmer Gavit's record of his experiences at the Geneva Conferences six years earlier. Gavit was the chief of the Washington Bureau of the Associated Press and a noted social activist. His original text, *"Opium,"* vigorously denounced the institution of the opium monopoly. "Shall we maintain, for the benefit of 'civilized' pockets, and even on the ground that we are saving 'inferior' native populations from other forms of taxation, a double standard: one for the protection of our own nationals, the other for 'east of Suez'?" Gavit demanded.[48] Though Gavit's opposition to gradual suppression was unequivocal, Andō's text expressed a more vague intention of nurturing international cooperation against opium. "Saving the world from the hell of the drug crisis would be considered an enormous contribution by the Japanese," declared his introduction.[49] Translated by moral entrepreneurs, critiques of opium policy became statements of support for the legitimacy of imperial rule.

MONOPOLY, MILITARISM, AND MORAL CRUSADE IN MANCHUKUO

While moral entrepreneurs veiled financial interests with the rhetoric of benevolence, the Kwantung Army quietly accumulated revenue from the drug traffic. Profits helped to fund expansionism, culminating in the invasion of Manchuria in September 1931 and the establishment of the state of Manchukuo six months later. Amid this political upheaval, the legal status of the Kwantung as a leased territory remained unchanged. Ongoing control of Dairen provided imperial Japan with leverage over the theoretically independent state of Manchukuo. The city was the busiest port in northeast Asia, handling 70 percent of trade in Manchuria and nearly a quarter of trade in China. Under the terms of a 1907 accord between the Japanese and Qing governments, goods for sale in the KLT could enter duty-free, but imports bound for China were subject to taxation. The customs commissioner, by law a Japanese national, remitted tariffs to the Chinese government. These monies were distributed among the great powers, which claimed them under the unequal treaties of the nineteenth century. For this reason, the Kwantung Army, which easily took over the Chinese-held customs houses of the Manchurian hinterland, could not seize the revenues of Dairen without provoking an international incident. American journalist Edgar Snow aptly described the situation as "ironic."[50]

In June 1932, the commander-in-chief of the Kwantung Army received the following telegram: "In view of the present situation of Manchukuo, it is very natural and a matter of urgent necessity that Manchukuo should take over the custom houses, including that at Dairen. Furthermore, we must keep the matter absolutely secret until its enforcement." The following August, the army informed the Japanese customs commissioner at Dairen, Fukumoto Junzaburō, that the state would consider the continued remittance of duties to China "highly provocative." Even if China asserted its legal right to the money, the Kwantung Army expected Fukumoto to withhold it. Upon receiving the military's instructions, Fukumoto notified the Chinese customs commissioner at Shanghai of his intention to comply. The latter dismissed Fukumoto for insubordination; sixty-five Japanese employees in Dairen resigned in his wake. All promptly accepted jobs with the Manchukuo customs service.[51]

Through these covert machinations, the Kwantung Army won control of the Dairen customs house. With the revenues of the legal drug traffic in military hands, the Manchukuo government prepared to establish a national opium monopoly. This plan alarmed the Kwantung Bureau, which anticipated that state control of the much larger drug market north of the KLT border might threaten its own profits. Merchants cautioned the army that the monopoly in the leased territory had failed to generate the anticipated revenues or justify the high start-up costs.[52] Although these warnings did not deter the military, the likelihood of competition between the KLT and Manchukuo monopolies sealed the fate of the Kwantung Bureau. In 1934, the Kwantung Army abolished the bureau, replacing it with the new Kwantung Division (Kantō-kyoku) in the Manchukuo capital of Xinjing (the renamed city of Changchun). This authority was placed under the supervision of the commander-in-chief of the Kwantung Army and Japan's ambassador to Manchukuo. Although the KLT opium monopoly continued to function, policymakers in the leased territory lost most of their independence.[53]

In November 1933, the Opium Law of Manchukuo established state control over the production and distribution of drugs. The legislation mandated examination, registration, and treatment for addicts; prevention of the spread of drug dependence; and penalties for infractions. Moral entrepreneurs identified the monopoly with benevolent government according to the Kingly Way. "The opium monopoly was not intended for profit, but rather for the welfare of the people, for moral motives: it is a 'people's monopoly,'" wrote one economist.[54] Oikawa Katsuzō, one of the first officials hired by the Manchukuo Opium Monopoly Bureau in 1933, claimed in a postwar interview that he had hoped to replicate Japan's benevolent extirpation of drugs in Taiwan.[55] Other merchants ignored the moral ramifications of drug sales. The state distributed retail licenses to tens of thousands of continental adventurers, seeking both their loyalty and their taxes. In contrast to the KLT, Manchukuo set no timeline for eliminating the opium trade. During the mid-1930s, the proceeds of the monopoly doubled to furnish nearly 10 percent of the national budget.[56] In the 1930s, the moral crusade against narcotics was not a critique of, but a smokescreen for, public profiteering in drugs.

Because the League of Nations did not recognize its sovereignty, Manchukuo was not a signatory to international anti-opium legislation or a sitting member of the OAC. The state nonetheless announced its intention to comply with the Hague Convention. Officials hoped that voluntary cooperation with the great powers would improve the image of the nation. "With regard to opium, our state can put forth a sincere effort to lead the way to global eradication. The world has unfortunately not recognized this true purpose of Manchukuo," contended the Monopoly Bureau.[57] Japan too pledged to continue participating in the OAC, despite having severed ties with the League of Nations in 1933. A metropolitan newspaper promised, "The Japanese government will go ahead and do it [support anti-opium legislation] whether it is asked to act by the League or not. To accuse Japan of tolerating the traffic in drugs is like accusing Japan of encouraging national suicide."[58] Miyajima Mikinosuke, a doctor and professor of public health who served on the committee in the early 1930s, even cautioned Japan against becoming a "nation that lagged behind global standards *[kōhijunkoku]*."[59]

The opium monopoly institution received a boost in credibility in 1934 when China, one of the most vociferous critics of gradual suppression at Geneva a decade earlier, itself placed the drug market under public control. Although leading anti-narcotics crusaders implacably opposed the monopoly, Chiang Kai-shek desperately needed funding for an ambitious modernization agenda and military offensive against the Chinese Communist Party. To Japanese moral entrepreneurs, the adoption of gradual suppression by the Chinese Republic sanctioned their own stance on drugs. Following his Chinese colleague's presentation of the new policy at the 1935 meeting of the OAC, a Japanese representative even proposed a resolution congratulating China on its "progressiveness." Portugal and Siam, which maintained opium monopolies themselves, supported the measure; Poland, which had no imperialist interest in Southeast Asia, quashed it.[60]

China's adoption of the opium monopoly did not shield the institution from attack. Euro-American critics of Manchukuo generally targeted the implementation rather than the principle of gradual suppression, which had finally brought about the near eradication of narcotics in most Southeast Asian colonies. A reporter for the *London Times* wrote, "The gap between precept, as embodied in the enlightened Opium Law, and practice, as reflected in the ubiquitous and well-frequented dens, may appear to those not inured to the disingenuous atmosphere of Manchukuo the symptom of a callous hypocrisy."[61] The British consul of Fengtian dismissed gradual suppression in Manchukuo as "at best a paper scheme." He informed the Foreign Office, "From inquiries made locally it seems that these provisions of the Opium Law and of the Regulations made thereunder are not treated seriously, and that any person who is prepared to pay for the privilege can smoke opium in one of the numerous licensed establishments, under conditions which do not suggest that the vice is discouraged."[62]

Among Japanese moral entrepreneurs of the 1930s, support for the opium monopoly was strong but not universal. The editor of a Chinese-language newspaper in Manchukuo admonished, "It is, after all, a shame for any civilised country to permit the open sale of narcotics."[63] In 1935, Miyajima Mikinosuke expressed his regret that the national promise to extirpate the drug economy was yet unfulfilled. He suggested a full revision of opium policy to "lift constraints on the happiness of the thirty million people and fulfill expectations of rule according to the Kingly Way."[64]

In 1938, Manchukuo announced a ten-year timeline for the complete shutdown of the drug market. For the first time, the state mandated the registration of morphine and heroin as well as opium users. The state induced barely twenty-five thousand alkaloid consumers to register for permits; nonetheless, they provided a convenient pretext for the construction of lucrative public refineries. The largest factory, located in a converted bank in the city of Fengtian, employed more than five hundred workers and produced upward of four tons of morphine and heroin annually. It was labeled *fushougao* (good luck and long life paste), and, as an American diplomat remarked, "certainly the appearance of the package is not calculated to impress the purchaser with the evil and destructive nature of the contents."[65]

State control of the refined narcotics market stimulated rather than suppressed consumption in the late 1930s and early 1940s. By 1944, an official survey estimated the Manchukuo drug user population at 1.2 million, but critics suggested that the actual number was more than 2.5 million and possibly as high as 4 million. Addiction cost as many as 179,000 lives during the thirteen-year lifespan of Manchukuo.[66] A Russian doctor who had lived in Harbin since the turn of the century declared, "Never, never have I seen anything like it. Under the Chinese we had opium, lots of it, and quite a number of the poor Chinese smoked it. But when the Japanese marched into Manchuria, everything took a turn for the worse. Their Monopoly Bureau doesn't even pretend to be suppressing the drug traffic. Instead, it actively promotes the planting and the smoking of opium."[67]

The Manchukuo government attempted to satisfy rising demand for drugs by encouraging poppy cultivation in the northern provinces of Jilin and Heilongjiang, in Rehe (annexed in 1933), and even across the border in colonial Korea. Still the state could not meet the domestic need for opium. Unable to import drugs from abroad and hampered by banditry and anti-Japanese resistance in procuring narcotics from north China, the military initiated operations to take over Inner Mongolia. In the late 1930s, the Kwantung Army established a string of Japanese puppet regimes in the region, allegedly in support of Mongolian self-determination. Under these governments, poppy production soared.[68] Moral entrepreneurs sought to justify new opium monopolies in the grasslands according to the familiar rhetoric of benevolence and racial harmony. In their argument, former authorities had depended on opium as a medium of exchange, forced the local population to grow poppies instead of food crops, and underpaid farmers or outright confiscated their harvest to fund the army. "Feudal" exploitation engendered poverty, ignorance, and addiction among the people. Moral entrepreneurs claimed that the Japanese invasion of the region "liberated" cultivators from their dual subjugation to opium and despotism by offering a fair price for poppies.[69] The opium economy was a moral economy.

Japanese puppet and collaborationist regimes in north and central China, established after the outbreak of fighting between the two nations in July 1937, also made simultaneous use of opium as a source of revenue and a justification for political legitimacy. Lacking the authority needed to enforce monopoly control of the drug market, these governments reverted to the outdated strategy of revenue farming. In 1938, Tokyo established the Kōain (Asia Development Board) to coordinate administrative, economic, and cultural measures throughout its expanding domains in China. Under the direction of the Kōain, Satomi Hajime, a longtime narcotics smuggler in Manchuria, took charge of the mainland drug market. Working quickly to restore order amid wartime chaos, Satomi co-opted the Shanghai branch of the Hongji Shantang as a Chinese façade for imperial management of the drug trade.[70] Like his predecessors in the KLT, Satomi deployed the charitable organization as a front for military revenue raising in the narcotics market, while asserting his intention to free China from oppression by drugs, feudalism, and the imperialism of the Western powers.[71]

In the context of total war on the Asian mainland, however, the pretense of Japanese benevolence had worn thin. When the OAC convened for the twenty-third time in Geneva in June 1938, China, the West, and colonies such as India and Egypt united in linking Japan's military invasion and occupation of China to surging narcotics trafficking and consumption. At the end of the session, delegates adopted a resolution asking Japan and China to cooperate in "the most vigourous action with a view to remedying the situation [the spread of drugs]."[72] The Japanese representative angrily protested that even this limited censure violated the "traditional policy of fairness and impartiality" upon which his nation's continuing participation in the OAC was predicated. Japan subsequently withdrew from the committee.[73]

In the early 1940s, Japan, no longer able to deny its status as an international pariah, attacked and occupied the European and American colonies of Southeast Asia, including Malaya, Singapore, the Philippines, the Dutch East Indies, Burma, and Indochina. By this time, the narcotic economy of the region had largely disappeared, although states continued to furnish opium to small numbers of registered, mostly Chinese smokers. These consumers provided a pretext for Japan to present its invasion as a rescue of the population from the "black plague" of narcotics and domination by the West.[74] Such rhetoric resonated among many Southeast Asian nationalists, who had long chafed under foreign rule and viewed Japan as both an inspiration and a potential ally against the great powers. With the empire in a state of total war, however, drug control in Southeast Asia remained largely a paper scheme.[75]

The opium economy of Manchukuo was a primary factor in Japan's motivation and means for waging war on the world. The deliberate nurturing of the domestic drug market for public profit grew demand beyond supply, leading the Kwantung Army to annex new regions for poppy cultivation. Expansionism, however, did not resolve the bottleneck, as military forces could not adequately stabilize occupied areas to establish long-distance distribution networks. The failure of conquest was in part an ideological one: puppet governments, suffering from the same problems of legitimacy as Manchukuo, could not adapt to changing global standards for drug regulation, civilized government, and nationhood. Born in and of a crisis of legitimacy, Manchukuo was one of the world's first fully realized narco-states—fiscally, socially, and above all morally dependent on opium.

CHAPTER SIX • Law Enforcement

Throughout the imperial age, merchants faced competition from unlicensed traffickers in the drug market. By the 1920s, Dairen had become the epicenter of the global narcotic economy, home to tens or even hundreds of thousands of dealers. One moral entrepreneur believed that up to three-quarters of the Japanese in southern Manchuria were somehow involved in illicit opium ventures. Other estimates ranged as high as 95 percent.[1] It was said that among Chinese, "only priests abstain from the traffic."[2] Illegal dealers drew business away from the revenue farms and the opium monopoly of the KLT, and damaged the reputation of the Japanese government in the international arena. To bring them to justice, the Kwantung Bureau created and supervised an elaborate network of police, courts, and corrections. Over time, however, mutual interest in Japanese expansion in Manchuria produced a symbiotic relationship between law enforcement and illicit dealers. Rather than arresting, prosecuting, and punishing traffickers to the full extent of the law, the Kwantung Bureau deliberately overlooked most violations of antinarcotics legislation, allowing the drug market to flourish with near impunity. The opium economy enriched the Japanese military financially, as many continental adventurers paid a portion of their profits as bribes and kickbacks. Surging drug crime also created a pretext to increase the ranks of police, instruments of "military rule in civil garb" and auxiliary agents of expansionism who fought alongside the Kwantung Army to subdue Manchuria in 1931.

In responding to illegal traffickers, officers of justice did not simply put into effect the moral regulations of others. They were entrepreneurs as well as enforcers of standards for legitimate nationhood in the moral crusade against narcotics of the high imperial age.[3] The judicial system consistently reflected the philosophy of benevolent government, in which treatment of violators was almost invariably lenient but far from impartial. Rather, each stage of justice, from the police station to the courthouse to the prison, represented an opportunity to address criminality according to the perceived level of civilization of the offender's race. Benevolence was not simply an abstract ideology of legitimacy for foreign audiences but an intimate attempt to inscribe the justification of Japanese rule on the bodies of imperial subjects.[4]

POLICING

Arrest by the police constituted the first stage of the narcotics offender's encounter with benevolent justice. In modern Japan, police functioned as both a symbol of enlightened Western modernity and an instrument of legitimate force on behalf of the authoritarian government. At the beginning of the Meiji period, the nation's "Father of Police," Kawaji Toshiyoshi, likened patrolmen to "a form of medical treatment for the state, just like everyday hygiene for the individual." Police, he continued, "protect good citizens and nurture the vigor of the national body." In Kawaji's view, the anthropomorphized nation was a fundamentally healthy patient whose continued well-being depended on ordinary medical maintenance. The policeman was his doctor, a provider of specialized knowledge and counsel. More famously, Kawaji also compared patrolmen to "nursemaids" of the people, benevolently awakening in their charges a sense of national consciousness and duty to the state.[5]

Kawaji's views were easily applied to the empire, where law enforcement endeavored to civilize subjects and cultivate goodwill toward Japan and the Japanese. The government invested more in recruiting and training this corps than did any of the Western empires, in which police served primarily to protect migrants from the metropole.[6] In contrast to British civil security in China, which consisted mainly of Sikhs, Scotsmen, and other non-English, nonelite groups, KLT police included predominantly of metropolitan Japanese.[7] Of the 931 officers hired by the Kwantung Bureau in 1906, over 70 percent had been born in the home islands. By 1927, the proportion of Japanese in the police force exceeded 80 percent.[8] The city-state established a training academy in Ryōjun to teach law, economics, and statistics, as well as practical skills such as horseback riding, martial arts, and firefighting. The school encouraged Japanese degree candidates to learn Chinese, Russian, and English; their Chinese counterparts took classes in Japanese. Students exhibiting particular commitment or leadership potential received grants to study in Tokyo.[9]

Japan's police force in Manchuria grew rapidly. From approximately 50 consular patrolmen stationed in the region prior to the Russo-Japanese War in 1904, manpower grew to 3,585 on the eve of the establishment of Manchukuo.[10] The intensity of policing in the KLT greatly surpassed that of any other imperial territory, reflecting the unique role of patrolmen as agents of expansionism as well as civil security. In 1931, the Kwantung Bureau employed one officer per 487 persons. By comparison, this ratio was 1:637 in Taiwan; 1:1,145 in the Japanese metropole; and 1:1,205 in Korea.[11] The cost of maintaining the KLT police force was considerable, totaling 5 million yen in 1929, or 86 percent of the Opium Monopoly Bureau's budget.[12]

Despite the intensity and expense of civil security in the KLT, police virtually ignored the drug traffic. In fact, the number of narcotics busts carried out annually in the city-state actually decreased from 207 (over 4 percent of all arrests) in 1906 to 109 (about 0.1 percent of all arrests) in 1932.

Even as law enforcement became more active, its efficiency against drug crime declined.[13] The Kwantung Army protected many traffickers, who paid bribes or kickbacks in exchange for near immunity from legal interference. The "victimless" nature of the drug trade, in which seeking redress exposes the illegal behavior of complainants, also hampered bringing dealers to justice. Yet these explanations do not sufficiently account for the stunning ineffectiveness of police in the narcotics market. With great perception, the British consul in Fengtian noted that the regime demonstrated "a remarkable reluctance, or a remarkable incapacity, to ensure that the police should not permit the manufacture and sale of illicit opium in the areas where they exercise control."[14] The growth of the narcotics market served Japanese imperialism in Manchuria by supplying a pretext for increasing the ranks of patrolmen, military rulers in civil garb who stretched imperial power beyond the areas of formal Japanese control. Less objectionable than army officers, police fulfilled the same function of absorbing people and territory into the Japanese empire. In the early 1930s, Dairen was the second-largest narcotics depot in the world, and drug-dealing continental adventurers and law enforcement fought alongside army troops to subdue the hinterland and establish the state of Manchukuo.[15]

In the early years of Japanese control, most drugs reached the KLT by sea. Dairen harbor, which remained ice-free in winter, was the primary gateway to landlocked Manchuria and north China. The city's status as a free port stimulated local growth but also gave rise to a significant smuggling problem involving not only banned substances but also legal, taxable commodities such as coal, cloth, and soybeans. Harbor police, numbering ninety-seven by 1928, intercepted incoming steamers at offshore quarantine stations and kept watch over small craft. They inspected all

TABLE 5 Imperial police officers, 1907–1932

Year	*Kwantung Bureau police*	*Consular police*	*Total police*
1907	981	34	1,015
1908	1,072	19	1,091
1909	1,075	18	1,093
1910	1,223	19	1,242
1911	1,250	23	1,273
1912	1,251	21	1,272
1913	1,183	18	1,201
1914	1,283	17	1,300
1915	1,228	21	1,249
1916	1,288	32	1,320
1917	1,437	35	1,472
1918	1,378	38	1,416
1919	1,496	52	1,548
1920	1,496	65	1,561
1921	2,055	68	2,123
1922	2,131	87	2,218
1923	2,132	85	2,217
1924	2,338	70	2,408
1925	2,414	71	2,485
1926	2,670	73	2,743
1927	2,784	83	2,867
1928	2,944	103	3,047
1929	3,012	107	3,119
1930	3,196	113	3,309
1931	3,435	150	3,585
1932	5,349	531	5,880

SOURCE: Ogino Fujio, *Gaimushō keisatsu shi* (Tokyo: Azekura shobō, 2005), 160.

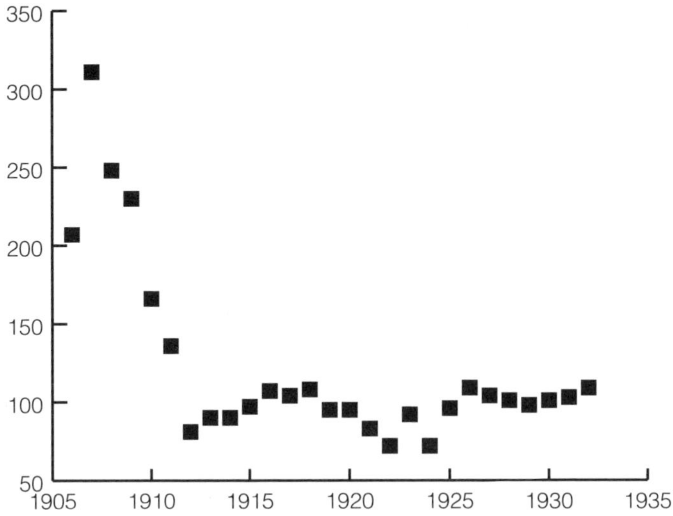

FIGURE 5.
Annual drug busts by KLT police, 1906–1932

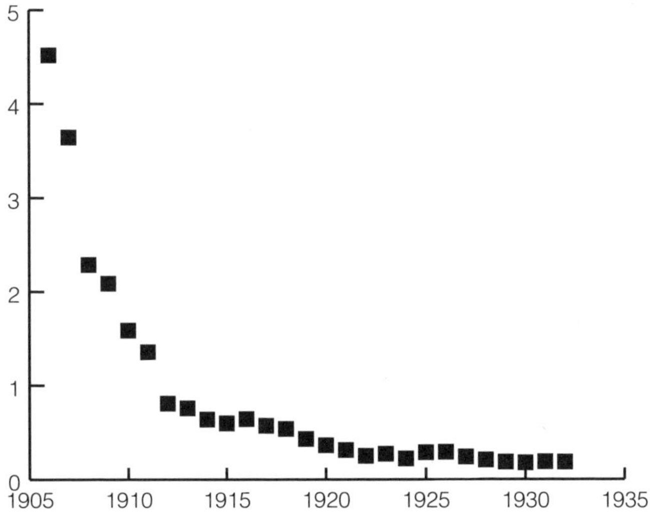

FIGURE 6.
Percentage of police actions involving narcotics, 1906–1932

vessels prior to docking or departure and searched all passengers upon landing.[16] Performance of these duties was scarcely earnest. In the opinion of the British consul of Dairen, "Cases in which opium has been smuggled on Japanese ships have as in the past continued to be brought to the notice of the authorities, but though the latter have invariably returned conciliatory replies . . . nothing of importance has ever been done."[17] In the five years from 1925 through 1929, only Shanghai superseded Dairen in terms of the volume of incoming narcotics. Yet harbor police arrested a mere 123 importers and exporters of opium, morphine, cocaine, and other drugs. Illicit substances were found hidden in cigarette and biscuit tins, bedsteads, blankets, barrels of carbolic acid, and cases of beer.[18]

After bringing narcotics into the KLT by ship, traffickers used the SMR to distribute them throughout Manchuria and north China. Stretching from Dairen to Harbin, the railway incorporated a steadily increasing network of cities and towns through branch lines. Traffickers circumvented security by unloading merchandise at the port, transporting it by rail to the KLT border, and crossing into the SMRZ by foot, motor vehicle, or oxcart. They then rejoined the railway at its next stop. Alternatively, they disguised their contraband, concealed it on their persons, or bribed SMR police. The Treaty of Portsmouth allowed Japan to station as many as thirteen thousand guards along the tracks from Dairen to Changchun. Despite their numbers, railway patrolmen were notoriously inattentive to drug trafficking. "Supervision of opium smoking and of the activities of smugglers of narcotics generally has been so lax as almost to suggest deliberate connivance followed, when the harm has been done, by frantic efforts to bring down the evil once more to reasonable limits," reported a consul in Fengtian, the largest city along the SMRZ.[19] In 1925, a continental adventurer transcribed his experiences smuggling "black" (opium) and "white" (heroin) on the SMR. His confidential report, submitted under the pen name Gionbō, testified to the deliberate inattentiveness and active complicity of police and the military.[20] A writer for the *China Medical Journal* alleged that railway patrolmen even protected the drug traffic at the expense of public health. When a cholera epidemic struck Manchuria, SMR inspectors ordered all carriages entering the city of Harbin to pass through a shallow pool of carbolic acid "so that *their wheels might be disinfected!*" "This farcical measure might benefit the business of drug dealers, but would certainly not affect the course of the vibrio along human intestines," commented the reporter.[21]

Along with the SMR, the Dairen postal system achieved notoriety as "the chief agency in the distribution of morphia in China."[22] Between 1911 and 1920, police caught three hundred senders and recipients of packages containing raw opium, morphine, heroin, and cocaine.[23] Many more escaped detection, including a Korean who wrote to notify a confederate that he had "received the packet [of morphine] without incident, to my relief. . . . Please send more."[24] To protect their identity, smugglers frequently mailed drugs in boxes without a designated recipient or return address. In suspicious cases, Japanese postal workers often protected dealers by withholding information from Chinese police, who chafed at their helplessness to crack down on the traffic.[25] "When a consignment is marked 'military supplies' or consigned to the Japanese military headquarters, we know it is morphine, heroin, or opium and we can do nothing," lamented a Chinese customs officer in a 1930s novel.[26]

Prior to World War I, imperial Japan relied on manufacturers in Europe to supply refined narcotics. The outbreak of the conflict, however, reduced the amount of morphine, heroin, and cocaine available for export, while global hostilities interfered with shipping. To meet legal demand, Japan sent chemists to Europe to learn how to prepare opium alkaloids. Many established illicit refineries upon returning to Dairen. By the late 1920s, manufacturers in the KLT synthesized enough narcotics to eliminate nearly all their Western competitors from the Asian mainland. Imperial Japan became the world's leading exporter of heroin, the fourth-largest manufacturer of morphine, and a significant producer of cocaine.[27] To avoid discovery, underground chemists worked in store basements, behind signboards and window displays indicating legitimate firms. They accepted customers only by introduction. Police "never interfered with the manufacture [of morphine and heroin], except in cases where it [became] absolutely necessary to save their face."[28] The Chinese novelist Lin Yutang described one such raid by the Chinese customs officer Afei and his uncle Lifu:

> Afei and Lifu went to the front door with some guards. A disguised guard knocked at the door, and, once it was open, the guards concealed at the sides rushed in and kept it from closing again. The servant opening the door was held by one of the guards and prevented from running in to give the alarm. Such plants were usually unguarded, depending more on secrecy and the protection of the Japanese.
>
> In the courtyard, Lifu saw on the floor rows of objects which looked exactly like cakes of toilet soap. Afei pointed out that these were cakes of heroin, to be packed and labeled "hygienic soap," "Coty Perfumed Soap," "Colgate's," and other foreign brand names.
>
> . . . They pushed the door open and Afei ordered the arrest of all present. Several girls, and four men with their mouths muffled by white handkerchiefs, were working at two long boards, serving as tables. On the floor were two

stoves. The house was full of an intoxicating and nauseating smell. On one of the tables were jars, bottles, large and small spoons, and the white powder on large pieces of white, crisp paper. Here the girls were working. Men were working at the other table, which was fitted with small wheeled machines with hornlike inlets and outlets for mixing and spraying the powder. Against the wall stood a special machine with an enameled top for pressing and cutting the drug into cakes.[29]

In addition to police intelligence, chemical disasters brought factories to light. The United States consul cabled the State Department, "I have been reliably informed that many of the rather frequent fires occurring in Dairen are caused by the explosion of materials used in illicit morphine plants. Very few of these cases are ever reported in the press or prosecuted because the obvious evidence is destroyed and the police do not care to bother with a difficult investigation." In 1931, patrolmen confiscated two hundred kilograms of morphine from two young men in a Dairen brothel. The arrest led to the discovery of an illicit factory run by three Japanese, including the entrepreneur Torii Mitsuyoshi. Torii was arrested, prosecuted, and assessed a nominal fine that did not approach the profits he had made in six months of manufacturing morphine. Undeterred, he reestablished his lab in a seaside resort near Dairen.[30] Only weeks later, a chemical blast demolished the factory, killing a number of Japanese employees. In the confusion, several others committed suicide or escaped. Arriving at the scene, police arrested two Chinese and six Japanese survivors, including Torii. A judge sentenced the ringleader to eight months in prison but allowed him to defer incarceration until after the impending birth of his child. "It is difficult to avoid the suspicion that Torii feels quite free to engage in the manufacture of morphine on the understanding that he will occasionally be arrested and sentenced to a nominal term of imprisonment," concluded the American consul.[31]

In addition to shielding dealers like Torii, some patrolmen became outright coconspirators in the drug market. In 1920, several Dairen police were arrested and imprisoned for quietly selling and pocketing the profits of narcotics confiscated from dealers.[32] Bribery was also common. Bingham Dai described a "raid" in 1929: "There came a friendly report that [a] Japanese police was coming. At once the opium pipes and lamps, etc. were all covered up. The police came, did his business, then off he went. The writer was told that every den had to bribe the Japanese police two or three times a year; usually Yen 2.00 or 3.00 at a time would satisfy them."[33] Chinese observers often derided co-national dealers as Japanese lapdogs *(zougou)*.[34]

Prior to the establishment of Manchukuo, Japanese citizens in Manchuria enjoyed extraterritoriality and immunity from arrest by Chinese police. In the Japanese-administered KLT and SMRZ, imperial patrolmen protected both Japanese and Chinese dealers. In 1913, the Chinese Foreign Ministry protested to the Japanese embassy in Beijing that trafficking by unruly migrants confounded the enforcement of China's antinarcotics legislation.[35] Although the Kwantung Bureau responded by criminalizing violations of Chinese drug regulations by KLT residents, China's quest to repeal extraterritoriality, continuing through the 1910s and 1920s, was unsuccessful.

The peculiar status of Korean migrants, by law Japanese citizens, contributed to rising friction between imperial and Chinese police. In the late 1920s, attempts by Chinese patrolmen to crack down on Korean drug traffickers frequently culminated in violence. In 1929, Chinese detectives entered and searched an opium retail establishment operated by a Korean in Harbin. They arrested a number of smokers and confiscated nearly seven pounds of illegally procured drugs. Japanese police hurried to the scene, where they accused the Chinese of robbery. When the Chinese patrolmen summoned backup, the Japanese officers opened fire. The matter was resolved with the handover of the Korean manager to the Japanese police. "Such cases can be multiplied; in fact, they are happening almost every day and almost everywhere in Manchuria," wrote Bingham Dai.[36] In some instances, violence resulted in tragedy: a 1932 raid on the vice quarter of Harbin by Chinese police led to the shooting deaths of two Korean retailers and two patrons.[37]

Although Koreans often benefited from defense by imperial police, many nonetheless resented their status as a pretext for the expansion of the empire that oppressed compatriots at home. A Korean employee at the SMR Research Bureau argued that "the Koreans in Manchuria receive no benefits of Japan's protection, but are, on the contrary, tramelled *[sic]* by the dual registration laws, Japan's policy to make use of the Koreans, and Japan's interference and control." A Korean member of the Institute for Pacific Relations, an international research organization, declared, "The charge is that wherever Koreans go, Japanese consular police follow them. This is resented by the Chinese and the Koreans are made to suffer. All we want here is that our Chinese friends . . . will see to it that the Koreans are given fair protection of life and property." His American colleague concluded, "Had the Koreans been assured of reasonable treatment in the Chinese courts of Manchuria, the great majority would probabl[y] have been quite willing to divest themselves completely of any dependence upon the Japanese consular authorities. In fact, it seems that, in spite of ill-treatment at the hands of the Chinese authorities, the majority of them preferred to throw in their lot with the Chinese."[38] Many Koreans applied to naturalize as Chinese, although legally they lacked the right to renounce Japanese citizenship.[39]

The problem of Korean nationality subsided after the 1932 creation of Manchukuo and the disestablishment of the Chinese police force. Moral entrepreneurs castigated the law enforcement corps of the deposed warlord administration for depravity, inefficiency, and corruption, including complicity in the drug traffic. They described Manchukuo police, by contrast, as "the embodiment of the Kingly Way" and the "pivot of harmony among the five races." Endō Ryūsaku, the chief of the general affairs board of Manchukuo and a publicist for Wangdao, declared police officers in the new state "peerless in the world for their impartiality and incorruptibleness."[40] As in the past, police served in a dual role as agents of Japanese benevolence and the vanguard of imperialism. Under the pretext of ending poppy cultivation in the adjacent Chinese province of Rehe, Manchukuo deployed patrolmen well beyond its borders. The encroachment of law enforcement prepared the way for Japanese military expansion in the region beginning in 1937.[41]

Kingly Way propaganda notwithstanding, the Manchukuo police force was honeycombed with drug traffickers. In 1938, more than eighty Harbin patrolmen were found to have personally profited from the sale of confiscated narcotics.[42] The English sailor Clifford Johnson, who was taken captive by pirates off the Chinese coast and ransomed to a gang of opium traffickers, reported that one of his captors was a Manchukuo police captain on a three-week leave.[43] The elevation of former continental adventurers to government positions further encouraged laxity in the enforcement of drug laws. By the late 1930s, offenders of anti-opium legislation accounted for less than 4 percent of all suspects taken into police custody.[44] In Fengtian, the largest city in Manchukuo, police closed down only three narcotics retailers in three years, despite the fact that there were "said to be fewer licensed than unlicensed shops."[45] Between 1938 and 1941, Harbin police removed more than two thousand corpses of morphine users from the streets of the "ghost district *[guishi]*." Of dozens of openly operating illegal dealers, however, they arrested only one.[46]

PROSECUTION

For most drug traffickers apprehended by the police, the court was the second point of contact with the judicial system.[47] The KLT adopted a streamlined version of the legal process in the Japanese metropole, which was in turn based on the French model. District courts exercised jurisdiction over the leasehold and handled some consular trials. The supreme court heard serious criminal cases and appeals of consular decisions. The civil governor of the city-state, who maintained executive authority over the courts, could appoint and dismiss judges at will.[48] Justice in the KLT thus reflected the ideology and volition of the Kwantung Bureau.

Between 1924 and 1941, the KLT prosecuted 1,137 defendants for violating the Opium Law. Over 90 percent were male. Of the 134 cases in which gender was recorded in trials involving refined narcotics, all except 8 involved men.[49] Males also predominated among defendants in the SMRZ. In 1917, the Harbin consular court adjudicated 74 opium and narcotics cases, 67 of which concerned a male defendant.[50] Gender imbalances in prosecution likely reflected a lower overall rate of female involvement in the drug market, as well as paternalism on the part of judges and male associates of women criminals. Some female dealers took advantage of this bias. Observing that "it was much easier for a woman—especially a young, oddly innocent woman—to smuggle contraband past the stringent customs," the heroin manufacturer depicted in Kuroshima Denji's 1930 novel *Militarized Streets* tasks his daughter with procuring supplies from abroad. Eventually, however, her frequent voyages and false baby bump arouse the suspicions of the authorities.[51]

Although the judicial system made allowances for gender, it distributed the burden of justice among Japanese, Chinese, Koreans, and Westerners alike, thus reinforcing stability in the diverse drug trafficker community and the population at large. Nationality was often correlated, however, to the substance found in the possession of the trafficker and the law under which he or she was charged. Throughout the period of imperial rule, Chinese accounted for a majority of those indicted for opium violations. Nearly 95 percent of defendants prosecuted under the KLT Opium Law of 1924, which proscribed smoking opium, were Chinese.[52] Conversely, Japanese defendants predominated in cases involving manufactured drugs, which were more lucrative due to their higher value by weight. Almost three-quarters of those charged with violating bans on refined narcotics were Japanese.[53]

The likelihood of indictment or conviction did not vary significantly according to the law allegedly violated by the defendant. Of all suspects arrested for offenses against the Opium Law, 88 percent of Japanese and 94 percent of Chinese went to trial. Among the more than 1,500 KLT drug case verdicts recorded in statistical yearbooks, nearly 96 percent were convictions.[54] A law professor explained the logic of the courts: "If an accused person is declared not guilty, then it is obvious that somebody, Procurator or Judge, or both, has blundered. As a person who is a public official *ipso facto* cannot blunder, therefore, the prisoner must be guilty, even if there is not sufficient evidence to sentence him."[55] Within the ideology of benevolent government, judicial officers enjoyed the presumption of superior morality, which they exercised against the threat to the public welfare posed by persons of lower status.

By giving officials discretion over the law, benevolence encouraged defense strategies that focused on the practical question of punishment rather than the abstract issue of guilt or innocence. Defendants generally accepted conviction as a foregone conclusion and sought leniency in sentencing based on personal circumstances and the expression of contrition. In 1927, police apprehended Zhang Mingcai, a Dairen-born Chinese, in the act of carrying about four pounds of raw opium worth approximately two hundred yen. Zhang had bought the drug from a Chinese dealer in Changchun and was attempting to sell it to a restaurant manager in the KLT. The court indicted Zhang under the Opium Law of 1924, reached a guilty verdict, and sentenced him to six months in prison. In an appeal, Zhang's Japanese lawyer acknowledged his client's culpability but contended that the offense was trifling. Moreover, Zhang's youth (he was twenty-three years old) and penury as a "boxcar boy" had prevented him from understanding and upholding moral conduct. If imprisoned, he would be unable to support his wife and small child. Above all, he was sorry for his actions. The lawyer concluded by suggesting that the experience of the trial had been adequate to civilize the defendant.[56]

Though Zhang was a petty offender, the benevolent justice he encountered also characterized the prosecution and sentencing of high-profile and large-scale narcotics dealers. In the mid-1920s, Dairen traffickers began importing benzoline, a morphine solution that had escaped prohibition on a technicality. In September 1927, following the discovery of a large shipment of benzoline from Germany at the Dairen post office, the Kwantung Bureau closed the loophole that had allowed the drug to circulate legally. Several prominent individuals connected to the Japanese military protested that they had already paid for imports of benzoline and the unexpected proscription would unfairly penalize them. As a compromise, the government allowed orders of the drug purchased prior to October 1927 to enter the leasehold. Taking advantage of this exception, Yamazaki Takeshi, an official in the Kwantung Bureau who maintained close ties to continental adventurers and the army, forged a series of backdated import permits. Between 1928 and 1931, approximately eight thousand kilograms of benzoline, worth over two million yen, entered Dairen under these false licenses. The exposure of Yamazaki's scam in early 1931 implicated numerous elite Japanese, including a graduate of the prestigious Tokyo Imperial University law department, a former member of the Japanese Diet, a chief of the Fengtian police, directors of the Dairen stock and merchandise exchanges, and others. Kawai Mataichi, the head of the Kwantung Bureau Sanitation Department, was charged with having accepted an expensive platinum watch "in token of . . . various facilities rendered in connection with the [smuggling enterprise]." Dr. Kuroi Tadaichi, chief of the Opium Monopoly Bureau, was said to have refused a similar bribe.[57]

The principal defendant of the case was Shirakawa Tomoichi, a former bank clerk, army officer, and merchant. Shirakawa had emigrated to Dairen to manage a construction business during the Russo-Japanese War. Through contacts in the military, he obtained a contract to provision a Japanese expeditionary force to Siberia in the late 1910s. Having acquired a vast personal fortune, he returned to Japan and successfully stood for election to the Diet.[58] Shirakawa's biography presents an interesting parallel to that of the Opium King, Ishimoto Kantarō, who was also born in Japan, built his career on opportunities created by war, and transmuted economic prowess into political power. The distinction between the merchant Ishimoto and the trafficker Shirakawa rested more on legal technicalities than conduct.

Shirakawa and his fellow defendants, all Japanese, stood trial from January through July 1931. The benzoline case generated tremendous publicity and outrage in Japan, prompting the prime minister himself to warn the court to exercise "strict neutrality" in judgment.[59] The announcement of the preliminary hearing spanned seven columns in Dairen's primary Japanese-language newspaper.[60] Owing to the sensitivity of the proceedings, the press was subsequently banned from the courtroom. In his opening statement, Shirakawa testified that he had been unaware of the change in regulations governing the importation of benzoline and had not understood the chemical composition of his merchandise. Lawyers for the defense questioned whether the drug he had imported was banned at all, claiming that it was a "salt" of benzoline and hence not covered by the prohibition of benzoline itself. Chemical experts, however, dismissed this sophistry.[61] Sensing his advantage, the chief prosecutor asked the judge to convict and imprison all the defendants, with Shirakawa receiving the longest sentence: eighteen months. Shirakawa and his lawyers responded by shifting from a defense based on legal grounds to a plea for benevolence. The accused dramatically assumed responsibility for the entire affair, asking the judge to punish him harshly and exonerate his coconspirators.[62] "I had no wish to make money by breaking the law," he testified. He expressed particular regret for the "misunderstanding" regarding the watch he had given Kawai. "I called on him occasionally and obtained various facilities, and intended it to be a gift. In this respect, I made a bad mistake and cast a gloom on the future of a promising young man, for which I feel very sorry," he apologized. In his defense, Kawai cited his humble background as the son of a farmer, his duty to his wife and two children, and his ignorance concerning the true nature of Shirakawa's bribe. He noted that he had attended Tokyo Imperial University with Shirakawa's son and "felt quite intimate towards him. So I thought it impolite to return the gift, and accepted it."[63]

On July 24, 1931, the judge presiding over the case appeared before the Dairen district court to announce his decision to acquit all the accused with the exception of Shirakawa, who was convicted on a nominal bribery charge. "Rather than viewing this decision as a verdict," the judge stated, "my mind is like 'the moon on an autumn night.'" He continued obliquely, "If I were to mind critics, nothing could be done. After all, I have to carry out my own convictions, independently of the opinions of others. Ten people have ten different perspectives. Some would say that I am right; others would say that I am wrong. My verdict may be criticized, but I think I have offered enough explanation."[64] The judge completely misread the public mood. Although Shirakawa's lawyers equated their client's acquittal with "fair and transparent government," most of the imperial legal community disagreed. The enraged prosecutor pointed out that "only in Dairen" could an acquittal take place in the context of such a clear violation. In response to the verdict, he demanded, "'Dairen morphine'—that is, benzoline—is it not a drug? Quite frankly, this is like saying a white horse is not a horse."[65] To many moral entrepreneurs, the outcome of the trial was a blot on the international honor of Japan and an open invitation to smugglers. In fact, within a year, several of the principal defendants in the benzoline case were caught dealing ecgonine, a banned derivative of cocaine.[66] In deference to the public outcry, the KLT supreme court retried the case and convicted all the accused; however, only two served time in jail.[67]

Westerners also took advantage of benevolent justice to profit from the KLT narcotics market. Europeans and Americans had a long history of selling opium on the Asian mainland. As Dairen developed into an epicenter of the global drug economy, the city attracted increasing numbers of smugglers from abroad. The United States Federal Bureau of Narcotics found evidence of opium trafficking in the leasehold by Americans, Germans, Russians, Greeks, Serbs, Poles, Austrians, Bulgarians, Czechs, and Italians. Jews accounted for about 10 percent of non-Asian dealers.[68] Religious commonality facilitated cross-national ties, linking wealthy Baghdadis with impoverished Russian refugees in cosmopolitan and lucrative partnerships. A foreign consul reported in 1927,

> The Central Hotel at Dairen is a den of smugglers. It is owned by a Russian Jew named Lerner who is a go-between for sellers and buyers of narcotics and gets a commission on the deals he puts through. His agent in Harbin is another Jew named Stavitsky, a former proprietor of the hotel who was deported by the Japanese in 1921 after several convictions for trafficking in drugs. The wealthier dealers have rooms at the Yamato Hotel, from whence they direct the movement of the traffic. There are also a number of small hotels run by Russian Jews at Changchun in the South Manchuria Railway area which are used as meeting places for the traffickers and the Chinese Eastern Railway Company's conductors and car-tenders, where goods are entrusted to the latter for safe delivery to Harbin.[69]

In the late nineteenth and early twentieth centuries, the Jews represented to Russia what the Koreans were to Japan: second-class citizens and the economic vanguard of imperialism in Asia. Like Korean migrants, Jews came to Manchuria in search of a haven from persecution at home and found the drug trade an accessible escape route from poverty.[70]

Westerners lost the right to extraterritoriality in Japanese sovereign territory in 1899, and were subject to the same laws and procedures as Asians in the KLT. Nonetheless, the courts often hesitated to indict them, partly because the Kwantung Bureau wished to avoid conflict with diplomatic representatives of the offenders' home countries. Between 1908 and 1936, KLT police arrested 111 Westerners (all males) for violation of local antidrug legislation. Of this group, 31 stood trial.[71]

One of the most noteworthy courtroom dramas involving Westerners began in September 1931, when the American consul in Dairen confidentially informed his supervisors in Washington, D.C., that Henri Bacri, a French Jew, had negotiated for the deposit of over two million francs in a French bank account. Although Bacri attributed this windfall to his silk import business, "a most reliable source" asserted that it was in fact payment for a shipment of drugs from Takushima Rokushi, a Japanese bicycle salesman whose firm had long been suspected of importing narcotics. Takushima was also alleged to have had dealings with Curt Smith, a Hamburg German and known trafficker whose movements were carefully monitored by the international authorities in his home base of Shanghai. Smith's trips to Dairen aroused suspicions that he was acting as a broker between the narcotics rackets of the two cities on behalf of "certain shady foreigners, all Russian Jews, who are confidently asserted to be regularly engaged in the drug traffic."[72] In November, police arrested Bacri, Takushima, two other Japanese, and two Jews of Russian origin: Jacob Lelchitsky and George I. Tribe.

Tribe, born in the Pale in 1902, grew up in Harbin and emigrated to the United States at the age of twenty. He settled in San Francisco, where he naturalized as an American citizen and worked as a dishwasher and waiter. In 1925, Tribe suffered a skull fracture in an automobile accident and was hospitalized. With five hundred dollars in compensation money, he left for Dairen and, together with a Russian partner, founded a company importing textiles and office equipment.[73] The American consul believed that he had become involved in drug trafficking through family connections in Harbin. Rather than seeking to exonerate Tribe on legal grounds, diplomatic representatives depicted him as the unwitting "tool" of his associates and "an amiable young man and not of the criminal type." One reported, "He is evidently of good social standing in the local Jewish community, for upon his arrest the Consulate received numerous inquires as to his welfare from reputable Jewish merchants."[74] At the conclusion of the trial, the court levied nominal fines on Tribe and Lelchitsky. Tribe subsequently fled to the protection of his brother in Harbin. Takushima, sentenced to prison for a year, successfully petitioned for a suspension. Bacri, given six months, forfeited his bond, escaped to Shanghai, and according to rumor, returned to Paris.[75] Amazed by this outcome, the British consul of Dairen offered a memorable summation of benevolent justice in the KLT: "The enormous steam-hammer at Woolwich Arsenal can be adjusted to descend so as to just fail to crush a watch laid beneath it. The leniency shown to convicted drug traffickers, after the ponderous machinery set in motion against them has brought them to justice, creates the same wonderment."[76]

PUNISHMENT

In contrast to the arrest and prosecution of suspects, which upheld stability in the drug market by distributing the burden of justice across all national groups, benevolence in punishment dictated different sentences for different nationalities. Moral entrepreneurs did not purport to treat all subjects equally, but rather to reform them according to the level of civilization attributed to their race. In practice, benevolence generally prescribed prison sentences for Japanese and Korean offenders. During the 1930s, Manchukuo also targeted some Korean drug dealers for forced resettlement from urban to rural areas. At the bottom of the imperial racial hierarchy, Chinese convicts often received the cheapest and most brutal form of justice: flogging.

The Kwantung Bureau inherited its penal infrastructure from the Russian administration of 1898–1905. The main prison, located in Ryōjun, incarcerated criminals convicted by the supreme court. A branch prison in Dairen held defendants awaiting trial, suspects under investigation by public procurators, inmates serving short-term sentences, and women.[77] In 1929, prisons received about 6 percent of the total operating budget of the Opium Monopoly Bureau—more than the courts but far less than the police.[78] Between 1908 and 1941, 722 offenders convicted of drug crimes were incarcerated. In 1933, the number of narcotics traffickers serving prison terms peaked at 104.[79] Statistical gazetteers for the city-state did not record the details of offenses or the criminal history of defendants; therefore, consistency in sentencing is impossible to assess. Consular court records are more informative, though fragmentary. Over the course of nine months in 1919, Japanese Foreign Ministry police in Changchun arrested 308 Chinese for dealing opium. They handed over 134 suspects to the Chinese authorities for justice. The quantity by weight of drugs in the possession of the arrested individual was recorded in 78 of the remaining 174 cases. Regression analysis on this sample suggests that the consular court did impose consistent prison sentences on Chinese offenders: each additional pound of opium found in the keeping of the accused increased the duration of his or her prison sentence by an average of about three days.[80]

Among KLT prisoners sentenced for drug trafficking, gazetteers recorded nationality in 687 cases, including 242 Japanese and 445 Chinese. Although Chinese inmates were more numerous overall, Japanese were approximately four times more likely to be imprisoned.[81] The dominance of continental adventurers within the ranks of imperial migrants undoubtedly contributed to the high rate of incarceration of Japanese, but the ideology of benevolence also played a role. Imperial Japan viewed imprisonment as a modern punishment suitable primarily for civilized subjects. The penitentiary provided a space for Japanese transgressors to repent of their behavior, mend their ways, and resume their position in the family state. In the case of the Chinese, viewed as racially inferior and unassimilable, the goal of incarceration was less clear. Japanese penologists even argued that Chinese convicts were incapable of understanding imprisonment as punishment, given the alleged poverty and degradation of their lifestyle in free society.[82]

To foster the reintegration of the Japanese offender into the national polity, penologists argued for favorable treatment of inmates. They consistently rejected the idea (intermittently popular in the early twentieth-century West) of "less eligibility": that is, that the living standards of prisoners should not exceed those of the state's least well-off noncriminal citizens. In the words of Masaki Akira, the second Japanese doctor of penology, "If only a prisoner were to be rehabilitated as a human being, he should be trusted, he should be loved and he should be given hope." Masaki believed "it was possible to reform criminals and also to make them work harder than ever only when prisoners were treated as human beings, and Japanese prisoners as Japanese."[83] Moral entrepreneurs cultivated contrition and industriousness through vocational training and ethical indoctrination. Inmates of the main penitentiary in Ryōjun grew crops and made shoes and bricks (including those used to renovate the cell blocks in 1916). According to gazetteers, juvenile offenders spent two hours in class per day, and adult prisoners enjoyed access to books and Buddhist and Shintō rites.[84]

The ideal of reform notwithstanding, security was the real concern of the penal system. In 1906, the Kwantung Bureau hired 90 surveillance personnel to supervise its 319 prisoners, bringing the guard-inmate ratio to 1:3.5. By 1931, the number of watchmen had grown to 127.[85] Despite this scrutiny, prisons in Japanese Manchuria maintained a flourishing underground traffic in drugs. SMR researcher Itō Takeo, who spent the late 1930s in custody following his arrest by the Kwantung Army, recalled his experience sharing a cell with a Korean morphine dealer:

> He had completely bought off the prison guards, and gradually more and more things were sent to us in prison. For example, since we were prisoners awaiting trials, we were held in a place where bedding was provided. On the pretext of having to resew the bedding he was given, the Korean had his bedding sent out and brought back once a week. All sorts of things would be crammed into it when it was brought back to him. Ordinarily these things would have been easily discernible, and they would have been confiscated, but since he had already greased the guards' palms, nothing was said.[86]

Between 1908 and 1941, 60 prison inmates, including 24 Japanese, 35 Chinese, and one foreigner, received treatment for overdose or chronic dependence on narcotics.[87]

Upon the establishment of Manchukuo in 1932, the state co-opted the penitentiary as a symbol of enlightened and legitimate government according to the Kingly Way. Policymakers declared their intention of overhauling the "miserable" facilities bequeathed by the warlord administration.[88] An investigation team, dispatched in 1933 to survey the national prison infrastructure, reported corruption, overcrowding, unsanitary living conditions, and starvation-level rations. At one institution, an inspector estimated that up to 60 percent of the funds allocated for inmate meals were disbursed as bribes. "Rations were so spoiled, I doubted they were even food!" he raged.[89] In 1937, the Manchukuo government enacted legislation to increase penal capacity, standardize sentencing practices, restore rights to prisoners, and improve education and moral reform programs.[90] However, Masaki Akira privately reported that the authorities believed "civilized" penal practices were "neither desirable nor possible" for Chinese prisoners.[91]

In Republican China, including Manchuria, violation of drug laws was the second most common reason for incarceration, following property crime. By contrast, after 1932 the Manchukuo judicial system imposed few prison sentences on opium offenders. On the last day of 1938, state prisons housed 15,826 inmates, of whom only 656, or about 4 percent, had been convicted for dealing drugs. These included 496 "Manchukuoans" and 178 Japanese, including Koreans. At less than 5 percent of the total population of Manchukuo, imperial migrants were vastly overrepresented among prisoners.[92]

For Chinese offenders of antinarcotics legislation, the most common punishment was flogging. Though corporal discipline was routine in early modern Japan, the Meiji state abolished the practice in 1872 in the hope of gaining recognition as a civilized nation-state and reclaiming jurisdiction over foreigners.[93] Like the West, however, Japan retained flogging for subjects of "inferior" races, who were seen as incapable of moral development except when prompted by physical pain. In 1908, the Kwantung Bureau passed a law allowing the conversion of prison terms of less than three months and fines below one hundred yen into floggings for Chinese.[94] In the words of a Dairen prison warden, "There is no better punishment for Chinese criminals than whipping. Even those who don't respond to imprisonment are easily affected this way."[95] In recognition of alleged progress toward assimilation on the part of subjects in the formal colonies, flogging was abolished in Korea in 1921 and Taiwan in 1922. In the KLT, by contrast, the state applied corporal discipline to Chinese offenders with increasing frequency during the interwar period. In the year preceding the foundation of Manchukuo, courts imposed floggings on nearly a thousand Chinese. Police also meted out physical punishment as part of summary justice.[96]

In 1936, Masaki Akira witnessed a flogging at the Dairen branch prison, an institution "noted for its whipping." He described the scene of the punishment as a hall of about fifteen square meters. A platform for the warden and other observers occupied about one-third of the floor space; a bed with a pillow filled the rest. At the appointed time, two guards led the offender into the hall, removed his underwear, and induced him to lie face down. Upon the order of a captain, the guards took turns striking the buttocks of the prisoner with split bamboo sticks wound with flax thread. The convict groaned with pain as his backside swelled. "How cruel the punishment was!" Masaki empathized.[97]

Violent flogging could bring about permanent injury or death. Guards administered the maximum sentence of ninety strokes over a three-day period because the pain was too great for the convict to endure in one session.[98] "I could hardly stand to keep watching, and wondered how the guards could stand such duty," Masaki recalled.[99] The penologist was not alone in his distaste for corporal punishment. Okamoto Shigeshirō, a Japanese lawyer, campaigned against flogging on legal grounds. He argued that KLT criminal justice applied to Chinese, not "Manchukuoans"—and that understanding Manchukuoans as Chinese for the purposes of punishment undermined the very basis of Manchukuo nationhood. Okamoto implored Japan to substitute prison sentences for flogging, which he characterized as a vestigial custom inimical to civilized and legitimate government.[100] The practice of flogging also came under criticism in the international arena, with China's representative to the OAC remarking pointedly, "It was a pity, in the matter of drug offences, that all were not treated alike."[101] In 1938, the KLT finally yielded to international pressure to abolish flogging.[102]

As Japanese citizens, Koreans in Manchuria were never subject to physical punishment. Instead, the Manchukuo government sought to "relieve" urban Korean drug dealers by removing them to rural areas. This plan dovetailed with a key imperial policy of the 1930s: the agricultural colonization of the vast Manchurian hinterland by Japanese subjects. In 1933, to gauge the need for resettlement programs at the local level, the Japanese embassy in Xinjing solicited information on the activities of Korean drug dealers. Diplomats received over twenty responses from consulates in six cities. Officials were unanimously enthusiastic about the prospect of ridding their jurisdictions of lawbreakers. The consul of Fengtian, who deemed drug dealers an immoral influence on "good" Koreans, appointed a commission to survey all Korean households in the city for potential candidates for removal. However, investigators encountered severe resistance and abandoned the project.[103] Another consul, whose jurisdiction included a majority Korean population, anticipated public opposition and preemptively objected to the forced entry of Korean homes.[104] Ultimately, the Manchukuo government identified approximately 20,000 targets for resettlement out of a total population of 150,000 to 200,000 Korean continental adventurers.[105]

Though initially promising, the scheme to resettle Korean dealers in agricultural communities failed. Military and civil police, the Kwantung Division, and the Manchukuo government proved unable to cooperate in implementing the plan.[106] The cost of relocation, moreover, exceeded the state's willingness or ability to pay. Even diplomats who amassed a sufficient budget encountered unexpected obstacles. In

October 1933, the consul of Harbin announced a scheme to move more than eight hundred Korean narcotics traffickers to the village of Hedong. With an existing population of approximately three hundred households, Hedong was utterly unable to accommodate the newcomers.[107]

As diplomats themselves realized, deportation simply promised to shift large numbers of "idle undesirables" from one place to another. In 1937, China lodged a formal protest with the Japanese embassy in Beijing against ongoing smuggling by continental adventurers, including Koreans. The embassy apologized and asserted a vague intention to "gradual[ly] absorb . . . these persons into other modes of life."[108] Later that year, the termination of extraterritorial privileges for Japanese nationals and the end of consular jurisdiction allowed Japan to relinquish further responsibility for the migrants.

By allowing all national groups in Manchuria to profit from opium sales, moral entrepreneurs furnished imperial and Chinese subjects alike with a common stake in the continuation of Japanese rule. Implicit state sanction of illegal dealing in the KLT allowed the narcotic economy to thrive, much to the benefit of the individual trafficker and the empire. The illicit drug market provided a pretext for the growth of quasi-military police, who facilitated the expansion of Japanese sovereignty on the Asian mainland. Prosecution and punishment, meanwhile, supplied the state with the opportunity to physically enact its legitimizing ideology of benevolence.

By filling a vital niche in the narcotics supply chain, unlicensed dealers facilitated the transfer of revenues to the expansion-minded Kwantung Army. Nonetheless, to depict all traffickers as imperialist collaborators, even unwitting collaborators, exaggerates the agency of the Japanese state and disregards the political leanings of dealers themselves.[109] Although opium revenue undergirded expansionism by the Kwantung Army, drug sales also funded various other political movements in Manchuria. As often happens in civil war, the major claimants to power and authority—warlord governments, the Nationalist Party under Chiang Kai-shek, and the Chinese Communist Party—all financed their opposition to Japan in part through narcotics trafficking.[110] For opponents of imperialism, participation in the illicit opium economy furnished both the means and mode of objection.

For many dealers, however, questions of collaboration and resistance were likely secondary to the problem of negotiating the challenging social topography of Japanese Manchuria. In 1939, Baek Hongyong was a twenty-seven-year-old housewife raising two children in her native Korea. Although her family was economically comfortable, her husband could not bear to live under Japanese colonial rule. At his urging, the couple and their children emigrated to Manchuria to escape the "slavery" of imperialism. When their small sesame oil business failed, Baek turned to drug trafficking to provide for her loved ones. Baek's husband considered himself a patriot, although he was more inclined to devote himself to the pursuit of material luxury and women than to the local resistance movement. But for Baek herself, opium was simply a means of furthering her family's fortunes. Through pragmatic cooperation with Japanese and Chinese in the drug market and the judicial realm, she was able to acquire wealth beyond her wildest imaginings. She did not forgive the Japanese for the colonization of her homeland and was not indifferent to its political fate. But survival came first, and she did not apologize for it.[111]

CHAPTER SEVEN • Laboratory Scientists

"Japan is a doctor responsible as a teacher of civilization," declared Fukuzawa Yukichi, one of the leading public intellectuals of Meiji Japan.[1] Medical metaphors abounded in the late nineteenth and early twentieth centuries, when the binaries of physican and patient, healthy and sick, and hygienic and unsanitary evoked the legitimate nation-state and its premodern past, recalled in the present by the various "backward" imperial territories. Public health *(eisei)* was a proxy for civilization and a duty of the moral nation.[2] Through scientific medicine, the state cultivated citizens able to appreciate and extend its power. The modernization of medical knowledge, care, and facilities, first at home and later in the empire, was a common feature of state building in all the great powers. Japan's emphasis on basic science, however, was unmatched in the empires of the West, where doctors were primarily clinicians, not scientists, and did not construct laboratory facilities of a quality equal to those in the metropole. To a greater extent than any other power, Japan used scientific medicine to justify imperial rule.[3]

Japanese scientists took on a new role as moral entrepreneurs following the enactment of the KLT Opium Law of 1924. Prior to this time, private doctors and organizations provided detoxification and cure services to drug users. The Opium Law claimed the medicalization of addiction for the state, as a manifestation of benevolent government. Interwar Japanese scientists accordingly transformed drug dependence, a source of shame and a symptom of racial inferiority, into a cause for exercising specialized expertise and political power. Cutting-edge studies gave career-minded researchers entry into a prestigious emerging network of scientists from around the world. Based in institutions of mutually acknowledged excellence, they interacted on terms of professional equality and adhered to certain common methodologies and principles. Japanese studies in physiology and pharmacology identified the imperial regime with the solution to, rather than the problem of, opium. Colonial medicine was not simply a three-way collaboration among doctors, the sick, and the state, but a fundamentally global project in which knowledge produced by a worldwide scientific community justified imperialism at both local and international levels.

In the 1930s, however, intellectual and political factors contrived to undermine the global network of addiction researchers. In Europe and the United States, many physicians came to view drug dependence as an issue of the psyche. Japanese scientists, by contrast, mostly remained wedded to a physiological understanding of addiction. This methodological disagreement reduced mutual interest in scholarly interchange. The establishment of the state of Manchukuo in 1932 also changed the stakes of imperial studies of drug dependence. Denied recognition by the League of Nations, Manchukuo had little hope of achieving legitimacy in the international forum. Drawing on the newly enshrined ideology of Pan-Asianism, a key element of the Kingly Way, Japanese scientists and policymakers cooperated to reformulate the study of addiction as the basis for an independent imperial research community. Terminating contact with colleagues in Europe, the United States, Republican China, and elsewhere, they concentrated on developing ties with scientists in the empire. By nurturing the nascent study of addiction in Taiwan, Korea, and the Japanese home islands, researchers positioned Manchukuo, generally considered "backward" relative to the metropole and formal colonies, at the top of a geo-scientific hierarchy of imperial spaces. They also solicited cooperation from a limited number of Chinese trained in Japanese institutions. The cultivation of subjects as laboratory researchers, which had no precedent or counterpart in the empires of the West, produced unique human symbols of benevolent government and legitimacy for Manchukuo.

Traversing the spectrum of medical activities, addiction researchers of high imperial Japan embodied the fundamental contradiction of colonial medicine: intellectuals at the cutting edge of science and humanitarianism were also race conscious to the point of overlooking the value of life.[4] The origins of the scientific study of addiction within the moral crusade against opium fatefully shaped the conduct and worldview of scientists, leaving relatively little space for goals incompatible with or simply irrelevant to the production of legitimacy for the Japanese empire and

Manchukuo nation-state. Yet despite embracing their political role, addiction researchers ultimately fell victim to the changing demands of the regime. In its death throes, Manchukuo scapegoated many ardent supporters, including moral entrepreneurs. The Kwantung Army rounded up numerous laboratory scientists and dispatched them to prison, combat divisions, or Unit 731, its notorious biological weapons development squad. The scientific study of drug dependence, like the state, came to an ignoble end.

THE ORIGINS OF ADDICTION SCIENCE

During most of the nineteenth century, compounds containing opium, such as laudanum and patent medicines, circulated almost without restriction throughout Europe and the United States. In the absence of laws requiring a prescription, doctors had few opportunities to observe drug dependence, although they did treat occasional overdoses or "poisonings" (often intended as suicide). When patients presented with symptoms of withdrawal from narcotics, physicians often attributed their suffering to independent causes and recommended additional drugs. By the end of the century, however, the use of morphine, a refined alkaloid of high purity, had largely supplanted less physiologically damaging opiates, greatly increasing rates of dependence. With the risks of narcotics increasingly apparent, many doctors turned against former pharmaceutical staples. They portrayed this stance as a moral position differentiating them from "quacks," who held no professional qualification and continued to supply opium-based painkillers and patent medicines.[5]

Prior to World War I, populations easily represented as "victims," such as middle- and upper-class native-born white women and Civil War battle veterans, predominated among American drug users.[6] The understanding of addiction as an affliction of the innocent and unfortunate undergirded the initiation of a medical research agenda on narcotics. Taking over scientific leadership from the traditional powerhouses of France and Germany, American researchers of the early twentieth century sought to understand the physiological bases of symptoms of opium habituation. Scientists captivated by the germ theory of disease assumed that drug dependency had a biological logic akin to that of cholera, typhus, and malaria.[7] Their work both drew upon and reinforced a new norm of research conducted in a laboratory by a credentialed professional.[8]

Following the Meiji Restoration, Japan seized on scientific medicine as one of many strategies in its quest to "catch up" to the West and secure international respect and power. Common scourges of the early modern period, such as smallpox and leprosy, left visible traces—signs of backwardness—on the human body. A healthy population, by contrast, reflected a powerful sovereign state able to guarantee subject welfare.[9] The Meiji authorities offered aspiring scientists relatively generous funding to train in French, German, and American institutions. Although the development of a research tradition at home was initially a lower priority, following World War I Japan established several world-class laboratories, including the Rikagaku Kenkyūjo (Research Institute for Physics and Chemistry, 1917) and the Kitasato Institute (1922). The acknowledged excellence of these facilities enabled imperial researchers to train students domestically and to interact with colleagues abroad on terms of professional equality.[10] Trailblazing research augmented individual and national glory. Scientific medicine was both the heritage and the legacy of interwar researchers—at home, in the empire, and in the world.

During these years, bureaucrats rather than technical experts tended to occupy positions of authority over the scientific community. Legal regulation engendered factional development and "feudalistic" behavioral norms within the academy. The years from about 1908 to 1924 (immediately preceding the KLT Opium Law) were a time of particular frustration for scientists despite major achievements in the laboratory.[11] Young medical graduates in the metropole faced a hostile research environment and narrowing career opportunities. The empire, by contrast, beckoned as a liberal haven for professional development and even political influence. In contrast to the colonies of Britain and France, where researchers often felt stifled and demoralized by bureaucratic oversight, the Japanese empire offered a virtually unbounded expanse of scientific possibilities.[12]

Owing partly to the legacy of Gotō Shinpei, Japan's "statesman of research," who equated knowledge with civilization and compared the colony to a laboratory, Manchuria provided a particularly supportive environment for institutional inquiry. According to one Dairen observer, "It is not too much to say that civilization [here] was born of scientific institutes."[13] During the early twentieth century, the most important medical research facility in Manchuria was the Mukden Medical College (MMC).[14] Founded in the SMRZ in Fengtian in 1911, the MMC sought to position itself at the forefront of global science, aspiring to the level of excellence of medical schools in Japan. Many leading faculty, in high demand as conference speakers and journal contributors, stayed for decades. The well-equipped laboratory was at once a prestigious symbol of modernity and a site of production of information with useful applications in the empire and beyond. "In all civilized countries," wrote one researcher, "such an institution is an indispensable one."[15] In the context of ethnic and cultural proximity of ruler and ruled, unparalleled in the empires of the

West, the laboratory also reinforced distinctions between producers and objects of knowledge, superiors and inferiors, and leaders and subjects. The simplified and controlled environment in which science took place was a microcosm of the imperium in the idealized imaginings of the Japanese.[16]

By contrast, research facilities in the Asian colonies and concessions of Great Britain, France, and Germany were mainly metropolitan outposts. Only a few of the largest colleges maintained even an improvised laboratory. Administrators funded academic inquiry to collect data for European institutions and to impress subjects with the technical and technological superiority of the colonizers. Scientists, meanwhile, rotated through overseas assignments in the hope of building a reputation that might enable them to secure more prestigious employment at home. In its use of medical research as a source of political legitimacy, imperial Japan had no parallels among the great powers.

In addition to producing cutting-edge knowledge, the MMC sought to win the respect and loyalty of the "primitive" Chinese population. "The mission to civilize demands the spread of modern medical science through Manchuria," proclaimed university publicity.[17] In contrast to many Japanese migrants, who viewed the region as a primitive but healthy zone where they could enjoy a simple and salubrious lifestyle, MMC students tended to see the landscape as diseased and in need of imperial benevolence.[18] The graduate rate offered an uncontroversial index of the progress of civilization. The four-year training program admitted only Japanese students between 1912 and 1922. During these years, the school awarded 130 medical degrees. In 1914, the KLT declared an MMC degree equal to a qualification earned at a Japanese university. As a result, a majority of students, including those born in Japan, sought employment in Manchuria after commencement. Meanwhile, Chinese who wished to learn medicine could enroll in a basic two-year Japanese language and scientific certification program. Between 1912 and 1922, fifty-five students completed this course.[19]

Following World War I, Great Britain, France, and Germany made some efforts to offer scientific education in their empires in accordance with their stated goal of preparing colonial subjects for self-rule (and for the practical purpose of relieving European doctors). However, curricula and facilities at local schools remained unsatisfactory. For most subjects, permanent migration to the West was the only alternative to discrimination and limited training and career opportunities at home.[20] "Higher learning had no place in higher education": colonial institutions emphasized technical over theoretical knowledge, and a university degree was viewed as barely equal to a secondary school certificate in the metropole.[21] Modern science was embedded in

Western attitudes toward the social and natural environment, and the philosophical distance between imperialists and subjects in the European empires impeded scholarly communication. Western scientists often interpreted culture shock as ineptitude, concluding that "natives" were incapable of logical reasoning. When non-Europeans did make path-breaking contributions to science, imperialists often denigrated their accomplishments as the mysterious intuition of a "mystic Oriental mind."[22]

Colonial subjects chafed under such discrimination. Viewing technological progress as the essence of nation building, many admired and sought to replicate Japan's transformation into the scientific equal of the great powers.[23] Japan, having experienced the transition from an Eastern to a Western intellectual tradition, was better equipped than any other empire to train subjects in modern science. Policymakers responded to the liberal ideal of colonial self-government and subjects' demands for increased political and professional opportunities by improving access to education in Taiwan, Korea, and Manchuria. In 1922, the MMC opened its four-year course to Chinese enrollment, becoming, in the words of the *China Medical Journal*, "an institution which aims at being really indigenous."[24] By the end of 1939, the number of scientifically trained doctors in the region stood at about 4,100; approximately half were Chinese. Of the total group, 1,615 had graduated from the MMC.[25] To a greater degree than any other imperial power, Japan sought to include its subjects in medical modernization and the justification of empire.[26]

LEGITIMIZING THE EMPIRE IN THE GLOBAL LABORATORY

During the first two decades of Japanese imperialism in Manchuria, scientists did not study addiction in the laboratory, despite mounting evidence of the impact of opium on public health.[27] But as Americans and Europeans refigured drug dependence as a disease to be understood and cured, Japan's disinterest came to seem backward. In addition to aligning state regulation of the narcotics market with international standards, the KLT Opium Law of 1924 added a medical dimension to drug control, mandating the establishment of a public clinic for detoxification and the inception of a research agenda on addiction. Students of opium were servants of the state, displaying the benevolence and legitimacy of the Japanese empire. The white coat clad a moral entrepreneur as well as a scientist.

Once initiated, research on drug dependence developed swiftly, aided by the aptitude of Japanese medicine in the study of local health issues. In working on global problems, Japanese scientists operated at a linguistic and resource disadvantage vis-à-vis their Western counterparts. By contrast, in the investigation of local phenomena, they capitalized on an unparalleled geographic and cultural proximity to their subjects. The tendency of Japanese doctors to focus on local medicine occasionally provoked the contempt of the West. In 1923, an English missionary divided researchers into two types: "First, there are the men of powerful original minds who are able to deduce . . . great laws, hypotheses or theories, which unify our knowledge and mark a distinct advance in human progress. . . . The other type is represented by the detail worker. Such individuals are easy to obtain. Here it is the Germans and the Japanese, who are so good in filling in the details of a larger plan."[28] Such views bespoke ongoing prejudices against the Japanese, a "yellow race," and the Germans, recent losers of World War I. Even as the international medical community came to accept non-Western participants, it formulated new bases for "white" supremacy. Japanese practitioners nonetheless found local medicine an effective means of winning international acclaim and avoiding charges of "borrowing."[29] The study of addiction, a local problem with global publicity, allowed moral entrepreneurs to legitimate the imperial regime before the great powers with a display of Japanese research prowess and before subjects with a show of benevolence.

Laboratory experiments made use of various animal subjects, including rabbits, rats, mice, marmots, guinea pigs, cats, and dogs. Scientists also conducted studies on humans. As imperial subjects in a global research community, doctors in Manchuria confronted a fundamental contradiction in their work on humans. The ideology of Japanese nation building explicitly distinguished between the racially superior Japanese and the inferior Chinese. Moral entrepreneurs accordingly rejected the possibility of learning about Japanese physiology from the Chinese body. Within the emerging worldwide scientific network, however, the belief that all phenotypes are identical for research purposes, known as biological or medical universalism, had by the 1920s achieved hegemony as the sole legitimate experimental methodology.[30] Biological universalism implicitly contravened the imperialist belief that addiction could afflict only the Chinese race. Japanese researchers, reliant on the state for funding and power, and on international colleagues for data and influence, never explicitly addressed this tension in their work.

Although biological universalism is often regarded as a triumph of science over racism, this ideal also served as a foundation for new forms of discrimination. To researchers worldwide, the utility of human subjects lay in their phenotypic representativeness of the larger population. Interchangeability made them expendable. At the other end of the hierarchy, scientists enjoyed almost superhuman status. Within the ideology of benevolence, high standing in society was equivalent to unimpeachable morality—that is, adherence to the values of the community. Across various types of political regimes, however, many early twentieth-century values were "unethical" or incompatible with universal and timeless "goodness" (insofar as such a quality may be said to exist). The prioritization of collectively useful knowledge over the well-being of individuals often resulted in "moral" conduct that flouted ethical standards. MMC researchers caused discomfort to patients by deliberately amplifying withdrawal symptoms for observation purposes and "very probably" carried out vivisections (dissections of live humans). Other practices deemed unethical by contemporary criteria were accepted (though not necessarily legal) throughout the prewar world. To secure cadavers, researchers raided tombs and petitioned judicial officials for the bodies of executed criminals and deceased penal inmates. Published experimental results on addiction openly referred to data collected from humans who gave no consent and derived no benefit from their participation.[31]

Early addiction scientists at the MMC coalesced around the laboratories of two professors: Morinaka Kiyoshi in internal medicine and Kubota Seikō in pharmacology. Both men were born in 1884 and received their medical degrees from Kyoto Imperial University in 1910. Morinaka, a native of southern Japan, accepted a professorship at the MMC in 1919. A year later, he earned his doctorate in physiology and departed for three years of study in Germany. Upon his return, he became the head of his own laboratory. Following the passage of the KLT Opium Law, Morinaka and his students in a range of subdisciplines began research on addiction. In 1930, the professor became the chief of the Dairen SMR Hospital, one of the most scientifically advanced institutions in Asia. Morinaka was a cosmopolitan figure with multicultural interests. His devotion to *nanga,* a Chinese-influenced style of Japanese painting that flourished in the early modern period, perhaps epitomized his desire for harmony between China and Japan. He frequently spoke out in favor of improving Sino-Japanese relations and deepening camaraderie between Japanese and Chinese medical students.[32] His Chinese colleagues at the MMC commended his sensitivity regarding the opium problem on the mainland.[33] Morinaka and his students collectively published about thirty scientific studies on the impact of narcotics on blood sugar regulation, adrenaline secretion, catalase production, and central nervous system functioning.[34]

Research on addiction in Manchuria also advanced within the pharmacology lab of Dr. Kubota Seikō. Kubota was one of the leading pharmacologists of his generation, a pioneer in a field that had only recently crystallized as a scientific discipline.[35] Kubota spent two and a half years studying histamines at Johns Hopkins

University prior to his recruitment by the MMC. His interest in addiction was a natural outgrowth of his personal commitment to improving public health in East Asia. Kubota deeply admired Gotō Shinpei, whose photograph hung on a wall of his office. In 1880, Gotō had proclaimed, "A regular physician can cure disease, a good physician will cure patients; however, a brilliant physician should manage the state."[36] Gotō's words inspired Kubota to cultivate legitimacy for the Japanese nation and empire through medical service. He led periodic visiting clinics to underserved parts of Mongolia and guided health missions to India, Siam, and Vietnam. Fearing the loss or destruction of irreplaceable texts on traditional medicine amid the political chaos of Republican China, Kubota petitioned the SMR for a grant to acquire over a thousand rare volumes for the MMC library. By 1930, Kubota was president of the college and frequently consulted by government officials on matters of public health.[37]

Over the course of his long career, Kubota trained multiple generations of devoted pharmacologists, including several luminaries of addiction research. Kubota's student Itō Ryōichi, like his mentor, hailed from the remote prefecture of Iwate in northern Japan. Their common, isolated birthplace provided a foundation for friendship between the two men. They also shared a dedication to their work. Like Kubota, Itō impressed colleagues as an extraordinary researcher. Itō studied the diffusion of opiates throughout the body. To simulate respiration, he built a machine that his technician "worked like a dog or horse" to pedal. In the late 1930s, Itō sought to establish a correlation between the strength of a dose of refined narcotics and the length of time needed to kill the recipient (a mouse). He derived a function relating morphine purity to time intervals from injection to convulsions and death. In 1940, Itō's renown as a researcher of addiction won him a chair in the pharmacology department of a new medical college in Xinjing.[38]

Terada Bunjirō, another noteworthy junior pharmacologist, joined the MMC faculty in 1928. He subsequently received a Rockefeller Foundation fellowship to study drug addiction at the University of Iowa. Upon his return to the MMC two years later, he took charge of an investigation of the pharmaceutical components, uses, and bodily impact of opium alkaloids. He also collaborated with Kubota to produce a film entitled *Ahen ka* (The opium crisis).[39]

In the late 1920s, the study of addiction in Manchuria stimulated similar scientific work in Taiwan. Drug controls implemented by the Japanese government of the colony had long provided an explicit model for policy in the KLT. The scientific investigation of addiction reversed the direction of imitation, exporting knowledge from Manchuria to Taiwan. The *Journal of the Taiwan Medical Association* published several papers by Manchuria-based researchers, including Kubota and Morinaka.[40] These scientists also helped train Tu Tsungming, Taiwan's most noteworthy addiction researcher and moral entrepreneur. In 1914, Tu and a classmate traveled through Manchuria and visited the Dairen SMR Hospital, where compatriot doctors welcomed them warmly. One of these physicians, Meng Tiancheng, was the third Taiwanese to have earned a degree from the medical school established by the Japanese colonial government in Taipei. By the time of Tu's visit, he had been working in the pathology ward of the SMR Hospital for several years.[41]

Following his trip to the mainland, Tu matriculated at the Kyoto Imperial University medical school in 1915. Initially intending to study physiology, he soon shifted his focus to pharmacology under the encouragement of disciplinary pioneer Morishima Kurata. Upon graduating in 1921, Tu returned to Taiwan to teach in the colonial medical college. In 1929, the government dispatched him to survey opium addiction treatment in Manchuria, Korea, and China. In Dairen, Tu sought out Meng, now the director of a detoxification clinic to which he had managed to attract several promising Taiwan-born doctors. Tu also appeared at the MMC for a meeting with Kubota Seikō, during which the two researchers discussed the state of the drug dependency field and Kubota's pet subject, traditional Chinese medicine. Upon his return to Taiwan, Tu presented the colonial administration with an overview of the state of addiction medicine in East Asia.[42]

Beyond the empire, Japanese scientists of the 1920s cultivated ties with Chinese and Western counterparts, nurturing a truly global community of medical researchers interacting on terms of professional equality. Kubota taught as a visiting professor at Peking University Medical College and lectured throughout South America.[43] Morinaka, Terada, and other scientists also spent time at the height of their careers working in China and the West. Itō Kōmao, a Japanese professor of neurology in the colonial medical college of Korea, undertook research at the Philadelphia General Hospital narcotic addiction ward. His findings appeared in the American journal *Archives of Internal Medicine* in 1929.[44] Tu Tsungming took a leave of absence to spend two and a half years studying at the University of Pennsylvania and Johns Hopkins University in the mid-1920s. His research brought him to the attention of United States commissioner of narcotics Harry J. Anslinger, who honored the doctor for his contributions to the international scientific community:

> Tu's name will long live, not only in the annals of medicine and science in his native land, but also in the international scene, for his untiring efforts and significant contributions to the research and literature on the complex subject

of narcotic addiction. . . . For many years I have benefited from the opportunity of intimately communicating with Dr. Tu in a free, frank, and instructive exchange of information and experiences concerning our mutual problems in the area of narcotic addiction and its attendant evils. . . . I especially cherish fond memories of our exceedingly pleasant personal meeting in my office several years ago during his tour of my country.[45]

To the end of his life, Tu regarded his highly publicized work in the field of addiction medicine as one of his proudest achievements.[46]

The bibliographies of imperial researchers indexed their growing importance within the global scientific community. Early students of addiction had few Japanese-language references at their disposal, but by the 1930s some articles cited only sources by Japanese authors.[47] The Opium Advisory Committee encouraged the translation of important results "to make this knowledge available to scientists in other parts of the world."[48] Periodicals such as the *Manshū igaku zasshi (Journal of Oriental Medicine*, henceforth referred to as the *MIZ*), the leading medical journal in Manchuria, published abstracts in English, French, German, and Chinese. Some journals, such as *Nihon no ikai (Japan Medical World)*, even produced a foreign-language version. Many Japanese researchers mastered Western languages and contributed directly to European and American publications. In 1928, on behalf of the United States Department of Social Hygiene, Dr. Charles E. Terry and his assistant Mildred Pellens compiled *The Opium Problem*, a landmark study encompassing "virtually everything that was scientifically known or believed about opiates at that time."[49] As part of their survey of the major literature on addiction, the authors discussed work by six Japanese researchers.[50] According to another bibliography, Japanese doctors produced almost 20 percent of all laboratory studies on the pharmacology of opium between 1924 and 1933.[51] Even Chinese doctors, who increasingly protested Japan's political and pharmaceutical encroachments in Manchuria, maintained that "cooperation with the Japanese medical profession is essential, because many of them have devoted much of their time to the study of this problem [addiction]." The *China Medical Journal*, the leading scientific medical publication of the Chinese Republic, devoted a monthly column to research in the Japanese empire.[52]

Laboratory studies of drug dependence brought Japan to the forefront of the global scientific community. In the proud words of Miyajima Mikinosuke, "In the past, we lacked communication among the government, research institutions, and academic networks, and there was a sense that the scientific system was incomplete. Was this not a great problem for our country? Now the progress in chemistry and medicine made by our nation is not a bit inferior to that of American academia, and research specifically concerning the drug problem is no less advanced."[53] Significantly, Miyajima compared Japanese productivity to that of other nations rather than praising the brilliance of MMC scholarship on its own terms. Much of the research in Manchuria and the Japanese empire was, like colonial science elsewhere, no more than form bereft of contribution—"trivial elaborations of accepted truths, pointless exercises dealing with established techniques, and articles filled with embarrassing mistakes."[54] Collectively, however, laboratory studies of addiction secured the position of Japanese scientists within a global community of knowledge and prestige, and that of Japan within an international society of civilized and legitimate empires.

LEGITIMIZING THE NATION IN THE IMPERIAL LABORATORY

In the early 1930s, scientific and political factors contrived to undermine the global community of addiction researchers. In many Western nations, shifting demographics of the narcotics consumer population eroded medical interest in drug dependence. Young male immigrant and minority "outsiders," who came to dominate the new cohort of users, commanded less public sympathy than prototypical opium addicts of the past. Drug dependence, like syphilis and other sexually transmitted infections, came to be seen as a "vice disease": the outcome of irresponsible and degenerate behavior on the part of afflicted individuals. Distaste for these "deviants" accelerated the retreat of European and American physicians from the study of narcotics.[55]

As the physiological basis of addiction came under attack, the field of psychiatry reformulated drug dependence as a psychological disorder. Psychiatrists, typically considered latecomers to the "professionalization revolution" of scientific medicine, took up the study of narcotics as part of a broader investigation of social deviancy. They sought to account for the appeal of opium in terms of psychopathology, degeneracy theory, eugenics, and personality science. By the mid-1930s, psychiatrists had positioned themselves at the forefront of addiction research in the West.[56] In Japan, by contrast, the discipline of psychiatry was neither well established nor greatly respected during the high imperial age. Psychotherapy, which dominated research and practice in Europe and the United States, generally failed to resonate within the East Asian cultural milieu. Moreover, compared to many medical subfields, Japanese psychiatry was relatively independent of state control—a circumstance that did not suit the politically entangled study of addiction.[57] Imperial Japan, which was determined to find a biological signifier of moral deficiency in the addict, invested the physiological model of drug dependence with inalienable legitimacy.

During the 1930s, global political rifts further undermined cooperation and interest in scholarly interchange between Japanese and Western researchers. In an age when nationalism was a key inspiration for science, the research world naturally reflected the polarization of states. Following the refusal of the League of Nations to recognize the sovereignty of Manchukuo, Japanese scientists grew increasingly isolated. Many disengaged from interactions with colleagues abroad, redirecting their energies toward developing an imperial network of colleagues. Perhaps they were grateful for the opportunity to exit the global scientific community: they generally did not share their Western counterparts' interest in psychiatry, and the rise of anti-Japanese attitudes throughout the world sparked various professional, personal, and perceived attacks on Japanese scholars. Periodicals that had once featured articles by imperial researchers on the physiology and pharmacology of addiction now drew attention to drug trafficking instead. "Not content with misleading the world in their relentless campaign of subjugating China through Manchuria, Shanghai and Jehol," the *Chinese Medical Journal* declared, "the Japanese Government and their propaganda machine have enlisted the help of even the medical profession."[58] For their part, Japanese who had formerly collaborated with scientists in the Chinese Republic now disdained the quality of their work. One research group in Dairen criticized Chinese scholars for "having failed to apply the scientific method to [their] own discoveries."[59]

The creation of Manchukuo in 1932 compensated researchers for the loss of their international profile in part by increasing their responsibilities as moral entrepreneurs. Scientists of the 1930s reinvented the study of addiction, formerly a justification of imperialism, as a rationale of Manchukuo statehood. Following the establishment of the new nation, Kubota Seikō, then president of the MMC, affirmed his dedication to serving the Kingly Way by eradicating the "backward" disease of addiction.[60] In 1934, Morinaka Kiyoshi submitted a report on drugs to a team of Kwantung Bureau policymakers, SMR representatives, and army generals. Noting that "fellow feeling *[nakama]*" among the nations of the world had facilitated the spread of opium, Morinaka stated that Manchukuo alone was prepared to take on the challenge of fighting addiction and called upon the state to allocate adequate resources for the task. Excluding researchers from outside the empire did not mean rejecting science altogether. "Medical studies must form the basis of future advances," Morinaka concluded.[61]

In addition to creating legitimacy for Manchukuo, scientists also used medicine to groom the surrounding region for takeover by Japan. Since the mid-1920s, the SMR had funded excursions of MMC professors and students to the grasslands west of Manchuria, where they investigated local conditions and provided basic health services to inhabitants. These trips also supported the political goal of extending the frontiers of civilization by dispensing benevolence. In 1934, the Kwantung Army sponsored three MMC faculty and a laboratory technician on a mission to Rehe, a newly annexed province where opium was intensively cultivated. By bringing addiction science to the region, the military hoped to nurture positive sentiment toward Japan. Departing Fengtian in July, the foursome spent six weeks traveling, carrying out fieldwork, and assessing local health conditions. They also met with representatives of the Rehe Opium Monopoly Bureau to discuss narcotics consumption in the area. The team returned to the MMC six weeks later, satisfied with its "cultural contribution" to the imperial periphery.[62]

Having demonstrated the political value of their work, scientists laid claim to the financial resources of Manchukuo. In 1938, the government, persuaded of the need for more doctors to treat rising numbers of narcotics users, agreed to fund the construction of a new public medical college in the capital of Xinjing.[63] The reformulation of research on addiction as a signifier of Manchukuo's political legitimacy also engendered opportunities for a limited number of Chinese trained in Japanese institutions to take part in the scientific community. The Kingly Way principle of "cooperation among the five races" generated a vision of science as a Pan-Asian rather than solely Japanese production. In the late 1930s, several Chinese-born researchers collaborated with Japanese professors or studied addiction on their own. In dual author projects, the name of the non-Japanese scientist invariably appeared second.[64] Integration was not equality. Nonetheless, imperial laboratories offered Chinese scientists unprecedented opportunities for experimental inquiry and professional progress.

Although some Chinese researchers were later viewed as traitors to their nation, in the 1930s and early 1940s most did not understand career development within imperial institutions as incompatible or even in competition with loyalty to the Chinese Republic. Common assumptions about drugs, race, and experimental methodology provided a foundation for cooperation with Japanese colleagues even in an age of political tension and war. Many physicians believed that imperial rule offered the most realistic framework for promoting scientific medicine and ultimately regaining control of the biological destiny of the Chinese national body.[65] From this perspective, colonial medicine was nothing more than an expedient path to independence on the part of both the individual and the state. And if Japanese researchers maintained a different view of the paramount significance of studying addiction—that is, the subjugation rather than the self-revitalization of China—scientists of both nationalities agreed on the institutionalization of modern medicine as an indispensable first step. Research on drug dependence thus collapsed the distinction between support for and opposition to imperialism, enticing Chinese scientists in Manchuria with the promise of national reform even as it secured their acceptance of Japanese rule.

Despite the inclusion of subjects within the scientific community, the small imperial research world inevitably tended toward insularity.[66] To combat self-referential tendencies, MMC faculty and students increased outreach to local colleagues. Study societies, traditionally concentrated in Fengtian and Dairen, extended their reach to cities such as Fushun and Harbin. Scholars of addiction at the MMC shared their work with the national medical community at an annual conference.[67] Through Japanese-language journals and conferences, they also nurtured the study of drug dependence throughout the empire. In late colonial Korea, opium loomed large as a topic of research in the neurology and neuropathology department of the state medical college. Annual scientific conferences in Seoul typically featured a handful of presentations on drug dependence, delivered by both Japanese and Koreans, sometimes in collaboration.[68] Taiwanese researchers, led by Tu Tsungming, likewise contributed to the burgeoning imperial community of addiction specialists. As the head of the pharmacology laboratory at the Taiwan Imperial University medical college, Tu supervised more than twenty "outstanding" Japanese and Taiwanese junior scientists. He was a warm and engaged patron, frequently asked to speak (in formal Japanese) at their graduations, weddings, and funerals.[69] Tu dispatched his mentees to conferences in cities throughout the empire and encouraged them to publish their findings in prestigious metropolitan journals. He himself worked closely with Itō Ryōichi during the latter's days at the medical college of Xinjing.[70]

In the Japanese home islands, insistence that opium was not a domestic problem initially deterred scientists from giving much consideration to drug dependence. During the 1930s, however, they followed their colleagues in Manchuria, Korea, and Taiwan in taking up the study of narcotics. Tu Tsungming's advisor, the towering Kyoto Imperial University professor emeritus Morishima Kurata, served with Kubota Seikō on a joint committee on opium cosponsored by the Japanese and Chinese governments and the League of Nations. Morishima lectured frequently on Japan's duty to spread benevolence throughout Asia. He also collaborated in founding an organization to institutionalize medical modernity on the continent. In

1939, during a trip to Taipei for an imperial pharmacology conference, he asked Tu Tsungming to show him around the Opium Monopoly Bureau laboratory, a popular tourist destination.[71] Other key figures in the development of an addiction research agenda in the Japanese home islands included Sakai Yoshio and Abe Shōma, a schoolmate of Morinaka Kiyoshi who taught at Tokyo's Keiō University. In 1935, Abe traveled to Taiwan to present his findings on the physiology of various symptoms of drug dependence in dogs, cats, birds, and marmots. He continued to publish on the topic through the end of the war, joined by at least two colleagues.[72] The study of addiction, having spread throughout the empire, at last came home to Japan. Yet Manchuria remained the fulcrum of opium physiology and pharmacology. Alone among the great powers, Japan nurtured a basic science network that included but did not invariably privilege the metropole.[73]

The imperial research community, however, did not last long. In the early 1940s, as Manchukuo approached collapse, the Kwantung Army launched a purge of the intellectual elite. Victims claimed not to understand the reasons for their arrest, torture, and imprisonment. Contemporary scholars can only speculate that Manchukuo, like other failing totalitarian and fascist regimes in history, sought scapegoats for its failures among those closest to the center of power.[74] In the 1920s, interactions with Western colleagues were a standard practice, even a raison d'être of Japanese science. Ironically, when Japan declared war on the Allied powers, these valued earlier ties furnished a pretext for assertions of disloyalty on the part of scientists. Voluntarily estranged from international colleagues who might have acted to save them, addiction researchers proved all too vulnerable to the polity they had sought to legitimize. Charged as subversives, spies, and saboteurs, moral entrepreneurs lost their laboratories, jobs, and freedom. A foreign observer reported the arrest and torture of several professors "on suspicion of anti-Manchukuo activities."[75] Other researchers were dispatched to work for secret biological weapons development squads, including Unit 731. Kinoshita Tetsuo, a pharmacology student who had conducted experiments on opium with Terada Bunjirō, received orders to join the unit so suddenly and unexpectedly that he left his desk at the MMC in a state of disorder, not realizing that he would never return.[76]

Unit 731, to date the most intensively investigated topic in the medical history of Manchuria, perpetrated perhaps the most extreme abuses of human subjects in the Japanese empire. Headed by microbiologist Ishii Shirō, the research corps, properly known as the Epidemic Prevention and Water Purification Bureau of the Kwantung Army, purported to study contagious diseases such as cholera. Supported by the imperial house and the proceeds of illicit drug trafficking by the Japanese military,

Ishii opened a laboratory in Pingfang, a village south of Harbin. This facility ultimately served as the blueprint for bases throughout Manchuria, occupied China, and beyond. Thousands of Chinese as well as smaller numbers of Taiwanese, Koreans, Mongolians, Russians, and Japanese political prisoners perished as experimental fodder at the hands of these biological weapons development squads.[77]

In addition to cultivating germs and poisons to subdue civilians, Kwantung Army researchers experimented with the lethal properties of narcotics. A senior sergeant captured by the Soviet army during the fall of Manchukuo testified:

> At the end of August 1944 . . . I put as much as a grain of heroin into some porridge and gave this porridge to an arrested Chinese citizen who ate it; about thirty minutes later he lost consciousness and remained in that state until he died 15–16 hours later. We knew that such a dose of heroin is fatal, but it did not make any difference to us whether he lived or died. . . . On one of the prisoners I experimented five to six times, testing the action of Korean bindweed, heroin, bactal, and castor-oil seeds.[78]

Biological warfare was neither a natural nor an inevitable outcome of the scientific study of narcotics in early twentieth-century Manchuria. The stated goal of drug dependence research in imperial Japan—that is, civilizing the opium user through benevolent medical intervention—was inimical to Unit 731's mission of developing weapons to exterminate life. Unlike Ishii and his henchmen, doctors who studied addiction in the laboratory were scientists. Their exposure to a global community of medical professionals furnished modes of thinking and responsibilities in scholarship and practice that had to be respected even when they superseded or contravened imperial interests. The conduct of these men reflected all the complexities, problems, and attitudes of early twentieth-century science, determined far beyond any single institution or political unit. Yet Ishii Shirō was not an isolated madman who single-handedly brought the practice of "medicine" to its wartime nadir but the product of an imperial environment that supported his work in ideological and material terms.[79] Addiction scientists of the Japanese empire belonged to a tightly integrated community that held the Unit 731 doctor in high regard. Ishii was a graduate of Kyoto Imperial University, one of the most prestigious institutions of higher education in Japan and the alma mater of a majority of senior MMC researchers. After Ishii was transferred from Pingfang to Nanjing in 1942, the Kwantung Army appointed MMC professor Kitano Masaji as his replacement.[80] Insofar as Unit 731 reflected the values, however inhuman, of its place and time, Ishii and his fellow researchers were not "immoral." But they were incontrovertibly unethical.

In his memoirs, Kinoshita Tetsuo wrote nothing of his service to Unit 731 beyond the bare mention of his orders to leave Fengtian for Pingfang. Upon his release from the unit, he was deployed as a doctor to the Japanese armed forces in Java and Burma. His former colleagues dispersed among various military hospitals in Manchuria and north China. By 1945, Terada Bunjirō, ill with typhus, had only two assistant professors and one technician working under him in the MMC pharmacology laboratory.[81] The addiction researchers of Manchuria were left with nothing more than the satisfaction of having served the empire to the end: conveying Japanese brilliance to the global community, reformulating science from a legitimation of imperialism to a justification of nation, and finally offering themselves along with their subjects as human fodder in the great experiment of Manchukuo.

CHAPTER EIGHT · Medical Doctors

As moral entrepreneurs, laboratory researchers sought to demonstrate the civilization of imperial Japan by creating scientific knowledge and institutions. Clinical doctors, by contrast, inscribed benevolence directly on the body of the subject. To facilitate this process, the 1924 KLT Opium Law established the Dairen Kyūryōsho (Kwantung Government Home for Opium Addicts). This clinic did not attempt to transform Chinese addicts into Japanese abstainers—an impossible task according to imperial ideology. Rather, doctors endeavored to liberate drug users from their "enslavement" to opium, thus increasing their biological "fitness" in social Darwinist terms. Detoxification therapy also demonstrated the legitimacy of Japanese rule to the great powers. As the world's first scientific medical hospital for the treatment of opium addiction, the Dairen Kyūryōsho inspired imitation throughout the United States and Asia, normalizing state attempts to cure drug users as a criterion of civilization.

When Manchukuo came into being in 1932, moral entrepreneurs co-opted the addiction clinic as a justification of nationhood, replicating it throughout the state to demonstrate attentiveness to subject welfare before a skeptical world and the benefits of the Kingly Way to a dubious domestic population. But the reproduction of the hospital also made visible its failure to cure addiction—a failure that belied the regime's commitment to benevolent government and ultimately undermined its political legitimacy. Imperial doctors purposefully ignored the ineffectiveness of their treatment and united against alternative medical approaches to addiction. To confront the inadequacy and futility of their efforts was to hold the regime accountable for the crisis it had created and to admit their own culpability as representatives of modern scientific medicine. Doctors could not abandon their role as moral entrepreneurs without sacrificing their professional identity. They failed along with the state.

ADDICTION TREATMENT BEFORE THE KLT OPIUM LAW OF 1924

Well before the establishment of Japanese rule in Manchuria, various local medical traditions explored the "craving *[yin]*" for opium as a health problem. Chinese doctors of the late Qing period understood the drug as a drain on the *qi* and *jing* (vital essence) of the body. One anodyne, proposed in the eighteenth-century fiction masterpiece *Courtesans and Opium,* consisted of varieties of ginseng and licorice root mixed into a paste. The author, the so-called Fool of Yangzhou, was not optimistic about the remedy: the characters in the work experience drug dependence as "a lifelong burden, one from which only death can free [them]."[1] In the nineteenth century, Christian missionaries such as Dugald Christie of Fengtian provided smokers with "Jesus opium": remedies for drug dependence that contained narcotics themselves and often simply shifted addiction from one substance to another.[2]

Upon taking possession of the Kwantung leasehold, Japan established several scientific medical hospitals that treated various maladies, including opium overdose and the symptoms of prolonged drug use. During the first quarter century of Japanese administration over the KLT, the Red Cross, which had long served as a symbol of civilization and enlightenment in Meiji Japan, treated almost 800 Japanese and more than 1,700 *gaikokujin* ("foreigners," including Chinese) for dependence on opium.[3] Missionary hospitals also provided free or low-cost relief to drug users. Between 1906 and 1940, the Japanese-run Mercy of Christ Hospital admitted 854 addiction cases, of whom nearly 97 percent were Japanese.[4] The free clinic of the Hongji Shantang treated almost 400 Chinese for chronic dependence or acute overdose on opium during the 1910s.[5] Many future moral entrepreneurs were active in these institutions. Morinaka Kiyoshi provided consulting services to the Mercy of Christ Hospital. Kwantung Bureau civil administrator Ōuchi Ushinosuke assisted in raising funds for the construction of new premises. Kuroi Tadaichi, later the director of the Opium Monopoly Bureau, was a board member of both the Christian clinic and the Hongji Shantang.[6] Formative experiences with addiction in a medical setting likely provided these physicians with a reservoir of interest and skill for later work. Encounters with patients who largely depended on free care may also have predisposed doctors to view themselves as agents of benevolence—a role that coincided with the use the regime wished to make of them.[7]

THE FIRST SCIENTIFIC MEDICAL ADDICTION CLINIC IN THE WORLD

The KLT Opium Law of 1924 explicitly transformed addiction medicine from charity into science. By the terms of the legislation, the Hongji Shantang hospital became a state institution under the name Dairen Kōsai Zendō Kyūryōsho (henceforth referred to as the Dairen Kyūryōsho).[8] The Dairen Kyūryōsho was not the first addiction clinic in the world, Asia, or even the Japanese empire, but it was the earliest institution of its kind to deploy Western science both to treat the individual and to seek a universal cure. At the Dairen Kyūryōsho, the physician was not only a healer but also a researcher and producer of specialized knowledge through controlled experimentation. In early twentieth-century Europe and the United States, many clinical doctors believed that scientific training hampered rather than enhanced their ability to provide humanitarian care to patients and encouraged junior colleagues to "forget all [their] physiology" when beginning to practice.[9] In imperial Japan, by contrast, research, whether in the laboratory or the hospital, was the moral duty of every doctor.

The physical layout of the Dairen Kyūryōsho reflected its purpose as a showplace of imperial benevolence. The hospital occupied a three-story structure in Xiaogangzi, a predominantly Chinese neighborhood west of the city center. As in the migrant labor barracks of Hekizansō, the brick façade of the hospital signified modernity. The luxurious interior of the clinic, meanwhile, emphasized Japan's adherence to the conventions of civilization. Hospital propaganda displayed images of its Western-style parlor, furnished with a mantle, coffee table, and array of patterned sofas surmounted by spotless white doilies. Curtains adorned the windows, and framed illustrations decorated the walls. The room was shown empty, free of its "morally diseased and socially so dangerous" occupants, sources of potential disorder within a highly regulated artificial world.[10] Other visuals depicted interaction between doctors and patients, but the former remained distinguishable by their professional attire and did not touch the drug users they sought to help. One particularly revealing image showed the clinic receptionist seated at his desk. Wearing spectacles and a white coat, he was indistinguishable from the institution's doctors. Around him clustered one female and eight male presumed patients, variously clad in Western-style suits, mandarin collars, and rough jackets. While several members of the group gazed distractedly at the camera, others stared fixedly at the receptionist through the glass windows of his office, perhaps

FIGURE 7.
Dairen Kyūryōsho exterior.
SOURCE: "Kantō Kyūryōsho yōran," in Shin Kitsu and Nagaoka Masami, eds., *Shokuminchi shakai jigyō shiryō shū: "Manshū, Manshūkoku" hen 9: Kantōshū no bu: Iryō to eisei* (Tokyo: Kin-gendai shiryō kankōkai, 2005), 111. Reprinted with permission from the Kin-gendai shiryō kankōkai.

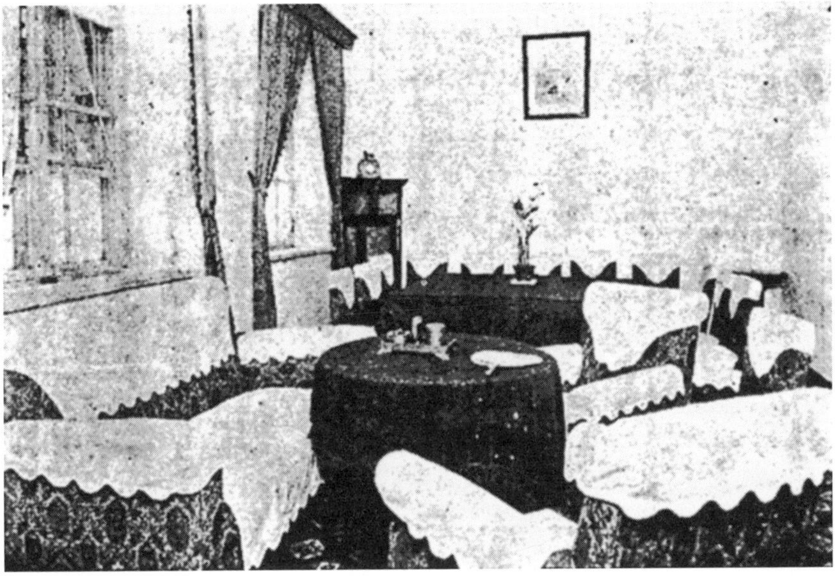

FIGURE 8.
Dairen Kyūryōsho waiting room.
SOURCE: "Kantō Kyūryōsho yōran," in Shin Kitsu and Nagaoka Masami, eds., *Shokuminchi shakai jigyō shiryō shū: "Manshū, Manshūkoku" hen 9: Kantōshū no bu: Iryō to eisei* (Tokyo: Kin-gendai shiryō kankōkai, 2005), 114. Reprinted with permission from the Kin-gendai shiryō kankōkai.

willing him to look up from the files on his desk. Preoccupied with the mission to civilize, yet distanced from actual engagement with the subjects he sought to help, the receptionist was the embodiment of benevolence in the Japanese empire.[11]

The initial staff of the Dairen Kyūryōsho included the receptionist, a pharmacist, several nurses, two manual workers, and the Tokyo-born physician Dr. Ozawa Atsuji. Ozawa began studying addiction following his graduation from medical school, testing remedies on both animals and human subjects, mostly laborers. From European and American scientists, Ozawa inherited the belief that narcotics were toxins for which the stomach lining might be stimulated to produce antitoxins. The ideal treatment involved a short-term hospital stay, during which drugs were administered to counter the physical effects of addiction and withdrawal.[12] Many researchers in the West considered the development of analgesics an incremental and often thankless process beneath their talents.[13] Taking up the challenge, Japanese doctors like Ozawa transformed

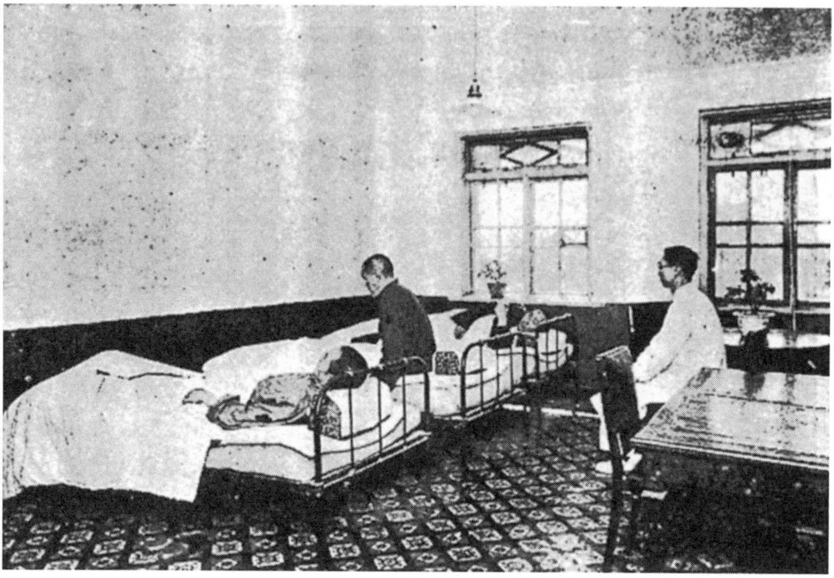

FIGURE 9.
Dairen Kyūryōsho patient ward.
SOURCE: "Kantō Kyūryōsho yōran," in Shin Kitsu and Nagaoka Masami, eds., *Shokuminchi shakai jigyō shiryō shū: "Manshū, Manshūkoku" hen 9: Kantōshū no bu: Iryō to eisei* (Tokyo: Kin-gendai shiryō kankōkai, 2005), 112. Reprinted with permission from the Kin-gendai shiryō kankōkai.

unobtrusive piecemeal advances into a source of international scientific acclaim. Ozawa began by combining iodine, arsenious acid, calcium chloride, and other ingredients. In one early study, he reported eight patients returned to health, nine unaffected cases, and one relapse. Based on these findings, Ozawa revised dosages to correlate with the patient's habitual daily intake of narcotics, the duration of addiction, and the findings of a baseline physical examination. Eventually he settled on a preparation that owed much to American research on spermatin and Vitamin A. Using this compound, he achieved a remission of withdrawal symptoms, the standard for a cure, in 75 percent of patients. Ozawa, like his colleagues around the world, strategically avoided any postdischarge follow-up that could compromise the appearance of success.[14]

The Dairen Kyūryōsho spared drug users from some of the more bizarre addiction treatments, such as those involving the application of goat feces and licorice, to which many drug users in "opium refuges" in rural China were subjected.[15] Yet

FIGURE 10.
Dairen Kyūryōsho receptionist.
SOURCE: "Kantō Kyūryōsho yōran," in Shin Kitsu and Nagaoka Masami, eds., *Shokuminchi shakai jigyō shiryō shū: "Manshū, Manshūkoku" hen 9: Kantōshū no bu: Iryō to eisei* (Tokyo: Kin-gendai shiryō kankōkai, 2005), 114. Reprinted with permission from the Kin-gendai shiryō kankōkai.

"scientific" remedies also traumatized patients. Scopolamine, an injectible compound developed in the West for use in obstetrics, not only proved useless in detoxifying addicts but also engendered a number of unpleasant side effects, including flushing, dilated pupils, hallucinations, partial amnesia, and finally, addiction.[16] In addition to these discomforts, patients experienced the symptoms of narcotic withdrawal: digestive distress, headache, nervous agitation, skin rash, and other health issues. From the perspective of the moral entrepreneur, the sufferings induced by unproven and experimental "cures" were a matter of little concern. The ideology of benevolence legitimated the use of brutality in the name of reform. To ensure that addicts understood the motives of the state in asking them to bear pain, the Dairen Kyūryōsho offered spiritual education alongside detoxification therapy.[17]

Between 1924 and 1940, the Dairen Kyūryōsho admitted a total of 8,435 patients. Together, Chinese, Manchurians, and Manchukuoans accounted for nearly 96 percent of the total. Although the clinic did accept a token number of Japanese and Koreans, it was to all intents and purposes a Chinese institution. It was also a predominantly male world, with men furnishing more than 90 percent of admissions. Fluctuations in patient numbers followed the seasonal pattern of labor migration, declining during the summer months when many natives of north China returned home. Of all occupational groups, however, unskilled workers spent the shortest average time in the clinic.[18]

According to clinic records, patients left the hospital under three circumstances: "total cure *[zenchi]*," "accident *[jiko]*," or death. Like penal inmates, they lacked the privilege of voluntary departure. "There are those who cannot withstand the temptation of drugs and dare to escape from the center just like prisoners," observed visiting penologist Masaki Akira.[19] Between 1924 and 1940, nearly 20 percent of admissions left the Dairen Kyūryōsho without medical authorization. They averaged less than seven days in treatment, compared to nearly twenty days for "cured" cases.[20]

Within months of the establishment of the Dairen Kyūryōsho, the great powers convened at Geneva for the Opium Conferences of 1924–25. After the Japanese representative described the new hospital as "an excellent method . . . to cure inveterate smokers," the assembly affirmed "that addicts, whose physical and mental state is diseased, should be treated accordingly, since they cannot be expected to relinquish the deep-rooted habit simply by law and regulation and by punishment."[21] The Japanese model of addiction treatment not only helped mitigate negative publicity surrounding drug trafficking by presenting imperial rule as the solution to, rather than the source of, opium addiction, but also inspired doctors around the world. The export of knowledge from Manchuria reversed traditional flows of information and imitation, both within the Japanese empire and vis-à-vis the West. Following his 1929 tour of addiction research and treatment facilities in the KLT and SMRZ, Tu Tsungming recommended buinding a Dairen Kyūryōsho–style clinic in Taiwan. In 1930, the colonial government closed the informal and temporary facilities that had previously offered treatment to local drug users. It purchased a defunct former hospital to house the new Taibei Kangshengyuan (Japanese, Taihoku Kōseisho; English, Taipei Healthy Life Institute) and mandated compulsory detoxification for all opium users in Taiwan. Those who resisted curing were liable to large fines and imprisonment with hard labor. The clinic reported that most patients admitted themselves willingly, although the circumstances under which they "volunteered" for treatment are not known.[22]

By offering a considerably higher salary than other public hospitals, the Taipei Healthy Life Institute attracted many of the best and brightest doctors in colonial

Taiwan. In 1930, Tu established a program to educate similarly qualified nurses. Over eighty applicants competed for admission to the first class. One successful candidate, Chen Shiu-Chiau, was born to Taiwanese parents in 1913. Chen had earned a high school diploma, an unusual accomplishment for a woman at that time. In addition to working at the Healthy Life Institute, she trained as a midwife, passing a government exam in the subject in 1935. When Chen died suddenly of illness in 1936, Tu himself gave the funeral address.[23]

Tu and fellow moral entrepreneurs at the Taipei Healthy Life Institute upheld the ideology of benevolence that inspired addiction treatment in the KLT. Although the doctor professed to favor a gentle, nonpunitive model of treatment, his clinic hospitalized patients for six weeks, subjecting them to police-style supervision during their recovery and watching them "like criminals" even after their release.[24] To alleviate withdrawal symptoms over time, Tu administered decreasing doses of a cocktail of morphine, Scopolamine, arsenic, and codeine. He also sought to improve the moral condition of the drug user. Observing that many patients were uneducated and unable to communicate in Japanese, the colonial lingua franca, Tu suggested that the clinic hold language classes. As a result, he claimed, "when they leave the hospital, addicts who could only speak the language of their native land *[hontō go]* are able to use Japanese, and having been lovingly warned away from the custom of opium smoking, they relapse only rarely."[25] For Tu, the Taiwanese doctor educated in the metropole, linguistic ability and abstinence from narcotics were mutually reinforcing aspects of the Japanese identity that his institution aimed to instill.

Within six years of the establishment of the Taipei Healthy Life Institute, a burgeoning network of clinics, some with a capacity of fewer than ten beds, had treated nearly sixteen thousand opium users in Taiwan.[26] Tu's work won accolades from addiction specialists around the world. A delegation from the OAC visited his hospital in 1930 and was impressed by the cure of a patient identified as S. H. So. Five years earlier, So, a merchant, had taken the advice of an uncle to use opium to relieve abdominal pain. When So's drug use cost him his fiancée, he sought admission to the Taibei Kangshengyuan. He detoxified and departed within fourteen days—just in time for the world to marvel at his success story.[27]

Moral entrepreneurs in Korea also followed the KLT model of benevolent addiction treatment, constructing a network of clinics under state control. Shūhō Masasue, the chief of the Sanitation Bureau and a faculty member at the government medical college, established the colony's first detoxification hospital, with eight sickrooms, in Seoul in 1925.[28] Within months, Shūhō's experiments on human subjects had produced an anti-addiction preparation called Antimol. Japan presented the drug to the OAC in the winter of 1926. By May, Shūhō claimed to have detoxified about a hundred opium users, "too many to remember their names." He had even cured a seventy-two-year-old man, restoring his joie de vivre and mobility after two weeks' hospitalization. Based on Shūhō's glowing reports, the colonial government supplied Antimol to hundreds of narcotics users throughout Korea in the late 1920s.[29]

In 1930, treatment became compulsory for opium consumers in the colony, with the state vowing to round up and forcibly detoxify all addicts "to the best of its ability."[30] As a result, the patient population rose dramatically. In a single year, two Seoul hospitals alone took in nearly ten thousand drug users. Korean males accounted for about 78 percent of total admissions; Korean females, 21 percent. Most of the remaining patients were Japanese women, said to be prostitutes. Tu Tsungming, who visited Korea in 1933, deemed its cure facilities the most systematic in Asia.[31] Clinics remained open through the 1930s, despite periodic government pronouncements that addiction had been eradicated.[32]

In the Japanese home islands, the perception that addiction afflicted only Korean and Chinese migrants initially discouraged doctors from addressing the issue. In 1933, Protestant reformer Namae Takayuki, inspired by Kikuchi Yūji, collaborated with a fellow Christian, Dr. Majima Kan, to establish a private addiction treatment facility in the latter's home in Tokyo. By this time, Majima, who had studied medicine in Chicago, had been experimenting with detoxification therapies for nearly a decade.[33] To raise funding for the new clinic, Namae founded the Mayaku chūdoku kyūgokai (Drug Addiction Relief Association). Capitalizing on his renown within political and humanitarian circles, the longtime bureaucrat solicited donations from a former superintendent of the metropolitan police, a representative in the House of Peers and former mayor of the city of Yokohama, a vice-minister of the imperial household, the Home Ministry, the Tokyo municipal administration, and the colonial government of Korea.

During its first decade in operation, Namae's clinic treated hundreds of drug users. Upon admission, patients underwent immediate and unmediated detoxification. After two weeks, when the worst symptoms of withdrawal had passed, convalescents followed a strict daily schedule intended to inculcate them with the "Japanese" traits of self-discipline, industriousness, and morality. Rising before 7 A.M., they breakfasted, cleaned their rooms and the local Shintō shrine, swept the neighborhood streets, did laundry, and sorted wastepaper for wages. After lunch at noon, patients returned to work until 5 P.M. (4:30 in winter). In the evenings, they participated in "wholesome" activities like playing Ping-Pong, listening to the radio, and learning martial arts from the Korean manager, Cho Sei-ki. Bedtime was 9:40 P.M. Within three months, Namae declared, patients had developed the skills needed to resist relapse and live independently.[34]

Despite Namae's charitable intentions, he and his staff perpetuated negative stereotypes of Koreans as lazy and dependent. According to Cho Sei-ki, "Following in the path of the Chinese . . . Korean youths were utterly enslaved . . . by the irresistible power of drugs." As a Korean in the home islands, Cho had himself suffered from racial discrimination. Nonetheless, he viewed the social problem of drug use as the primary obstacle to the economic success of colonial migrants to Japan.[35] Numerous hospital inmates absorbed and repeated this perspective, remembering Cho as a hero on their path to redemption. In addition to helping them gain entry to the clinic, he supported many cured patients after departure, even providing one woman with capital to open a small business.[36] "Kyo," a twenty-eight-year-old Korean woman who had worked as a geisha in Japan, reflected, "You know the drug habit is a horrible thing, but you can not *[sic]* get away from it once you acquire it. At first you may conceal from your friends that you are addicted to morphine, but later you don't mind what your friends think. They may be shocked, despise you and finally desert you. It is a sad thing, but what of it. You simply have to have another injection when the effect of the last begins to dissipate." Like many former patients, Kyo ultimately resolved to remain permanently at the clinic as an assistant.[37] Namae's intentions notwithstanding, his treatment tended to replace physical dependence on opiates with psychological attachment to the hospital. His institution accordingly came to serve as a showcase of Korean unfitness for self-rule, suggesting that only benevolent supervision could save the addict from social Darwinist elimination in the outside world.[38]

Over time, however, Japanese patients actually came to outnumber Koreans in the clinic. By 1940, Namae and Majima had treated 637 drug users, including 377 Koreans and 260 Japanese.[39] Repatriates from Manchuria and social elites such as doctors, dentists, nurses, company employees, and priests made up a rising percentage of inmates. To meet the growing need for addiction treatment, Namae hoped to expand the hospital and build a second facility on a nearby island. Although his declining health and the outbreak of war stymied these plans, the original institution remained open through 1943, praised by politicians, university professors, doctors, researchers, youth groups, and Manchukuo Opium Monopoly Bureau officials.[40]

Following in Namae's footsteps, in 1935 Tokyo's Musashino Hospital opened a ward for narcotics users. Administered by Dr. Sakai Yoshio under the direction of the municipal Police Sanitation Bureau, the hospital accommodated up to thirty addiction cases at a time. During the first year, nearly eight hundred patients, including more than five hundred Koreans, completed the two-week detoxification program. To improve the effectiveness of treatment, the hospital dispatched Masaki Akira to observe medical practices at the Dairen Kyūryōsho. Upon his return, Masaki reported, "I was able to find several methods [of detoxifying drug users] in the Kantō [Kwantung] . . . district of Manchuria which could be copied by our country."[41]

In addition to visitors like Masaki, medical missionaries in the Dōjinkai spread the Dairen Kyūryōsho model of addiction treatment through the empire. Advertisements in Dōjinkai journals disseminated information about analgesic remedies, which competed for the hospital market and private business of doctors. Many alleged cures were indistinguishable from patent medicines: secret compounds marketed with extravagant and unverified claims to effectiveness. In the United States, patent medicines fell from favor after the passage of the Pure Food and Drug Act of 1906, which required manufacturers to enumerate the ingredients of comestibles.[42] In China, the Republican government of Chiang Kai-shek enacted similar legislation in 1930, but patent medicines remained readily available.[43] R. Y. Lo contended in 1933, "That the Japanese are responsible for . . . the manufacture of different preparations, chiefly in the form of pills, which are advertised as panaceas for relieving pain or opium cure . . . is almost common knowledge to all."[44] Backed by credentialed physicians and the might of the Japanese empire, these remedies flourished in the mainland market. Advertisements capitalized on public veneration for Western medicine by explicitly identifying the researcher and institution responsible for the compound. They declared products effective, efficient, and above all, scientific. Early remedies generally offered to eliminate cravings by mimicking the effects of opiates.[45] By the 1930s, many had expanded their claims to include the suppression of drug withdrawal symptoms. A few boasted endorsements from political authorities: a 1930 ad for Spamidol, for example, alleged that the analgesic had cured all eighty patients at a state clinic in colonial Korea.[46]

Most advertisements occupied a full page and conformed to a basic aesthetic template. Large, stylish Roman letters spelled out illuminating names such as Narcopon, Narcopol, Nonmorphin, Neomohin, and Mordyne. The text was commonly adorned with images such as blooming poppies and the syringe, alluring as both a "modern" device and a traditional tool of East Asian medicine. A 1928 advertisement for Mophyzalin, a prescription for morphine, heroin, and cocaine users, featured an attractively configured pyramid of hypodermic needles, their tips touching at the apex and their shadows forming the base.[47] Many remedies could be ingested in multiple ways—by smoking, eating, or injecting—according to the preference of the drug user. Some analgesics appeared in advertisements in multiple publica-

FIGURE 11.
Advertisement for Pantopon.
SOURCE: *Man-Sen no ikai* 109 (1930).

tions over a period of ten years or more, indicating a certain level of market confidence and demand. Even as journals streamlined in response to diminishing resources available for nonmilitary purposes in an age of war, ads for addiction cures continued to occupy valuable page space.

Although Chinese doctors grew increasingly skeptical of Japanese addiction medicine during the 1920s, they remained avid contributors to and consumers of Dōjinkai publications. They also adopted the Dairen Kyūryōsho prototype of

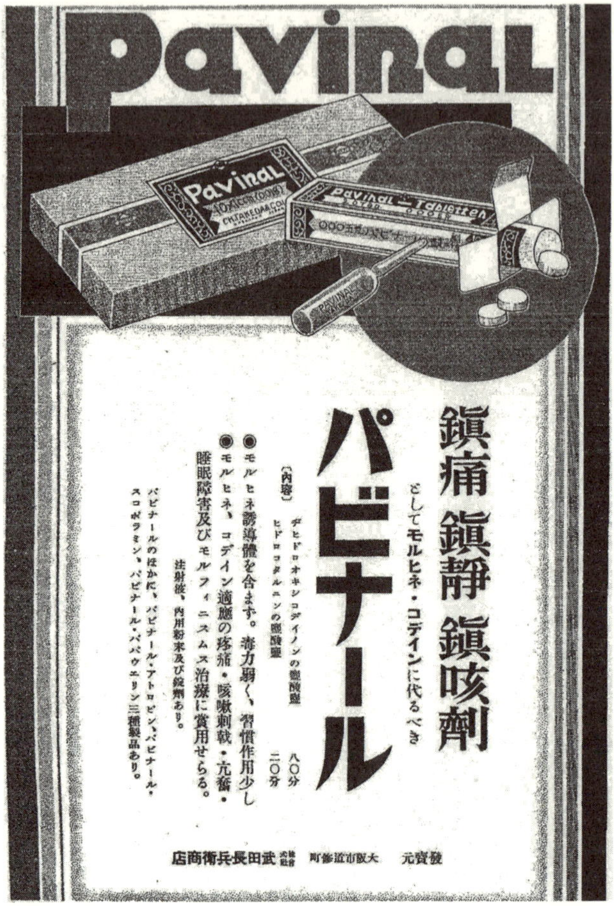

FIGURE 12.
Advertisement for Pavinal.
SOURCE: *Manshū igaku zasshi* 12, no. 4 (1930).

addiction treatment. In 1927, Manchurian warlord Zhang Zuolin established hospitals for drug users in the cities of Fengtian, Jilin, Changchun, and Harbin. These clinics imposed a cold-turkey cure over a three-week period. Recovering addicts then completed a vocational training program, learning carpentry, metalworking, printing, sewing, or weaving. The proceeds from these occupations supported the hospitals, which had a capacity of hundreds.[48]

Chiang Kai-shek's Nationalist government also adopted the strategy of benevolent confinement and treatment of drug users in provinces beyond Manchuria. On the eve of the Mukden Incident, the state maintained over forty cure institutions.[49] At meetings of the OAC in Geneva, Chinese representatives praised imperial Japan, where "the excellent service provided by government and society for the amelioration of addicts is in a large measure responsible for the disappearance of the evil." They entreated their Japanese colleagues to provide advice on conducting research and clinical work at the Metropolitan Reformatory Hospital in Beijing (then Beiping).[50] China's medical campaign against opium accelerated in the mid-1930s during Chiang's attempt to strengthen the nation by eradicating the "three vices": gambling, prostitution, and drug use. By 1937, the national Anti-Smoking Bureau supervised 1,160 public addiction treatment centers. These facilities, like the Dairen Kyūryōsho, sought to civilize and reform the addict through sex-segregated confinement, compulsory labor, uniform clothing, heavy surveillance, and other prison-style practices.[51]

Beyond Asia, the Dairen Kyūryōsho model of benevolent care of addicts also influenced doctors in North America. Canada, home to a burgeoning narcotics user population (concentrated in Vancouver), purchased a film from the Japanese government on the cure of drug dependence.[52] In the United States, the idea of treatment as a civilizing mission grew in appeal as narcotics consumers, once dominated by "respectable" middle-aged white women, came to encompass mostly immigrants, male drifters, and the urban underclass. In the 1919 case *Webb v. United States*, the Supreme Court validated public distaste for these social Others by outlawing addiction maintenance, or the medical supply of narcotics to habituated individuals whose sole reason for consuming drugs was dependence thereupon. Over the next six years, the government closed the approximately sixty treatment facilities then in operation and adopted a more punitive approach to opium control.[53]

Within a few years, however, American doctors had reinvented the hospital to complement an increasingly criminal view of addiction, addressing not only physiological symptoms but also the racial and personality traits presumed to hinder the drug user's integration into normative white working society. After receiving reports of the success of Ozawa Atsuji's cure in 1928, American physicians cabled the Dairen consulate for further information.[54] In response, a diplomat enclosed a copy of a report by Opium Monopoly Bureau director Kuroi Tadaichi and informed the State Department, "It is understood that the treatment, as well as the general direction of the [Kwantung Government] Home [for Opium Addicts], is both humane and intelligent."[55] At the eighteenth meeting of the OAC, the Japanese representative furnished a full report on the Dairen Kyūryōsho. An American delegate expressed his appreciation for "the interesting and useful exposé" and noted,

"This problem [curing drug dependence] was at present the subject of study in the United States of America with a view to the establishment of similar institutions."[56]

In 1929, the federal government authorized the creation of two addiction research and treatment centers for convicted felons and volunteer patients in Lexington, Kentucky, and Fort Worth, Texas. Though referred to as "farms," these institutions were in fact prisons, in which every aspect of life was ordered and regulated. In addition to providing drugs and psychotherapy to ease recovery, the hospitals put inmates to work, inculcating a socially useful ethic of productivity through training in agriculture, carpentry, barbering, drafting, printing, repairing musical instruments, and other trades.[57] Japan showed significant reciprocal interest in the narcotics farms, even dispatching a Tokyo police chief to visit Lexington.[58] The Japanese delegate to the OAC expressed his hope of collaborating with American doctors in advancing the medical treatment of addiction.[59] After listening to a presentation on the narcotics farms, he commended the "remarkable scientific and practical contribution" made by doctors at Lexington.[60] Miyajima Mikinosuke even translated information about the farms for Japanese physicians. In his opinion, "If one surveys the modern world, it may be said that only the United States and our country are adequately conscious of the drug problem, and have created the institutions needed to treat addicts."[61]

In contrast to American doctors, Europeans decisively rejected the Dairen Kyūryōsho model of benevolent treatment of addiction. In Great Britain, narcotics use was mostly confined to the middle-aged and the middle class, and could not be presented as a moral defect or a cultural characteristic of Otherness. The 1926 decision to uphold maintenance for addicts who could live a normal life while taking drugs became part of a stance toward narcotics regulation dubbed the "British System." Far from a coherent approach to drug control, the British System was, in the frequently quoted and pithy description of one historian, a response of "masterly inactivity in the face of a non-existent problem."[62] With the domestic drug user population estimated at less than seven hundred citizens, narcotic addiction was simply too uncommon to warrant much attention from doctors. On the European continent, interest was similarly minimal. In France, the notorious Ullmo Affair of 1907, involving a drug-dependent would-be spy, provoked a flurry of public anxiety regarding narcotics and national degeneration. Yet the state remained aloof from addiction, which was associated with deviant groups including alienated youths, artists, and military and civilian personnel "contaminated" by residence in colonial Indochina. In Weimar Germany, meanwhile, steadily decreasing rates of cocaine and morphine use, even among "traditional" consumers such as demimonde writers, painters, intellectuals, and the working class, relieved pressure for the state to intervene against drugs.[63]

In the European colonies of Southeast Asia, Western doctors maintained a similarly laissez-faire stance toward addiction, despite the reality of significant narcotics consumption.[64] In 1930, as part of its evaluation of gradual prohibition, the League of Nations Commission of Enquiry in Opium-Smoking Territories surveyed medical efforts to address addiction throughout Asia. Most doctors interviewed by the commission expressed scant interest in the issue. In the British realm, drug users occasionally appeared for treatment at general hospitals, but only one colony, Sarawak, maintained a special facility for curing addiction. In the year preceding the league's visit, this institution admitted a mere forty patients. In Hong Kong, where the population of opium smokers was broadly estimated at two hundred thousand, the colonial government cited the very scale of the problem as a justification of inaction. Investigators in French Indochina criticized not only the dearth of treatment facilities but also the generally disinterested stance of the government.[65] According to one physician in Hanoi, most drug users recovered on their own, weaning themselves off opium by substituting diluted solutions of narcotics, morphine-based pills, or traditional pharmaceutical products.[66] Only the "Ethical Policy" (Ethische Politiek) administration of the Dutch East Indies came close to implementing the KLT model of benevolent treatment of addiction. In 1931, the Dutch East Indies boasted nineteen publicly funded hospitals, which claimed to collectively detoxify nearly two thousand patients annually.[67]

Alone among the imperial territories visited by the Commission of Enquiry, the KLT received praise for its medical stance against drug dependence. Investigators interviewed ten doctors—more than anywhere else—and an unspecified number of patients at the Dairen Kyūryōsho. They concluded, "Considerable work has been and is being done in the leased territory in regard to the curing of opium-smokers, both in the form of scientific study of the problem of morphinism and the practical question of cures. Several medical practitioners in the service of the Government and of the South Manchuria Railway Company are devoting much of their time to the problem." The survey team further suggested that the research agenda of Japanese doctors in the city-state might serve as a model for the rest of Asia.[68] OAC disapproval of inaction in the European colonies indicated that, by the early 1930s, the obligation of the government to support medical intervention against drug dependence had become a norm of civilized rule. Governments admired the state-sponsored addiction treatment approach embodied by the Dairen Kyūryōsho even if they did not implement it. Within a decade of the passage of the KLT Opium Law, Japan set the standard of addiction medicine to which the great powers were held.

MEDICAL AND MORAL FAILURE IN MANCHUKUO

Upon the creation of Manchukuo in 1932, moral entrepreneurs replicated the addiction clinic throughout the state as a symbol of benevolent rule according to the Kingly Way. In 1933, the central government opened 10 clinics with a total of 330 beds. An additional 36 facilities, each staffed by 2–4 doctors, were established at the provincial level.[69] At peak capacity in 1942, about 200 hospitals detoxified 200,000 patients annually. Thereafter, total war constrained the material resources available for addiction treatment: at the time of Japan's defeat in 1945, only two-thirds of the institutions remained operational.[70]

To cement the public addiction clinic as a representation of the legitimacy of Manchukuo, moral entrepreneurs mobilized against treatment alternatives. In the late 1920s, the Lishan qinjie yanjiuhui (Society for Promoting Abstinence from Wine and Opium), a Chinese organization, offered a traditional cure to drug users in Manchuria. The society encouraged adherents to pledge themselves to substance-free living and provided food, clothing, shelter, and burial services to the poor. It sought to "arouse the moral sense and willpower of drug addicts, so they [could] drop the evil habit voluntarily and permanently." Curing involved a bowel cleanse followed by light, simple meals. In 1929, Bingham Dai observed, "Inspired by the elders of the society and encouraged by the religious environment and fellowship, most addicts are cured in a week or less."[71]

Like the Feiluan jingbihui of early colonial Taiwan, the Lishan society alarmed Japanese policymakers as a potential locus of resistance to Manchukuo. In 1932, the Kwantung Army banned all esoteric groups. However, recognizing the potential of "good" organizations to carry out the will of the government, rather than abolishing Lishan, the military stripped it of its involvement in addiction treatment and expanded it as a vehicle of publicity for the Wangdao paradise. Within a decade, 23,398 members had joined 508 branches throughout Manchukuo.[72]

Meanwhile, moral entrepreneurs asserted their determination to cure drug users through a scientific medical regimen identified with the Kingly Way and the justification of Manchukuo statehood. However, the expansion of facilities could not keep pace with the population of registered opium users, which ballooned to nearly one million during the thirteen-year lifespan of Manchukuo. Dr. Sakai Yoshio estimated that, at the current rate, the clinics would require a century to cure all publicly acknowledged drug users.[73] The KLT faced a similar crisis: serving an average of fewer than five hundred patients per year, the Dairen Kyūryōsho would have needed over sixty years to treat all registered addicts in the KLT.[74] The hospital received less than 1 percent of the total funds allocated to the opium regulatory regime, including the police, the monopoly administration, and courts and prisons.[75] Chronic underfinancing led many observers to dismiss addiction treatment as mere propaganda for the Wangdao state. In 1940, an American diplomat cabled his home government, "Heretofore more lip-service than action has been given to the general problem of aiding, treating, and rehabilitating addicts, and so-called sanitaria for treating addicts, operated by municipalities and philanthropic bodies, have generally been scrofulous places . . . avoided by decent people."[76]

Historians have likewise often dismissed Manchukuo's intention to treat addiction as a "pose" disguising its hunger for authority beneath a veneer of concern for subject welfare. However, many individual doctors seem to have sincerely sought to cure drug dependence.[77] Copious and meticulous documentation of experiments, treatments, and patient progress bespoke a reverence for science, if not for human beings, that transcended a crudely political agenda. It was not because moral entrepreneurs were satisfied with symbolic treatment that hospitals fell short in the quest to relieve drug dependence. Failure derived, rather, from the problems of the cure model itself. During the 1930s, both components of the standard addiction treatment strategy—the analgesic and the hospital—came under scrutiny as ineffective, even exacerbating, factors in the social problem of opium.

In their search for a chemical remedy for the symptoms of narcotic withdrawal, the doctors of Japanese Manchuria won the acclaim of contemporaries around the world but accomplished little for their patients. Nearly all "cures" were eventually exposed as habit forming despite their creators' protests to the contrary. As one remedy after another lost credibility, physicians found themselves treating dependence on an expanding range of substances. Advertisements for Arimalin claimed that the product could detoxify users of Pavinal, a formerly popular analgesic found to be addictive.[78] But even as doctors conducted clinical trials on Pavinal consumers, medical journals persisted in featuring advertisements for the drug. Even more flagrant was a 1930 advertisement for Pantopon placed between the pages of a clinical study of a treatment for addicts of opium, heroin, morphine, cocaine, Scopolamine, Pavinal, Narcopon—and Pantopon.[79]

The production and prescription of ineffective and even harmful remedies for addiction reflected the dual role of the doctor as both healer and dealer, motivated by morality on the one hand and commercialism on the other. The pursuit of profit gave rise to a multilateral struggle for treatment hegemony. In the mid-1930s, Dr. Sakai Yoshio of the Tokyo Imperial University medical college sought to leverage the authority of his name and position into market power. Sakai tested his analgesic, known by its abbreviation IM, in addiction clinics maintained by the Police Sanitation Bureau in Tokyo. By the early 1940s, the Japanese government had declared IM a "miracle cure" to the OAC and decided to promote it in China. Sakai traveled to Nanjing to advise the Japanese puppet regime and establish a factory for the production of his remedy. In the postwar period, the International Military Tribunal of the Far East characterized IM as opium by another name, a variant means of drugging the Chinese population into submission.[80]

Although IM underwent testing in Manchuria, in 1943 the Manchukuo authorities selected a competing compound to produce and distribute on a monopoly basis. The government was likely able to acquire the formula for this analgesic, a white powder known as Tōkōzai (Chinese, Dongguangji), on comparatively favorable terms. A bacteriologist at the Harbin Medical School and a pharmacist who had worked for the college's pathology lab jointly developed Tōkōzai, or "Shining East." Newspapers claimed that the medicine could cure drug dependence permanently in only four days. The formula for the remedy was lost in the chaos of Japan's defeat, and its contemporary obscurity suggests that it was no more than one of many pharmaceutical preparations that promised to resolve one addiction and in fact substituted another.[81]

The profitability and prestige of analgesic production naturally disincentivized doctors to scrutinize their success. Prior to the establishment of Manchukuo, studies that followed drug users after treatment were extremely rare: the patient interested the physician only until the moment of discharge. However, in the 1930s, scientists in the West, frustrated by their own inability to resolve addiction and increasingly hostile to Japan for political reasons, became skeptical of imperial accomplishments. The OAC openly challenged the high cure rates regularly reported by Japanese doctors. At the annual meeting of the committee in 1933, a Swiss representative wondered aloud if discharged addiction patients were "real or only apparent cures." With a touch of cynicism, he added that lasting detoxification "would be really remarkable." British delegate Malcolm Delevingne chimed in, "Was there any system of following up those completely cured? The removal of the craving was not difficult. The restoration of the patient's morale was the hard thing. . . . How many had relapses?" To these challenges, the Japanese representative could only respond that he had no information but "would endeavor to obtain it."[82]

In the mid-1930s, a landmark survey by three MMC-trained Chinese doctors employed at public addiction treatment clinics in two Manchukuo cities tackled the question of relapse statistically for the first time. Of nearly one thousand patients who were cured and released between September 1935 and November 1936, approximately 40 percent had resumed drug use by the time of follow-up in early 1938. Amid this depressing news, the authors of the study nonetheless found grounds for self-congratulation, noting that over 90 percent of patients relapsed following hospitalization in German institutions.[83]

In 1938, Manchukuo publicly acknowledged a relapse rate of 70 percent.[84] At the Dairen Kyūryōsho, Ozawa's calcium cure failed to achieve lasting results in at least half the cases.[85] Even the much-vaunted eradication of drug use in Taiwan, Japan's OAC representative confessed, was due to the natural attrition of elderly addicts over time rather than clinical care.[86] A 1939 study under the direction of Tu Tsung-ming found that less than half of "cured" patients had not resumed narcotics consumption—yet.[87] In Japan, 80 percent of Namae Takayuki's patients relapsed, and the bureaucrat reported a general sense of disillusionment among doctors regarding the existence of a permanent cure for drug dependence.[88]

Given the close relationship between addiction medicine and political legitimacy in Manchukuo, ineffective treatment inevitably damaged the credibility of the state. In 1935, Chinese novelist Xiao Jun (1908–88) published *Bayue de xiangcun* (*Village in August*), a novel widely hailed as the first anti-Japanese fiction of the Fifteen Years' War. In a key passage, Lao Ba (Old Eight), a sympathetic character who hopes to join the resistance movement, juxtaposes sham addiction remedies with the Pan-Asianist rhetoric of the Kingly Way:

> [The Japanese] sold morphine, they sold opium. . . . [T]hey came down to the village selling a "foreign medicine" that they had invented to cure people of the opium habit, and when you got through taking it you were a heroin addict. . . . [T]hat's what a Japanese was like.
>
> Old Eight could neither read nor write, but he was a tough-minded fellow. He knew absolutely that there was no good in the Japanese. And sometimes he heard people who had come back from a trip to town telling about how the Japanese claimed they wanted to be brothers of the Chinese! It reminded him of the proverb, "When the weasel bids the hen a happy New Year, it can't be because he means her well."[89]

Village in August was an immediate bestseller in China and the first work of modern Chinese fiction to be translated into English.[90]

Testimony by drug users themselves further discredited the "benevolence" of addiction treatment. "No one could give up smoking in the hospital," former patients alleged; doctors subverted the entire process of curing by extorting money in exchange for drugs. To enter an addiction clinic, Xia Shulan paid a hefty deposit of one hundred Manchukuo yuan. "Tortured" almost beyond endurance, she emerged "half alive and half dead *[ban si bu huo]*" and uncured.[91] In 1938, Chen Yi's district constructed a detoxification facility with four hundred beds and forcibly hospitalized his relative. The patient later recounted that he and his fellow inmates could not even speak without permission. Contact with the outside world, including family members, was prohibited. A package Chen sent was inspected; some items were confiscated, and the recipient did not dare to ask for their return. Convalescents who did not follow rules were beaten, cursed, and deprived of sleep and food. Twice-daily meals consisted mainly of coarse grain and soup "without a drop of oil." Despite their hunger, inmates were made to run and do exercises while singing anti-opium songs (including those made popular by Ri Kōran). Unable to withstand this regimen, they fled the clinics in droves. One hospital lost over a third of its patients to escapes in the mid-1930s. Chen's relative, who endured until formal discharge, emerged emaciated, seemingly on the verge of death, and uncured.[92]

In 1940, the state renamed the addiction hospitals "Healthy Life Institutes" (Japanese, Kōseiin; Chinese, Kangshengyuan) to attract patients and emphasize the positive aspects of Manchukuo rule. In a play on the new name, Chinese derided the clinics as *kangsiyuan* ("resist death institutes"), *kengshengyuan* ("cheating life institutes"), and *shengkangyuan* ("raising resistance institutes").[93] To arrest the decline in political credibility, moral entrepreneurs began providing follow-up services to prevent relapse, according to the new philosophy that "careful surveillance after the addicts are cured is more important and painstaking than the actual curing procedure itself."[94] In June 1943, representatives of the Manchukuo Opium Monopoly Bureau met with the heads of public addiction treatment centers to discuss postdischarge procedures. They resolved to release convalescents directly to mines and factories for six-month terms of employment in "Support Life and Protect the Nation Brigades *[Kangsheng baoguodui]*."[95] Supervised labor not only enabled the state to monitor former patients and continue their moral indoctrination but also addressed the growing shortage of workers in a time of total war. "A hospital, on the one hand, and an employment office, on the other," scoffed an American observer.[96] Following the collapse of Manchukuo in 1945, some moral entrepreneurs were executed by Chinese seeking retribution for the exploitation and mistreatment they had suffered in Healthy Life Institutes.[97]

Although follow-up programs implicitly acknowledged the importance of environmental factors in drug addiction, doctors remained reluctant to tackle these issues openly. During the age of imperialism, Japanese, Europeans, and Americans who traveled to the distant peripheries of their realm encountered a host of unfamiliar illnesses. Many doctors attributed these diseases to the allegedly primitive and unsanitary lifestyle of indigenous populations. However, as settlers from the metropole also succumbed to local complaints, the environment as well as the subject came under scrutiny as a source of sickness. The rising incidence of addiction among Japanese migrants to Manchukuo generated expectations that the state would adopt a more comprehensive approach to public health. In 1938, the American consul of Dairen remarked, "The fact that the number of Japanese addicts is showing an increase, deplorable as it is, may contain a certain promise of hope for future improvement. As long as the victims of the traffic were only Chinese and Koreans, the authorities were inclined to be complacent. But a marked increase in opium addiction among the Japanese themselves, who have hitherto been accounted largely free from the habit, will rouse the authorities to action as nothing else would."[98]

The consul's prediction, however, proved incorrect. Although moral entrepreneurs feared and deplored the contagion of drug use among the Japanese of Manchuria, they nonetheless resisted consideration of environmental causes. This conceptual block did not result from lack of capacity: successful containment of cholera and bubonic plague in early twentieth-century Manchuria demonstrated that the state could, when it chose, mobilize society and geography against disease.[99] But opium addiction was inscribed in the political justification of Japanese rule in a way that other scourges were not. Targeting the environment contradicted orthodox views of addiction as a racial and moral failing. It implicitly attributed blame for the social problem of narcotics to the Japanese regime, which was responsible for the environment. Like the Dairen Kyūryōsho receptionist, staring resolutely down at the files before him, deliberately unaware of the multitude of patients clamoring for his attention, imperial doctors purposefully ignored of the futility of their cure and resisted alternative models of treatment. To look up, to confront the inadequacy and ineffectiveness of their efforts, was to hold themselves accountable for the crisis they had created as moral entrepreneurs. For these reasons, addiction in Manchukuo failed to complete the transition from vice disease to environmental condition, from an issue of morality and race to a problem of public health.

Unable to abandon their treatment model, moral entrepreneurs of the late Manchukuo years could do no more than attempt to contain the public relations damage of the failing clinics. The addiction hospital gradually disappeared from state propaganda. Instead, doctors presented their inability to cure drug dependence as evidence of Chinese dereliction, which overwhelmed even modern medical science. A 1943 editorial in the *Manchuria Daily News* argued, "The time is past when habitually ailing persons could plead that they are victims of fate or of untoward environment or circumstances. In almost all cases, persons in ill-health have only themselves to blame for their affliction. . . . They have brought their poor health upon themselves. Such is the unanimous opinion of all reputable physicians today in all civilized lands."[100]

Situating Manchukuo firmly within the ranks of "civilized" nations, moral entrepreneurs may have derived a certain grim satisfaction in this final confirmation of Chinese incorrigibility. Or perhaps, as the paradise of the Kingly Way crumbled, they felt only regret at the wasted enterprises of addiction medicine and Manchukuo.

CHAPTER NINE · Moral Panic in Postwar Japan

The defeat of Japan in August 1945 brought an end to the moral crusade of the high imperial age. Within weeks, the victorious Allied powers disestablished the wartime state and occupied the home islands. Under American leadership, the government of the Supreme Commander of the Allied Powers (SCAP) enjoyed virtually unlimited power to reconfigure Japan as a Western-style democracy and ally in the increasingly tense environment of the nascent Cold War.

Almost seven years later, in April 1952, Japan celebrated the departure of SCAP and the restoration of independence. Despite the festive public mood, the resumption of sovereignty exposed deep-seated anxieties regarding Japan's ability to function as nation.[1] In the aftermath of the Occupation, Japan had to re-create itself according to new criteria: to differentiate the present from the past, to maintain American friendship without becoming a U.S. puppet, and to modernize a second time, after the first attempt had failed so spectacularly and tragically. Amid a renewed sense of national crisis, the familiar trope of narcotics reemerged as a purported manifestation of deviance and danger. During the "hiropon (philopon) age *[hiropon jidai]*," which lasted from about 1952 to 1956, the very real social problem of methamphetamine surged to the forefront of national attention.[2]

In contrast to opium, long viewed as an affliction of the Other, hiropon was a domestic affair. For the first time, Japan experienced and acknowledged a breach of its invented tradition of abstinence from narcotics. In response, the very grassroots of society mobilized against hiropon. The movement to suppress stimulants in 1950s

Japan was not simply a moral crusade—a zealous attack by moral entrepreneurs against a (constructed) source of deviance. It was a moral panic: a sudden spike of popular concern regarding a social phenomenon seen to represent a collapse in collective values. Through the growing mass-media industry of postwar Japan, panic about drugs spread swiftly throughout virtually every sector of society.[3]

Although methamphetamine was a significant phenomenon in economic, medical, and political terms, stimulant drugs were only one of many issues facing Japan in the mid-1950s, and scarcely the most pressing constraint on domestic recovery. Yet owing to the ideological framing of narcotics in the prewar era, hiropon occupied a disproportionate share of the national mind. The addict, a stereotype of powerlessness, was a fitting symbol of a defeated country adrift from its value system. He or she was at once a helpless victim, a prisoner of anxiety, a bullied inferior, and above all, a deeply flawed, even strange personality. The collective response to hiropon, which transformed the dependent addict into an independent citizen, provided a measurable index of progress in legitimizing a new national identity for postwar Japan: a confident, cooperative, moral member of global society.

THE "HIROPON AGE"

In 1888, the Japanese chemist Nagai Nagayoshi synthesized methamphetamine for the first time. The drug became commercially viable after World War I as a bronchodilator for asthmatics but ultimately achieved market success as a stimulant. During World War II, the major belligerents, including Germany, Great Britain, the United States, and Japan, produced and stockpiled stimulants to distribute to pilots on long flights, soldiers in combat, and workers in factories.[4] After the war, SCAP took control of Japan's drug caches, which were scattered throughout the archipelago in caves, supply depots, army and navy hospitals, and military and industrial bases. In late 1945, the Occupation confiscated and itemized these resources, allocating a limited quantity to public dispensaries for distribution as medicine.[5] Evidence suggests that the remains were secretly filtered to the black market, rather than destroyed as planned.[6]

In 1946, SCAP created the forty-person Narcotics Section (Mayaku bu) within the Ministry of Welfare (Kōseishō). Under the direction of this agency, more than two hundred American-trained Japanese patrolmen dispersed throughout the nation to enforce restrictions on opiates and marijuana.[7] Hiropon, by contrast, remained fully legal. The United States military personnel responsible for policymaking in Occupation-era Japan tended to perceive methamphetamine as benign. American troops had used stimulants extensively in recent combat, and the Federal Bureau of Narcotics, influenced by pharmaceutical producers, did not yet recognize consumption of these drugs as a health risk.

In the late 1940s, some twenty Japanese companies produced and marketed hiropon as a cure for low blood pressure, sleepiness, and sluggishness.[8] Successful advertising and the absence of controls set the stage for the explosive popularity of methamphetamine. In 1949, in response to an ordinance prohibiting the production of stimulant powder and tablets, manufacturers began making hiropon in solution form, for delivery by syringe. The transformation of methamphetamine into an injectable drug greatly boosted consumption among a population that valued the hypodermic needle both as a modern scientific technology and as a traditional tool of East Asian medicine. One Occupation official marveled, "The public display and sale of hypodermic needles in even the most remote small town and their general use by the Japanese layman have, in a sense, conditioned the Japanese as a people to have no bad association with the hypodermic needle. Indeed, even young people know what it is and they know how to use it."[9] Nearly all methamphetamine users in early postwar Japan consumed the drug by injection.[10]

Alarmed by the growing demand for hiropon, the Japanese Diet, convening for its tenth postwar session in June 1951, enacted the Ban on Stimulant Drugs *(Kakuseizai torishimari hō)*. This legislation, which came into force the following month, stipulated fines and prison terms for the production, distribution, possession, and use of methamphetamine in the home islands. By December, police had arrested nearly ten thousand suspected violators, more than 80 percent of the total number of drug offenders taken into custody in Japan that year.[11] Beyond offenses involving direct contact with stimulants, hiropon was also implicated in various robbery, arson, rape, extortion, assault, fraud, and larceny cases. In two months of 1954 alone, police linked thirty-one murders to methamphetamine.[12]

As a growing consumer base exhausted wartime stockpiles of hiropon, domestic dealers learned to manufacture the stimulant. On the evening of May 26, 1953, police searched the Tokyo residence of forty-six-year-old Tanaka Seiji and his common-law wife. Finding about ten thousand doses of stimulants and injection paraphernalia, they took the couple into custody. An investigation revealed that the pair had been making upward of 1,500 doses of hiropon per day, each with a retail value of six to ten yen.[13] The Tanaka couple typified the "mom and pop" nature of most early 1950s methamphetamine operations. Of eighty-seven laboratories exposed by police in the city of Osaka in 1953, nearly a third employed only two people, and barely 10 percent involved more than four people. Production averaged five hundred to six hundred doses daily, with few factories capable of making more than two thousand doses.[14] The scale of some operations, however, shocked the public. In late 1955, Tokyo police rounded up nearly seventy suspects in connection with a single manufacturing ring that had earned tens of millions of yen. During the preceding two years, the group had synthesized methamphetamine in nearly a dozen locations, including a former air raid shelter.[15] Law enforcement found methamphetamine labs hidden in factories making paint, tuberculosis remedies, ice cream, window casings, cold perm solution, cosmetics, hair dye, and chemicals. They even identified several plants for producing imitation hiropon. Drug manufacturers were not limited to chemists, pharmacists, and doctors, but also included bureaucrats, company presidents, university graduates, Manchurian repatriates, housewives, electronics repairmen, mechanics, noodle sellers, and the unemployed.[16]

Suppliers and consumers in the methamphetamine market overlapped considerably. In 1952, 42.9 percent of suspects arrested for violating the Ban on Stimulant Drugs showed signs of hiropon addiction. This rate rose to 51 percent in 1952, 56.2 percent in 1953, and 58.1 percent in the first half of 1954.[17] In May 1954, the Ministry of Welfare distributed anonymous census cards to conduct a national survey of drug use. Of 127,142 respondents, 9,108, or 7.5 percent, had sampled hiropon. Almost three-quarters of users injected five or more ampoules daily.[18] The national newspaper *Asahi Shinbun* estimated at the end of the year that 1.5 million Japanese were methamphetamine consumers, of whom 20 percent were so seriously dependent that they could not function without the drug.[19]

Stimulants initially attracted prominent figures in the postwar creative world, such as comedienne "Miss Wakana" (Kawamoto Kikuno) and "decadence" writers Dazai Osamu, Sakaguchi Ango, Tanaka Hidemitsu, and Oda Sakunosuke. By the mid-1950s, these artistic luminaries had all succumbed to a death in which drugs were a contributing factor, and hiropon had passed into mainstream society.[20] Free of the racial baggage of opium, methamphetamine spread rapidly through the population. Students, factory technicians, company employees, entertainers, and night workers reported using stimulants to increase productivity and alertness on the job. According to one drug expert, the public taste for methamphetamine reflected the "hard-working Japanese national character."[21] Amid the urgency of domestic economic recovery, some users may have viewed consuming hiropon as almost an act of patriotism. Others took stimulants to kill hunger pangs, alleviate boredom, and face disappointment and despair under the desperate conditions of the early postwar period. In late 1954, police arrested the elderly Dr. Masui Ryūhei for drug possession. Masui, who had earned a doctorate at the University of Chicago more than three decades earlier, was a renowned tuberculosis specialist. During the war, his hospital was bombed into rubble and his wife died of illness. Unable to continue his career as a physician, he supported himself by selling drugs and at some point became addicted. By the time Masui was picked up by police, he was living as a vagrant in a Tokyo park.[22]

MEANINGS OF METHAMPHETAMINE

Moral entrepreneurs of the mid-1950s looked backward to overcoming the past, as well as forward to creating a new identity. During World War II, Chinese and Westerners controversially alleged that the Japanese empire had deliberately encouraged addiction to narcotics among conquered populations in order to undermine their capacity to resist imperial rule. Following Japan's defeat, however, the International Military Tribunal for the Far East, consisting of representatives from the former Allied powers, declined to indict former traffickers as war criminals. In general, Japan's atrocities against other Asians received little attention at the Tokyo Trials of 1945–48, owing both to a tendency to emphasize the prosecution of crimes against Westerners and to postwar geopolitical factors. As American relations with the Soviet Union deteriorated, SCAP came to prioritize the swift recovery and reconstitution of Japan as an effective ally against communism in East Asia.[23] Rather than holding the Japanese accountable for past offenses, Occupation officials sought to absolve complicity on the part of "ordinary" citizens by presenting humanitarian offenses as the unsupported or unknown actions of an all-powerful military establishment. By the early 1950s, SCAP secretary of labor Richard Deverall had shifted blame for the alleged imperial policy of drugging Asian subjects into submission from the Japanese people and nation to the army. In his view, "The opium-pushing activities of the Japanese Army in Korea, Manchuria, and, later, in China proper was *[sic]* part of the planning of a military group that at times behaved as if it were beyond the control of the civilian government in Tokyo."[24]

Having re-envisioned the Japanese as war victims, SCAP proceeded to blame a new enemy for the spike in hiropon consumption. In 1949, Mao Zedong declared the establishment of the People's Republic of China (PRC), the first communist state in Asia. The passionately right-wing Deverall declared, "Thousands and tens of thousands of Japanese are becoming addicted to drugs smuggled in from Red China—and drugs that will surely kill them as if they were shot on the field of battle or died under an Atomic Bomb detonation." In his view, "Drug users have been turned into human slaves whose self-degradation earns dollars for the war economy of Mao Tze-tung . . . a deliberate murderer of human souls infinitely worse than the worst of the war criminals!"[25] The following year, commissioner of narcotics Harry J. Anslinger testified before the American Congress regarding the danger of "red dope" in Japan.[26] Drugs became the foundation of a political script for the postwar period that aligned Japan and the United States, erstwhile enemies mutually forgiven, against an immoral communist world.

Deverall's allegations notwithstanding, in the early 1950s China finally succeeded in purging narcotics from the domestic social and economic landscape. When Mao Zedong defeated Chiang Kai-shek to proclaim the foundation of the People's Republic in 1949, a national survey counted as many as twenty million drug users, three hundred thousand manufacturers and dealers, and more than one million hectares of poppy fields.[27] Following a long line of political authorities, including the government of Manchukuo, Mao declared the eradication of narcotics to be one of his paramount objectives. The Chinese Communist Party adopted a zero-tolerance approach to drug control, characterized by public mobilization and education, mass surveillance, coercive rehabilitation, and harsh punishment, including the death penalty, for convicted suppliers and users who resisted curing. Between 1949 and 1953, the courts tried approximately 220,000 narcotics cases, sentencing 80,000 defendants and executing over 800. By 1953, Mao had proclaimed China a drug-free nation *(wu du guo)*.[28] When the left-leaning Japan Teachers Union visited the mainland the following year, it dismissed Deverall's depiction of the People's Republic as a narco-state: "It is quite impossible for us, who visited Red China, though our trip was very short, to believe what he asserts."[29] A study of trafficking by Japan's Narcotics Section reached a similar conclusion.[30] By the early 1950s, national economic policy experts had come to see trade with the PRC as a potential solution to chronic deflation. Whatever the American agenda, Japan was reluctant to inflame its mainland neighbor with unsubstantiated allegations about drugs. Some moral entrepreneurs even wrote enviously of the "ironic contrast" between a physically and morally exhausted Japan and the "healthy, newly constructed China of today."[31]

As the political cleavages of the looming Cold War hardened, SCAP also accused the newly revived and increasingly popular Japan Communist Party (JCP) of spreading drugs throughout the country. In 1950, a Tokyo police detective apprehended a branch chairman and two party members in the act of carrying narcotics they claimed to have acquired from the People's Republic.[32] Two years later, patrolmen arrested a Tokyo-based communist organizer for manufacturing over one hundred thousand doses of hiropon and distributing them through Korean brokers.[33] In another incident in 1955, a group of twelve men and women, including a member of the JCP, were caught using stimulants.[34] The Narcotics Section also charged one of its own typists with alerting communist traffickers of impending raids.[35] By some accounts, as many as two thousand cadres, disguised as merchants and students, sold drugs in the home islands as a tactic of psychological warfare.[36] Much of the evidence against party figures was reported in the American or strongly pro-American press. The Japanese media, by contrast, mostly gave the impression that party figures were responsible for only a tiny fraction of the hiropon in circulation. The anticommunist ideology of SCAP did not strongly influence moral entrepreneurs in the hiropon age.

In fact, to many Japanese of the mid-1950s, the occupiers appeared more complicit in the illegal drug trade than the communists. The *Asahi Shinbun,* a national newspaper, characterized U.S. military installations in the home islands as "hiropon bases" and accused GIs of spreading stimulants from large cities to small towns and even the countryside.[37] The Narcotics Section reported that 16 percent of all arrests for drug trafficking in 1953 (including 623 American soldiers) took place in the vicinity of U.S. bases.[38] Films such as the 1953 *Akasen kichi* (Red line base) and 1954 *Kyō en* (Feast of maniacs) depicted American soldiers as sources of drugs and corruption. In response, Deverall wrote defensively, "*Not military bases but the drug pushing of Red China to Japanese is the root of the problem.* . . . [A] leading Japanese narcotics official has informed this writer that if every last GI were suddenly to leave the country, the narcotic drug traffic would be practically as bad as it is now." In his view, "Addiction is spread among a small minority of troopers by men already addicted, by girl friends and prostitutes, and by peddlers who have a political motive. . . . Obviously, if the men had never come to the Far East most of them would never have fallen victim to the dirty drug habit.[39] The *Nippon Times,* "the organ if not the creature" of Japan's pro-American Foreign Ministry, sought to reinforce the impression of military innocence through stories about troops led astray by depraved locals.[40] In one such case, reported in 1956, a third-class naval officer died from a heart attack after injecting himself with hiropon in the home of his Japanese girlfriend.[41]

In deference to censorship and American-Japanese friendship, most drug scandals involving the United States received relatively little publicity in the mainstream press. Instead, the Japanese media renewed accusations of drug trafficking by former imperial subjects in the home islands, now euphemistically referred to as "third-country nationals *[dai san kokujin]*." The characterization of Chinese and Korean denizens as methamphetamine traffickers allowed postwar Japanese to cast themselves in a morally superior light, as the victims of "pollution *[osen]*" by those they had wronged. This depiction implicitly obviated guilt for imperial opium operations on the Asian mainland. The media provided almost daily coverage of narcotic "conspiracies" on the part of "debauched third-country nationals."[42] In June 1953, police arrested two unemployed males, one Japanese and one Korean, for the manufacture and sale of hiropon. Despite the dual nationalities of the principals, the *Asahi Shinbun* titled the story, "Korean Caught in Manufacture of Stimulants."[43] In mid-1955, the newspaper dubbed Korean-born Ryang Hae-ryong the "Hiropon King *[Hiropon Ō]*" following the discovery of his enormous methamphetamine factory, containing over five hundred million yen worth of raw materials and equipment. Ryang and seven collaborators, including Koreans and Japanese repatriated from Manchuria, had been producing stimulants for more than a year. In the chaos of the police raid that put an end to his operation, Ryang managed to flee the scene, remaining at large for over a month until the authorities found him living under a false name.[44]

A police task force on methamphetamine concluded that third-country nationals "knew all too well the dangers of stimulants" but provided them to children anyway. According to one research organization, "Seventy percent of the manufacturers of hiropon are Korean, and they do not become addicted themselves—only among Japanese is drug dependence a problem."[45] Others rejected this claim, portraying Koreans as equal victims of hiropon. One doctor noted, "The world believes that stimulant use in Japan is due to a Korean plot . . . but although the absolute number of Japanese addicts is higher, as a percentage of the total denizen Korean population, the number of Korean addicts is unsurpassed." Koreans accounted for 12 percent of the patients he had treated for drug dependence, a rate that far exceeded their representation within the population of Japan.[46] Many moral entrepreneurs further argued that foreigners produced hiropon out of economic necessity. At the end of the Occupation, approximately six hundred thousand former imperial subjects who did not repatriate to their newly liberated home countries lost their Japanese citizenship and suffered exclusion from most types of legitimate employment.[47] Beset by deprivation and discrimination, they, like many Japanese, supported themselves through the black market, including the drug traffic. In the words of one sympathetic observer, "If we look at arrests for manufacturing [drugs] up to now, Koreans make up the majority. Just as in the era of Prohibition in America, when alcohol was mostly distilled by blacks *[kokujin]*, ethnic minorities here are treated without mercy and can't find legal work. Today within Tokyo there are fifty thousand Koreans, among whom three thousand are known manufacturers."[48]

Recalling the characterization of opium during the imperial age, some moral entrepreneurs depicted methamphetamine as a racial poison that would inevitably lead to the extermination of the Japanese.[49] For most writers, however, the moral panic over hiropon was about nationhood, not race. Foreigners were scapegoats or at most exacerbating factors in a fundamentally domestic crisis. A government task force on stimulants reported, "After the end of the war, people lost their spirit, the country was catapulted into extreme economic disorder, and both hope for tomorrow and the dreams of the past were lost; so people drifted into nihilism and decadence, and turned to the powder that could make them forget [i.e., hiropon]."[50] The novelist Dazai Osamu furnished perhaps the most enduring representation of this national "sickness of the spirit." In his most famous work *Shayō* (*The Setting Sun*, 1948), the author's lightly fictionalized alter ego, Naoji, a war veteran recently returned from combat in the Pacific, is tormented by "'the anxiety of the age'—men frightened by one another, every known principle violated, effort mocked, happiness denied, beauty defiled, honor dragged down. . . . I trembled with fear, felt shy and embarrassed, whatever I attempted to do, throbbed ceaselessly with anxiety, and was powerless to act. I needed more than ever the momentary peace that the vertigo of drink and drugs could afford."[51] Redolent with the victim consciousness that suffused society, *The Setting Sun* was an immediate bestseller.[52]

Despite occasional references to smaller outbreaks of stimulant use in Germany, Scandinavia, the United Kingdom, the United States, and other nations, the Japanese of the 1950s generally regarded the hiropon crisis as a unique national phenomenon—in the words of one minister of welfare, "our country's special situation *[waga kuni nomi no tokushu jijō]*."[53] "The methamphetamine epidemic was the first experience of epidemic drug use and dependence among the Japanese. This was also the first epidemic of methamphetamine abuse and dependence in the world," Katō Masaaki, a professor of psychiatry at the University of Tokyo medical college, informed participants in an international conference on drug abuse.[54] Hiropon, as the public seemed to realize, was an inextricable part of Japan's postwar culture of defeat. Following the departure of SCAP, a Tokyo professor wrote, "After losing the war, Japan has at last regained independence, but we cannot say that the social foundations are entirely solid; the nation as a whole has no confidence in itself."[55] Invoking Buddhist concepts of salvation, psychiatrist Kaneko Junji declared that the Japanese had lost agency *[jiriki]* and sought the external power *[tariki]* of stimulants to overcome a collective sense of hopelessness. He likened the Japanese of his day to the Chinese after the Opium War: "In the past, we criticized China for its opium problem, saying, 'China has fallen into a grievous state of addiction,' and 'China can't eradicate its narcotic economy and will disintegrate.' But if we replace the word 'opium' with 'hiropon,' we have a picture of Japan's current situation."[56]

The comparison between postwar Japan and nineteenth-century China engaged many moral entrepreneurs, including Narcotics Section director Nagahama Masamutsu and Opium War historian Ushikubo Ainoshin. Salvation for the nation, anthropomorphized as an addict, lay in restoring an autonomous drug-free identity. "We must steadfastly believe in the fact that Japan is an independent state, and drive a wedge between ourselves and this threat of extermination [i.e., hiropon]," Ushikubo urged.[57] The association of methamphetamine with the undesirable condition of dependence established the elimination of stimulants as a high priority for Japan, above and beyond many other social agendas in the post-Occupation period. To regain a sense of nationhood, Japan had to be drug-free.

STIMULATING SOCIAL AGENCY

In contrast to moral crusades against opium, which were led by a diverse but limited cohort of moral entrepreneurs, the 1950s moral panic against hiropon mobilized society from the grassroots. Antimethamphetamine messages saturated virtually every aspect of the public domain, including the law, media, education, community organizations, and medicine. Accessible to all, the campaign against hiropon ultimately served to restore a sense of social agency and nationhood in a defeated and traumatized people.

During the Occupation, SCAP decentralized public security and decommissioned former officers. Although the remainder of the police force continued to patrol the home islands, the association of law enforcement with wartime repression fostered a general loss of respect for authority among Japanese citizens. Offended by popular hostility and forced by inadequate pay to participate in the black market they were charged with eradicating, police suffered from low morale and limited effectiveness. In the 1950s, however, with American manpower strained by the outbreak of the Korean War, SCAP sought to increase efficiency by reestablishing central control over internal security. In June 1954, the post-Occupation Japanese government continued this trend by consolidating municipal and prefectural law enforcement under a national agency.[58] At the same time, the Diet increased the scope of the Ban on Stimulant Drugs and mandated heavier punishments for violators.

Taking action against hiropon allowed Japan's police to jettison their prewar role as "nursemaids of the people" in favor of a new image as defenders of democracy. Protecting the population from the threat of methamphetamine through highly publicized drug busts, patrolmen restored their public credibility and power. In evening raids on "hiropon nests" in the black markets of north Tokyo, they found narcotics concealed in food, clothing, school satchels, fish baskets, and apple crates. One all-night investigation in Osaka in July 1954 mobilized two thousand officers to search nearly eight hundred buildings in various neighborhoods and netted over three hundred arrests.[59] In 1954, the number of suspects taken into custody for violating the Ban on Stimulant Drugs increased approximately 150 percent from the preceding year to peak at 54,104, representing more than 96 percent of all drug crime in Japan, or 613 arrests per 100,000 population.[60] Approximately 70 percent of suspects were Korean, a ratio that likely reflected discriminatory targeting of third-country nationals.[61] The rate of indictment also surged, from approximately 43 percent in 1953 to over 63 percent in 1954 and 1955. Almost all convicted offenders received penal sentences. Between 1951 and 1956, nearly nine thousand violators of the Ban on Stimulant Drugs served time in prison.[62]

Both the public and private sectors supplemented this legal crackdown with antidrug education. In January 1955, the Ministry of Welfare established the General Headquarters for the Promotion of Policy against Amphetamines (Kakuseizai taisaku honbu) as an advisory body and liaison between state and society. In 1955 alone, the task force of over two hundred spent sixteen million yen circulating 225,000 antihiropon pamphlets, 470,000 leaflets, and 385,000 posters.[63] One poster distributed in Osaka showed the crouching figure of a drug user covered with injection punctures and shivering in long underwear. A man in a business suit and tie extended his hand in the direction of the addict, with the caption, "Let's wipe out the evil of stimulant drugs!"[64] In cooperation with newspapers and the film industry, the agency also produced an educational video entitled *Kakuseizai no kyōfu* (The stimulants crisis). Nationwide broadcasts on the government radio station, NHK, addressed topics such as "Can hiropon addiction be cured?" and "The hard work of stimulants researchers." At the local level, moral entrepreneurs organized lectures, roundtable discussions, and presentations in schools, corrective institutions, professional organizations, welfare centers, factories, and even nightclubs throughout Japan.[65] *Asahi Shinbun*, *Yomiuri Shinbun*, and *Tokyo Shinbun*, the three newspapers with the largest circulation in early postwar Japan, made drug crimes headline news fifty-one times in 1954 (including forty-three times between the months of July and December). One doctor recalled of spring 1954, "For three straight days there were no newspapers without articles about the central stimulants."[66] Publicity peaked that November, designated "Antihiropon Month." In addition to lurid exposés and images of illicit drug activity, newspapers printed interviews, editorials, and cautionary tales by ex-users, doctors, psychologists, and public figures such as Sugahara Tsumi, a popular movie actor, author, arts patron, and leader in campaigns against narcotics, prostitution, and venereal disease.[67]

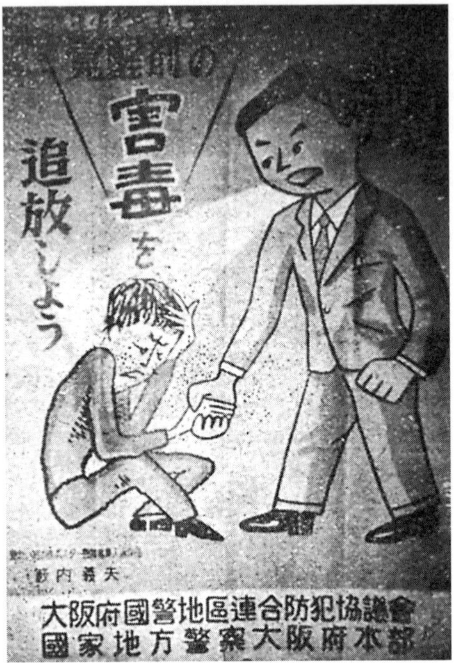

FIGURE 13.
"Let's wipe out the evil of stimulant drugs!"
SOURCE: Richard L.-G. Deverall, *Red China's Dirty Drug War* (Tokyo: Toyoh Printing and Book Binding, 1954).

The moral panic against methamphetamine proved particularly instrumental to the revitalization and spread of newspapers in 1950s Japan. During the war years, the press was widely viewed as a mouthpiece of state propaganda. After 1945, despite ongoing censorship, SCAP promoted newspapers "as the most effective instrument of adult education, giving leadership to the process of democratization."[68] As a result, the industry sought to improve its credibility and cultivate new readers through social and cultural reform campaigns. In the case of hiropon, newspaper coverage achieved its intended result of public awareness. In 1955, the government questioned three thousand individuals in thirty cities and thirteen villages on their knowledge of methamphetamine. Only 3 percent (1 percent of urban residents) claimed total ignorance of hiropon. The remainder reported learning about stimulants from newspapers, radio broadcasts, social acquaintances, movies, billboards, lectures, and other methods.[69]

Public receptivity toward antihiropon messages rested partly on the perception that stimulants posed a particular threat to youth. As early as 1950, police estimated that Tokyo alone contained more than twenty-five thousand juvenile methamphetamine users. A psychiatrist at an addiction clinic claimed that 80 percent of hiropon consumers were under the age of twenty-five, and 60 percent were younger than twenty. According to one survey, nearly 30 percent of respondents twenty to twenty-two years old had used or at least experimented with stimulants. Of one hundred methamphetamine psychosis patients in a mental ward, more than 50 percent had first sampled hiropon between the ages of fifteen and twenty-four.[70]

In identifying drug use as a youth problem, moral entrepreneurs reflected a tradition of concern for juvenile behavior dating back to the late nineteenth century. Meiji-era politicians, professionals, penologists, reformers, religious leaders, and others viewed the proper cultivation of youth as essential to the future of an economically and militarily strong nation. By the time of Japan's defeat in 1945, society had institutionalized the belief that every aspect of adolescence should be subjected to intensive government surveillance and regulation.[71] In the hiropon age, as the state confronted the challenge of postwar reconstruction, society naturally shifted its attention to the next generation, which would shoulder the responsibility of restoring Japan to the ranks of first-rate global powers. Narcotics Section chief Nagahama Masamutsu wrote, "As most of the victims are youths in their twenties and the ones to lead the world of tomorrow, it must be realized that this [i.e., hiropon] effects the decline of morals and the tragedy it will bring upon society."[72] Particularly worrying was the growing tendency of young men and women to use drugs not only for temporary relief from a prevailing sense of impotence *(impotentsu)*, but also as a means of suicide—the ultimate withdrawal from the national community.[73]

In the years after World War II, the United States also experienced rising public anxiety regarding juvenile delinquency, symbolized by an alluring youth "scene" of pegged pants, disc jockeys, and backseats. The Occupation transmitted postwar popular culture and its critics to Japan. Japanese and American observers of the 1950s concluded that youth were unsophisticated and likely to be led astray by temptation if not firmly guided.[74] In Japan, the legacy of war and defeat compounded this mindset. Moral entrepreneurs viewed adolescents and young adults as "doubly innocent"—not only naive in the ways of the world but also free from culpability in the crimes of imperialism committed by older generations. As one psychiatrist pointed out, youth were the purest victims of the hiropon age, suffering from "frustration, collapse, loss of confidence, and doubt concerning humanity due to defeat in the war."[75] Typical was the case of a juvenile delinquent given the pseudonym "Yoshio." When Yoshio's father lost his job at an iron mine, the youth dropped out of school to help support his family by selling newspapers outside a

Tokyo train station and known hiropon market. He subsequently joined a street gang, escaped from his parents, and became a vagrant and petty thief. By the time he was found by a researcher at a child welfare organization, he had been selling and using methamphetamine for several years.[76]

Yoshio was undeniably a victim of circumstances beyond his control, but he was also a criminal threat to society. A unique feature of Japanese law, which enabled the judicial system to monitor "problem children" who exhibited disturbing behavior but had not committed any crimes, prompted a retroactive inquiry into the background of juvenile hiropon users like Yoshio. A study of 160 underage consumers found that only 5 percent had a positive attitude toward school, and nearly 90 percent had failed to achieve grades of C or higher or had dropped out.[77] Another survey deemed 80 percent of youths arrested for methamphetamine consumption "of the type easily led astray *[aku ni mo somari yasui],*" and claimed that seven out of ten had demonstrated abnormal behavior prior to drug use. Like Yoshio, a quarter had run away from home. Between the early 1940s and mid-1950s, the number of juvenile delinquents nationwide quadrupled, and approximately half of all youth in detention admitted to regular use of stimulants.[78] Doctors theorized that methamphetamine exacerbated a natural tendency toward criminality. The 1954 rape and murder of primary schoolgirl Hosoda Kyōko by a twenty-year-old hiropon user seemed to confirm this fear. The media covered the story for weeks, stirring the outrage of the nation and reinforcing an understanding of the stimulant user as the source as well as the victim of moral menace.[79]

The protection of youth from hiropon and safeguarding of the general population from juvenile delinquents were uncontroversial goals in which diverse social and professional groups could cooperate, rebuilding a sense of unity and collective purpose in the process.[80] In June 1954, a prefectural youth council in southern Japan staged ten days of antihiropon events and speeches by police, pharmaceutical representatives, educational association leaders, and fishermen (the dominant occupational group in the region). The fourth meeting of the All-Japan Youth Problems Forum (Seishōnen mondai zenkoku kaigi), held in February 1955, attracted 195 participants, including police officials, cabinet members, and representatives of the Ministries of Welfare, Justice, Finance, Commerce, Labor, and Self-Defense. In May 1955, the journal *Seishōnen mondai* (Youth matters) devoted a special issue entirely to hiropon. Films such as *Hiropon wa akuma da* (Hiropon is the devil) and *Ushinawareta seishun* (Lost youth) doubled as publicity and entertainment, reinforcing the message against drugs in an increasingly available media likely to appeal to a juvenile audience.[81]

Mothers also organized against hiropon. Maternal associations dated back to the prewar period, when they sought to strengthen the nation by training women in how to raise morally and physically fit children.[82] In September 1954, mere weeks after the capture of Hosoda Kyōko's murderer, the Tokyo Haha no rengōkai (Tokyo Alliance of Mothers) assembled three thousand women to call for stricter punishment of hiropon traffickers, the expansion of addiction treatment facilities, and the complete eradication of the drug.[83] Meanwhile, teachers brought the antimethamphetamine message into the classroom. One article in an education journal encouraged homeroom instructors, "who have a special love for their students," to work closely with parents to reinforce the idea that "even one injection is dangerous." The author recommended suspending or expelling students who showed signs of hiropon use.[84] In February 1955, the Ministry of Education outlined a comprehensive plan for antinarcotics activities in schools. It tasked teachers with four responsibilities: 1) disseminating information and providing guidance to pupils, 2) offering extra help to weak-willed or "strange *[ijō seikaku]*" students, 3) detecting symptoms of drug use, and 4) working with families and neighborhoods to keep children safe.[85]

Block associations *(chōkai* or *chōnaikai)* facilitated cooperation between schools and communities. Voluntary neighborhood organizations originated in Japan's early modern age, when they served as instruments of self-policing and tax collection. During the Meiji period, modern law enforcement gradually took over many of these functions. In the early twentieth century, however, block associations emerged "from below" as channels of community solidarity, mutual aid, friendship, and communication with the national bureaucracy. Following the outbreak of total war, the government incorporated block associations into the administrative apparatus of the state to facilitate the spiritual unification and collective monitoring of the population.[86] Upon Japan's defeat, SCAP denounced *chōkai* as a means by which "the government reached into the lives of every citizen through a means more effective than the very effective police system." By 1951, however, the Occupation had come to view neighborhood associations as potential vehicles of democratization and "a broad base upon which Japan can create a civilization of fundamental newness."[87] During the early postwar years, *chōkai* membership was optional, but social pressure to join was so strong that participation was virtually universal. In a classic study of a Tokyo ward in the 1960s, sociologists Hiroshi Wagatsuma and George A. De Vos attributed Japan's low rate of juvenile delinquency partly to these local organizations.[88]

Like members of block associations, doctors and scientists found antimethamphetamine activism an effective means of restoring a sense of solidarity and professionalism. The study of addiction provided researchers with a means of joining the global scientific community from which they had become estranged during the war years. During the Occupation, heavy American influence in all disciplines, including medicine, bolstered the credibility of psychiatry, a languishing subfield in imperial Japan. Doctors who had resolutely upheld a physiological construction of addiction in the age of empire came to believe that prewar cures had failed because they had not addressed the psychological condition of the drug user: "Up until today . . . our efforts have been focused upon only such a treatment as to remove the addiction symptoms, and almost nothing else has been done in the psychological aspect of the victims to keep them, physically and mentally, away from their injurious habit of using narcotics. . . . Accordingly, there have been many cases in which those who have once been discharged . . . have had to repeat ineffective hospitalization, time and again."[89] By claiming the high-profile issue of methamphetamine addiction as their specialty, Japanese psychiatrists built professional credibility and demonstrated their value to society. In the words of Hemmi Takemitsu, "We psychiatrists of Japan learned many things from this nation-wide movement toward the abuse of central stimulants, particularly how we experts might participate in the activities of ordinary citizens. It can be said that this seemed to be the dawn of community psychiatry in Japan."[90]

In 1950, the National Diet passed the Mental Hygiene Law *(Seishin eisei hō)*. Drafted by Kaneko Junji, a former professor of criminal psychiatry and longtime moral entrepreneur, this legislation expanded the social and political role of psychiatrists by mandating the institutionalization of individuals suffering from various psychological disorders in new, state-subsidized mental facilities.[91] The following year, the government amended the law to add hiropon addicts to the roster of patients subject to involuntary confinement. By 1954, concerned citizens had identified over 4,000 candidates for hospitalization, but only 263 of the 37,849 beds in the nation's 224 mental asylums were available to drug users. The Diet allocated funding for 3,750 new places for recovering methamphetamine consumers in psychiatric clinics, but openings remained insufficient, compelling doctors to treat many stimulant users on an outpatient basis.[92]

Within asylums, physicians sought to provide a secure environment for methamphetamine withdrawal, a process often accompanied by sweating, insomnia, irregular appetite, anxiety, and signs of psychosis, including hallucinations, depression, and paranoia. Defining *addicts* as "persons who, of their own free will, are unable to give up the use of drugs," doctors plied convalescents with personality and intelligence tests and interviews, seeking to understand their motivation in consuming hiropon. They also attempted radical interventions such as electric and insulin shock treatment, lobotomy, and psychotherapy. To prevent relapse, asylums attempted to improve the social adjustment of recovering drug users through job training and family counseling.[93]

Doctors also responded to encouragement by the Japan Medical Association (Nihon Ishikai), the leading professional organization of its kind, to undertake laboratory research on methamphetamine addiction.[94] Eager to efface past estrangement and methodological differences with European and American physicians, Japanese scientists courted global publicity for their research on stimulants. Like their predecessors in the 1920s, they published studies in English- and German-language periodicals and collaborated with colleagues in the West.[95] During the 1950s, Dr. Maurice Seevers of the University of Michigan visited Japan eight times as the American coordinator of a cooperative research program on drug abuse, a venture cosponsored by the National Science Foundation and the Japan Society for the Promotion of Science. Seevers also hosted thirty-five Japanese postdoctoral researchers in Ann Arbor.[96]

In 1956, Tatetsu Seijun, Gotō Akio, and Fujiwara Takeshi, doctors at the Matsuzawa Mental Hospital, Japan's flagship psychiatric asylum and hiropon addiction treatment facility, published a book-length summary of their research findings over the preceding eight years. The authors argued that because methamphetamine consumption was first noticed as a social issue in Japan, Japanese psychiatrists had a responsibility to the world to develop the field.[97] Dr. Hirose Tetsuya received a one-year residential fellowship from the Narcotic Addiction Control Commission of New York to translate the text into English. In the preface of his work, Hirose observed, "Since the experience of the West is still far smaller than that in Japan with respect to methamphetamines, and far briefer, it would seem that there is much to be gained from an intensive study of that epidemic, its outcome, and any [lessons] which may be identified."[98] Some psychiatrists in Europe and the United States did in fact look to Japan for a model response to stimulants. In the context of rising methamphetamine consumption in Scandinavia, Swedish psychiatrist Nils Bejerot suggested, "The Japanese have shown how to combat a mass epidemic of advanced drug addiction."[99]

Reinserting Japan into the international scientific community after the rift of the 1930s and 1940s was the real accomplishment of Japanese addiction psychiatrists, who were unable to cure most or even many methamphetamine users. After eight years of clinical research, Tatetsu, Gotō, and Fujiwara could only conclude that the success of treatment "depended on the individual." Most of the case studies they presented—an orphaned harmonica player, an unemployed school dropout, a middle-aged bar hostess—failed to leave the hospital environment or relapsed and were returned by relatives or police.[100] Another asylum found that only eighteen out of sixty-eight patients remained drug-free six months after discharge.[101] Disillusioned, Hemmi began advocating the institutionalization of incorrigible addicts in jails and correctional facilities instead of mental hospitals.[102] In 1955, one psychiatrist published a cartoon depicting an addict crouching on the ground, a syringe poised above his big toe. Next to him, a burly policeman, mouth open in speech, thrust forward a pair of handcuffs. A doctor, identifiable through his signature white coat, stood in the distance behind the two figures.[103] Even in their own view, psychiatrists played only a background role in addressing the hiropon crisis.

POSTWAR, POSTNARCOTICS

By 1956, the moral panic over hiropon had passed its peak. Under headlines such as "Japan Gradually Winning Battle against Philopon," the media encouraged a cautious optimism regarding the disappearance of methamphetamine.[104] Violations of the Ban on Stimulant Drugs declined to about 6,700—less than 13 percent of the 1954 total. By 1958, the number of arrests had fallen below one thousand; barely two hundred suspects were indicted. Less than a quarter of all narcotics offenses involved stimulants, compared to over 90 percent in 1952–55.[105] Why did Japan succeed so completely and immediately in eradicating stimulants in the 1950s, when past crusades against drugs had mostly failed?

Hiropon was exceptional. The use of the phrase *hiropon age* in its own time suggests society's awareness that the drug was characteristic of a specific and passing temporal frame: the aftermath of war, defeat, and occupation.[106] Unlike opium, alcohol, or tobacco, hiropon never generated communities of interest to anchor it to the changing social landscape, transforming it from an artifact of exhaustion into a financial or psychological tool of recovery.[107] On the contrary, the long-standing connotation of dependence attached to addiction generated comprehensive efforts to remodel sick and helpless hiropon users as empowered and self-reliant citizens.

As high-speed growth created jobs and put an end to ubiquitous participation in the black market, drug trafficking shifted from the mainstream to the margins of society. By the end of the hiropon age, Japan's organized crime families, the yakuza, had laid claim to the stimulant trade. They found reluctant allies among many third-country nationals, similarly excluded from participation in public life. Over time, the yakuza also developed links to criminal syndicates in South Korea, Taiwan,

China, and Southeast Asia, as well as narco-states such as North Korea and Myanmar. By pushing the market into the hands of gangsters, the resolution of the hiropon crisis gave rise to a political economy and subculture based on narcotics. Policymakers have found this racket far more dangerous and difficult to combat than the petty operations of the hiropon age.[108]

The shift of the narcotics traffic to illegal organizations paralleled the demographic transformation of narcotics users into social Others. In the wake of the hiropon age, methamphetamine addicts, once the very incarnation of the nation, found themselves on its fringes. The figure of the emaciated, rag-clad youth injecting stimulants to quell hunger disappeared from public view and the popular imagination. Society no longer accepted juvenile delinquents as piteous victims of war. Rather, stimulant consumers came to be regarded as spoiled children in whom the experience of luxury had awakened a pernicious hedonism and indifference to the collective welfare.[109] For Kurosawa Akira's 1962 suspense drama *High and Low (Tengoku, jigoku)*, screenwriter Oguni Hideo, who had collaborated with producer Matsuzaki Keiji on *The Opium War* in 1943, scripted a scene in which the young suspect in an attempted kidnapping seeks a murder victim on Skid Row. The site of iniquity is plastered with signs in English and Korean. "You don't belong here," one addict admonishes the villain, a Japanese male, as he observes a woman writhing in the throes of withdrawal. At the end of the film, however, he becomes identified with the drug users, crumpling in the manner of an addict as he confesses his guilt and faces permanent exclusion from the national community through the ultimate punishment: execution.[110]

In the mid-1970s, following two decades of relatively minimal narcotics crime, the market for illegal substances experienced a sudden surge. During what became known as the "second stimulant epidemic," police took tens of thousands of suspects into custody annually for trafficking and consumption of *shabu*, a new variant of methamphetamine.[111] The outbreak aroused some concern among policymakers but failed to spark a moral panic comparable to the hiropon age. By this time, high-speed growth had transformed Japan into an advanced industrial capitalist state with the second-largest GDP in the world. Although illegal drugs were hardly a source of pride for the nation, they reflected Japan's attainment of the coveted status of a First World superpower, with all the social problems thereof. Murakami Ryū's 1976 novel *Kagiri naku tomei ni chikai buru- (Almost Transparent Blue)* won the Akutagawa Prize, a distinguished literary award for first-time authors, for its depiction of drug use as an inevitable outcome of Japan's participation in the global economy and (counter)culture. Within the work, only the narrator, Ryū, is clearly identifiable as Japanese. Other characters include a nude model of mixed descent, a hairdresser from Okinawa, a white prostitute, an African-American GI, and "foreigners" of various descriptions.[112] Drugs, Murakami suggested, were neither exceptional nor inimical to Japan, but simply a consumer choice in a borderless consumer society.

By the mid-1980s, the second stimulant epidemic had waned, but narcotics use in Japan remained far from minimal or marginal. Today, authorities count casual consumers in the millions, in addition to a *shabu* "addict" community of about four hundred thousand. In 2003, one study claimed that 1.7 percent of the nation's population age fifteen through sixty-four had abused methamphetamine.[113] American reporter Christopher Seymour concluded from an extended period of fieldwork, "There is no sector of Japanese society that doesn't pull its weight in [stimulant] consumption. Businessmen, politicians, housewives, laborers, students, entertainers, cabbies, pachinko players and yakuza themselves love the stuff."[114] A collection of testimonies from "reformed" drug users, edited by the government, included narratives by members of all of the above categories, as well as real estate agents, fishermen, Buddhist priests, farmers, state employees, and college students.[115] And yet, with the foundations of nationhood secure, postwar Japan has not witnessed the recrudescence of moral panic over methamphetamine.

Over the course of Japan's first century of participation in modern international relations, moral entrepreneurs called attention to drugs as a social problem and source of deviance in response to three distinct crises of political legitimacy. In the 1890s, alleged abstinence from opium allowed Japan to "leave Asia and enter the West"—to distinguish itself from its historical Other, China, in favor of alignment with the great powers of Europe and America. During the high imperial age between the end of World War I and Japan's defeat in World War II, moral entrepreneurs framed the very real issue of narcotics to reflect changing justifications of nationhood and empire. Cultural producers, merchants, judicial officers, scientific researchers, and medical doctors came together in a moral crusade against opium, legitimizing the empire through the rhetoric of benevolence and the nation-state of Manchukuo according to the Kingly Way. Finally, in the 1950s, methamphetamine addiction came to symbolize a collective identity of despair, defeat, and dependence. A public campaign against stimulants, the outcome of Japan's first and only moral panic concerning drugs, yielded measurable achievement in the quest for rejuvenation as a confident, cooperative, and legitimate nation-state. Overcoming hiropon allowed Japan to develop and demonstrate the global values of contemporary international society—to become, again, a moral nation.

NOTES

INTRODUCTION

1. "Japanese in the Dope-Drug Trade," *Peiping Chronicle*, Mar. 17, 1934.

2. Gerrit W. Gong, *The Standard of "Civilization" in International Society* (Oxford: Clarendon Press, 1984).

3. I use the term *values* to describe ideals of human thought and behavior. Values may or may not be ethical—that is, aligned with an abstract and universal standard of goodness. Societies have at times upheld unethical values leading to, for instance, eugenics, discrimination, and persecution. *Morality* refers to individual or group attempts to meet the values of a community. Morality, therefore, is only as ethical as the values it seeks to realize. On the relationship among morality, values, and ethics, see Arthur Kleinman, *What Really Matters: Living a Moral Life amidst Uncertainty and Danger* (New York: Oxford University Press, 2006).

4. In the classic formulation of Max Weber, legitimacy is "an order that enjoys the prestige of being considered binding . . . the readiness to conform with rules which are formally correct and have been imposed by accepted procedure." Max Weber, *The Theory of Social and Economic Organization*, trans. A. M. Henderson and Talcott Parsons (New York: Oxford University Press, 1947), 125.

5. I choose the term *crusade* because it encompasses not only the recognition of a problem but an active stand against it. The religious overtones of *crusade*, moreover, capture both the zeal and the salvationist aspirations of this type of social reaction. In the classic formulation of sociologist Howard Becker, "The crusader is not only interested in seeing to it that other people do what he thinks right. He believes that if they

do what is right it will be good for them." The alleged humanitarian objectives of moral crusades do not preclude and can even encourage participation motivated by self-interest. Howard Becker, *Outsiders: Studies in the Sociology of Deviance* (New York: Free Press, 1963), 148–49.

6. Scientifically speaking, narcotics are a class of poppy-based sedatives. In common parlance, the category typically encompasses any mind-altering substance subject to criminal regulation. Public health officers have at times even classified alcohol as a narcotic, although I do not do so here. For recent scholarship on the deviantization of drug use, see Erich Goode and Nachman Ben-Yehuda, *Moral Panics: The Social Construction of Deviance*, 2nd ed. (Malden, MA: Wiley-Blackwell, 2009), 197–217.

7. For the sake of variety, I use the term *drugs* interchangeably with *narcotics* (except in cases where greater clarity is desirable). On the problem of defining *drugs*, see Andrew Sherratt, "Introduction: Peculiar Substances," in Jordan Goodman, Paul E. Lovejoy, and Andrew Sherratt, eds., *Consuming Habits: Global and Historical Perspectives on How Cultures Define Drugs*, 2nd ed. (New York: Routledge, 2007), 1–10.

8. Carl Trocki, *Opium, Empire and the Global Political Economy: A Study of the Asian Opium Trade, 1750–1950* (New York: Routledge, 1999); David T. Courtwright, *Forces of Habit: Drugs and the Making of the Modern World* (Cambridge, MA: Harvard University Press, 2001); and Paul Gootenberg, *Andean Cocaine: The Making of a Global Drug* (Chapel Hill: University of North Carolina Press, 2008).

9. For an overview of commodity-led globalization, see Kenneth Pomeranz and Steven Topik, *The World That Trade Created: Society, Culture, and the World Economy, 1400 to the Present* (Armonk, NY: M. E. Sharpe, 2006). On specific commodities, see Sidney Mintz, *Sweetness and Power: The Place of Sugar in Modern History* (New York: Viking, 1985); Zhong Weimin, *Chaye yu yapian: Shijiu shiji jingji quanqiuhua zhong de Zhongguo* (Beijing: Sanlian shudian, 2010); Carol Benedict, *Golden-Silk Smoke: A History of Tobacco in China, 1550–2010* (Berkeley: University of California Press, 2011); and Michael R. Dove, *The Banana Tree at the Gate: A History of Marginal Peoples and Global Markets in Borneo* (New Haven, CT: Yale University Press, 2011).

10. Andre Schmid, *Korea between Empires, 1895–1919* (New York: Columbia University Press, 2002), 61. Although Japan had no real tradition of slavery, historian Daniel V. Botsman has shown that notions of freedom were deeply rooted in Japanese history, undergirding the emergence of the slave as a metaphor for coolies, prostitutes, outcastes, and other disenfranchised groups in the modern period. Daniel V. Botsman, "Freedom without Slavery? 'Coolies,' Prostitutes, and Outcastes in Meiji Japan's 'Emancipation Movement,'" *American Historical Review* 116, no. 5 (2011): 1323–47.

11. Quoted in R. Y. Lo, *The Opium Problem in the Far East* (Shanghai: Commercial Press, 1933), 56.

12. On geographic and political controversies regarding *Manchuria* as a place name, see Mark C. Elliott, "The Limits of Tartary: Manchuria in Imperial and National Geog-

raphies," *Journal of Asian Studies* 59, no. 3 (2000): 603–46; and Nakami Tatsuo, "Rekishi no naka no 'Manshū' zō," in Nakami Tatsuo, ed., *Manshū to wa nandatta no ka* (Tokyo: Fujiwara shoten, 2004). Chinese historians today often prefer to substitute *Dongbei* ("the Northeast") for *Manchuria,* or to preface the toponym with *wei* ("false") to signify its association with Japanese imperialism. In deference to pre-1945 primary sources and conventions in English-language scholarship, I use *Manchuria* to signify the imagined region of China that was the object of Japanese expansionism during the imperial age.

13. Kuroba Kiyotaka, *Jūgo nen sensō shi josetsu* (Tokyo: Sanshōtō, 1979), 203–51.

14. Alice Conklin, *A Mission to Civilize: The Republican Ideal of Empire in French West Africa, 1895–1930* (Stanford, CA: Stanford University Press, 1997), 7; Michael Adas, *Machines as the Measure of Men: Science, Technology, and Ideologies of Western Dominance* (Ithaca, NY: Cornell University Press, 1989), 200.

15. Historians have challenged the idea that consumption can be value-neutral, arguing that the figure of the "consumer" is inextricably embedded in a critique of capitalist immorality dating back to the nineteenth century. I use the word *consumer* here in the most basic sense, to signify physical ingestion. See Frank Dikötter, *Exotic Commodities: Modern Objects and Everyday Life in China* (New York: Columbia University Press, 2006), 11; and Frank Trentmann, "The Modern Genealogy of the Consumer: Meanings, Identities and Political Synapses," in John Brewer and Frank Trentmann, eds., *Consuming Cultures, Global Perspectives: Historical Trajectories, Transnational Exchanges,* 19–69 (New York: Berg, 2006). In sociological theory, the addict would occupy the position of a "folk devil." See Stanley Cohen, *Folk Devils and Moral Panics: The Creation of the Mods and Rockers,* 3rd ed. (New York: Routledge, 2002).

16. Sheldon Garon, *Molding Japanese Minds: The State in Everyday Life* (Princeton, NJ: Princeton University Press, 1997), 18–20.

17. Sociological studies of moral entrepreneurs have focused mainly on cultural producers or "the media." Chas Critcher, *Moral Panics and the Media* (Buckingham, PA: Open University Press, 2003), 17–18. In examining merchants, law enforcement, scientists, and doctors as moral entrepreneurs, I am broadening the category beyond its traditional scope.

18. Erez Manela, *The Wilsonian Moment: Self-Determination and the International Origins of Anticolonial Nationalism* (New York: Oxford University Press, 2007).

19. Susumu Fukui, Kiyoshi Wada, and Masaomi Iyo, "Epidemiology of Amphetamine Abuse in Japan and Its Social Implications," in Arthur K. Cho and David S. Segal, eds., *Amphetamine and Its Analogs: Psychopharmacology, Toxicology, and Abuse* (New York: Academic Press, 1994), 459–78.

20. On the concept of imagined communities, see Benedict Anderson, *Imagined Communities: Reflections on the Origin and Spread of Nationalism* (New York: Verso, 2006).

CHAPTER 1

1. Thomas De Quincey, *The Confessions of an English Opium Eater* (Tokyo: Hokuseido Press, 1928), 9.

2. James M. Polachek, *The Inner Opium War* (Cambridge, MA: Harvard University Council on East Asian Studies, 1992); Joyce Madancy, *The Troublesome Legacy of Commissioner Lin: The Opium Trade and Opium Suppression in Fujian Province, 1820s to 1920s* (Cambridge, MA: Harvard University Asia Center, 2003); David Anthony Bello, *Opium and the Limits of Empire: Drug Prohibition in the Chinese Interior, 1729–1850* (Cambridge, MA: Harvard University Asia Center, 2005).

3. Timothy Brook and Bob Tadashi Wakabayashi, "Introduction: Opium's History in China," in Timothy Brook and Bob Tadashi Wakabayashi, eds., *Opium Regimes: China, Britain, and Japan, 1839–1952* (Berkeley: University of California Press, 2000), 8; Elizabeth Kelly Gray, "The Trade-Off: Chinese Opium Traders and Antebellum Reform in the United States, 1815–1860," in James H. Mills and Patricia Barton, eds., *Drugs and Empires: Essays in Modern Imperialism and Intoxication, c. 1500–c. 1930* (New York: Palgrave Macmillan, 2007), 220–42.

4. William B. McAllister, *Drug Diplomacy in the Twentieth Century: An International History* (New York: Routledge, 2000), 27. On the Second Opium War, see J. Y. Wong, *Deadly Dreams: Opium, Imperialism, and the Arrow War (1856–1860) in China* (New York: Cambridge University Press, 1998).

5. Satō Saburō, *Kindai Nit-Chū kōshōshi no kenkyū* (Tokyo: Yoshikawa Kōbunkan, 1984), 185–220; Tan Romi, *Ahen no Chūgokushi* (Tokyo: Shinchōsha, 2005), 144–46.

6. Quoted in Hans Derks, *History of the Opium Problem: The Assault on the East, ca. 1600–1950* (Boston: Brill, 2012), 495.

7. Yamawaki Teijirō, *Kinsei Nihon no iyaku bunka* (Tokyo: Heibōsha, 1995), 173–98.

8. *Control of Opium in Japan: Report of the Japanese Delegates to the International Opium Commission* (Shanghai, 1909), 3–16.

9. Joshua A. Fogel, *Politics and Sinology: The Case of Naitō Konan (1866–1934)* (Cambridge, MA: Harvard University Council on East Asian Studies, 1984), 11; Joshua A. Fogel, *The Literature of Travel in the Japanese Rediscovery of China, 1862–1945* (Stanford, CA: Stanford University Press, 1996), 74–82.

10. Oka Senjin, *Kankō kiyū* (Tokyo, 1886), 10.

11. Sōmu-chō tōkei-kyoku, *Nihon chōki tōkei sōkan*, vol. 1 (Tokyo: Nihon tōkei kyōkai, 1987), 52.

12. "Shina imin," in Tani Mitsutaka, ed., *Tō-A Dōbun Shoin ahen chōsa hōkokusho*, CD-rom (Toyohashi: Aichi Daigaku Tō-A Dōbun Shoin Daigaku kinen senta-, 2007).

13. On the discovery of "society" and social problems in Meiji Japan, see Carol Gluck, *Japan's Modern Myths: Ideology in the Late Meiji Period* (Princeton, NJ: Princeton University Press, 1985).

14. On social Darwinism in Japan, see Julia Adeney Thomas, *Reconfiguring Modernity: Concepts of Nature in Japanese Political Ideology* (Berkeley: University of California Press, 2002); and Yuehtsen Juliette Chung, *Struggle for National Survival: Eugenics in Sino-Japanese Contexts, 1896–1945* (New York: Routledge, 2002).

15. On opium as "poison" in nineteenth-century Europe, see Louise Foxcroft, *The Making of Addiction: The 'Use and Abuse' of Opium in Nineteenth-Century Britain* (Burlington, VT: Ashgate, 2007), 110; and Howard Padwa, *Social Poison: The Culture and Politics of Opiate Control in Britain and France, 1821–1926* (Baltimore, MD: Johns Hopkins University Press, 2012).

16. Oka, *Kankō kiyū*, 35.

17. Margaret Pelling, "The Meaning of Contagion: Reproduction, Medicine and Metaphor," in Alison Bashford and Claire Hooker, eds., *Contagion: Historical and Cultural Studies* (New York: Routledge, 2001), 20; Angela Ki Che Leung, "The Evolution of the Idea of *Chuanran* Contagion in Imperial China," in Angela Ki Che Leung and Charlotte Furth, eds., *Health and Hygiene in Chinese East Asia: Policies and Publics in the Long Twentieth Century* (Durham, NC: Duke University Press, 2010), 25–50.

18. Andō Akimichi, *Kokusai ahen mondai kenkyū* (Dairen: Kantō-chō zaimubu, 1931), 1.

19. Tazawa Shingo, ed., *Ahen shiryō* (Taihoku: Tazawa kagaku kōgyō kenkyūjo, 1932), 93.

20. Although the Hartley case is generally understood as an abuse of the privilege of extraterritoriality, Richard T. Chang has argued that the historical record generally "fails to sustain the interpretation that the Western consular courts in Japan as a rule did not render evenhanded justice." Richard T. Chang, *The Justice of the Western Consular Courts in Nineteenth-Century Japan* (Westport, CT: Greenwood Press, 1984), 79.

21. "Nagasaki no gaikokujin inryūchi ni te Shinajin ga bōkō to hataraku koto," *Yomiuri Shinbun*, Sept. 30, 1883, 2.

22. James L. Huffman, *Creating a Public: People and Press in Meiji Japan* (Honolulu: University of Hawai'i Press, 1997), 59–66.

23. For example, see "Ahen han," *Yomiuri Shinbun*, June 16, 1887, 3; "Ahen mitsu yunyū," *Yomiuri Shinbun*, Sept. 20, 1887, 2; and "Ahen mitsu yunyū no roken," *Yomiuri Shinbun*, Apr. 27, 1890, 3. On Chinese conscript laborers and opium addiction, see Curtis Marez, *Drug Wars: The Political Economy of Narcotics* (Minneapolis: University of Minnesota Press, 2004), 39–69.

24. Matsui Kokichi, *Ei-Shin ahen sen shi* (Tokyo: Hakubunkan, 1895), 1, 5.

25. Wilbur F. Crafts, *Intoxicants & Opium in All Lands and Times: A Twentieth-Century Survey of Temperance, Based on a Symposium of Testimony from One Hundred Missionaries and Travelers* (Washington, DC: International Reform Bureau, 1911), 257; "The Japanese and Opium," *Journal of the American Medical Association* 36, no. 13 (1900): 896–97.

26. H. L. E. Johnson, "Medicine in the Far East," *Journal of the American Medical Association* 34, no. 5 (1900): 310; Crafts, *Intoxicants & Opium in All Lands and Times*, 231.

27. Noriko Kamachi, "The Chinese in Meiji Japan: Their Interactions with the Japanese before the Sino-Japanese War," in Akira Iriye, ed., *The Chinese and the Japanese: Essays in Political and Cultural Interactions* (Princeton, NJ: Princeton University Press, 1980), 58–73.

28. The agreements Japan signed with the West gave foreign nationals the right to reside only in segregated neighborhoods in the treaty ports. The desire of the great powers to terminate these restrictions gave Japan leverage in its quest to overturn the unequal treaties. In the 1890s, when Europe and the United States relinquished extraterritoriality and other privileges, Japan ended its isolation policy for Westerners. Eiji Oguma, *A Genealogy of "Japanese" Self-Images*, trans. David Askew (Melbourne: Trans Pacific Press, 2002), 16–30.

29. "Shinajin zakkyo no kyohi," "Shina rōdōsha," "Shina rōdōsha no kaigai yusō ni oite," and "Shinajin zakkyo mondai," in Tani, ed., *Tō-A Dōbun Shoin ahen chōsa hōkokusho.*

30. Miyajima Mikinosuke, "Opium Abuse and Its Control in Japan," *Japan Medical World* 3, no. 2 (1923): 29.

31. *Nihon teikoku tōkei nenkan*, vols. 11–32 (Tokyo: Tōkei kyōkai, 1892–1913). This statistical yearbook was called the *Dai Nihon teikoku tōkei nenkan* from 1937 to 1941 (vols. 55–59). To avoid confusion, I refer to it throughout as the *Nihon teikoku tōkei nenkan.*

32. Quoted in Tazawa, ed., *Ahen shiryō*, 80.

33. Mori Gōin, *Hoku-Man chihō no ahen* (Harbin: Harupin shohin chinritsu kan, 1925).

34. Kikuchi Yūji, "Ahen mondai ni kanshite (2)," *Dōjin* 4, no. 4 (1929): 25.

35. Gotō Asatarō, *Shina kidan: Ahen shitsu* (Tokyo: Marikaku shobō, 1928), 6.

36. United States Philippine Commission Opium Investigation Committee, *Use of Opium and Traffic Therein: Message from the President of the United States, Transmitting the Report of the Committee Appointed by the Philippine Commission to Investigate the Use of Opium and the Traffic Therein, and the Rules, Ordinances, and Laws Regulating Such Use and Traffic in Japan, Formosa, Shanghai, Hongkong, Saigon, Singapore, Burma, Java, and the Philippine Islands, and Inclosing a Letter from the Secretary of War Submitting the Report for Transmission* (Washington, DC: Government Printing Office, 1906), 22.

37. Osamu Dazai, *Self-Portraits: Tales from the Life of Japan's Great Decadent Romantic*, trans. Ralph F. McCarthy (New York: Kodansha International, 1991), 162.

38. Mayaku chūdokusha kyūgokai, *Mayaku chūdokusha kyūgokai nenpō* (*Shōwa 16*) (Tokyo: Mayaku chūdokusha kyūgokai, 1941), 32.

39. Keith McMahon, *The Fall of the God of Money: Opium Smoking in Nineteenth-Century China* (Lanham, MD: Rowman & Littlefield, 2002), 8.

40. Wilbur F. Crafts, *Opium Cures: Opinions of American and European Physicians in China as to the Medical and Governmental Aid That Should Be Given to Those Compelled by*

Anti-Opium Legislation in Many Lands to Break Off the Opium Habit, and to Others Voluntarily Turning from It (Washington, DC: International Reform Bureau, 1907), iv, 4.

41. Aoki kyozai zaidan, ed., *Shusei mondai kenkyū* (Tokyo: Aoki Shōzō, 1926), 50.

42. "Ahen gyōsei no nanji," *Taiwan Nippō*, Feb. 6, 1898, 2.

43. Padwa, *Social Poison*, 6–7.

44. United States Philippine Commission Opium Investigation Committee, *Use of Opium and Traffic Therein*, 71.

45. On antinarcotics legislation in Germany, see Robert P. Stephens, *Germans on Drugs: The Complications of Modernization in Hamburg* (Ann Arbor: University of Michigan Press, 2007). For the United States, see David F. Musto, *The American Disease: Origins of Narcotic Control*, 3rd ed. (New York: Oxford University Press, 1999). On the British case, see Terry M. Parssinen, *Secret Passions, Secret Remedies: Narcotic Drugs in British Society, 1820–1930* (Philadelphia: Institute for the Study of Human Issues, 1983); and Virginia Berridge, *Opium and the People: Opiate Use in Nineteenth-Century England* (New Haven, CT: Yale University Press, 1987).

46. *The Opium War* (Tokyo: Maruya and Kigyōsha, 1890), 5.

47. Joshua Rowntree, *The Imperial Drug Trade: A Restatement of the Opium Question in Light of Recent Evidence and New Developments in the East* (London: Methuen, 1906), 253, 255.

48. Homi Bhabha, *The Location of Culture* (New York: Routledge, 1994), 125–28.

49. Shimpei Gotō, "The Administration of Formosa (Taiwan)," in Shigenobu Ōkuma and Marcus B. Huish, eds., *Fifty Years of New Japan* (New York: E. P. Dutton, 1909), 2:530.

50. Edward I-te Chen, "The Attempt to Integrate the Empire: Legal Perspectives," in Ramon Myers and Mark Peattie, eds., *The Japanese Colonial Empire, 1895–1945* (Princeton, NJ: Princeton University Press, 1984), 240–74; Asano Toyomi, *Teikoku Nihon no shokuminchi hōsei: Hōiki tōgō to teikoku chitsujo* (Nagoya: Nagoya Daigaku shuppankai, 2008).

51. Mizuno Jun, *Taiwan ahen shobun* (Tokyo: Mizuno Jun, 1898), 22.

52. Mizobe Hideaki, "Gotō Shinpei ron: Tōsōteki sekai zō to 'risei no dokusai,'" *Hōgaku ronsō* 100, no. 2 (1976): 62–96.

53. Liu Jin-tan, Liu Jin-long, and Chow Shin-yi, *The Demand for Opium in Colonial Taiwan, 1914–1942* (Taipei: Academia Sinica Institute of Economics, 1996), 5.

54. For a comprehensive account of Japanese regulation of opium in colonial Taiwan, see Ryū Meishū, *Taiwan tōchi to ahen mondai* (Tokyo: Yamakawa shuppansha, 1983).

55. Kaku Sagatarō, *Opium Policy in Japan* (Geneva: Albert Kundig, 1924), 19; Tsurumi Yūsuke, *Gotō Shinpei den: Taiwan tōchi hen* (Tokyo: Taiheiyō kyōkai shuppanbu, 1943), 604.

56. Mizuno Jun, "Shina ahen en haishi ron," *Yomiuri Shinbun*, Nov. 29, 1895, 1.

57. Mizuno, *Taiwan ahen shobun*, 11, 18, 10. For an analysis of Mizuno's perspective on opium, see Yamada Gōichi, "Taiwan senbai shi josetsu: Mizuno Jun 'Taiwan ahen

shobun' to Gotō Shinpei 'Taiwanjima ahen seido ni kansuru iken,'" *Shakai kagaku tōkyū* 38, no. 4 (1992): 31–68.

58. Katō Hisayuki, *Taiwan ni okeru ahen* (Taihoku, 1906), 37, 1–3, 7.

59. Ishiguro Tadanori, "Taiwan ni okeru ahen en ni oite," *Yomiuri Shinbun*, Jan. 24, 1897, 3.

60. "Ahen hōan," *Yomiuri Shinbun*, Mar. 12, 1897, 3.

61. *Control of Opium in Japan*, 65.

62. *Nihon teikoku tōkei nenkan* 27 (1908), 925.

63. "Taiwan seiji no dai mokuteki," *Taiwan Nippō*, Aug. 7, 1897; "Taiwan seiji no dai mokuteki," *Taiwan Nippō*, Aug. 11, 1897, 1.

64. "Ahen rei jisshi oite chūi," *Taiwan Nippō*, Aug. 25, 1897, 2; "Ahen gyōseki no genkyō," *Taiwan Nippō*, July 6, 1897, 1; "Shinminsei-kyoku chō to ahen rei," *Taiwan Nippō*, Mar. 13, 1898, 1.

65. Takekoshi Yosaburō, *Japanese Rule in Formosa*, trans. George Braithwaite (Taipei: SMC, 1907), 154.

66. Yamada Gōichi, "Taiwan senbai sei no tenkai katei," *Shakai kagaku tōkyū* 44, no. 1 (1998): 1–37; Hui-yu Caroline Tsai, *Taiwan in Japan's Empire-Building: An Institutional Approach to Colonial Engineering* (New York: Routledge, 2009), 113–39.

67. Uga Jirō, *Taiwan ahen shi* (Taihoku: Taiwan Sōtokufu senbai-kyoku, 1926), 405.

68. "Ahen inja to Taihoku Iin," *Taiwan Nippō*, Oct. 14, 1897, 2.

69. Kimura Kingo, "Ahen inja taikaku kensa dai ichi hōkoku," *Taiwan Igakkai zasshi* (hereafter *TIZ*) 2, no. 3 (1903): 1–5.

70. Between 1911 and 1929 (vols. 10–28), the *TIZ* did not publish any research on opium addiction by doctors practicing in Taiwan.

71. *Taiwan no ahen seido* (Taihoku: Taiwan Sōtokufu keimu-kyoku, 1939), 3–5; Taiwan Sōtokufu, *Taiwan tōkei sho* 8–15 (Taihoku: Sōtokufu, 1904–11).

72. Quoted in Rowntree, *The Imperial Drug Trade*, 253.

73. Crafts, *Intoxicants & Opium in All Lands and Times*, 144.

74. Rowntree, *The Imperial Drug Trade*, 260.

75. "Savage Island of Formosa Transformed by Japanese: Wonders Worked in a Few Years with a People That Others Had Failed to Subdue—A Lesson for Other Colonizing Nations," *New York Times*, Sept. 24, 1904.

76. United States Philippine Commission Opium Investigation Committee, *Use of Opium and Traffic Therein*, 25.

CHAPTER 2

1. To emphasize the distinction between the KLT and Japan's formal colonies, such as Taiwan and Korea, I refer to it as a leasehold or city-state.

2. League of Nations Advisory Committee on the Traffic in Opium and Other Dangerous Drugs (OAC), "Annual Report on the Traffic in Opium and Other Dangerous Drugs for the Year 1935" (Geneva, 1937), 25.

3. Cohen, *Folk Devils and Moral Panics,* xxviii.

4. The impulse to seek order and reassurance of political legitimacy through "facts" has been documented in many modern states and empires; yet, in the words of one historian, "no other colonial power in the world invested more energy in knowing the colonized" than Japan. Yao Jin-to, "The Japanese Colonial State and Its Form of Knowledge in Taiwan," in Liao Ping-Hui and David Der-Wei Wang, eds., *Taiwan under Japanese Colonial Rule 1895–1945: History, Culture, and Memory* (New York: Columbia University Press, 2006), 41. On knowledge and power, see Michel Foucault, "Governmentality," trans. Rosi Braidotti, in Graham Burchell, Colin Gordon, and Peter Miller, eds., *Studies in Governmentality: The Foucault Effect* (Chicago: University of Chicago Press, 1991), 87–104; and Arjun Appadurai, *Modernity at Large: Cultural Dimensions of Globalization* (Minneapolis: University of Minnesota Press, 1996), 115–17.

5. This gazetteer was titled *Kantō Totokufu tōkei sho* for the years 1906–17 inclusive (vols. 1–12), *Kantō-chō tōkei sho* from 1918 to 1933 (vols. 13–28), and *Kantō-kyoku tōkei sho* for 1934 to 1941 (vols. 29–36). For the sake of consistency, I refer to it as the *Kantō tōkei sho.* After 1941, the constraints associated with total war likely prevented the publication of the gazetteer.

6. I have found no references to the gazetteers in the writings of moral entrepreneurs. The data, moreover, were not assembled in a way that suggests an intention to make longitudinal calculations. Measures change year to year, categories are unclear, and the collection process is not described. On the use of numbers in moral crusades, see Joel Best, *Damned Lies and Statistics: Untangling Numbers from the Media, Politicians, and Activists* (Berkeley: University of California Press, 2001).

7. *Kantō tōkei sho* 3 (1908).

8. Totokufu Minsei-chō, "Ahen torishimari ni kansuru kettei," Aug. 12, 1911, in *Manshū ni okeru enkan toba hanzai shobun iken.*

9. "1938 Manchukuo Annual Report," in R. L. Jarman, ed., *Japan and Dependencies: Political and Economic Reports 1906–1960*, vol. 16, *Manchukuo: Political and Economic Reports 1937–1941* (Oxford: Archive Editions, 1993), 68.

10. Chian-bu keimu-shi, *Eisei keisatsu* (Shinkyō: Manshūkoku keisatsu kyōkai, 1938), 59.

11. Naimushō, "Kantōshū ahen rei ni oite," in *Ahen sono ta dokuzaiyaku oyobi kyūshoku kigu torishimari kankei zakken: Honpō no bu—Kantōshū, Seitō, Taiwan ni okeru ahen seido teppai mondai.*

12. Letter from Koga Renzō to Shidehara Kijūrō, Jan. 30, 1918, in *Ahen sono ta dokuzaiyaku oyobi kyūshoku kigu torishimari kankei zakken: Honpō no bu—Kantōshū, Seitō, Taiwan ni okeru ahen seido teppai mondai.*

13. Matsubara Nobuyuki, *Kantōshū ahen seido shi* (Dairen: Kantō-chō senbai-kyoku, 1932), 466–67.

14. David T. Courtwright, *Dark Paradise: Opiate Addiction in America before 1940* (Cambridge, MA: Harvard University Press, 1982), 117. Investigating the extent to which the KLT registration system undercounted narcotics consumers, sociologist Bingham Dai visited a government pharmacy in Dairen in April 1929 and found "not a single case in which the buyer or smoker was required to show his smoking permit." Bingham Dai, "The Opium Condition in Manchuria: The Report of an Investigation Conducted in May and June, 1929," *Opium: A World Problem* 3, no. 2 (1929): 10.

15. When the great powers convened in 1899 to establish a common classification system for diseases, they excluded addiction to narcotics. William Johnston, *The Modern Epidemic: A History of Tuberculosis in Japan* (Cambridge, MA: Harvard University Council on East Asian Studies, 1995), 71. Doctors today generally deem chronic addiction to narcotics a contributing factor rather than an acute cause in mortality.

16. For example, see R. K. Newman, "Opium Smoking in Late Imperial China: A Reconsideration," *Modern Asian Studies* 29, no. 4 (1995): 765–94.

17. The unusually high death rate in 1916 may reflect conditions associated with Japan's declaration of war on Germany and attack on the German colony of Jiaozhou Bay, located due south of Dairen. Mortality is calculated from data in *Kantō tōkei sho*, vols. 3–36 (1908–41). By comparison, the death rate from opium overdose in early twentieth-century England has been estimated at 0.2 per one hundred thousand population. Berridge, *Opium and the People*, 236.

18. Kin Juhō, "Dairen to watashi wo tsunagu unmei no kei," in Nakami, ed., *Manshū to wa nandatta no ka*, 505.

19. D. M. B. Collier and Lt.-Col. L'E. Malone, *Manchoukuo: Jewel of Asia* (London: George Allen & Unwin, 1936), 155; "1936 Manchukuo Annual Report," in Jarman, ed., *Japan and Dependencies*, vol. 15, *Manchukuo—Political and Economic Reports 1935–1937*, 149.

20. On the concept of superfluous men, see Hannah Arendt, *The Origins of Totalitarianism* (New York: Harcourt Brace Jovanovich, 1951), 187–88. On *tairiku rōnin*, see Nakami Tatsuo, "Gaikokujin ni wa rikai shigatai: Nihon shi no kotoba 'tairiku rōnin' to sono shūben," *Nihon rekishi* 704 (2007): 126–31.

21. Kuroshima Denji, *A Flock of Swirling Crows and Other Proletarian Writings*, trans. Zeljko Cipris (Honolulu: University of Hawai'i Press, 2005), 147–48. *Busō seru shigai* was set in Qingdao (Seitō), which was administered by Japan in 1916–22.

22. *Kantō tōkei sho*, vols. 3–36 (1908–41). Data is not available for 1932.

23. Data is not available for 1932 and 1933. Chinese historians have estimated that, in the 1930s, up to 85 percent of the Chinese in Dairen were drug users. If accurate, this figure would include one-time and casual users as well as heavy and dependent consumers. Wang Jinxiang, *Zhongguo jindu jianshi* (Beijing: Xuexi chubanshe, 1996), 231; Gao

Shaoyu, "Qianxi Riben diguo zhuyi dui Hua de yapian qinlüe," in Li Lilun, ed., *Dalian jindai shi yanjiu*, vol. 2 (Dalian: Dalian shi jindai shi yanjiusuo, 2005), 89.

24. Kantō-chō, "Kantōshū ahen oyobi mayaku seido gaiyō," in Kurahashi Masanao, ed., *Benzoirin fusei yunyū jiken kankei shiryō* (Tokyo: Fuji shuppan, 2003), 104.

25. Jonathan Spence, "Opium Smoking in Ch'ing China," in Frederic E. Wakeman Jr. and Carolyn Grant, eds., *Conflict and Control in Late Imperial China* (Berkeley: University of California Press, 1975), 145.

26. Kuroi Tadaichi, "Ahen moruhine chūdokusha ni taisuru henshitsuzai no chiryō seiseki," *Jūzenkai zasshi* 33, no. 8 (1928): 1–64.

27. Thomas Szasz, *Ceremonial Chemistry: The Ritual Persecution of Drugs, Addicts and Pushers*, rev. ed. (New York: Syracuse University Press, 2003), 202.

28. This figure was obtained by dividing Kuroi's tally of doctors with opium smoking permits (227) by the number of medical personnel in the KLT in 1930 (6,481), as reported in Kantō-chō, *Shōwa go nen Kantō-chō kokusai chōsa kekka hyō* (Ryōjun: Kantō-chō chōkan kanbō chōsaka, 1933), 70.

29. Shūhō Masasue, "'Morufuin' mata wa 'heroin' chūdokusha no 'morufuin' mata wa 'heroin' no teikōryoku ni oite," *Chōsen Igakkai zasshi* 22, no. 9 (1932): 108–12.

30. International Labor Office, *Opium and Labor: Being a Report on a Documentary Investigation into the Extent and Effects of Opium Smoking among Workers* (Geneva: League of Nations, 1935), 9, 42.

31. "Dongsan yanguo shikuang," *Judu yuekan* 42 (1930): 23–32.

32. OAC, "Report by the Kwantung Bureau for the Calendar Year 1937 on the Traffic in Opium and Other Dangerous Drugs" (Geneva, 1939), 19; OAC, "Report by the Kwantung Bureau for the Calendar Year 1938 on the Traffic in Opium and Other Dangerous Drugs" (Geneva, 1940), 44.

33. Kurahashi Masanao, "Nazo no ahen tokkō yaku: Tōkōzai," *Kiyū: Chiiki kenkyū* 40 (2008): 63–85; "Jin Mingshe zhengci," in Zhongguo di'er lishi dang'anguan, Zhongyang dang'anguan, and Jilin sheng shehui kexueyuan, eds., *Riben diguo zhuyi qin Hua dang'an ziliao xianpian* (Beijing: Zhonghua shiyu chuban, 1991), 14:820; Chen Yi, "Wei-Man fandu he xishi yapian yan jianwen," in Wenshi jinghua bianjibu, ed., *Jindai Zhongguo yandu xiezhen* (Shijiazhuang: Hebei renmin chubanshe, 1997), 250–52.

34. "Dairen Kyūryōsho yōran," in Shin Kitsu and Nagaoka Masami, eds., *Shokuminchi shakai jigyō kankei shiryō shū—Manshū, Manshūkoku*, vol. 9, *Kantōshū no bu: Iryō to eisei* (Tokyo: Kindai shiryō, 2005), 135. The physiological risks of alkaloid consumption, which greatly exceeded those of smoking opium, likely contributed to the rising dominance of refined narcotics consumers among hospital admissions.

35. Tawara Yutaka, *Man-Mō fūzoku taikan* (Tokyo: Otani Tokunosuke, 1939), 237; Dai, "The Opium Condition in Manchuria," 1–23.

36. Inoue Kōbai, *Chūka mangekyō* (Tokyo: Umiushisha, 1993), 172.

37. Amleto Vespa, *Secret Agent of Japan* (Boston: Little, Brown, 1938), 103.

38. Itō Ryōichi, "Hōten fujin ni oite mitsubai seraruru mayaku 'hakumenyaku' ni oite," *MIZ* 27, no. 4 (1937): 523–33.

39. Satō Shin'ichirō, *Daikan'en no kaibō: Kan minzoku shakai jittai chōsa* (Tokyo: Hara shobō, 2002), 69.

40. Richard L.-G. Deverall, *Red China's Dirty Drug War* (Tokyo: Toyoh Printing, 1954), 170. Deverall's observation dates from his service (1945–1948) in the United States occupation.

41. "Japan, and Opium in China," *Journal of the American Medical Association* 52, no. 17 (1909): 1339; Ruth Rogaski, "Vampires in Plagueland: The Multiple Meanings of *Weisheng* in Manchuria," in Leung and Furth, eds., *Health and Hygiene in Chinese East Asia*, 132–59.

42. Frank Dikötter, *Narcotic Culture: A History of Drugs in China* (London: Hurst, 2004), 146–72; Henrietta Harrison, "Narcotics, Nationalism and Class in China: The Transition from Opium to Morphine and Heroin in Early Twentieth-Century Shanxi," *East Asian History* 32/33 (2006/2007): 151–76.

43. Yangwen Zheng, *The Social Life of Opium in China* (New York: Cambridge University Press, 2005), 78. The bannermen were a hereditary elite tasked with defending China under the Qing dynasty (1644–1911). They were demobilized following the establishment of the Chinese Republic.

44. *Courtesans and Opium: Romantic Illusions by the Fool of Yangzhou*, trans. Patrick Hanan (New York: Columbia University Press, 2009), 6.

45. Dai, "The Opium Condition in Manchuria," 19.

46. Xavier Paulès, "Drogue et transgressions socials: Les femmes et l'opium à Canton dans les années 1930," *Clio* 28 (2008): 225–44.

47. Shenyang jingcha-ting weishengke, "Shenyang jingcha-ting san nian weisheng nianjian," *Dongfang yixue zazhi* 15 (1937): 40. For more on "hostesses" in opium retail establishments, see Norman Smith, *Intoxicating Manchuria: Alcohol, Opium, and Culture in China's Northeast* (Vancouver: University of British Columbia Press, 2012), 111–33.

48. Kō Toriu, "Mansei ahen mayaku chūdoku no josei seiki ni oyobosu eikyō no shikenteki narabi ni rinshōteki kenkyū," *MIZ* 30, no. 5 (1939): 876.

49. Ibid., 877.

50. Manshū Ika Daigaku, *Manshū Ika Daigaku gyōseki shū dai ni ken (Shōwa 14–16)* (Hōten: Manshū Ika Daigaku, 1942), 30.

51. *Kantō tōkei sho*, vols. 12–36 (1912–41). Data are not available for 1932.

52. Sakai Yoshio, *Kokka minzoku wo metsubō seshimuru ahen no maryoku* (Tokyo: Shintō kagaku kenkyūjo, 1938), 17.

53. Kuroi, "Ahen moruhine chūdokusha ni taisuru henshitsuzai no chiryō seiseki," 25.

54. International Labor Office, *Opium and Labor*, 45.

55. C. Walter Young, "Chinese Colonization and the Development of Manchuria," in J. B. Condliffe, ed., *Problems of the Pacific: Proceedings of the Third Conference of the Institute of Pacific Relations* (Chicago: University of Chicago Press, 1930), 430.

56. Yanagisawa Asobu, "Dairen kō no rōdō," in Matsumura Takao, Jie Xueshi, and Eda Kenji, eds., *Mantetsu rōdō shi no kenkyū* (Tokyo: Nihon keizai hyōronsha, 2002), 249–84; Fukusho kakō kabushiki kaisha, "Hekizansō seikatsu fuku," in Shin and Nagaoka, eds., *Shokuminchi shakai jigyō kankei shiryō shū—Manshū, Manshūkoku*, vol. 5, *Kantōshū no bu: Shakai jigyō no jissen*, 217.

57. Minami Manshū tetsudō kabushiki kaisha chōsabu, *Mantetsu tōkei nenpō* (Dairen: Minami Manshū tetsudō kabushiki kaisha, 1911), 346–83; Fukusho kakō kabushiki kaisha, "Hekizansō seikatsu fuku," 219; Paul H. Kratoska, ed., *Asian Labor in the Wartime Japanese Empire: Unknown Histories* (Armonk, NY: M. E. Sharpe, 2005); Mark Driscoll, *Absolute Erotic, Absolute Grotesque: The Living, Dead, and Undead in Japan's Imperialism, 1895–1945* (Durham, NC: Duke University Press, 2010), 25–56.

58. Fukusho kakō kabushiki kaisha, "Hekizansō seikatsu fuku," 211; Eda Izumi, "Seikatsu," in Matsumura, Jie, and Eda, eds., *Mantetsu rōdō shi no kenkyū*, 375–415; Takenaka Ken'ichi, *Dairen rekishi sanpō* (Tokyo: Kōseisha, 2008), 117.

59. Kobayashi Hideo and Zhang Zhiqiang, eds., *Ken'etsu sareta tegami ga kataru: Manshūkoku no jittai* (Tokyo: Shōgakkan, 2006), 97–98.

60. Su Zhiliang, *Zhongguo dupin shi* (Shanghai: Shanghai renmin chubanshe, 1997), 391.

61. Kantō-kyoku kanbō bunshoka, *Kantō-kyoku yōran* (Dairen: Kantō-kyoku kanbō bunshoka, 1939), 183.

62. Thomas Gottschang and Diana Lary, *Swallows and Settlers: The Great Migration from North China to Manchuria* (Ann Arbor: University of Michigan Press, 2000).

63. On labor resistance, see Tanaka Tsunejirō, *"Manshūkoku" ni okeru han-Man kō-Nichi undō no kenkyū* (Tokyo: Rokuin shobō, 1997); and Matsumura, Jie, and Eda, eds., *Mantetsu rōdō shi no kenkyū.*

64. James C. Scott, *Weapons of the Weak: Everyday Forms of Peasant Resistance* (New Haven, CT: Yale University Press, 1985); Ted Goldberg, *Demystifying Drugs: A Psychosocial Perspective* (New York: St. Martin's Press, 1999); Daniel Bradburd and William Jankowiak, "Drugs, Desire, and European Expansion," in William Jankowiak and Daniel Bradburd, eds., *Drugs, Labor, and Colonial Expansion* (Tucson: University of Arizona Press, 2003), 27.

65. W. S. Caldwell, "Medicine in the Far East," *Journal of the American Medical Association* 34, no. 10 (1900): 637–38; International Labor Office, "Opium and Labor," 57.

66. Iijima Wataru, *Mararia to teikoku: Shokuminchi igaku to Higashi Ajia no kōiki chitsuryō* (Tokyo: Tokyo Daigaku shuppankai, 2005), 343.

67. These numbers do not include the vast numbers of migrants who arrived in Dairen by foot, rail, or (in rare cases) air. In 1927, C. Walter Young of the Institute for Pacific

Relations estimated that 20 percent of incoming Chinese reached the city via a land route. The South Manchuria Railway Company Research Bureau calculated that over half of Chinese laborers leaving Manchuria between 1924 and 1933 boarded trains from Dairen. Young, "Chinese Colonization and the Development of Manchuria," 430; Keizai chōsabu, *Manshū no kuri* (Dairen: Minami Manshū tetsudō kabushiki kaisha, 1934), 24.

68. Louise Young, *Japan's Total Empire: Manchuria and the Culture of Wartime Imperialism* (Berkeley: University of California Press, 1998), 263.

69. Dai, "The Opium Condition in Manchuria," 13.

70. Gotō Asatarō, *Shina oyobi Manshū ryokō annai* (Tokyo: Shun'yōdō, 1932), 360. On Japanese writers who sampled the mainland drug scene, see Driscoll, *Absolute Erotic, Absolute Grotesque*, 161–202; and Liu Jianhui, *Demon Capital Shanghai: The "Modern" Experience of Japanese Intellectuals*, trans. Joshua A. Fogel (Portland, ME: MerwinAsia, 2012).

71. Zhou Jue, "'Manzhouguo' he yapian lingbaisuo," in Tao Kangde, ed., *Yapian zhi jinxi* (Shanghai: Yuzhou feng she chuban, 1937), 9–13.

72. Jeffrey E. Hanes, *The City as Subject: Seki Hajime and the Reinvention of Modern Osaka* (Berkeley: University of California Press, 2002), 176. On the social and economic world of Japanese migrants to Dairen, see Yanagisawa Asobu, *Nihonjin no shokuminchi keiken: Dairen Nihonjin shōkōgyōsha no rekishi* (Tokyo: Aoki shoten, 1999); and Tsukase Susumu, *Manshū no Nihonjin* (Tokyo: Yoshikawa Kōbunkan, 2004).

73. Keizai chōsabu, *Manshū no kuri*, 44. From the 1890s through the end of World War II, approximately 25 million Chinese migrated from the overpopulated and arid plains of northern China to Manchuria; two-thirds eventually returned home. Gottschang and Lary, *Swallows and Settlers*, 1–12; James Reardon-Anderson, *Reluctant Pioneers: China's Expansion Northward, 1644–1937* (Stanford, CA: Stanford University Press, 2005), 147–59. On the migrants themselves, see Matsushige Mitsuhiro, "Shokuminchi Dairen ni okeru Kajin shakai no tenkai: 1920 nendai shotō Dairen Kashōdantai no katsudō wo chūshin ni," in Soda Saburō, ed., *Kindai Chūgoku to Nihon—Teikei to tekitai no han seiki* (Tokyo: Ochanomizu shobō, 2001), 107–37; Uchiyama Masao, "Minkoku shoki no Santō kara no tōhoku imin," in Honjō Hisako, ed., *Nihon no Seitō senryō to Santō no shakai keizai* (Tokyo: Tōyō Bunko, 2006), 325–46; and Matsushige Mitsuhiro, "Dai ichiji taisen sengo ni okeru Dairen no 'Santō hō,'" in Honjō, ed., *Nihon no Seitō senryō to Santō no shakai keizai*, 347–68.

74. Shūsaku Endō, *The Final Martyrs*, trans. Van C. Gessel (New York: New Directions, 2009), 122.

75. *Kantō tōkei sho*, vols. 7–20 (1912–25).

76. On urban planning in Dairen, see Koshizawa Akira, "Dairen no toshi keikaku shi," *Nit-Chū keizai kyōkai kaikoku* 134/135/136 (1984): 1–50; Robert John Perrins, "'Great Connections': The Creation of a City, Dalian, 1905–1931: China and Japan on the Liaodong Peninsula" (PhD diss., York University, 1997); Nishizawa Yasuhiko,

Zusetsu Dairen toshi monogatari (Tokyo: Kawade shobō shinsha, 1999); Inoue Hisashi, *Inoue Hisashi no Dairen: Shashin to chizu de miru Manshū* (Tokyo: Shōgakkan, 2002); Hashiya Hiroshi, *Teikoku Nihon to shokuminchi toshi* (Tokyo: Yoshikawa Kōbunkan, 2004); and Christian A. Hess, "From Colonial Jewel to Socialist Metropolis: Dalian 1895–1955" (PhD diss., University of California at San Diego, 2006).

77. Marshall Berman, *All That Is Solid Melts into Air: The Experience of Modernity* (New York: Simon and Schuster, 1982), 5–12; James C. Scott, *Seeing Like a State: How Certain Schemes to Improve the Human Condition Have Failed* (New Haven, CT: Yale University Press, 1998), 103–46.

78. Carl Schorske, *Fin-de-Siècle Vienna: Politics and Culture* (New York: Alfred A. Knopf, 1980), 40.

79. T. Philip Terry, *Terry's Guide to the Japanese Empire* (Boston: Houghton Mifflin, 1930), 757.

80. South Manchuria Railway Company, *Third Report on Progress in Manchuria to 1932* (Dairen: South Manchuria Railway Company, 1932), 128.

81. For example, see Kiyooka Takayuki, "Akashiya no Dairen," in *Kiyooka Takayuki Dairen shōsetsu zenshū* (Tokyo: Bungeisha, 1992), 65–156.

82. Nishihara Kazumi, "Shashin ni miru 'Manshū' ime-ji," in Nakami, ed., *Manshū to wa nandatta no ka,* 113–26; Tomita Shōji, "Yamato Hoteru to teikoku hoteru," in Yoshida Yōji and Fujiwara Yoshio, eds., *Mantetsu to wa nandatta no ka* (Tokyo: Fujiwara shoten, 2006), 206–7.

83. H. W. Kinney, *Modern Manchuria* (Dairen: South Manchuria Railway Company, 1928), 44–45.

84. Berman, *All That Is Solid Melts into Air,* 5.

CHAPTER 3

1. On Japan's post–World War I crisis of legitimacy, see Frederick R. Dickinson, *War and National Reinvention: Japan and the Great War, 1914–1919* (Cambridge, MA: Harvard University Asia Center, 1999).

2. In the empires of the West, the "mission to civilize" was born of liberal republican ideals, including a universalistic rejection of tyranny and clericalism; the ardent patriotism of a loyal, disciplined, and enlightened citizenry; capitalist individualism; and faith in reason, science, and the perfectibility of mankind. "Progress" on the part of colonial subjects involved substituting the values of modern "civilization" for "backward" practices that transgressed Euro-American norms. Never coherently transcribed, the mission to civilize nonetheless functioned as an essential rationalization of imperialism for all the great powers. Conklin, *A Mission to Civilize,* 1–10.

3. James H. Mills and Patricia Barton, "Introduction," in Mills and Barton, eds., *Drugs and Empires,* 1–16.

4. Zhai Xin, *Tō-A Dōbunkai to Chūgoku: Kindai Nihon ni okeru taigai rinen to sono jissen* (Tokyo: Keiō Daigaku shuppankai, 2001), 15.

5. Douglas R. Reynolds, "Training Young China Hands: Tōa Dōbun Shoin and Its Precursors, 1886–1945," in Peter Duus, Ramon H. Myers, and Mark R. Peattie, eds., *The Japanese Informal Empire in China, 1895–1945* (Princeton, NJ: Princeton University Press, 1989), 227.

6. "'Yuehan' ensen keizai chōsa han," "Min yori Shō e," in Tani, ed., *Tō-A Dōbun Shoin ahen chōsa hōkokusho.*

7. Kishū han, "Hōmyō nikki," in ibid.

8. Tō-A Dōbun Shoin, "Kōyaku chōsa hōkoku sho," *Aichi Daigaku kokusai mondai kenkyūjo kiyō tokushū gō* 93 (1991): 134.

9. Reynolds, "Training Young China Hands," 263.

10. Dōjinkai, *Dōjinkai yonjū nen shi* (Tokyo: Dōjinkai zaidan hōjin, 1943), 195, 205.

11. Shintō kagaku kenkyūjo, ed., *Ahen oyobi ruiji "arukaroido" mansei chūdokushō no kōkateki chiryō to sono hōsaku* (Tokyo: Shintō kagaku kenkyūjo, 1936), 1.

12. Sakai Yoshio, "Mayaku mansei chūdokushō," *Dōjin* 9, no. 11 (1935): 34–39.

13. Shintō kagaku kenkyūjo, ed., *Ahen oyobi ruiji "arukaroido" mansei chūdokushō no kōkateki chiryō to sono hōsaku,* 10.

14. Sakai, *Kokka minzoku wo metsubō seshimuru ahen no maryoku,* 21–22.

15. Yoshihisa Tak Matsusaka, *The Making of Japanese Manchuria, 1904–1932* (Cambridge, MA: Harvard University Asia Center, 2001), 17–59.

16. John Young, *The Research Activities of the South Manchuria Railway, 1907–1945: A History and Bibliography* (New York: Columbia University East Asian Institute, 1966), 1–33.

17. Itō Takeo, *Life along the South Manchuria Railway: The Memoirs of Itō Takeo,* trans. Joshua Fogel (Armonk, NY: M.E. Sharpe, 1988), 80.

18. Keizai chōsabu, *Manshū no kuri,* 25–27.

19. William Jankowiak and Daniel Bradburd, eds., *Drugs, Labor, and Colonial Expansion* (Tucson: University of Arizona Press, 2003); Moon-Ho Jung, *Coolies and Cane: Race, Labor, and Sugar in the Age of Emancipation* (Baltimore, MD: Johns Hopkins University Press, 2006).

20. Kantō-kyoku kanbō bunshoka, *Kantō-kyoku shisei sanjū nen gyōseki chōsa shiryō* (Dairen: Kantō-kyoku bunshoka, 1937), 671.

21. Erving Goffman, *Asylums: Essays on the Social Situation of Mental Patients and Other Inmates* (New York: Anchor Books, 1961), 5–6.

22. "Stevedore Coolies of Dairen," *Milestones of Progress* 2 (1938): 92.

23. *The Directory of Manchoukuo* (Dairen: Oriental Publishing, 1936), 54.

24. Keizai chōsabu, *Manshū no kuri,* 71.

25. Goffman, *Asylums,* 9.

26. Itō, *Life along the South Manchurian Railway*, 49. In Chinese, the coolie boss was also referred to by the terms *toumu, kulitou,* and *touer.*

27. Itō Kazuhiko, "Mantetsu rōdōsha to rōmu taisei," in Matsumura, Jie, and Eda, eds., *Mantetsu rōdō shi no kenkyū*, 123–76.

28. David Tucker, "Labor Policy and the Construction Industry in Manchukuo: Systems of Recruitment, Management, and Control," in Kratoska, ed., *Asian Labor in the Wartime Japanese Empire*, 31.

29. "Dairen Kyūryōsho yōran," 121.

30. Keizai chōsabu, *Manshū no kuri*, 56.

31. Fukusho kakō kabushiki kaisha, "Hekizansō seikatsu fuku," 217.

32. Michael A. Weiner, "The Invention of Identity: 'Self' and 'Other' in Pre-War Japan," in Michael A. Weiner, ed., *Japan's Minorities: The Illusion of Homogeneity* (New York: Routledge, 1997), 4.

33. Yosano Akiko, *Travels in Manchuria and Mongolia: A Feminist Poet Encounters Prewar China*, trans. Joshua A. Fogel (New York: Columbia University Press, 2001), 14–15. Following scholarly convention in writing about Yosano Akiko, I refer to her as Akiko.

34. Ibid., 45–46.

35. Ibid., 127.

36. Steve Rabson, *Righteous Cause or Tragic Folly: Changing Views of War in Modern Japanese Poetry* (Ann Arbor: University of Michigan Center for Japanese Studies, 1998), 109–39.

37. Copies of Gotō's works were acquired, for example, by the SMR public library in Dairen.

38. See, for example, Gotō Asatarō, *Shina bunka no kaibō* (Osaka: Osaka yago shoten, 1921); *Omoshiroi Shina no fūzoku* (Osaka: Osaka yago shoten, 1923); and *Shina shumi no hanashi* (Osaka: Osaka yago shoten, 1924).

39. Gotō Asatarō, *Shina kidan*, 18.

40. Ibid., 47.

41. Ibid., 468–69.

42. Gotō Asatarō, *Shina kokuminsei kōwa* (Tokyo: Gansuidō shoten, 1927), 9.

43. Takeuchi Yoshimi and Hashikawa Bunsō, *Kindai Nihon to Chūgoki (shita)* (Tokyo: Asahi Shinbunsha, 1974), 27–45; Fogel, *The Literature of Travel in the Japanese Rediscovery of China*, 200–208; Katsuragawa Mitsumasa, "Gotō Asatarō, Chūgoku, ahen," *Ōsaka Sangyō Daigaku ronshū* 113 (1999): 57–65.

44. Inoue Kōbai, "Ahen kyūshoku taiken ki," *Dōjin* 4, no. 6 (1930): 14–23.

45. Inoue Kōbai, *Shina fūzoku* (Shanghai: Nihondō shoten, 1920), 377.

46. Inoue Kōbai, *Sake, ahen, majan* (Tokyo: Marikaku shobō, 1930), 19.

47. Karen Laura Thornber, *Empire of Texts in Motion: Chinese, Korean, and Taiwanese Transculturations of Japanese Literature* (Cambridge, MA: Harvard University Asia Center, 2009), 135.

48. Inoue Kōbai, "Ahen to tabako," in Imai Toshiki and Ozaki Hotsumi, eds., *Ajia mondai kōza dai kyū moku: Shakai, shūzoku hen* (Tokyo: Sōgensha, 1940), 270.

49. Takeuchi and Hashikawa, *Kindai Nihon to Chūgoku (shita)*, 27–45. For more on the career and writings of Inoue Kōbai, see Liu Jianhui, "Demon Capital Shanghai: The 'Modern' Experience of Japanese Intellectuals: Taishō Writers Who Indulged in the Demon Capital," trans. Joshua A. Fogel, *Sino-Japanese Studies* 16 (2009): 184–204.

50. Matsui Yoshio, *Mayaku to bungaku* (Tokyo: Kōshinsha, 1938), 4. On the place of De Quincey in European and American literature, see Alethea Hayter, *Opium and the Romantic Imagination: Addiction and Creativity in De Quincey, Coleridge, Baudelaire and Others* (Wellingborough, Northamptonshire, UK: Crucible, 1988), 101–31; Barry Milligan, *Pleasures and Pains: Opium and the Orient in Nineteenth-Century British Culture* (Charlottesville: University Press of Virginia, 1995); and Marcus Boon, *The Road of Excess: A History of Writers on Drugs* (Cambridge, MA: Harvard University Press, 2002).

51. On the confessional mode in Japanese literature, see Karatani Kōjin, *Origins of Modern Japanese Literature*, ed. and trans. Brett de Bary (Durham, NC: Duke University Press, 1993), 76–96.

52. De Kuinshii, *Ahen dekiaisha no kokuhaku*, trans. Tsuji Jun (Tokyo: Shunjūsha, 1925); Do Kuinzui, *Ahen fukuyōsha no zange: Sono ta*, trans. Isobe Yaichirō (Tokyo: Eibungakusha, 1929); Do Kuinshi, *Ahenzuki na ichi Eijin no kokuhaku*, trans. Suzuki Ken'ichirō (Tokyo: Tōhō shoin, 1934); Dei Kuinshii, *Ahen jōyōsha no kokuhaku*, trans. Tanabe Jūji (Tokyo: Iwanami shoten, 1937).

53. Ise Ryūsuke, "Ahen kyokuyaku, ahen jigoku," *Dōjin* 4, no. 10 (1930): 34–46; Ise Ryūsuke, "Ahen kyokuyaku, ahen jigoku (shita)," *Dōjin* 4, no. 11 (1930): 43–52.

54. Thomas De Quincey, *"Confessions of an English Opium-Eater" and "The English Mail-Coach,"* ed. E. Nagasawa (Tokyo: Kenkyūsha, 1923); Thomas De Quincey, *Confessions of an English Opium-Eater*, ed. Y. Otagiri (Tokyo, 1928).

55. Sunaga Asahiko, "Dekadan no dōwa," in Sunaga Asahiko, ed., *Satō Haruo* (Tokyo: Kokusho kankōkai, 1992), 255–70.

56. Takaki Mamoru, *Tsuji Jun: "Ko" ni ikiru* (Tokyo: Taimatsusha, 1979), 182. Following publication of his translation of *Confessions*, Tsuji became a noted anarchist, nihilist, and Japan's first self-identified Dadaist. Toward the end of his life, amid the tightening regulation of thought and ideology in wartime Japan, he was persecuted by police and jailed repeatedly. Tsuji's original works attracted immediate and enduring attention from scholars, but his significance as a translator has been largely overlooked.

57. Satō Haruo, "Shimon," in Sunaga, ed., *Satō Haruo*, 15.

58. Ibid., 14.

59. Ibid., 13.

60. Ibid., 34.

61. Ibid., 72.

62. Ibid., 70.

63. Edgar Allan Poe, *The Tell-Tale Heart* (New York: J. H. Eggers, 1916), 1.

64. Noriko Lippit, "Natsume Sōseki on Poe," *Comparative Literature* 14, no. 1 (1977): 30–37.

65. Ōshita Udaru, *Ōshita Udaru shū* (Tokyo: Heibonsha, 1930), 705.

66. Ibid., 708.

67. Ibid., 714.

68. Ibid., 717.

69. Ibid., 723–24.

70. On the ideal of the "good wife, wise mother" in modern Japan, see Sharon H. Nolte and Sally Ann Hastings, "The Meiji State's Policy toward Women, 1890–1910," in Gail Lee Bernstein, ed., *Recreating Japanese Women, 1600–1945* (Berkeley: University of California Press, 1991), 151–74.

71. Christine L. Marran, *Poison Woman: Figuring Female Transgression in Modern Japanese Culture* (Minneapolis: University of Minnesota Press, 2007), xiii–xxi.

72. Ōshita, *Ōshita Udaru shū*, 742.

73. Yokomitsu Riichi, *Shanghai,* trans. Dennis Washburn (Ann Arbor: University of Michigan Press, 2001), 216.

74. Ibid., 233.

75. Marek Kohn, *Dope Girls: The Birth of the British Drug Underground* (London: Lawrence & Wishart, 1992).

76. Yokomitsu, *Shanghai,* 241.

77. Kuroshima Denji, *Kuroshima Denji shū* (Tokyo: Shin Nihon shuppansha, 1984), 312.

78. Ibid., 408.

79. Zeljko Cipris, "Introduction," in Kuroshima, *A Flock of Swirling Crows and Other Proletarian Writings,* 7.

80. Anzai Fuyue, "Gunkan Mari," in Itō Shinkichi, ed., *Kitagawa Fuyuhiko, Anzai Fuyue, Kitasono Katsue, Haruyama Yukio, Takenaka Iku* (Tokyo: Chūo kōronsha, 1975), 93–95.

81. Jos Ten Berge, "The *Belle Epoque* of Opium," in Sander L. Gilman and Xun Zhou, eds., *Smoke: A Global History of Smoking* (London: Reaktion Books, 2004), 108–17.

82. Charles W. Inglehart, *A Century of Protestant Christianity in Japan* (Rutland, VT: Charles E. Tuttle, 1959), 337.

83. Jon Thares Davidann, *A World of Crisis and Progress: The American YMCA in Japan, 1890–1930* (Bethlehem, PA: University of Lehigh Press, 1998).

84. Robert Cornell Armstrong, "The Second Meeting of the N. C. Council," *Kirisutokyō renmei* 8 (1924): 4.

85. Robert Cornell Armstrong, "English Bulletin," *Kirisutokyō renmei* 20 (1925): 8.

86. Robert Cornell Armstrong, "English Bulletin," *Kirisutokyō renmei* 11 (1925): 4.

87. Kikuchi Yūji, "Ahen mondai to Nihonjin no sekinin," *Kirisutokyō renmei* 40 (1927): 1–2.

88. Kikuchi, "Ahen mondai ni kanshite (2)," 25–32.

89. Michael A. Weiner, *The Origins of the Korean Community in Japan, 1900–1923* (Atlantic Highlands, NJ: Humanities Press International, 1989), 12.

90. Kikuchi Yūji, "Shina ni taisuru ahen no haidoku hōshi undō," *Dōjin* 2, no. 5 (1928): 7–12.

91. Kikuchi Yūji and Song Zhifu, "Riben yapian zhengce zhi jiepou," *Judu yuekan* 25 (1928): 33–35; Kikuchi Yūji, "Riben zhuanjia dui yu Zhong-Ri yapian wenti guancha," trans. Zhu Yuanwen, *Judu yuekan* 27 (1928): 25–34; Kikuchi Yūji, "Riren zai Hua zhi dubin mishu," trans. Zhu Xizhou, *Judu yuekan* 43 (1930): 31–34.

92. Kikuchi Yūji, "Ahen han no tōkei ten ni oite," *Keisatsu Kyōkai zasshi* 333 (1928): 60–65; Kikuchi Yūji, "Shina ni okeru ahen no haidoku," in Kikuchi Yūji, ed., *Ahen mondai no kenkyū* (Tokyo: Kokusai renmei kyōkai, 1928), 12–24; Kikuchi Yūji, "Ahen mondai to Kirisutosha no sekinin," *Raifu* 10 (1928): 16–21.

93. "Ahen haidoku hōshikai," *Yomiuri Shinbun*, Apr. 17, 1930, 4.

94. "Jinyan jinian ri," *Xinmin Ribao*, June 4, 1929. The date of the celebration, June 3, 1929, marked the ninetieth anniversary of Chinese trade commissioner Lin Zexu's public burning of British opium stocks in Canton, an incident directly implicated in the outbreak of the Opium War.

95. Kikuchi, "Ahen mondai ni kanshite (2)," 25–32; Kikuchi Yūji, "Ahen mondai ni kanshite," *Dōjin* 4, no. 3 (1929): 11–16; Kikuchi Yūji, "Jinzō ahen no kansei," *Tongren yixue* 4, no. 11 (1931): 972–979.

96. On the life and work of Kikuchi Yūji, see Kurahashi Masanao, *Nihon no ahen senryaku: Kakureta kokka hanzai* (Tokyo: Kyōei shobō, 1996), 204–35; and Kurahashi Masanao, *Ahen, teikoku, Nihon* (Tokyo: Kyōei shobō, 2008), 172–206.

97. Kudase Kentarō, "Shina ni okeru Kirisutokyō senkyōshi no igakuteki katsudō," *Dōjin* 5, no. 12 (1931): 15–30.

98. "Report on Formosa," in Jarman, ed., *Japan and Dependencies*, vol. 9, *Formosa: Political and Economic Reports 1906–1926*, 328.

99. *Taiwan no ahen seido*, 3–5.

100. OAC, "Summary of Annual Reports of Governments on the Traffic in Opium and Other Dangerous Drugs for the Years 1929 and 1930" (Geneva, 1932), 114.

101. Nakatani Yoshisaburō, "Nakatani Yoshisaburō wo kakonde," in Kubo Ken, ed., *Zai-Sen Nihonjin yakugyō kaikō shi* (Tokyo, 1961), 7.

102. Imamura Yutaka, *Chōsen ni okeru jinkō ni kansuru sho tōkei* (Keijō: Chōsen kōsei kyōkai, 1943), 77–80.

103. "1922 Annual Report," in Jarman, ed., *Japan and Dependencies*, vol. 11, *Korea: Political and Economic Reports 1906–1923*, 415.

104. Kikuchi Yūji, "Shina no genjō to ahen haidoku mondai (1928)," in *Ahen sono ta dokuzaiyaku oyobi kyūshoku kigu torishimari kankei zakken: Shina no bu.*

105. Do Sōmei, "Chōsen ni okeru 'moruhine' rui mansei chūdoku mondai ni oite," *Rikagaku kyōshitsu ronshū* 30 (1933): 217–25.

106. Elazar Barkan, *The Retreat of Scientific Racism: Changing Concepts of Race in Britain and the United States between the World Wars* (New York: Cambridge University Press, 1992).

107. On *dōka*, see Mark R. Peattie, "Japanese Attitudes toward Colonialism, 1895–1945," in Ramon H. Myers and Mark R. Peattie, eds., *The Japanese Colonial Empire, 1895–1945* (Princeton, NJ: Princeton University Press, 1984), 80–127; Oguma Eiji, *'Nihonjin' no kyōkai: Okinawa, Ainu, Taiwan, Chōsen, shokuminchi shihai kara fukki undō made* (Tokyo: Shin'yōsha, 1998); Komagome Takeshi, *Shokuminchi teikoku Nihon no bunka tōgō* (Tokyo: Iwanami shoten, 1996); Ishida Takeshi, *Kioku to bōkyaku no seijigaku: Dōka seisaku, sensō sekinin, shūgōteki kioku* (Tokyo: Akashi shoten, 2000); and Mark E. Caprio, *Japanese Assimilation Policies in Colonial Korea, 1910–1945* (Seattle: University of Washington Press, 2009).

108. Kaku, *Opium Policy in Japan*, 36.

109. OAC, "Report to the Council on the Work of the Eighteenth Session" (Geneva, 1934), 84; Yoshiki Yasaburō, "Ahen no hanashi," *Chōsen oyobi Manshū* 166 (1921): 45–47.

110. Yokomitsu Riichi, "Aoi taii," in *Yokomitsu Riichi zenshū dai ni ken* (Tokyo: Kawade shobō shinsha, 1981), 335–49. For an English translation, see Yokomitsu Riichi, *"Love" and Other Stories of Yokomitsu Riichi*, trans. and intro. Dennis Keene (Tokyo: University of Tokyo Press, 1974), 97–108.

111. Shōji Sōichi, *Chin fujin* (Tokyo: Tsūbunkaku, 1940), 188.

112. Sakai Yoshio, *Ahen kyūin ni kansuru eiseiteki chōsa* (Kōain Kachū renrakubu, 1941), 1–2.

113. Kim Rin-song, "Heian Nandō ni okeru kako nana nenkan no mayaku rui chūdokusha chiryō no tōkeiteki kansatsu," *Man-Sen no ikai* 183 (1936): 7–8.

114. Kubo Kiyoji and Gwang Shin-haeng, "Chōsen ni okeru mayaku chūdoku ni kansuru kenkyū," *Chōsen Igakkai zasshi* 30, no. 6 (1940): 1–13.

115. Herbert Samuel Middlemiss, ed., *Narcotic Education: Edited Report of the Proceedings* (Washington, DC: World Conference on Narcotic Education, 1927), 70.

116. Ibid., 231.

117. Lü Heruo, "Gōka heian," in *Seishū* (Tokyo: Yumani shobō, 2001), 188. On Lü's political position, see Tarumi Chie, "An Author Listening to Voices from the Netherworld: Lü Heruo and the *Kuso* Realism Debate," in Liao Ping-Hui and David Der-wei Wang, eds., *Taiwan under Japanese Colonial Rule, 1895–1945*, 262–78.

118. On Koreans in imperial Japan, see Weiner, *The Origins of the Korean Community in Japan;* and Ken C. Kawashima, *The Proletarian Gamble: Korean Workers in Interwar Japan* (Durham, NC: Duke University Press, 2009).

119. Tazawa, ed., *Ahen shiryō*, 83.

120. Kim X Ki, "Kutsu wo shikkei suru no ga senmon," in Majima Kan, *Mayaku chūdokusha to naku: Tō-A wo ahen kara kaikō seyo* (Tokyo: Ajia seisaku kenkyūjo, 1935), 6–9.

121. Kim X Joo, "Hanayaka no koshō kara suri no tsuma ni," in Majima, ed., *Mayaku chūdokusha to naku,* 17–26.

122. OAC, "Minutes of the Twenty-Second Session" (Geneva, 1937), 50.

123. Sakai Yoshio, *Tō-A no reimei wa mayaku no genzetsu yori* (Tokyo: Shintō kagaku kenkyūjo, 1939), 20–22.

124. "Ushijima umare no akufu," *Chūgai Shōgyō Shinbun,* Nov. 10, 1936.

125. "Mohi kanja wo atsumari: Senjin ga settōdan," *Yomiuri Shinbun,* Feb. 6, 1931, 7.

126. *Nihon teikoku tōkei nenkan,* vols. 7–63 (1888–1944).

127. On Koreans in Manchuria under Japanese occupation, see Barbara J. Brooks, "Peopling the Japanese Empire: The Koreans in Manchuria and the Rhetoric of Inclusion," in Sharon A. Minichiello, ed., *Japan's Competing Modernities: Issues in Culture and Democracy, 1900–1930* (Honolulu: University of Hawai'i Press, 1998), 25–44; and Hyun Ok Park, *Two Dreams in One Bed: Empire, Social Life, and the Origins of the North Korean Revolution in Manchuria* (Durham, NC: Duke University Press, 2005).

128. Taiwanese migrants to Manchuria occupied a similar position in the drug market but were much less numerous. Man-houng Lin, "The Power of Culture and Its Limits: Taiwanese Merchants and Asian Commodity Flows, 1895–1945," in Eric Tagliacozzo and Wen-Chin Chang, eds., *Chinese Circulations: Capital, Commodities, and Networks in Southeast Asia* (Durham, NC: Duke University Press, 2011), 305–35.

129. Eguchi Keiichi, *Nit-Chū ahen sensō* (Tokyo: Iwanami shoten, 1988), 181; Kobayashi Motohiro, *Kindai Chūgoku no Nihon iryūmin to ahen* (Tokyo: Yoshikawa Kōbunkan, 2012), 225–26.

130. "Koreans a Problem in North Manchuria," *New York Times,* Jul. 3, 1932.

131. Satō Shin'ichirō, *Daikan'en no kaibō,* 140–43.

132. Helie Lee, *Still Life with Rice: A Young American Woman Discovers the Life and Legacy of Her Korean Grandmother* (New York: Scribner, 1996), 121.

133. Ibid., 122.

134. Yao Yunpeng, Yang Shangqing, and Wei Dan, "'Da Qiao lüguan' de yangui," in Wenshi jinghua bianjibu, ed., *Jindai Zhongguo yandu xiezhen,* 240.

135. Yamazaki Masao, "Senjin wo chūshin to seru Harupin no kōsatsu," *Chōsen oyobi Manshū* 193 (1923): 33–36.

136. "Osorubeki heroin no haidoku to zen-Man ni man'en suru inja," *Dairen Jihō,* Feb. 15, 1934, 7.

CHAPTER 4

1. In Japanese, this incident is referred to as the "Manchurian Incident *[Manshū jihen]*." In Chinese, it is often called *Jiu-yi-ba* (9/18), after the date on which it took place.

2. Janis Mimura, *Planning for Empire: Reform Bureaucrats and the Japanese Wartime State* (Ithaca, NY: Cornell University Press, 2009), 48.

3. Motosada Zumoto, *Lytton Commission on China and Manchuria* (Tokyo: Herald Press, 1932), 4. On the history of Manchu ethnicity, see Pamela Kyle Crossley, *Orphan Warriors: Three Manchu Generations and the End of the Qing World* (Princeton, NJ: Princeton University Press, 1990); Mark C. Elliott, *The Manchu Way: The Eight Banners and Ethnic Identity in Late Imperial China* (Stanford, CA: Stanford University Press, 2001); and Shao Dan, *Remote Homeland, Recovered Borderland: Manchus, Manchoukuo, and Manchuria, 1907–1985* (Honolulu: University of Hawai'i Press, 2011).

4. Shintō kagaku kenkyūjo, *Ahen oyobi ruiji "arukaroido" mansei chūdokushō no kōkateki chiryō to sono hōsaku*, 13.

5. Although historians have traditionally dismissed the Kingly Way as propaganda, recent scholarship has convincingly presented the doctrine as a logical culmination of long-standing intellectual trends. See Prasenjit Duara, *Sovereignty and Authenticity: Manchukuo and the East Asian Modern* (Lanham, MD: Rowman & Littlefield, 2003); Han Suk-Jung, "The Problem of Sovereignty: Manchukuo, 1932–1937," *positions* 12, no. 2 (2004): 457–78; and Yamamuro Shin'ichi, *Manchuria under Japanese Domination*, trans. Joshua Fogel (Philadelphia: University of Pennsylvania Press, 2006).

6. *The Manchoukuo Year Book* (Tokyo: Tō-A keizai chōsa-kyoku, 1934), 101–2.

7. Minami Manshū kyōikukai kyōkasho henshūbu, "Xin shidai guoyu duben," in Takenaka Ken'ichi, ed., *"Manshū" shokuminchi Chūgokujin yō kyōkasho shūsei* (Tokyo: Rokuin shobō, 2005), 4:370–71.

8. *The Manchoukuo Year Book* (1934), 101–2.

9. On Pan-Asianism among Chinese thinkers, see Prasenjit Duara, "Transnationalism and the Predicament of Sovereignty: China, 1900–1945," *American Historical Review* 102, no. 4 (1997): 1030–51. For a general overview of Pan-Asianism, see Eri Hotta, *Pan-Asianism and Japan's War 1931–1945* (New York: Palgrave Macmillan, 2007).

10. Stefan Tanaka, *Japan's Orient: Rendering Pasts into History* (Berkeley: University of California Press, 1993), 115–52.

11. Sources disagree regarding the groups included in the five races. Most commonly, the roster included Japanese, Koreans, Han Chinese, Manchus, and Mongolians. On ethnic, racial, and national categories in the history and historiography of Manchukuo, see Mariko Asano Tamanoi, "Knowledge, Power, and Racial Classifications: The 'Japanese' in 'Manchuria,'" *Journal of Asian Studies* 59, no. 2 (2000): 248–76.

12. Zai-Man kyōkashobu, "Seinen gakkō tettei kyōkasho: Shūshin oyobi kōmin ka," in Takenaka, ed., *"Manshū" shokuminchi Chūgokujin yō kyōkasho shūsei*, 9:79.

13. T. Nagashima, "Opium Administration in Manchukuo," *Milestones of Progress* 3, no. 1 (1939): 18–44, 27.

14. Nichi-Man jitsugyō kyōkai, "Manshūkoku ahen seido to ahen no gainen," in Okada Yoshimasa, Tatai Yoshio, and Takahashi Masae, eds., *Ahen mondai* (Tokyo: Misuzu shobō, 1986), 224.

15. *The Manchoukuo Year Book* (1934), 706.

16. Okabe Makio, Yanagisawa Asobu, and Xing Bailin, "Kyōwakai to gozoku kyōwa," in Shokuminchi bunka gakkai, ed., *"Manshūkoku" to wa nandatta no ka* (Tokyo: Shōgakkan, 2008), 215–36.

17. Tsukase Susumu, *Manshūkoku 'minzoku kyōwa' no jisshō* (Tokyo: Yoshikawa Kōbunkan, 1998), 83–84; Duara, *Sovereignty and Authenticity*, 103–5.

18. This song, originally in Chinese, appeared in Japanese translation in Taniyama Tsuneki, *Manshū no fūzoku to densetsu min'yū* (Tokyo: Matsuyama bō, 1938), 387–88. The English translation is my own.

19. Kazama Hideto, ed., *"Kyōwa undō" bessatsu kaitei, sō mokuroku, sakuin* (Tokyo: Rokuin shobō, 1995), 6–13.

20. Wang Yunzhi, "Jindu ganyan," *Kyōwa undō* 3, no. 6 (1941): 174.

21. Chen Yingbin, "Gaishan guomin sixiang yu duanjin yapian," *Kyōwa undō* 3, no. 4 (1941): 158–62.

22. Baba Shachi, *Ahen tōzenshi* (Shinkyō: Manshū jigyō annaisho, 1941), 202–3.

23. Kikuchi Yūji, "Shina ni okeru ahen no haidoku," in *Ahen mondai no kenkyū* (Tokyo: Kokusai renmei kyōkai, 1928), 14–15.

24. "Chō Gakuryō shi jūtai," *Yomiuri Shinbun*, Jun. 6, 1931, 4.

25. Contemporary historians remain critical of warlord rule in Manchuria. See Gavan McCormack, *Chang Tso-lin in Northeast China, 1911–1928: China, Japan and the Manchurian Idea* (Stanford, CA: Stanford University Press, 1977); and Ronald Suleski, *Civil Government in Warlord China: Tradition, Modernization and Manchuria* (New York: Peter Lang, 2002).

26. Charles de Secondat, baron de Montesquieu, *The Spirit of the Laws*, trans. Anne M. Cohler, Basia Carolyn Miller, and Samuel Harold Stone (New York: Cambridge University Press, 1989); James Stuart Mill, *The History of British India*, abridged by William Thomas (Chicago: University of Chicago Press, 1975).

27. *The Manchoukuo Year Book* (1934), 702.

28. Kurahashi Masanao, "Chō Sakurin seiken no ahen kaikin seisaku (1927 nen)," *Aichi Kenritsu Daigaku bungaku ronshū* 44 (1995), 80–56.

29. Nagashima, "Opium Administration in Manchukuo," 27.

30. Miyajima Mikinosuke, "Manshū no ahen to mayaku," in Okada, Tatai, and Takahashi, eds., *Ahen mondai*, 106.

31. Tanaka Tadao, *Ahen mondai to Shina nōson keizai* (Tokyo: Tō-A kenkyūkai, 1933).

32. Mantetsu chōsabu, *Ahen sensō ni yoru dentōteki Shina kokka no hōkai to fukoku kyōhei undō* (Shinkyō: Mantetsu chōsabu, 1941).

33. Among Chinese scholars, too, the Opium War loomed large as a subject of research during the 1930s and 1940s. Chinese historians, however, did not generally present the conflict in ways that suggested a political agenda. For example, see Cai Yuanpei and Wu Jingheng, eds., *Yapian zhanzheng shi* (Shanghai: Shangwu yinshuguan, 1931); and Yao Weiyuan, *Yapian zhanzheng shi shikao* (Guiyang: Wentong shuju, 1942).

34. For example, see Murayama Tomoyoshi, *Ahen sensō: Yonmaku hachiba* (Tokyo: Nitteishutsu, 1934).

35. Ema Shū, *Ahen sensō* (Tokyo: Yumani shobō, 2004), 151–52.

36. Ibid., 163.

37. Ibid., 170.

38. Ibid., 244.

39. Uranishi Kazuhiko, "Josetsu," in Ema, *Ahen sensō,* 1–4.

40. Ushikubo Ainoshin, *Ahen ka: Eikoku Tōyō shinryaku shi* (Tokyo: Akatsuki shoin, 1933), 2, 389.

41. Yano Jin'ichi, *Ahen sensō to Honkon* (Kyoto: Kōbundō shobō, 1939), 1–4. Contemporary scholars evaluate Yano as "the epitome of a political scholar who served imperialist aims." Shao, *Remote Homeland, Recovered Borderland,* 133–34.

42. Takeuchi Chūji, *Ahen sensō to Eikoku no tai-Shi shinryaku* (Tokyo: Takeuchi Chūji, 1939), 28.

43. Ōizumi Kokuseki, *'Bai gui lai': Ahen sensō wa kaku tatakarareta* (Tokyo: Daishinsha, 1942).

44. Osaragi Jirō, *Ahen sensō* (Tokyo: Modan Nihon shahan, 1942), 379. Osaragi's real name was Nojiri Haruhiko.

45. Ibid., 243.

46. Ōhara Masatoshi, *Ahen sensō* (Taihoku: Morioka shuppanbu, 1944), 1–2.

47. Matsuzaki Keiji, *Ahen sensō: Sono shijitsu to monogatari* (Tokyo: Takayama shoin, 1942), 7.

48. Ibid., 259–60.

49. Nakamine Manahito, "Gijutsu jihyō: 'Ahen sensō,' 'Kaizen zenya,'" in Makino Mamoru, ed., *"Nihon eiga": Fukkokuban* (Tokyo: Yumani shobō, 2002), 28:36–39; Ueno Ichirō, "Ahen sensō," in Makino Mamoru, ed., *"Eiga junpō": Fukkokuban* (Tokyo: Yumani shobō, 2004), 26:291.

50. Ueno, "Ahen sensō," 292.

51. John W. Dower, *Japan in War and Peace: Selected Essays* (New York: New Press, 1993), 40; Peter B. High, *The Imperial Screen: Japanese Film Culture in the Fifteen Years' War, 1931–1945* (Madison: University of Wisconsin Press, 2004), 346–71.

52. Washitani Hana, "The Opium War and the Cinema Wars: A Hollywood in the Greater East Asian Co-Prosperity Sphere," *Inter-Asia Cultural Studies* 4, no. 1 (2003): 74.

53. Michael Baskett, *The Attractive Empire: Transnational Film Culture in Imperial Japan* (Honolulu: University of Hawai'i Press, 2008), 77–79.

54. *Wan shi liu fang*, directed by Bu Wancang (Shanghai: Tōhō and China United, 1943).

55. Chan Airin, "'Man se ryū hō' hyō," in Yomota Inuhiko, ed., *Ri Kōran to Higashi Ajia* (Tokyo: Tokyo Daigaku shuppankai, 2001), 167.

56. Yamaguchi Yoshiko and Fujiwara Sakuya, *Ri Kōran: Watashi no hansei* (Tokyo: Shinchōsha, 1990), 298.

57. Poshek Fu, "The Ambiguity of Entertainment: Chinese Cinema in Japanese-Occupied Shanghai, 1941–1945," *Cinema Journal* 37, no. 1 (1997): 75.

58. Yamaguchi Takeshi, "Hō to iu kannen kara mita Man'ei no tokuisei to Amakasu Masahiko," in Nakami, ed., *Manshū to wa nandatta no ka*, 188–99; Aaron Gerow, "Narrating the Nation-ality of a Cinema: The Case of Prewar Japanese Film," in Alan Tansman, ed., *The Culture of Japanese Fascism* (Durham, NC: Duke University Press, 2009), 195–98.

59. Yamaguchi and Fujiwara, *Ri Kōran*, 295–98.

60. Alan Baumler, *The Chinese and Opium under the Republic: Worse Than Floods and Wild Beasts* (Albany: State University of New York Press, 2007), 5.

61. Lo, *The Opium Problem in the Far East*, 16.

62. Wie T. Dunn, "The Opium Traffic in Its International Aspects" (PhD diss., Columbia University, 1920), 9. On the image of the addict in the Chinese anti-opium movement, see Xavier Paulès, "Anti-Opium Visual Propaganda and the Deglamorisation of Opium in China, 1895–1937," *European Journal of East Asian Studies* 7, no. 2 (2008): 229–62.

63. *Opium: A World Problem* 1, no. 2 (1927): 15.

64. Wang King Ky, "China's Opium Problem," *Opium: A World Problem* 3, no. 1 (1929): 21.

65. "Riben dui Hua zhi si da zhengce," *Judu yuekan* 78 (1934): 4.

66. Aiguoshe, "Riben qintun Man-Meng duhua zhi da pilü," in Jilin sheng tushuguan Wei-Manzhouguo shiliao bianweihui, ed., *Wei-Manzhouguo shi liao* (Beijing: Quanguo tushuguan wenxian suowei fuzhi zhongxin, 2002), 24:55, 57.

67. Mei Gongren, *Wangguo miezhong de yapian yanhuo* (Beijing: Beijing zhongxian tuofang keji fazhan youxian gongsi, 2007), 32, 26–27.

68. Norman H. Smith, "Opiate Addiction and the Entanglements of Imperialism and Patriarchy in Manchukuo, 1932–1945," *Social History of Alcohol and Drugs* 20 (2005): 66–104.

69. Lin Yutang, *Moment in Peking* (New York: John Day, 1939), 717.

70. Xu Daolin, "Nihon wa teki ka mikata ka?" in Tani, ed., *Tō-A Dōbun Shoin ahen chōsa hōkoku*.

71. "1934 Manchukuo Annual Report," 235–470, in Jarman, ed., *Japan and Dependencies*, vol. 14, *Manchukuo: Political and Economic Reports 1933–1935*, 238; "1935 Manchukuo Annual Report," in Jarman, ed., *Japan and Dependencies*, vol. 15, *Manchukuo:*

Political and Economic Reports 1935–1937, 135; "1938 Manchukuo Annual Report," in Jarman, ed., *Japan and Dependencies*, vol. 16, 51.

72. *American Student Party's Visit to Manchoukuo* (Dairen: South Manchuria Railway Company Information and Publicity Department, 1938), 8.

73. Mark Gayn, *Journey from the East: An Autobiography* (New York: A. A. Knopf, 1944), 410, 418–19.

74. Vespa, *Secret Agent of Japan*, 108.

75. "Drug Addicts Increasing: Local Authorities Urged to Take Strict Action," *Japan Chronicle*, Dec. 2, 1934.

76. Frederick Merrill, *Japan and the Opium Menace* (New York: International Secretariat, Institute for Pacific Relations, and the Foreign Policy Association, 1942), 63.

77. Yuma Totani, *The Tokyo Trials: The Pursuit of Justice in the Wake of World War II* (Cambridge, MA: Harvard University Asia Center, 2008), 154.

78. F. C. Jones, *Manchuria since 1931* (London: Royal Institute of International Affairs, 1949), 134.

CHAPTER 5

1. In 1915, China consented to extend the term of the lease to ninety-nine years.

2. Kantō-chō, *Kantō-chō yōran* (Ryōjun: Kantō-chō, 1934), 307.

3. Kobayashi Michihiko, "Mantetsu to Gotō Shinpei," in Yoshida and Fujiwara, eds., *Mantetsu to wa nandatta no ka*, 39–49; Nishinomiya Kō, "Gotō Shinpei no Manshū keiryaku," in Nakami, ed., *Manshū to wa nandatta no ka*, 225–43.

4. *Kantō tōkei sho*, vol. 3 (1908).

5. John Butcher, "Revenue Farming and the Changing State in Southeast Asia," in John Butcher and Howard Dick, eds., *The Rise and Fall of Revenue Farming: Business Elites and the Emergence of the State in Southeast Asia* (New York: St. Martin's Press, 1993), 42; Howard Dick, "A Fresh Approach to Southeast Asian History," in Butcher and Dick, eds., *The Rise and Fall of Revenue Farming*, 8.

6. Katsuragawa Mitsumasa, "Kantōshū ahen seido no seitai to Chūgoku shōnin: Kantōshū no tōchi wo meguru kōsatsu," *Shirin* 91, no. 2 (2008): 69–94.

7. Tsurumi Yūsuke, *Gotō Shinpei den*, 2:635–36; Xu Jielin, "Gotō Shinpei to sono ahen mōryaku," *Shokuminchi bunka kenkyū* 4 (2005): 47–53.

8. Lü Yonghua, *Wei-Man shiqi de Dongbei yandu* (Changchun: Jilin renmin chubanshe, 2004), 32. Katsuragawa Mitsumasa has argued that Shen remained the real force behind the opium economy in the 1910s. Katsuragawa, "Kantōshū ahen seido no seitai to Chūgoku shōnin," 71.

9. Kantō-chō, *Kantō-cho yōran*, 307; Yamada Gōichi, *Manshūkoku no ahen senbai: Waga Man-Mō no tokushu ken'eki ron* (Tokyo: Kyūko shoin, 2002), 15.

10. Takenaka, *Dairen rekishi sanpo*, 34.

11. Kurahashi, *Nihon no ahen senryaku*, 155.

12. Harumi Gotō-Shibata, "The International Opium Conference of 1924–1925 and Japan," *Modern Asian Studies* 36, no. 4 (2002): 969–91; Kashiwara Jun, "Shanhai ni okeru 'Kokusai ahen chōsa iinkai' to Nihon no ahen seisaku: Taiwan Sōtokufu no ahen senbai seido wo chūshin to shite," *Kindai Nihon kenkyū* 28 (2011): 3–50.

13. Nonami Shizuo, *Kokusai ahen mondai* (Tokyo: Heibōsha, 1925), 234.

14. Matsubara Nobuyuki, *Kantōshū ahen seido shi*, 53.

15. Gao, "Qianxi Riben diguo zhuyi dui Hua de yapian qinlüe," 87.

16. Ōuchi Ushinosuke, *Shina ahen mondai kaiketsu iken* (Tokyo, 1917); Zaidan hōjin Dairen Kōsai Zendō, "Dairen Kōsai Zendō yōran," in Shin and Nagaoka, eds., *Shokuminchi shakai jigyō kankei shiryō shū*, 5:253.

17. "Manshū meibutsu ahen kai no rimen," *Chōsen oyobi Manshū* 113 (1916): 127–29.

18. Takenaka, *Dairen rekishi sanpo*, 99; Minami-Manshu tetsudō kabushiki kaisha Dairen Iin, *Dairen Iin shinchiku rakusei kinen igakkai shi* (Dairen: Minami-Manshu tetsudō kabushiki kaisha, 1927), 14; Matsushige, "Dai ichiji taisen sengo ni okeru Dairen no 'Santō hō Chūgokujin shōnin,'" 357.

19. Yamada, *Manshūkoku no ahen senbai*, 24–27; Hess, "From Colonial Jewel to Socialist Metropolis," 139. Zhang's relationship with the Japanese military continued long after his involvement in the Hongji Shantang opium traffic. When war broke out between China and Japan in 1937, he supplied the Kwantung Army with ships and capital. In 1947, Zhang, eighty-six, was tried and executed as a Japanese collaborator and "traitor to the Han race *[Hanjian]*."

20. Yamada, *Manshūkoku no ahen senbai*, 24.

21. *The Kwantung Government: Its Functions and Works* (Dairen: Kwantung Government, 1934), 142.

22. Matsubara Kazue, *Maboroshi no Dairen* (Tokyo: Shinchōsha, 2008), 76. The *Kantō tōkei sho* records 205 admissions for addiction treatment at the Dairen Iin in 1916–20. *Kantō tōkei sho*, vols. 11–15 (1916–20). For more on Ishimoto's career after the loss of his opium farm, see Emer Sinead O'Dwyer, "People's Empire: Democratic Imperialism in Japanese Manchuria" (PhD diss., Harvard University, 2007), 50, 81, 124.

23. "Charge That Japan Aids Opium Trade," *New York Times*, Feb. 14, 1919.

24. These articles were collected and presented to a Japanese readership in Okauchi Hanzō, ed. and trans., *Sekai wo fubi seru ahen no ryūkō* (Dairen: Ryōtō shōtōsha, 1920).

25. Katō Kiyofumi, "Hara Kei to Mantetsu," in Kobayashi Hideo, ed., *Kindai Nihon to Mantetsu* (Tokyo: Yoshikawa Kōbunkan, 2000), 53; Ken'ichirō Hirano, "The Japanese in Manchuria 1906–1931: A Study of the Historical Background of Manchukuo" (PhD diss., Harvard University, 1983), 84.

26. Fujiwara Tetsutarō, "Ahen seido chōsa hōkoku," in Okada, Tatai, and Takahashi, eds., *Ahen mondai*, 162–92; Fujiwara Tetsutarō, "Kantōshū ahen seido kansei

iken," in *Ahen sono ta dokuzaiyaku oyobi kyūshoku kigu torishimari kankei zakken: Honpō no bu—Kantōshū, Seitō, Taiwan ni okeru ahen seido teppai mondai.*

27. On this scandal and the policy changes leading up to it, see John M. Jennings, *The Opium Empire: Japanese Imperialism and Drug Trafficking in Asia, 1895–1945* (Westport, CT: Praeger, 1997), 48–50; Kathryn Meyer and Terry Parsinnen, *Webs of Smoke: Smugglers, Warlords, Spies, and the History of the International Drug Trade* (Lanham, MD: Rowman & Littlefield, 1998), 177–78; Matsubara Kazue, *Dairen dansu ho-ru no yoru* (Tokyo: Chūō kōronsha, 1998), 13–30; and Yamada, *Manshūkoku no ahen senbai*, 62–73.

28. "1923 Kwantung Annual Report," in Jarman, ed., *Japan and Dependencies*, vol. 13, *Kwantung: Political and Economic Reports 1906–1923*, 293.

29. Oi Shizuo, *Ahen jiken no shinsō* (Tokyo: Ōi Shizuo, 1923), 219.

30. Quoted in *Manchuria Daily News*, Aug. 10, 1922, in United States Department of State, *Records of the Department of State Relating to the Internal Affairs of Japan, 1910–1929*.

31. Matsubara Nobuyuki, *Kantōshū ahen seido*, 329.

32. "The Annual Report of the International Anti-Opium Association" (Peking, 1924), in *Ahen nado mayaku rui seisan torihiki jōkyō chōsa*.

33. League of Nations, "First Opium Conference: Minutes and Annexes" (Geneva, 1925), 118.

34. For more on the management of opium in the colonial Philippines, see Anne L. Foster, "Opium, the United States, and the Civilizing Mission in Southeast Asia," *Social History of Alcohol and Drugs* 24, no. 1 (2010): 6–19.

35. Ellen N. La Motte, *The Opium Monopoly* (New York: Macmillan, 1920), 73–74.

36. League of Nations, "First Opium Conference: Minutes and Annexes," 81.

37. League of Nations, "Resolutions of the Assembly, the Council and the Advisory Committee in Traffic in Opium and Other Dangerous Drugs" (Geneva, 1926), 21.

38. Nonami, *Kokusai ahen mondai*, 219.

39. Ibid., 233.

40. "Editorial: What about the Hague Convention?" *Opium: A World Problem* 2, no. 3 (1929): 4.

41. "Where China Needs International Cooperation," *Opium: A World Problem* 2, no. 4 (1929): 3.

42. "1929 Annual Report," in Jarman, ed., *Japan and Dependencies*, vol. 2, *Japan: Political Reports 1923–1931*, 397.

43. William O. Walker III, *Opium and Foreign Policy: The Anglo-American Search for Order in Asia, 1912–1954* (Chapel Hill: University of North Carolina Press, 1991), 21.

44. "1930 Annual Report," in Jarman, ed., *Japan and Dependencies*, 2:462.

45. The name Fujitsuru referenced two of Japan's most important symbols: Mount Fuji and the crane.

46. OAC, "Minutes of the Fourteenth Session" (Geneva, 1931), 126; "Investigation of Mr. J. Slattery, Deputy Inspector-General of Police, Punjab, India," Sept. 13, 1930,

in United States Department of State, *Records of the Department of State Relating to the Internal Affairs of Japan, 1930–1939*; "1931 Annual Report," in Jarman, ed., *Japan and Dependencies*, 2:557. For more on this incident, see James H. Mills, "Drugs, Consumption, and Supply in Asia: The Case of Cocaine in Colonial India, 1900–1930," *Journal of Asian Studies* 66, no. 2 (2007): 345–62.

47. Report, June 6, 1931, in *Records of the United States Department of State Relating to the Internal Affairs of Japan, 1930–1939*.

48. John Palmer Gavit, *"Opium"* (New York: Brentano's, 1927), 9.

49. John Palmer Gavit, *Ahen*, trans. Andō Akimichi (Tokyo: Nihon hyōronsha, 1931), 4.

50. Edgar Snow, *Far Eastern Front* (New York: Harrison Smith & Robert Haas, 1933), 267–70.

51. R. John Pritchard and Sonia M. Zaide, eds., *The Tokyo War Crimes Trial: The Complete Transcripts of the Proceedings of the International Military Tribunal for the Far East in Twenty-Two Volumes* (New York: Garland Publishing, 1981), 2837–44.

52. Thomas David Reins, "China and the International Politics of Opium, 1909–1937: The Impact of Reform, Revenue, and the Unequal Treaties" (PhD diss., Claremont Graduate University, 1981), 257.

53. Park Kang, *Zhong-Ri zhanzheng yu yapian*, trans. You Juanhuan (Taipei: Guoshiguan, 1998), 51.

54. Miyauchi Isamu, ed., *Manshū kenkoku sokumenshi* (Tokyo: Shin keizaisha, 1942), 167.

55. Eguchi Keiichi, *Shōgon: Nit-Chū ahen sensō* (Tokyo: Iwanami shoten, 1991), 13.

56. Lü Yonghua, *Wei-Man shiqi de Dongbei yandu*, 42.

57. Nichi-Man jitsugyō kyōkai, "Manshūkoku no ahen seido to ahen no gainen," in Okada, Tatai, and Takahashi, eds., *Ahen mondai*, 238.

58. Quoted from *Osaka Mainichi*, in Report, May 31, 1936, United States Department of State, *Records of the Department of State Relating to the Internal Affairs of Japan, 1930–1939*.

59. Miyajima Mikinosuke, *Kokusai ahen mondai no keii* (Tokyo: Nihon kokusai kyōkai, 1935), 87.

60. OAC, "Minutes of the Nineteenth Session" (Geneva, 1935), 65–66.

61. Peter Fleming, "A Far Eastern Inquiry Part V: The Opium Monopoly," *Times* (London), Mar. 8, 1935, 17.

62. "1939 Manchukuo Annual Report," in Jarman, ed., *Japan and Dependencies*, 16:284; "Harbin Intelligence Report (to September 1933)," in Jarman, ed., *Japan and Dependencies*, 4:211–12.

63. OAC, "Minutes of the Twenty-Second Session," 59–60.

64. Miyajima, "Manshū no ahen to mayaku," 110.

65. "Yapian yinzhe guanli guize," in Zhongguo di'er lishi dang'anguan, Zhongyang dang'anguan, and Jilin sheng shehui kexueyuan, eds., *Riben diguo zhuyi qin Hua dang'an*

ziliao xianpian, 14:834–35; "Developments in the Opium Monopoly of the Kwantung Leased Territory," Mar. 24, 1938, in United States Department of State, *Records of the Department of State Relating to the Internal Affairs of Japan, 1930–1939.*

66. "Jin Mingshe zhengce," in Zhongguo di'er lishi dang'anguan, Zhongyang dang'anguan, and Jilin sheng shehui kexueyuan, eds., *Riben diguo zhuyi qin Hua dang'an ziliao xianpian,* 14:822; Lü Yonghua, *Wei-Man shiqi de Dongbei yandu,* 150.

67. Gayn, *Journey from the East,* 413.

68. Eguchi, *Nit-Chū ahen sensō,* 60–90.

69. Mantetsu Hoku-Shi keizai chōsajo, "Mōkyō ni okeru ahen," in Eguchi Keiichi, ed., *Shiryō Nit-Chū sensō ki ahen seisaku: Mōkyō seiken shiryō wo chūshin ni* (Tokyo: Iwanami shoten, 1985), 202–95.

70. On Japan's management of China's opium market in the late 1930s and early 1940s, see Senda Kakō, *Kōgun "ahen bōryaku"* (Tokyo: Sekibunsha, 1980); Yamada Gōichi, *Ō-rudo Shanhai no ahen jijō* (Tokyo: Aki shobō, 1995); Timothy Brook, "Opium and Collaboration in Central China, 1938–1940," in Brook and Wakabayashi, eds., *Opium Regimes,* 323–43; Motohiro Kobayashi, "An Opium Tug-of-War: Japan versus the Wang Jingwei Regime," in Brook and Wakabayashi, eds., *Opium Regimes,* 344–59; Mark Eykholt, "Resistance to Opium as a Social Evil in Wartime China," in Brook and Wakabayashi, eds., *Opium Regimes,* 360–79; and Ota Naoki, *Tōjō Hideki: Ahen no yami, Manshū no yume* (Tokyo: Kadogawa gakugei shuppan, 2009). Satomi Hajime is the subject of two recent biographies: Senga Motofumi, *Ahen Ō ichidai: Chūgoku ahen shijō no teiō Satomi Hajime no shōgai* (Tokyo: Kōjinsha, 2007); and Sano Shin'ichi, *Ahen Ō: Manshū no yoru to kiri* (Tokyo: Shinchōsha, 2008).

71. Satō Hiroshi, "Dai Tō-A no tokushu shigen: 'Ahen,'" in Okada, Tatai, and Takahashi, eds., *Ahen mondai,* 13–31.

72. OAC, "Minutes of the Twenty-Third Session" (Geneva, 1939), 21.

73. Ibid., 46, 111.

74. Nanhō kaihatsu kinko chōsaka, "Kyōeiken no ahen jijō," in Okada, Tatai, and Takahashi, eds., *Ahen mondai,* 193–207.

75. On Japanese management of the drug market in Southeast Asia in the early 1940s, see Steven B. Karch, "Japan and the Cocaine Industry of Southeast Asia, 1864–1944," in Paul Gootenberg, ed., *Cocaine: Global Histories* (New York: Routledge, 1999), 146–64.

CHAPTER 6

1. Kikuchi Yūji, "Ahen haidoku undō ni kansuru iken," 7.

2. "1935 Manchukuo Annual Report," in Jarman, ed., *Japan and Dependencies,* 15:497.

3. Scholars have not traditionally understood law enforcers as moral entrepreneurs, instead viewing their emergence as an outcome of moral crusades. Becker, *Outsiders,* 157.

4. On law as a signifier of legitimacy for Japanese imperialism, see Tay-Sheng Wang, *Legal Reform in Taiwan under Japanese Colonial Rule, 1895–1945: The Reception of Western Law* (Seattle: University of Washington Press, 2000); and Alexis Dudden, *Japan's Colonization of Korea: Discourse and Power* (Honolulu: University of Hawai'i Press, 2005).

5. Kawaji Toshiyoshi, "Kengi sōron," in Yamamoto Kazuo, *Nihon keisatsu shi* (Tokyo: Shōkadō shoten, 1934), 132; Elise K. Tipton, *The Japanese Police State: The Tokkō in Interwar Japan* (Honolulu: University of Hawai'i Press, 1990), 35–51.

6. James R. Rush, *Opium to Java: Revenue Farming and Chinese Enterprise in Colonial Indonesia, 1860–1910* (Ithaca, NY: Cornell University Press, 1990), 114; Brian G. Martin, *The Shanghai Green Gang: Politics and Organized Crime, 1919–1937* (Berkeley: University of California Press, 1996), 23.

7. Frederic E. Wakeman Jr., *Policing Shanghai: 1927–1937* (Berkeley: University of California Press, 1995), 116–31; Robert Bickers, "Who Were the Shanghai Municipal Police, and Why Were They There? The British Recruits of 1919," in Robert Bickers and Christian Henriot, eds., *New Frontiers: Imperialism's New Communities in East Asia, 1842–1953* (Manchester: Manchester University Press, 2000), 38–54.

8. South Manchuria Railway Company, *Report on Progress in Manchuria* (Dairen: South Manchuria Railway Company, 1929), 55.

9. Kantō-chō bunshoka, *Kantō-chō shisei nijū nenshi* (Dairen: Kantō-chō, 1926), 291–93.

10. Ogino Fujio, *Gaimushō keisatsu shi* (Tokyo: Azekura shobō, 2005), 160.

11. *Nihon teikoku tōkei nenkan*, vol. 51 (1931), 401.

12. Kantō-chō keimu-kyoku eiseika, *Kokusai renmei Kyokutō ahen chōsa no shitsumon ni taisuru tōbensho* (Dairen: Kantō-chō keimu-kyoku eiseika, 1930), 73.

13. *Kantō tōkei sho*, vols. 3–32 (1908–37).

14. "1936 Manchukuo Annual Report," in Jarman, ed., *Japan and Dependencies*, 15:149.

15. Erik Esselstrom, *Crossing Empire's Edge: Foreign Ministry Police and Japanese Expansionism in Northeast Asia* (Honolulu: University of Hawai'i Press, 2009), 93.

16. League of Nations, "Commission of Enquiry into the Control of Opium-Smoking in the Far East" (Geneva, 1931), 456–57.

17. "1926 Annual Report," in Jarman, ed., *Japan and Dependencies*, 2:191.

18. Dairen keisatsu sho, "Ahen oyobi masuizai mitsu yushutsunyū nenbetsu chō," in Kurahashi, ed., *Benzoirin fusei yunyū jiken kankei shiryō*, 141; "1924 Kwantung Annual Report," in Jarman, ed., *Japan and Dependencies*, 13:312.

19. "1938 Manchukuo Annual Report," in Jarman, ed., *Japan and Dependencies*, 16:182.

20. Kurahashi, *Ahen, teikoku, Nihon*, 37–103.

21. "Medical Work in Manchuria," *Chinese Medical Journal* 47, no. 2 (1933): 187–89, 189 (italics in original). Sewage from boxcars was often emptied onto the train tracks, accounting for the attempt to disinfect the wheels.

22. "Charge That Japan Aids Opium Trade," *New York Times*, February 19, 1919.

23. Gaimushō, *Ahen mondai* (Tokyo: Gaimushō tsūshō-kyoku, 1922), 228–29.

24. Kobayashi and Zhang, eds., *Ken'etsu sareta tegami ga kataru*, 98–99.

25. "1925 Kwantung Annual Report," in Jarman, ed., *Japan and Dependencies*, 13:333–34; Memorandum to the Japanese Legation at Beijing, Jun. 10, 1920, in *Ahen sono ta dokuzaiyaku oyobi kyūshoku kigu torishimari kankei zakken: Honpō no bu—Kantōshū, Seitō, Taiwan ni okeru ahen seido teppai mondai.*

26. Lin Yutang, *Moment in Peking*, 720.

27. Kurahashi, *Nihon no ahen senryaku*, 121–30.

28. "Communication from Manchurian Agent to U.S. Commissioner of Customs," Apr. 16, 1935, in United States Department of State, *Records of the Department of State Relating to the Internal Affairs of Japan, 1930–1939.*

29. Lin Yutang, *Moment in Peking*, 722.

30. Report, Feb. 10, 1933, in United States Department of State, *Records of the Department of State Relating to the Internal Affairs of Japan, 1930–1939*; Commissioner Report, Jun. 7, 1932, in ibid.

31. Report, Sept. 14, 1934, in ibid.

32. "1914 Dairen Trade Report," in Jarman, ed., *Japan and Dependencies*, 13:260.

33. Dai, "The Opium Condition in Manchuria," 20.

34. Sun Bang, ed., *Wei-Man shehui* (Changchun: Jilin renmin chubanshe, 1993), 450.

35. Guojia jindu weiyuanhui bangongshi zuzhi pianxie, *Zhongguo jindu shi ziliao* (Tianjin: Tianjin renmin chubanshe, 1998), 597.

36. Dai, "The Opium Condition in Manchuria," 6.

37. Vespa, *Secret Agent of Japan*, x.

38. C. Walter Young, *Korean Problems in Manchuria as Factors in the Sino-Japanese Dispute: An Analytical and Interpretive Study* (Supplementary Documents to the Report of the Commission of Enquiry, 1933), 23.

39. Mizuno Naoki, "Kokuseki wo meguru Higashi Ajia kankei: Shokuminchi ki Chōsenjin kokuseki mondai no isō," in Yamamuro Shin'ichi and Furuya Tetsuo, eds., *Kindai Nihon ni okeru Higashi Ajia mondai* (Tokyo: Yoshikawa Kōbunkan, 2001), 211–37; Brooks, "Peopling the Japanese Empire," 25–44.

40. R. Endo, *Japan, China, and Manchukuo: The Kingly Way* (Tokyo: East Asiatic Society Press, 1933), 15.

41. Makuuchi Mitsuo, *Manshūkoku keisatsu gaishi* (Tokyo: San'ichi shobō, 1996), 256–58, 288.

42. "1938 Manchukuo Annual Report," in Jarman, ed., *Japan and Dependencies*, 16: 253.

43. Clifford Johnson, *Pirate Junk: Five Months' Captivity with Manchurian Bandits* (New York: Charles Scribners' Sons, 1934), 111.

44. *The Manchoukuo Year Book* (Tokyo: Tō-A keizai chōsa-kyoku, 1942), 380.

45. Shenyang jingcha-ting weishengke, "Shenyang jingcha-ting sannian weisheng nianjian," *Dongfang yixue zazhi* 15 (1937): 40–48; "1934 Manchukuo Annual Report," in Jarman, ed., *Japan and Dependencies*, 14:355.

46. Satō Shin'ichirō, *Daikan'en no kaibō*, 141.

47. The consular police sentenced some petty dealers directly rather than remanding them to court. Although the severity of consular justice varied by time and place, harsh punishment was exceptional. Kuratsuka Yoshio, "Ahen kara mita Nit-Chū kankei," *Kikan Chūgoku* 57 (1999): 7.

48. Kwantung Government, *Outline of the Kwantung Government* (Dairen: Manchuria Daily News, 1926), 7.

49. *Kantō tōkei sho*, vols. 19–36 (1924–41). Data is unavailable for 1934 and 1935.

50. "Ahen en oyobi 'moruhine' 'kokain' ni kansuru hanzai hyō," 1918, in *Ahen sono ta dokuzaiyaku oyobi kyūshoku kigu torishimari kankei zakken: Ryōjikan rei no bu.*

51. Kuroshima, *A Flock of Swirling Crows and Other Proletarian Writings*, 148, 161–62.

52. *Kantō tōkei sho*, vols. 19–36 (1924–41). Data is unavailable for 1935.

53. Ibid., vols. 13–36 (1918–41).

54. Ibid., vols. 19–36 (1924–41). Data is unavailable for 1926–28 inclusive and 1940.

55. A. M. Pooley, *Japan at the Cross Roads* (London: George Allen & Unwin, 1917), 333.

56. Kantō-chō kōtō hōin, chihō hōin, "Ahen saiban hanketsu bun," in Okada, Tatai, and Takahashi, eds., *Ahen mondai*, 85–91. The ultimate outcome of Zhang's case was not recorded.

57. "Drug Smuggling Ring Which Sold 2,200,000 Yen Worth of Dope: Trial in Dairen," *Japan Chronicle*, Feb. 4, 1931.

58. Dairen chihō hōin, *Masuizai torishimari kisoku ihan nami sōshūwai hikoku jiken kokan sokki* (Dairen: Dairen chihō hōin, 1931), 1–43.

59. Ibid., 1.

60. "Benzoirin mitsuyu jiken honjitsu yoshin shūketsu su," in Kurahashi, ed., *Benzoirin fusei yunyū jiken kankei shiryō*, 13.

61. "Dairen Drug Scandal: Expert Declares Drug Covered by Regulations," *Japan Chronicle*, Feb. 5, 1931.

62. Dairen chihō hōin, *Masuizai torishimari kisoku ihan nami sōshūwai hikoku jiken kokan sokki*, 43.

63. "Dairen Drug Scandal," *Japan Chronicle*, Feb. 5, 1931.

64. Dairen chihō hōin, *Masuizai torishimari kisoku ihan nami sōshūwai hikoku jiken kokan sokki*, 2–3.

65. Ibid., 128.

66. Kurahashi, *Ahen, teikoku, Nihon*, 208–23.

67. Dispatch, Aug. 28, 1933, in United States Department of State, *Records of the Department of State Relating to the Internal Affairs of Japan, 1930–1939*.

68. Alan A. Block, "European Drug Traffic and Traffickers between the Wars: The Policy of Suppression and Its Consequences," *Journal of Social History* 23, no. 2 (1989): 315–37.

69. Quoted in Richard Davenport-Hines, *The Pursuit of Oblivion: A Global History of Narcotics 1500–2000* (London: Weidenfield & Nicolson, 2001), 217–18.

70. Chiara Betta, "Marginal Westerners in Shanghai: The Baghdadi Jewish Community, 1842–1945," in Bickers and Henriot, eds., *New Frontiers*, 38–54; Joshua A. Fogel, "The Japanese and the Jews: A Comparative Analysis of Their Communities in Harbin, 1898–1930," in Bickers and Henriot, eds., *New Frontiers*, 88–108.

71. *Kantō tōkei sho*, vols. 4–36 (1909–41). Data is incomplete for 1913, 1930–35, and 1937–38.

72. "Memorandum Handed to Mr. Kawai, Director of Foreign Affairs, Kwantung Government," Sept. 16, 1931, in United States Department of State, *Records of the United States Department of State Relating to the Internal Affairs of Japan, 1930–1939*; "1934 Manchukuo Annual Report," in Jarman, ed., *Japan and Dependencies*, 14:291.

73. "Letter to A. A. Elliott, Acting District Supervisor of San Francisco," Mar. 4, 1932, in United States Department of State, *Records of the United States Department of State Relating to the Internal Affairs of Japan, 1930–1939*.

74. Report, Dec. 28, 1931, in United States Department of State, *Records of the Department of State Relating to the Internal Affairs of Japan, 1930–1939*; "Arrest of George I. Tribe, American Citizen and Narcotic Trafficker," in United States Department of State, *Records of the Department of State Relating to the Internal Affairs of Japan, 1930–1939*.

75. Report, Jun. 12, 1933, in United States Department of State, *Records of the United States Department of State Relating to the Internal Affairs of Japan, 1930–1939*.

76. "1932 Kwantung Annual Report," in Jarman, ed., *Japan and Dependencies*, 13:456.

77. *The Kwantung Government: Its Functions and Works* (Ryōjun: Kwantung Government, 1929), 12.

78. Kantō-chō keimu-kyoku eiseika, *Kokusai renmei Kyokutō ahen chōsa iin no shitsumon ni taisuru tōbensho*, 73.

79. *Kantō tōkei sho*, vol. 28 (1933).

80. "Chōshun tetsudō fuzokuchi ni okeru Shinajin ni ahen en han," in *Ahen sono ta dokuzaiyaku oyobi kyūshoku kigu torishimari zakken: Honpō no bu—Kantōshū, Seitō, Taiwan ni okeru ahen seido teppai mondai*. Numbers do not suffice to analyze sentencing patterns among Japanese and Korean suspects arrested for narcotics violations.

81. *Nihon teikoku tōkei nenkan*, vols. 31–48 (1912–29).

82. Richard Mitchell, *Thought Control in Prewar Japan* (Ithaca, NY: Cornell University Press, 1976), 127; Chulwoo Lee, "Modernity, Legality, and Power in Korea under Japanese Rule," in Gi-Wook Shin and Michael Robinson, eds., *Colonial Modernity in Korea* (Cambridge, MA: Harvard University Asia Center, 1999), 21–51.

83. Masaki Akira, *Reminiscences of a Japanese Penologist* (Tokyo: Japanese Criminal Policy Association, 1964), 38, 67–68.

84. Kantō-kyoku bunshoka, *Kantō-kyoku shisei nijū nen shi*, 251.

85. Kantō-kyoku kanbō bunshoka, *Kantō-kyoku shisei sanjū nen gyōseki chōsa shiryō*, 148, 134.

86. Itō Takeo, *Life along the South Manchurian Railway*, 196.

87. *Kantō tōkei sho*, vols. 3–36 (1908–41).

88. South Manchuria Railway Company, *Sixth Report on Progress in Manchuria* (Dairen: South Manchuria Railway Company, 1939), 15. Ironically, the modern Chinese penal system was largely based on the Japanese model. Frank Dikötter, *Crime, Punishment, and the Prison in Modern China* (New York: Columbia University Press, 2002), 114.

89. *Man-Mō tokushu ken'eki ron* (Tokyo: Nihon hyōron shuppan, 1933), 318.

90. South Manchuria Railway Company, *Sixth Report on Progress in Manchuria*, 15.

91. Masaki, *Reminiscences of a Japanese Penologist*, 81–82.

92. Dikötter, *Crime, Punishment, and the Prison in Modern China*, 126; *The Manchoukuo Year Book* (1942), 383, 117.

93. Daniel V. Botsman, *Punishment and Power in the Making of Modern Japan* (Princeton, NJ: Princeton University Press, 2005), 141–64.

94. Kantō-chō bunshoka, *Kantō-chō shisei nijū nenshi*, 302.

95. Masaki, *Reminiscences of a Japanese Penologist*, 91.

96. *Nihon teikoku tōkei nenkan*, vols. 27–63 (1908–44).

97. Masaki, *Reminiscences of a Japanese Penologist*, 91.

98. In Taiwan and Korea, by contrast, no more than twenty-five strokes were administered per day. Chulwoo Lee, "Modernity, Legality, and Power under Japanese Colonial Rule," 34–35.

99. Masaki, *Reminiscences of a Japanese Penologist*, 91.

100. Okamoto Shigejirō, "Manshūkokujin ni kei wo kasuru koto wo eru ya," *Hōritsu Shinbun*, Jul. 8, 1936, 3–4.

101. OAC, "Minutes of the Twentieth Session" (Geneva, 1935), 75.

102. Thomas David DuBois, "Inauthentic Sovereignty: Law and Legal Matters in Manchukuo," *Journal of Asian Studies* 69, no. 3 (2010): 763.

103. Letter from Consul Morioka to Foreign Minister Uchida, May 24, 1933, in *Ahen sono ta dokuzaiyaku torishimari kankei zakken: Manshūkoku no bu*.

104. Letter from Consul Nagai to Foreign Minister Uchida, Feb. 15, 1933, in ibid.

105. Letter from General Mutō to Foreign Minister Uchida, Sept. 26, 1933, in ibid.

106. Letter from Consul Kajiwara to Foreign Minister Uchida, Aug. 1, 1933, in ibid.

107. Letter from Consul Morishima to Foreign Minister Hirota, Oct. 1933, in ibid. On comparable schemes to relocate Korean drug dealers in the north China port of Tianjin, see Kobayashi Motohiro, "Drug Operations by Resident Japanese in Tianjin," in Brook and Wakabayashi, eds., *Opium Regimes,* 162–63.

108. "Japanese Opium Policy in China," *Chinese Medical Journal* 52, no. 1 (1937): 122–23.

109. On the complexities of "collaboration" in Japanese Manchuria, see Rana Mitter, *The Manchurian Myth: Nationalism, Resistance, and Collaboration in Modern China* (Berkeley: University of California Press, 2000).

110. On warlords and opium, see Xiaoxing Li, *Poppies and Politics in China: Sichuan Province, 1840s to 1940s* (Newark: University of Delaware Press, 2009). On the stance of Chiang Kai-shek and the Nationalist Party regarding opium, see Edward Slack, Jr., *Opium, State and Society: China's Narco-Economy and the Guomindang, 1924–1937* (Honolulu: University of Hawai'i Press, 2001); and Baumler, *The Chinese and Opium under the Republic.* On opium trafficking by the CCP, see Chen Yung-fa, "The Blooming Poppy under the Red Sun: The Yan'an Way and the Opium Trade," in Tony Saich and Hans van de Ven, eds., *New Perspectives on the Chinese Communist Revolution* (Armonk, NY: M. E. Sharpe, 1995), 263–98.

111. Helie Lee, *Still Life with Rice,* 107–8.

CHAPTER 7

1. Quoted in Christopher T. Nieh, "Japan's Manchuria Policy from the Kwantung Leased Territory to the Formation of Manchukuo" (PhD diss., Johns Hopkins University, 1993), 36.

2. Ruth Rogaski, *Hygienic Modernity: Meanings of Health and Disease in Treaty-Port China* (Berkeley: University of California Press, 2004), 136–64.

3. Iijima, *Mararia to teikoku,* 390.

4. Richard C. Keller, *Colonial Madness: Psychiatry in French North Africa* (Chicago: University of Chicago Press, 2007), 8.

5. Timothy A. Hickman, *The Secret Leprosy of Modern Days: Narcotic Addiction and Cultural Crisis in the United States, 1870–1920* (Amherst: University of Massachusetts Press, 2007), 33–58.

6. Courtwright, *Dark Paradise,* 38–43.

7. Michael Bourdaghs, "The Disease of Nationalism, the Empire of Hygiene," *positions* 6, no. 3 (1998): 637–73.

8. Nakayama Shigeru has defined Western or scientific medicine as "modern approaches to treatment on the basis of physiological and pathological theories that are

grounded in anatomy." The East Asian tradition, by contrast, emphasizes the development of techniques through experience. Nakayama Shigeru, *Academic and Scientific Traditions in China, Japan and the West*, trans. Jerry Dusenbury (Tokyo: University of Tokyo Press, 1984), 198.

9. Susan Burns, "Contemplating Places: The Hospital as Modern Experience in Meiji Japan," in Helen Hardacre with Adam L. Kern, eds., *New Directions in the Study of Meiji Japan* (New York: Brill, 1997), 702–18; Johnston, *The Modern Epidemic*, 189; Ann Bowman Jannetta, *The Vaccinators: Smallpox, Medical Knowledge, and the Opening of Japan* (Stanford, CA: Stanford University Press, 2007), 9.

10. Hiromi Mizuno, *Science for the Empire: Scientific Nationalism in Modern Japan* (Stanford, CA: Stanford University Press, 2009), 12.

11. James Bartholomew, *The Formation of Science in Japan: Building a Research Tradition* (New Haven, CT: Yale University Press, 1989), 125–95.

12. Deepak Kumar, *Science and the Raj 1857–1905* (New York: Oxford University Press, 1995), 111; Lewis Pyenson, *Civilizing Mission: Exact Sciences and French Overseas Expansion, 1830–1940* (Baltimore, MD: Johns Hopkins University Press, 1993), 341.

13. M. Matsuo, *The Development of Science and Culture in Manchuria: Japan's Contributions* (Dairen: Research Committee of Pacific Relations in SMR, n.d.), 1.

14. The Mukden Medical College (so called in the West) was founded as a public institution by the SMR as the Minami-Man Igakudō, but became a private institution in 1922 and changed its name to Manshū Ika Daigaku. This shift notwithstanding, the SMR continued to support the MMC financially.

15. M. Tsurumi, *Public Hygiene in Manchuria and Mongolia* (Dairen: *Manshū Nichinichi Shinbun*, n.d.), 5.

16. On the significance of the colonial laboratory, see Warwick Anderson, *Colonial Pathologies: American Tropical Medicine, Race, and Hygiene in the Philippines* (Durham, NC: Duke University Press, 2006), 5–6.

17. Minami-Man Igakudō, "Minami-Man Igakudō ikken," in Shin and Nagaoka, eds., *Shokuminchi shakai jigyō kankei shiryō shū—"Manshū, Manshūkoku"* vol. 41, *Iryō to eisei*, 227.

18. Rogaski, "Vampires in Plagueland,"134.

19. Nan-Man Igakudō, *Nan-Man Igakudō jū nen shi* (Hōten: Nan-Man Igakudō, 1923), 40.

20. Laurence Monnais, "'Modern Medicine' in French Colonial Vietnam: From the Importation of a Model to Its Nativisation," in Hormoz Ebrahimnejad, ed., *The Development of Modern Medicine in Non-Western Countries: Historical Perspectives* (New York: Routledge, 2009), 127–59; Douglas M. Haynes, "The Persistence of Privilege: British Medical Qualifications and the Practice of Medicine in the Empire," in Kevin Grant, Philippa Levine, and Frank Trentmann, eds., *Beyond Sovereignty: Britain, Empire, and Transnationalism, c. 1880–1950* (New York: Palgrave Macmillan, 2007), 214–39.

21. Pyenson, *Civilizing Mission*, 65.

22. Pratik Chakrabarti, *Western Science in Modern India: Metropolitan Models, Colonial Practices* (Delhi: Permanent Black, 2004), 185.

23. Kumar, *Science and the Raj 1857–1905*, 212.

24. *China Medical Journal* 40, no. 7 (1926): 743.

25. Saenaga Keiko, *Senji igaku no jittai* (Tokyo: Seiunsha, 2005), 9.

26. The one comparable case may be the Dutch East Indies, which boasted a number of premier educational and scientific institutes and offered a limited number of Indonesian students the opportunity to earn a medical degree or doctorate and pursue a career in research. Lewis Pyenson, *Empire of Reason: Exact Sciences in Indonesia 1840–1940* (Leiden: Brill, 1989).

27. Scholarly indexes attest to the lack of research on addiction in Japanese Manchuria prior to 1924. For example, see Manshū Ika Daigaku, *Manshū Ika Daigaku gyōseki shū dai isshū* (Hōten: Manshū Ika Daigaku, 1940); and Manshū Ika Daigaku, *Manshū Ika Daigaku gyōseki shū dai ni shū* (*Shōwa 14–16*).

28. "Medical Research in the Orient," *China Medical Journal* 37, no. 5 (1923): 412.

29. Chung, *Struggle for National Survival*, 37.

30. Barkan, *The Retreat of Scientific Racism*, xi.

31. Susan E. Lederer, *Subjected to Science: Human Experimentation in America before the Second World War* (Baltimore, MD: Johns Hopkins University Press, 1995); Steven Epstein, *Inclusion: The Politics of Difference in Medical Research* (Chicago: University of Chicago Press, 2007), 30–52; Ken'ichi Tsuneishi, "Unit 731 and the Human Skulls Discovered in 1989: Physicians Carrying Out Organized Crimes," in William La Fleur, Gernot Bihme, and Susumu Shimazono, eds., *Dark Medicine: Rationalizing Unethical Medical Research* (Bloomington: Indiana University Press, 2007), 73–84; Nancy D. Campbell, J. P. Olsen, and Luke Walden, *The Narcotic Farm* (New York: Abrams, 2008); Hsu Hung Bin, "From Smokers to Addicts: A History of Opium and Its Uses in Taiwan" (PhD diss., School of Oriental and African Studies, 2008), 354; Saenaga Keiko, "Jūgo nen sensō ki no daigaku ni okeru igaku kenkyū—Kyū Manshū Ika Daigaku wo jirei to shite," *Nihon no kagakusha* 43, no. 2 (2008): 16–21.

32. *Nobiyuki Dairen* (Dairen: Achō shuppan kyōkai, 1935), 115; Sasaki Tōichirō, "Nit-Shi kyōgaku no shin'i tettei ni tsutomerareta Morinaka Kiyoshi gakuchō," in Hōjin Dōsōkai, ed., *Manshū Ika Daigaku yonjū shūnen kinen shi* (Tokyo: Hōjin Dōsōkai, 1952), 924–25.

33. Wang Shigong, "Chūgoku ahen kōshū," *Dōjin* 10, no. 2 (1936): 47–50.

34. *MIZ*, vols. 1–39 (1924–43).

35. Susan Reynolds Whyte, Sjaak van der Geest, and Anita Hardon, *Social Lives of Medicines* (New York: Cambridge University Press, 2002).

36. Quoted in Liu Shi-yung, "Medical Reform in Colonial Taiwan" (PhD diss., University of Pittsburgh, 2000), 70.

37. Kinoshita Tetsuo, "Yakurigaku kyōshitsu," in Hōjin Dōsōkai, ed., *Manshū Ika Daigaku yonjū shūnen kinen shi,* 38–40.

38. Kinoshita, "Yakurigaku kyōshitsu," 41–43; Itō Ryōichi, "Ketsuen yō ahen ni kansuru keitōteki kenkyū, dai ni hō: Dai ichi ji shiken seiseki," *MIZ* 26, no. 1 (1937): 23–37; Itō Ryōichi, "Ketsuen yō ahen ni kansuru keitōteki kenkyū, dai san hō: Dai ni ji shiken seiseki," *MIZ* 26, no. 2 (1937): 219–28; Itō Ryōichi, "Ketsuen yō ahen ni kansuru keitōteki kenkyū, dai yon hō: Dai san ji oyobi dai yo ji shiken seiseki," *MIZ* 26, no. 3 (1937): 347–68.

39. Terada Bunjirō and Honda Masato, "Amai nezumi shiriage hannō yori mitaru ahen 'arukaroido' no yakuri kisen ni oite," *MIZ* 22, no. 4 (1936): 677–85; Kinoshita, "Yakurigaku kyōshitsu," 47.

40. Nakajima Seikichi and Kubota Seikō, "Ahen en chū ni fukumaru, yūkō seibun ni oite," *TIZ* 26, no. 265 (1927): 522.

41. Du Congming, *Huiyi lü* (Taipei: Du Congming boshi jiangxuejijinhui, 1982), 65.

42. Du Congming, "Kanto-chō oyobi Chūgoku ni okeru ahen oyobi moruhine rui chūdokusha oyobi sono chiryō shūyōsho no jōtai ni kansuru chōsa hōkoku sho," in *Du Congming yanlun ji* (Taipei: Du Congming boshi huanli jinian jiangxuejin guanli weiyuanhui, 1955), 194.

43. Kinoshita, "Yakurigaku kyōshitsu," 39.

44. Itō cited his paper in the following publication: Itō Kōmao, "Mayaku chūdokushō no kyōdō ni oite," *Man-Sen no ikai* 179 (1936): 21–24.

45. Du, *Huiyi lü,* 130.

46. Ibid., 51.

47. For example, see Takano Toranosuke and Xiang Naixi, "Mansei ahen oyobi 'heroin' chūdoku kanja no kessei yokudo sanchi ni oite," *MIZ* 29, no. 3 (1938): 761–767.

48. Herbert L. May, *Survey of Smoking Conditions in the Far East: A Report to the Executive Board of the Foreign Policy Association* (New York: Opium Research Committee of the Foreign Policy Association, 1927), 138.

49. Sarah W. Tracy and Caroline Jean Acker, "Psychoactive Drugs: An American Way of Life," in *Altering American Consciousness: The History of Alcohol and Drug Use in the United States, 1800–2000* (Amherst: University of Massachusetts Press, 2004), 15. Terry and Pellens's work (Charles E. Terry and Mildred Pellens. *The Opium Problem* [New York: Bureau of Social Hygiene, 1928]) "remains a classic and standard reference today." Caroline Jean Acker, *Creating the American Junkie: Addiction Research in the Classic Era of Narcotic Control* (Baltimore, MD: Johns Hopkins University Press, 2002), 56.

50. Terry and Pellens, *The Opium Problem,* 223–465.

51. Hugo Martin Krueger, *The Pharmacology of the Opium Alkaloids* (Washington, DC: Government Printing Office, 1943), 1089–448. An earlier edition of this work appeared in Japanese translation as *Ahen arukaroido kagaku,* trans. Takamoto Ryūji (Tokyo: Nankōdō, 1937).

52. "Japan and the Opium Scourge in China," *Opium: A World Problem* 1, no. 4 (1928): 17.

53. Miyajima, *Kokusai ahen mondai no keii,* 109.

54. Lewis Pyenson, *Cultural Imperialism and Exact Sciences: German Expansion Overseas, 1900–1930* (New York: Peter Lang, 1984), 306–7.

55. Acker, *Creating the American Junkie,* 17.

56. Edward Shorter, *A History of Psychiatry* (New York: John Wiley & Sons, 1997), 145–89. Psychiatrists are the only medical specialists regularly studied as moral entrepreneurs.

57. Janice Matsumura, "Mental Health as Public Peace: Kaneko Junji and the Promotion of Psychiatry in Modern Japan," *Modern Asian Studies* 38, no. 4 (2004): 899–930. Even prewar psychiatrists who wrote about addiction, such as Kaneko Junji, considered the condition a moral rather than psychological problem. Kaneko Junji, *Hanzai no shinri* (Tokyo: Kuresu shuppan, 2008), 28–29.

58. "Medical Work in Manchuria," *Chinese Medical Journal* 47, no. 2 (1933): 189.

59. Matsuo, *The Development of Science and Culture in Manchuria,* i.

60. Kubota Seikō, "Ahen no hanashi," in Manshū Ika Daigaku, ed., *Manshū Ika Daigaku jutsu kōenkai kōenshū* (Shinkyō: Manshū Ika Daigaku, 1934), 26.

61. Manshū Ika Daigaku, *Manshu Ika Daigaku gyōseki shū dai isshū,* ii.

62. Kotani Keisuke, *Kantōgun shūsai Manshū Ika Daigaku Nekka chihōbyō kenkyūdan kōdō no gaiyō* (Hōten: Manshū Ika Daigaku, 1934), 134.

63. "Manchoukuo to Have a New Medical College," *Contemporary Manchuria: A Bi-Monthly Review of Manchuria* 2, no. 2 (1937): 113–14.

64. For example, see Wang Zujie, "Shōshū chūdoku kanja no tōkeiteki kansatsu," *MIZ* 29, no. 5 (1938): 1012; Morinaka Kiyoshi and Liu Maochun, "Manxing mafei zhongduzheng zhi weichang zhanggai," *Tongren yixue* 4, no. 8 (1931): 713–30; and Takano and Xiang, "Mansei ahen oyobi 'heroin' chūdoku kanja no kessei yokudo sanchi ni oite."

65. Ming-cheng Lo refers to these doctors as "national physicians." Ming-cheng Miriam Lo, *Doctors within Borders: Profession, Ethnicity, and Modernity in Colonial Taiwan* (Berkeley: University of California Press, 2002), 109–50.

66. Manshū Ika Daigaku, *Manshū Ika Daigaku gyōseki shū dai isshū,* 36–38.

67. "Harupin shi bu rekkai," *MIZ* 29, no. 6 (1938): 1134; "Fushun shi bu rekkai," *MIZ* 31, no. 6 (1939): 1355; "Dai roku Manshū Igakkai sōkai," *MIZ* 31, no. 4 (1939): 169.

68. Programs for the medical conference appeared annually in the September issues of *Man-Sen no ikai* in 1928–33. See *Man-Sen no ikai,* nos. 78, 103, 114, 126, 138, and 151.

69. Between 1934 and 1944, Du gave at least seven commencement addresses, one wedding toast, and two eulogies for his staff. Du, *Du Congming yanlun ji,* 234–384.

70. Du, *Huiyi lü,* 86; Du Congming, "Morishima Kurata-sensei ni sashiageta tegami, 1939-nen go gatsu sanjū nichi," in *Du Congming yanlun ji,* 313–14.

71. Du Congming, "Yue Morishima Kurata-sensei yōchōshiki chōji," in *Du Congming yanlun ji*, 374–75; Du Congming, "Morishima-sensei wo shinobu," in *Du Congming yanlun ji*, 380–82; "Japan," *Journal of the American Medical Association* 97, no. 10 (1931): 719–20.

72. For a compilation of Sakai's writings on opium addiction, see Shintō kagaku kenkyūjo, ed., *Ahen oyobi ruiji 'arukaroido' mansei chūdokushō no kōkateki chiryō to sono hōsaku*. For examples of Abe's research, see his four-part study, "Guanyu manxing mafei zhongdu zhi yanjiu," *Tongren yixue* 2, no. 4 (1929): 205–18; and Abe Shōma, "Moruhine shōhan no gen'in nami ni kindan genshō no gen'in," *TIZ*, no. 365 (1935): 2177.

73. For comparison cases, see Roy MacLeod, "On Visiting the 'Moving Metropolis': Reflections on the Architecture of Imperial Science," in Nathan Reingold and Marc Rothenberg, eds., *Scientific Colonialism: A Cross-Cultural Comparison* (Washington, DC: Smithsonian Institution Press, 1987), 217–51; and David Arnold, *Science, Technology, and Medicine in Colonial India* (New York: Cambridge University Press, 2000), 14.

74. The voluminous literature analyzing the rationale behind Stalin's purges in the Soviet Union in the 1930s may offer some theoretical perspectives for understanding the Kwantung Army's seemingly illogical turn against the intellectual elite of Manchukuo. Hannah Arendt, one of the earliest and most famous commentators on totalitarianism, has written, "None of these immense sacrifices in human life was motivated by a *raison d'état* in the old sense of the term." Purges "lacked political sense," given that "none of the liquidated social classes was hostile to the regime or likely to become hostile in the foreseeable future." Arendt, *The Origins of Totalitarianism*, 321–22.

75. F. C. Jones, *Manchuria since 1931*, 215.

76. Kinoshita, "Yakurigaku kyōshitsu," 47.

77. Unit 731 is now the subject of hundreds of popular and scholarly books and articles. For a full-length treatment of the subject in English, see Sheldon H. Harris, *Factories of Death: Japanese Biological Warfare, 1932–1945, and the American Cover-Up* (New York: Routledge, 1994).

78. *Materials on the Trial of Former Servicemen of the Japanese Army Charged with Manufacturing and Employing Bacteriological Weapons* (Moscow: Foreign Languages Publishing House, 1950), 80.

79. Saenaga, *Senji igaku no jittai*, 9.

80. Harris, *Factories of Death*, 105.

81. Kinoshita, "Yakurigaku kyōshitsu," 49.

CHAPTER 8

1. *Courtesans and Opium*, 6, 245.

2. Paul Wilson Howard, "Opium Suppression in Qing China: Responses to a Social Problem, 1729–1906" (PhD. diss., University of Pennsylvania, 1998), 144.

3. Kantō-chō, *Kantō-chō kannai shakai jigyō yōran* (Dairen: Kantō-chō naimu-kyoku chihōka, 1925); *Kantō tōkei sho,* vols. 12–24 (1917–29). On the history of the Red Cross in Japan, see Caroline Reeves, "From Red Crosses to Golden Arches: China, the Red Cross, and the Hague Peace Conference, 1899–1900," in Jerry H. Bentley, Renate Bridenthal, and Anand A. Yang, eds., *Interactions: Transregional Perspectives on World History* (Honolulu: University of Hawai'i Press, 2005), 70.

4. *Dairen Seiai Iin sanjūgo shūnen shi* (Dairen: Seiai Iin, 1941), 98. The nationality of four patients was not reported.

5. *Kantō tōkei sho,* vols. 5–14 (1910–19).

6. The hospital was founded as the Kirisuto Jie Byōin and changed its name to the Dairen Seiai Byōin in 1930.

7. The SMR Dairen Hospital also treated about two hundred drug users, mostly Japanese, between 1916 and 1920. Due to its position at the cutting edge of public health in the Japanese empire and East Asia, the hospital has been the subject of much contemporary scholarship. See Shimada Hiroshi, *Mantetsu no isan Dairen Byōin* (Nijū seiki Dairen kaigi, 2004); and Robert J. Perrins, "Doctors, Disease, and Development: Engineering Colonial Public Health in Southern Manchuria, 1905–1926," in Morris Low, ed., *Building a Modern Japan: Science, Technology, and Medicine in the Meiji Era and Beyond* (New York: Palgrave Macmillan, 2005), 103–32.

8. The institution founded under the name Dairen Kōsai Zendō Kyūryōsho became known as the Kantō-chō Kyūryōsho in 1928, in conjunction with the establishment of the KLT opium monopoly. When the Kantō-chō was abolished and replaced with the Kantō-kyoku in 1934, the name of the hospital was changed to Dairen Kyūryōsho. In 1938, it became known as the Kantō Kyūryōsho. To minimize confusion, I consistently refer to it as the Dairen Kyūryōsho. Kantōshū kōsei jigyō kyōkai, "Kantōshū shakai jigyō gaiyō," in Shin and Nagaoka, eds., *Shokuminchi shakai jigyō kankei shiryō shū—"Manshū, Manshūkoku,"* vol. 4, *Shakai jigyō sōran,* 303.

9. Gerald L. Geison, "Divided We Stand: Physiologists and Clinicians in the American Context," in Morris J. Vogel and Charles E. Rosenberg, eds., *The Therapeutic Revolution: Essays in the Social History of American Medicine* (Philadelphia: University of Pennsylvania Press, 1979), 71.

10. Michel Foucault, *The Birth of the Clinic: An Archaeology of Medical Perception,* trans. A. M. Sheridan Smith (New York: Pantheon Books, 1973), 85.

11. "Dairen Kyūryōsho yōran," n. p.

12. Thomas Dormandy, *Opium: Reality's Dark Dream* (New Haven, CT: Yale University Press, 2012), 268.

13. Acker, *Creating the American Junkie,* 94.

14. Kuroi, "Ahen moruhine chūdokusha ni taisuru henshitsuzai no chiryō seiseki," 10.

15. Dikötter, *Narcotic Culture,* 141.

16. Acker, *Creating the American Junkie,* 35.

17. "Dairen Kyūryōsho yōran," 122.

18. Ibid., 131.

19. Masaki, *Reminiscences of a Japanese Penologist,* 86.

20. "Dairen Kyūryōsho yōran," 125.

21. League of Nations, "Records of the Second Opium Conference" (Geneva, 1925), 159; League of Nations, "First Opium Conference: Minutes and Annexes," 19.

22. Chen Zhimin, *Du Congming yu Taiwan yiliao shi yanjiu* (Taipei: Guoli Zhongguo yiyue yanjiusuo, 2005), 107.

23. Du Congming, "Taihoku Kōseiin kangofu Chen Shiu-Chiau kokubutsushiki no chōji," in *Du Congming yanlun ji,* 251.

24. OAC, "Annual Reports of Governments on the Traffic in Opium and Other Dangerous Drugs for the Year 1936" (Geneva, 1938), 27; and Taiwan Sōtokufu keimu-bu eiseika, "Taiwan ahen inja no kōsei," in Okada, Tatai, and Takahashi, eds., *Ahen mondai,* 65.

25. Du Congming, "Taiwan kara ahen doku wo issō suru kōsei jigyō," in *Du Congming yanlun ji,* 348.

26. Taiwan Sōtokufu keimu-kyoku, *Taiwan no ahen seido,* 26.

27. Du Congming, "The Medical Treatment of Opium Addicts in the Government Central Hospital for Opium Addicts in Taipeh," in *Du Congming yanlun ji,* 200–202.

28. Shūhō Masasue, "Mansei 'morufuin' chūdoku ni kansuru kenkyū," *Man-Sen no ikai* 114 (1930): 35–36.

29. "Keijō dōchō no mohi chūdoku kanja chiryōsho wo otonau," *Chōsen oyobi Manshū* 272 (1926): 42–43; Tazawa, ed., *Ahen shiryō,* 16.

30. Mantetsu keizai chōsakai dai go bu, *Chōsen ahen mayaku seido chōsa hōkoku* (Dairen: Minami Manshū tetsudō kabushiki kaisha, 1932), 1.

31. Du Congming, "Chōsen ni okeru 'moruhine' rui mansei chūdoku mondai ni oite," in *Du Congming yanlun ji,* 217–24.

32. John M. Jennings, "The Forgotten Plague: Opium and Narcotics in Korea under Japanese Rule, 1910–1945," *Modern Asian Studies* 29, no. 4 (1995): 795–815.

33. Majima, *Mayaku chūdokusha to naku,* 1–2; Sally Ann Hastings, *Neighborhood and Nation in Tokyo, 1905–1937* (Pittsburgh, PA: University of Pittsburgh Press, 1995), 61, 183–84.

34. Mayaku chūdokusha kyūgokai, *Mayaku chūdokusha kyūgokai nenpō* (*Shōwa 14/15*) (Tokyo: Mayaku chūdokusha kyūgokai, 1940), 17–20.

35. Cho Sei-ki, "Akuma wo kugurite," in Majima, ed., *Mayaku chūdokusha to naku,* 101.

36. Kim X Joo, "Hanayaka na koshō kara suri no tsuma ni." In 1938, Cho and four other hospital staff were anonymously accused of manhandling patients and committing

other human rights violations. To Namae's chagrin, they were convicted at trial. Namae Takayuki, *Waga kyūjū nen no shōgai* (Tokyo: Ōzorasha, 1988), 162.

37. "Successful First Year for Anti-Drug Clinic Brings Plans to Extend Free Cure Facilities," *Japan Advertiser,* Oct. 20, 1936.

38. "Rescue Home Aids Victims of Drugs," *Japan Advertiser,* June 14, 1935.

39. Namae, *Waga kyūjū nen no shōgai,* 165.

40. Mayaku chūdokusha kyūgokai, *Mayaku chūdokusha kyūgokai nenpō* (*Shōwa 16*), 15, 29.

41. Masaki, *Reminiscences of a Japanese Penologist,* 87.

42. Courtwright, *Dark Paradise,* 56.

43. Sherman Cochran, "Marketing Medicine and Advertising Dreams in China, 1900–1950," in Wen-hsin Yeh, ed., *Becoming Chinese: Passages to Modernity and Beyond* (Berkeley: University of California Press, 2000), 84.

44. Lo, *The Opium Problem in the Far East,* 43.

45. "Oitorumin," *Nan-Man Igakkai zasshi* 11, no. 11 (1922): n.p.

46. "Spamidol," *Man-Sen no ikai* 107 (1930): n.p.

47. "Mophyzalin," *Tongrenhui yixue zazhi* 1, no. 3 (1928): n.p.

48. Dai, "The Opium Condition in Manchuria," 3–4.

49. Baumler, *The Chinese and Opium under the Republic,* 206.

50. Neizhengbu, "Jiejin yiyuan zhangcheng," in Zhu Wenyuan, ed., *Guomin zhengfu jinyuan shiliao* (Taipei: Guoshiguan, 2006), 4:587–88; Wang, "China's Opium Problem," 21; OAC, "Minutes of the Fifteenth Session" (Geneva, 1932), 165.

51. Dikötter, *Narcotic Culture,* 125–45.

52. OAC, "Minutes of the Twenty-Second Session," 34. On addiction in early twentieth-century Canada, see Catherine Carstairs, *Jailed for Possession: Illegal Drug Use, Regulation, and Power in Canada, 1920–1961* (Toronto: University of Toronto Press, 2006).

53. Musto, *The American Disease,* 151–82.

54. "Claim Opium Cure: Japanese Scientists Say Experiments Have Been Success." *Washington Star,* May 7, 1928.

55. Dispatch, Oct. 3, 1935, in United States Department of State, *Records of the Department of State Relating to the Internal Affairs of Japan, 1930–1939.*

56. OAC, "Minutes of the Eighteenth Session" (Geneva, 1934), 27.

57. Campbell, Olsen, and Walden, *The Narcotic Farm,* 15–18.

58. Harry J. Anslinger, "Memorandum for Assistant Secretary Gibbons," Oct. 12, 1937, in United States Department of State, *Records of the Department of State Relating to the Internal Affairs of Japan, 1930–1939.*

59. OAC, "Minutes of the Sixteenth Session" (Geneva, 1933), 18.

60. OAC, "Report to the Council on the Work of the Twenty-Third Session" (Geneva, 1938), 22.

61. Miyajima, *Kokusai ahen mondai no keii,* 109.

62. Quoted in Virginia Berridge, "'The British System' and Its History: Myth and Reality," in John Strang and Michael Gossop, eds., *Heroin Addiction and the British System: Origins and Evolution*, vol. 1 (New York: Routledge, 2005), 15.

63. Alex Mold, *Heroin: The Treatment of Addiction in Twentieth-Century Britain* (DeKalb: Northern Illinois University Press, 2008), 14–26; Padwa, *Social Poison*, 78–84, 139–74; Stephens, *Germans on Drugs*, 14–15.

64. The findings of the Commission of Enquiry notwithstanding, some scientific research on addiction did take place in the European colonies. See C. Rangé, "L'intoxication par l'opium," in the Far Eastern Association for Tropical Medicine, ed., *Transactions of the Second Congress* (Hong Kong: Noronha, 1912), 219–28; David J. Galloway, "Opium Smoking," in the Far Eastern Association for Tropical Medicine, ed., *Transactions of the Fifth Congress* (London: John Bale, Sons & Danielsson, 1923), 864–85; R. N. Chopra and Khem Singh Grewal, "Opium Habit in India," in the Far Eastern Association for Tropical Medicine, ed., *Transactions of the Seventh Congress*, vol. 3 (Calcutta: Thacker's Press & Directories, 1927), 568–75.

65. League of Nations, "Commission of Enquiry into the Control of Opium-Smoking in the Far East," 324.

66. Laurent Gaide, *L'Assistance médicale et la protection de la santé publique* (Hanoi: Imprimerie d'Extrême Orient, 1931), 372.

67. OAC, "Report to the Council on the Work of the Eighteenth Session," 87.

68. League of Nations, "Commission of Enquiry into the Control of Opium-Smoking in the Far East," 138.

69. *Japan-Manchoukuo Year Book* (Tokyo: Asia Statistics, 1938).

70. Lü, *Wei-Man shiqi de Dongbei yandu*, 119; Su, *Zhongguo dupin shi*, 407. Kurahashi Masanao has suggested that many addiction treatment clinics in Manchukuo existed in name only. See Kurahashi, "Nazo no tokkō yaku," 63–85.

71. Dai, "The Opium Condition in Manchuria," 5, 13.

72. Minami Manshū tetsudō kabushiki kaisha keizai chōsabu, *Manshū rōdō jigyō shūkan* (Dairen: Manshū bunka kyōkai, 1936), 227–28; Minseibu kōsei jigyōka, "Kyōka dantai gaiyō," in Shin and Nagaoka, eds., *Shokuminchi shakai jigyō kankei shiryō shū—"Manshū, Manshūkoku,"* vol. 37, *Shakai jigyō no jissen*, 184.

73. Shintō kagaku kenkyūjo, ed., *Ahen oyobi ruiji "arukaroido" mansei chūdokushō no kōkateki chiryō to sono hōsaku*, 27.

74. Kantō-kyoku keimubu eiseika, ed., *Eisei gaikan* (Shinkyō: Kantō-kyoku keimubu eiseika, 1937), 94.

75. Kantō-chō, *Kantō-chō kannai shakai jigyō yōran*, 42.

76. Dispatch, Feb. 12, 1940, in United States Department of State, *Confidential State Department Central Files: Internal Affairs of China, 1940–1944*.

77. Lü, *Wei-Man shiqi de Dongbei yandu*, 118–41; Kurahashi, *Ahen, teikoku, Nihon*, 107; Driscoll, *Absolute Erotic, Absolute Grotesque*, 227–63.

78. "Arimalin," *Tongren yixue* 2, no. 9 (1929): n.p.

79. Abe Tokujirō, "Mansei 'moruhine' chūdoku kanja no tōkeiteki kansatsu," *Man-Sen no ikai* 109 (1930): 9–28.

80. Shintō kagaku kenkyūjo, ed., *Ahen oyobi ruiji "arukaroido" mansei chūdokushō no kōkateki chiryō to sono hōsaku,* 41–57; Sakai, *Tō-A no reimei wa mayaku no genzetsu yori,* 23; Pritchard and Zaide, eds., *The Tokyo War Crimes Trial,* 4768–70.

81. Kurahashi, *Ahen, teikoku, Nihon,* 106–41.

82. OAC, "Minutes of the Sixteenth Session," 26–27.

83. Nai Shixiang, Yu Qinghan, and Guo Wentai, "Mansei mayaku chūdoku no yogo ni oite," *MIZ* 33, no. 1 (1940): 57–65.

84. Nagashima, "Opium Administration in Manchukuo," 33.

85. Reported in Sakai, *Tō-A no reimei wa mayaku no genzetsu yori,* 3.

86. OAC, "Minutes of the Sixteenth Session," 27.

87. Uga, *Taiwan ahen shi,* 31.

88. Namae Takayuki, "Mayaku chūdokusha kyūgo mondai," *Dojin* 8, no. 12 (1934): 35–41; Namae, *Waga kyūjū nen no shōgai,* 178.

89. T'ien Chün, *Village in August* (Cleveland, OH: World Publishing, 1944), 283.

90. Ibid., ix–xvii.

91. Wang Dianling, "Wei-Man shiqi jianxin de shehui duliu," in Wenshi jinghua bianjibu, ed., *Jindai Zhongguo yandu xiezhen,* 242.

92. Guo Wentai, "Mansei ahen oyobi 'moruhine' chūdokushō kanja no rinshōteki kansatsu," *MIZ* 26, no. 5 (1937): 911–19; Chen Yi, "Wei-Man shiqi de 'Kangshengyuan' he yapian xiaomaisuo," in Wenshi jinghua bianjibu, ed., *Jindai Zhongguo yandu xiezhen,* 250–52.

93. Chen, "Wei-Man shiqi de 'Kangshengyuan' he yapian xiaomaisuo," 252.

94. Nagashima, "Opium Administration in Manchukuo," 19.

95. "Opium Control Officers Meet," *Manchuria Daily News,* June 10, 1943, 4; Lü, *Wei-Man shiqi de Dongbei yandu,* 125.

96. "Japan," *Journal of the American Medical Association* 102, no. 8 (1934): 632–33.

97. Sun Bang, ed., *Wei-Man shehui,* 449.

98. Dispatch, Nov. 29, 1938, in United States Department of State, *Confidential State Department Central Files: Internal Affairs of Japan, 1940–1944.*

99. Carl F. Nathan, *Plague Prevention and Politics in Manchuria, 1910–1931* (Cambridge, MA: Harvard University East Asian Research Center, 1967); Iijima Wataru, "Shokuminchi shugi to igaku," in Nakami, ed., *Manshū to wa nandatta no ka,* 134–39; Sean Hsiang-lin Lei, "Sovereignty and the Microscope: Constituting Notifiable Infectious Disease and Containing the Manchurian Plague," in Leung and Furth, eds., *Health and Hygiene in Chinese East Asia,* 73–106; William C. Summers, *The Great Manchurian*

Plague of 1910–1911: The Geopolitics of an Epidemic Disease (New Haven, CT: Yale University Press, 2012).

100. "Good Health Great Asset," *Manchuria Daily News*, December 12, 1943, 3.

CHAPTER 9

1. In contrast to the increasingly rich scholarship on the trauma Japan experienced during its first and only period of foreign administration, the tensions and uncertainties accompanying the restoration of independence in 1952 remain for the most part unstudied. On the Occupation era, see John W. Dower, *Embracing Defeat: Japan in the Wake of World War II* (New York: W. W. Norton, 1999).

2. Hiropon (Philopon) was the registered trademark of the brand under which methamphetamine was marketed in Japan. Even after legal sales of the drug were banned, the public continued to use *hiropon* to refer to stimulants.

3. Moral panic is a key concept in the sociology of collective behavior and deviance. Stanley Cohen's original definition is often quoted in full: "A condition, episode, person or group of persons emerges to become defined as a threat to societal values and interests; its nature is presented in a stylized and stereotypical fashion by mass media; the moral barricades are manned by editors, bishops, politicians and other right-thinking people; socially accredited experts pronounce their diagnoses and solutions; ways of coping are evolved (or more often resorted to); the condition then disappears, submerges or deteriorates and becomes more visible. Sometimes the object of the panic is quite novel and at other times it is something which has been in existence long enough, but suddenly appears in the limelight. Sometimes the panic passes over and is forgotten, except in folklore and collective memory; at other times it has more serious and long-lasting repercussions and might produce such changes as those in legal or social policy or even in the way society conceives itself." Cohen, *Folk Devils and Moral Panics*, 1.

4. Nicholas Rasmussen, *On Speed: The Many Lives of Amphetamines* (New York: New York University Press, 1998), 53–58.

5. Allied Occupation, *History of the Non-Military Activities of the Occupation of Japan* (Washington, DC: National Archives, 1975), 221.

6. H. Richard Friman, *NarcoDiplomacy: Exporting the U.S. War on Drugs* (Ithaca, NY: Cornell University Press, 1996), 68.

7. Allied Occupation, *History of the Non-Military Activities of the Occupation of Japan*, 226.

8. Shōji Taichi, *Bindama tobaso* (Tokyo: Pareo, 1997), 17–18.

9. Deverall, *Red China's Dirty Drug War*, 171.

10. Katō Masaaki, "An Epidemiological Analysis of the Fluctuation of Drug Dependence in Japan," *International Journal of the Addictions* 4, no. 4 (1969): 596.

11. Hōmushō, *Kensatsu tōkei nenpō*, vol. 78 (Tokyo: Hōmushō, 1952).

12. Lester Grinspoon and Peter Hedblom, *The Speed Culture: Amphetamine Use and Abuse in America* (Cambridge, MA: Harvard University Press, 1975), 189.

13. "'Hiropon dzukuri' kenkyo," *Asahi Shinbun,* May 27, 1953, 3. At the official exchange rate of 360 Japanese yen to the U.S. dollar, each dose had a retail value of less than three cents.

14. Kondō Kōji, "Kakuseizai mitsuzō no seitai," *Seishōnen mondai* 2, no. 5 (1955): 34–40.

15. "Oyabun no yonjū-nana nin wo kenkyo," *Asahi Shinbun,* Oct. 3, 1955, 3.

16. *Asahi Shinbun,* 1951–57.

17. Honda Heisaburō, "Hanzai e hashiru kakuseizai jōyōsha no yokogao," in Shinkei eisei bunka kyōkai, ed., *Hiropon: Kakuseizai ka no higeki to sono taisaku* (Tokyo: Shinkei eisei bunka kyōkai, 1955), 139.

18. Morimoto Kiyoshi, "The Problem of the Abuse of Amphetamines in Japan," in United Nations Bureau of Social Affairs, ed., *Bulletin on Narcotics,* vol. 9 (Geneva: United Nations, 1957), 11.

19. "Hiropon ka issei e," *Asahi Shinbun,* Oct. 15, 1954, 3.

20. Nakano Kaichi, "Oda Sakunosuke—Hiropon to 'bungaku no kanōsei' no chōsen," *Kokubungaku: Kaishaku to kanshō* 48, no. 7 (1983): 343–49; Phyllis Lyons, *The Saga of Dazai Osamu: A Critical Study with Translations* (Stanford, CA: Stanford University Press, 1985); Ōkawa Wataru, "Hiropon, adorumu, Tanaka Hidemitsu," *Chikuma* 348 (2004): 26–29; James Dorsey and Douglas Slaymaker, eds., *Literary Mischief: Sakaguchi Ango, Culture, and the War,* trans. James Dorsey (Lanham, MD: Lexington Books, 2010), 3–20.

21. Muroo Tadashi, *Kakuseizai* (Tokyo: San'ichi shobō, 1982), 41.

22. "Zetsubō no ka no mayaku nagashi: Seikatsu gurushii kara 'tenraku no ihaku,'" *Asahi Shinbun,* Dec. 1, 1954, 7.

23. Tominaga Toshiharu and Nurita Nobuyuki, "Nihon no Chūgoku senryaku ni okeru ahen seisaku," in Mori Masataka, ed., *Chūgoku no daichi wa wasurenai: Shinryaku, katararenakatta sensō* (Tokyo: Shakai hyōronsha, 1995), 201–18; Jennings, *The Opium Empire;* Totani, *The Tokyo Trials.*

24. Richard L.-G. Deverall, *Mao Tse-Tung: Stop This Dirty Opium Business! How Red China Is Selling Opium and Heroin to Produce Revenue for China's War Machine* (Tokyo: Toyoh Printing and Book Binding, 1954), 7.

25. Ibid., 53, 79.

26. "Red Dope Damaging Japan," *Nippon Times,* Oct. 16, 1955, 1.

27. Hong Lu, Terence D. Miethe, and Bin Liang, *China's Drug Practices and Policies: Regulating Controlled Substances in a Global Context* (Surrey: Ashgate, 2009), 83.

28. Zhou Yongming, *Anti-Drug Crusades in Twentieth Century China: Nationalism, History, and State Building* (Lanham, MD: Rowman & Littlefield, 1999), 93–112; Peter Liu and Yingyi Situ, "Narcotics Control in China: A Growing Challenge," in Jianhong

Lu, Lening Zhang, and Steven F. Messner, eds., *Crime and Social Control in a Changing China* (Westport, CT: Greenview Press, 2001), 39. Some authors have claimed that China was likely not fully "drug-free" until 1955. Lu, Miethe, and Liang, *China's Drug Practices and Policies,* 85.

29. Deverall, *Red China's Dirty Drug War,* 4.

30. "Mayaku mondai no jijō chōsa," *Asahi Shinbun,* Nov. 4, 1953, 3.

31. Kaneko Mitsuzō, "Kakuseizai no mitsuzō no ru-to," in Shinkei eisei bunka kyōkai, ed., *Hiropon,* 188.

32. *The Illicit Narcotics Trade of the Chinese Communists* (Taipei: Asian Peoples' Anti-Communist League, 1957), 23.

33. "Hiropon jūman bon mitsuzō," *Asahi Shinbun,* Aug. 25, 1952, 3.

34. "Kyōsantō ra jūni mei hiropon torishimari de kenkyo," *Asahi Shinbun,* Jun. 8, 1955, 3.

35. Crawford F. Sams, *Medic: The Mission of an American Military Doctor in Occupied Japan* (Armonk, NY: M. E. Sharpe, 1998), 153–56.

36. *The Illicit Narcotics Trade of the Chinese Communists,* 25.

37. "Hiropon, chihō e mashu," *Asahi Shinbun,* April 17, 1955, 3.

38. Reported in Harry Emerson Wildes, *Typhoon in Tokyo: The Occupation and Its Aftermath* (New York: Macmillan, 1954), 178.

39. Deverall, *Red China's Dirty Drug War,* 115–17, 119. Italics in original.

40. Robert H. Berkov, "The Press in Postwar Japan," *Far Eastern Survey* 16, no. 14 (1947): 162.

41. "Navy Officer Dies after Philopon Shot," *Nippon Times,* Aug. 11, 1956, 3.

42. Ushikubo Ainoshin, *Mayaku dokuhon: Ahen, moruhine, hiropon no seitai* (Tokyo: Rokushinsha, 1955), 3.

43. "Kōfunzai wo mitsuzō: Chōsenjin wo taiho," *Asahi Shinbun,* Jun. 17, 1953, 3.

44. "'Hiropon dzukuri' kenkyo," *Asahi Shinbun,* May 27, 1955, 3.

45. Kokusai mondai kenkyū kyōkai, *Nihon wo mushibamu hiropon ka no jittai* (Tokyo: Kokusai mondai kenkyū kyōkai, 1954), 5.

46. Hirose Masaki, "Mansei kakuseizai chūdokusha no tōkeiteki jittai," *Ifu* 9, no. 2 (1955): 4–6.

47. Yukiko Koshiro, *Trans-Pacific Racisms and the U.S. Occupation of Japan* (New York: Columbia University Press, 1999), 89–122; Lori Watt, *When Empire Comes Home: Repatriation and Reintegration in Postwar Japan* (Cambridge, MA: Harvard University Asia Center, 2009), 90–95; Tessa Morris-Suzuki, *Borderline Japan: Foreigners and Frontier Controls in the Postwar Era* (New York: Cambridge University Press, 2011), 59–65.

48. Maruyama Shinobu, "Akuma no mayaku wa chōsen suru," *Seishōnen mondai* 2, no. 5 (1955): 24. On the characterization of non-Japanese Asians in Japan's postwar illegal drug market, see Jeffrey W. Alexander, "Japan's *Hiropon* Panic: Resident Non-

Japanese and the 1950s Meth Crisis," *International Journal of Drug Policy* 24, no. 3 (2013): 238–43.

49. See, for example, Kokusai mondai kenkyū kyōkai, *Nihon wo mushibamu hiropon ka no jittai*, 23.

50. Keishi-chō kakuseizai torishimari taisaku honbu, *Hiropon kakuseizai no gaiaku to sono taisaku* (Tokyo: Keishi-chō kakuseizai torishimari taisaku honbu, 1955), 19.

51. Dazai Osamu, *The Setting Sun*, trans. Donald Keene (New York: New Directions Books, 1956), 169.

52. Dower, *Embracing Defeat*, 158.

53. Kawasaki Hideji, "Kakuseizai mondai ni tsuite," *Seishōnen mondai* 2, no. 5 (1955): 6.

54. Katō Masaaki, "Epidemiology of Drug Dependence in Japan," in Chris J. D. Zarafonetis, ed., *Drug Abuse: Proceedings of the International Conference* (Philadelphia: Lea & Febinger, 1972), 67.

55. Isomura Eiichi, "Mayaku, hiropon mondai no shakaiteki haikei," *Toshi mondai* 46, no. 2 (1955): 254.

56. Kaneko Junji, "Hiropon," *Ifu* 9, no. 2 (1955): 17–23, 18.

57. Ushikubo, *Ahen ka*, 59, 66.

58. Christopher Aldous, *The Police in Occupied Japan: Control, Corruption and Resistance to Reform* (New York: Routledge, 1997), 208–16.

59. "Yaku sanbyaku nin kenkyo," *Asahi Shinbun*, Jul. 15, 1954, 3.

60. By comparison, in 1954 the FBI recorded 6,634 arrests for violations of antinarcotics legislation among the 38,642,183 people living in U.S. cities with more than 2,500 inhabitants. This figure equaled 172 arrests per 100,000 population—less than 30 percent of the arrest rate for stimulants violations alone in urban and rural Japan that year. Federal Bureau of Investigation, *Uniform Crime Reports for the United States* (Washington, DC: Government Printing Office, 1955).

61. Isomura, "Mayaku, hiropon mondai no shakaiteki haikei," 252.

62. Hōmushō, *Kensatsu tōkei nenpō*, vols. 78–83 (1952–57).

63. Morimoto, "The Problem of the Abuse of Amphetamines in Japan," 11.

64. Deverall, *Red China's Dirty Drug War*, 176.

65. Morimoto, "The Problem of the Abuse of Amphetamines in Japan," 10–11; Keishi-chō kakuseizai torishimari taisaku honbu, *Hiropon kakuseizai no gaiaku to sono taisaku*, 16–49.

66. Tatetsu Seijun, Gotō Akio, and Fujiwara Takeshi, *Kakuseizai chūdoku* (Tokyo: Igaku shoin, 1956), 10; Hemmi Takemitsu, "How We Handled the Problem of Drug Abuse in Japan," in Folke Sjökvist and Malcolm Tottie, eds., *Abuse of Central Stimulants: Symposium Arranged by the Swedish Committee on International Health Relations* (New York: Raven Press, 1969), 151.

67. Hemmi, "How We Handled the Problem of Drug Abuse in Japan," 193.

68. Berkov, "The Press in Postwar Japan," 166.

69. Naikaku sōri daijin kanbō shingi shitsu, "Kokumin no kanshi wa takamaru: Kakuseizai ninshiki ni kansuru yoron chōsa no kekka ni tsuite," *Seishōnen mondai* 2, no. 5 (1955): 60–64.

70. Arakawa Jūjirō, "Hiropon chūdoku ni tsuite," *Hanzai to igaku* 2, no. 3 (1950): 123–24; Takeyama Tsunetoshi, "Hiropon chūdoku no chiryō taisaku," *Seishōnen mondai* 2, no. 5 (1955): 8–12; Morimoto, "The Problem of the Abuse of Amphetamines in Japan," 11; Henry Brill and Tetsuya Hirose, "The Rise and Fall of a Methamphetamine Epidemic: Japan 1945–55," *Seminars in Psychiatry* 1 (1969): 4–6.

71. David Ambaras, *Bad Youth: Juvenile Delinquency and the Politics of Everyday Life in Modern Japan* (Berkeley: University of California Press, 2006).

72. Quoted in Deverall, *Red China's Dirty Drug War*, iii.

73. Funayama Takeshi, "Hiropon, adorumu, funōsha," *Shin shōsetsu* 5, no. 6 (1955): 19–21.

74. Hiroko Hara and Mieko Minagawa, "From Productive Dependents to Precious Guests: Historical Changes in Japanese Children," in David W. Schwalb and Barbara J. Schwalb, eds., *Japanese Childrearing: Two Generations of Scholarship* (New York: Guilford Press, 1996), 9–30.

75. Hemmi, "How We Handled the Problem of Drug Abuse in Japan," 148.

76. Inekura Satoru, "Hiropon jidō no jittai," *Shakai jigyō* 33, no. 2 (1950): 19–25.

77. Aoki Yoshiharu, "Kakuseizai chūdokushō no kankyō mondai," in Fukkōkai, ed., *Hiropon chūdoku ni oite Sōbu Byōin de no kansatsu* (Funabashi: Fukkōkai, 1954), 12.

78. Maruyama, "Akuma no mayaku wa chōsen suru," 14–24; Kokusai mondai kenkyū kyōkai, ed., *Nihon wo mushibamu hiropon no jittai*, 27; Arakawa, "Hiropon chūdoku ni tsuite," 123–24.

79. For more on this incident, see Akihiko Satō, "Methamphetamine Use in Japan after the Second World War: Transformation of Narratives," *Contemporary Drug Problems* 35 (2008): 717–40.

80. As sociologists observe, moral panics throughout the postwar world have often vilified youth, a marginal and ambiguously situated social group. See Kenneth Thompson, *Moral Panics* (New York: Routledge, 1998), 43.

81. "Soshiki ni yoru kakuseizai tsuihō undō," *Seishōnen mondai* 2, no. 1 (1955): 61–64; "Hiropon ka issō e," *Ifu* 9, no. 2 (1955): 9; "Kakuseizai ni tsuite no eiga wo go-shōkai shimasu," *Seishōnen mondai* 2, no. 5 (1955): 41.

82. Mark A. Jones, *Children as Treasures: Childhood and the Middle Class in Early Twentieth Century Japan* (Cambridge, MA: Harvard University Asia Center, 2010), 139.

83. "Hiropon ka issei e," *Asahi Shinbun*, Oct. 15, 1954, 3.

84. Taiiku hoken ka, "Hirogaru hiropon," *Kagoshima Kyōiku Iinkai geppō* 38 (1954): 114–17.

85. Monbushō shōtō chūtō kyōiku-kyoku hokenka, "Kakuseizai shiryō no haishi ni tsuite no Monbu jikan tsūtachi," *Seishōnen mondai* 2, no. 2 (1955): 39.

86. Henry D. Smith II, "Tokyo as an Idea: An Exploration of Japanese Urban Thought until 1945," *Journal of Japanese Studies* 4, no. 1 (1978): 66; Hastings, *Neighborhood and Nation in Tokyo,* 69–85.

87. Ralph Braibanti, "Neighborhood Associations in Japan and Their Democratic Potentialities," *Far Eastern Quarterly* 7, no. 2 (1948): 140, 164.

88. Hiroshi Wagatsuma and George A. De Vos, *Heritage of Endurance: Family Patterns and Delinquency Formation in Urban Japan* (Berkeley: University of California Press, 1984), 442–43.

89. Kōseishō yakumu-kyoku, *Kokuren Ajia Kyokutō mayaku kyōgikai* (Tokyo: Kōseishō yakumu-kyoku, 1964), 193.

90. Hemmi, "How We Handled the Problem of Drug Abuse in Japan," 153. On the medical discourse of methamphetamine addiction during the hiropon age, see Satō Akihiko, *Kakuseizai no shakai shi: Doraggu, disuko-su, tōchi gijutsu* (Tokyo: Tōshindo, 2006), 175–237.

91. Matsumura, "Mental Health as Public Peace," 921. Prior to 1950, families typically cared for the mentally ill at home.

92. Nagahama Masamutsu, "A Review of Drug Abuse and Counter Measures in Japan since World War II," *Bulletin on Narcotics* 20, no. 3 (1968): 21.

93. Akio Ishii and Nobuo Motohashi, "Drug Abuse in Japan," *Addictive Diseases: An International Journal* 3, no. 1 (1977): 112–13.

94. Kasamatsu Akira and Ritsuno Ryū, "Kakusei amine (hiropon) chūdokushō," *Nihon Ishikai zasshi* 24, no. 2 (1950): 92–101.

95. For example, see I. Sano, "Chronic Alerting Amine Addiction in Japan," *Fortschritte der Neurologie-Psychiatrie* 24, no. 7 (1956): 391–94; H. Utena, T. Ezoe, N. Katō, and H. Hada, "Effects of Chronic Administration of Methamphetamine in Enzymic Patterns in Brain Tissue," *Journal of Neurochemistry* 4, no. 2 (1959): 161–69.

96. Brill and Hirose, "The Rise and Fall of a Methamphetamine Epidemic," 192. On Seevers's influence over American constructions of addiction, see Nicolas Rasmussen, "Maurice Seevers, the Stimulants and the Political Economy of Addiction in American Biomedicine," *BioSocieties* 5, no. 1 (2010): 105–23.

97. Tatetsu, Gotō, and Fujiwara, *Kakuseizai chūdoku,* 5.

98. Brill and Hirose, "The Rise and Fall of a Methamphetamine Epidemic," 190.

99. Nils Bejerot, *Addiction and Society* (Springfield, IL: Charles C. Thomas, 1970), 71.

100. Tatetsu, Gotō, and Fujiwara, *Kakuseizai chūdoku,* 137–73.

101. Watsuji Tetsurō, *Gendai dōtoku no jittai: Nihon ni okeru sengo no ijō* (Tokyo: Koshutsu shobō, 1954), 267. Contemporary doctors generally also report low rates of success in permanently detoxifying methamphetamine consumers. Physicians at Hazelden, long renowned as a cutting-edge rehabilitation center in the United States, find that almost half of their methamphetamine cases relapse. Studies at other clinics report that over 90 percent of discharged patients subsequently return to the drug. Ralph

Weisheit and William L. White, *Methamphetamine: Its History, Pharmacology, and Treatment* (Center City, MN: Hazelden, 2009), 209.

102. Hemmi, "How We Handled the Problem of Drug Abuse in Japan," 153.

103. Takeyama Tsunetoshi, "Hiropon no osoroshisa," *Shōsetsu kōen* 6, no. 3 (1955): 233.

104. "Japan Gradually Winning Battle against Philopon," *Nippon Times*, Jun. 23, 1956, 3.

105. Hōmushō, *Nihon kensatsu nenpō*, vols. 79–85 (1953–59).

106. For example, see Okakura Yoshijirō, "Tsugi wa 'hiropon e-ji'?" *Bungaku* 19, no. 12 (1951): 77; and Shimoyama Akira, "Hiropon no haigo ni aru mono," *Seiki* 12 (1955): 45.

107. Both alcohol and tobacco use rose rapidly during the hiropon age and its aftermath. On alcohol in contemporary Japan, see Amy Borovoy, *The Too-Good Wife: Alcohol, Codependency, and the Politics of Nurturance in Postwar Japan* (Berkeley: University of California Press, 2005); and Nakamoto Shin'ichi, *Datsu 'aruko-ru izon shakai' wo mezashite: Nihon no aruko-ru seisaku e no teigen* (Tokyo: Akashi shoten, 2009). On tobacco, see Roddey Reid, *Globalizing Tobacco Control: Anti-Smoking Campaigns in California, France, and Japan* (Bloomington: Indiana University Press, 2005).

108. Masayuki Tamura, "The Yakuza and Amphetamine Abuse in Japan," in Harold H. Traver and Mark S. Gaylord, eds., *Drugs, Law and the State* (Hong Kong: University of Hong Kong Press, 1992), 99–117; David E. Kaplan and Alex Dubro, *Yakuza: Japan's Criminal Underworld* (Berkeley: University of California Press, 2003).

109. Annette Erbe, "Youth in Crisis: Public Perceptions and Discourse on Deviance and Juvenile Problem Behavior in Japan," in Gesine Foljanty-Jost, ed., *Juvenile Delinquency in Japan: Reconsidering the "Crisis"* (Boston: Brill, 2003), 51–73.

110. *Tengoku, jigoku*, directed by Kurosawa Akira (Tokyo: Tōhō Company, 1963), DVD.

111. Hōmushō, *Nihon kensatsu nenpō*, vols. 104–20 (1978–94).

112. Murakami Ryū, *Kagiri naku tomei ni chikai buru-* (Tokyo: Kōdansha, 1976). For an English-language translation of this novel, see Murakami Ryū, *Almost Transparent Blue*, trans. Nancy Andrews (Tokyo: Kodansha International, 1977).

113. Caterina Gouvis Roman, Heather Ahn-Redding, and Rita J. Simon, *Illicit Drug Policies, Trafficking, and Use the World Over* (Lanham, MD: Lexington Books, 2005), 174.

114. Christopher Seymour, *Yakuza Diary: Doing Time in the Japanese Underworld* (New York: Atlantic Monthly Press, 1996), 40.

115. Yakubutsu ran'yō taisaku shinpo honbu, ed., *Shiroi koma no kyōfu: Kakuseizai chūdokusha nado no koe* (Tokyo: Yakubutsu ran'yō taisaku shinpō honbu, 1977).

WORKS CITED

ARCHIVAL MATERIALS

ARCHIVES OF THE JAPANESE FOREIGN MINISTRY (GAIMUSHŌ SHIRYŌKAN)

Ahen nado mayaku rui seisan torihiki jōkyō chōsa

Ahen sono ta dokuzaiyaku oyobi kyūshoku kigu torishimari kankei zakken:

Honpō no bu—Kantōshū, Seitō, Taiwan ni okeru ahen seido teppai mondai

Ryōjikan rei no bu

Manshūkoku no bu

Shina no bu

Manshū ni okeru enkan toba hanzai shobun iken

LEAGUE OF NATIONS

International Labor Office. *Opium and Labor: Being a Report on a Documentary Investigation into the Extent and Effects of Opium Smoking among Workers.* Geneva: League of Nations, 1935.

League of Nations. "First Opium Conference: Minutes and Annexes." Geneva, 1925.

———. "Records of the Second Opium Conference." Geneva, 1925.

———. "Resolutions of the Assembly, the Council and the Advisory Committee in Traffic in Opium and Other Dangerous Drugs." Geneva, 1926.

———. "Commission of Enquiry into the Control of Opium-Smoking in the Far East." Geneva, 1931.

League of Nations Advisory Committee on the Traffic in Opium and Other Dangerous Drugs (OAC). "Minutes" and "Reports to Council." Sessions 14–23. Geneva, 1931–39.

———. "Annual Reports of Governments on the Traffic in Opium and Other Dangerous Drugs." Geneva, 1932–38.

———. "Reports by the Kwantung Bureau on the Traffic in Opium and Other Dangerous Drugs." Geneva, 1939–40.

NATIONAL ARCHIVES AND RECORDS ADMINISTRATION

Allied Occupation. *History of the Non-Military Activities of the Occupation of Japan.* Microfilm collection. Washington, DC: National Archives, 1975.

United States Department of State. *Confidential State Department Central Files: Internal Affairs of China, 1940–1944.* Microfilm collection. Washington, DC: National Archives, 1965.

———. *Records of the Department of State Relating to the Internal Affairs of Japan, 1910–1929.* Microfilm collection. Washington, D.C.: National Archives, 1965.

———. *Confidential State Department Central Files: Internal Affairs of Japan, 1940–1944.* Microfilm collection. Wilmington, DE: Scholarly Resources, 1986.

———. *Records of the Department of State Relating to the Internal Affairs of Japan, 1930–1939.* Microfilm collection. Wilmington, DE: Scholarly Resources, 1986.

PUBLISHED COLLECTIONS OF ARCHIVAL DOCUMENTS

Eguchi Keiichi, ed. *Shiryō Nit-Chū sensō ki ahen seisaku: Mōkyō seiken shiryō wo chūshin ni.* Tokyo: Iwanami shoten, 1985.

Guojia jindu weiyuanhui bangongshi zuzhi pianxie. *Zhongguo jindu shi ziliao.* Tianjin: Tianjin renmin chubanshe, 1998.

Jarman, R. L., ed. *Japan and Dependencies: Political and Economic Reports 1906–1960.* Oxford: Archive Editions, 1993.

Jilin sheng tushuguan Wei-Manzhouguo shiliao bianweihui, ed. *Wei-Manzhouguo shi liao.* Beijing: Quanguo tushuguan wenxian suowei fuzhi zhongxin, 2002.

Kurahashi Masanao, ed. *Benzoirin fusei yunyū jiken kankei shiryō.* Tokyo: Fuji shuppan, 2003.

Makino Mamoru, ed. *"Nihon eiga": Fukkokuban.* Tokyo: Yumani shobō, 2002.

———, ed. *"Eiga junpō": Fukkokuban.* Tokyo: Yumani shobō, 2004.

Okada Yoshimasa, Tatai Yoshio, and Takahashi Masae, eds. *Ahen mondai.* Tokyo: Misuzu shobō, 1986.

Pritchard, R. John, and Sonia M. Zaide, eds. *The Tokyo War Crimes Trial: The Complete Transcripts of the Proceedings of the International Military Tribunal for the Far East in Twenty-Two Volumes.* New York: Garland Publishing, 1981.

Shin Kitsu and Nagaoka Masami, eds. *Shokuminchi shakai jigyō kankei shiryō shū*. Tokyo: Kindai shiryō, 2005.

Sun Bang, ed. *Wei-Man shehui*. Changchun: Jilin renmin chubanshe, 1993.

Takenaka Ken'ichi, ed. *"Manshū" shokuminchi Chūgokujin yō kyōkasho shūsei*. Tokyo: Rokuin shobō, 2005.

Tani Mitsutaka, ed. *Tō-A Dōbun Shoin ahen chōsa hōkokusho*. CD-rom collection. Toyohashi: Aichi Daigaku Tō-A Dōbun Shoin Daigaku kinen senta-, 2007.

Wenshi jinghua bianjibu, ed. *Jindai Zhongguo yandu xiezhen*. Shijiazhuang: Hebei renmin chubanshe, 1997.

Zhongguo di'er lishi dang'anguan, Zhongyang dang'anguan, and Jilin sheng shehui kexueyuan, eds. *Riben diguo zhuyi qin Hua dang'an ziliao xianpian*. Beijing: Zhonghua shiyu chuban, 1991.

Zhu Wenyuan, ed. *Guomin zhengfu jinyuan shiliao*. Taipei: Guoshiguan, 2006.

PERIODICALS

NEWSPAPERS

Asahi Shinbun

Chūgai Shōgyō Shinbun

Dairen Jihō

Hōritsu Shinbun

Japan Advertiser

Japan Chronicle

Manchuria Daily News

New York Times

Nippon Times

Peiping Chronicle

Taiwan Nippō

Times (London)

Washington Star

Xinmin Ribao

Yomiuri Shinbun

JOURNALS

Bungaku

China Medical Journal / Chinese Medical Journal

Chōsen Igakkai zasshi

Chōsen oyobi Manshū

Contemporary Manchuria

Dōjin

Dongfang yixue zazhi

Hanzai to igaku

Ifu

Japan Medical World

Journal of the American Medical Association

Judu yuekan

Jūzenkai zasshi

Kagoshima Kyōiku Iinkai geppō

Keisatsu Kyōkai zasshi

Kirisutokyō renmei

Kyōwa undō

Man-Sen no ikai

Milestones of Progress

Nan-Man Igakkai zasshi / Manshū igaku zasshi (MIZ)

Nihon Ishikai zasshi

Opium: A World Problem

Raifu

Rikagaku kyōshitsu ronshū

Seiki

Seishōnen mondai

Shakai jigyō

Shin shōsetsu

Shōsetsu kōen

Taiwan Igakkai zasshi (TIZ)

Tongren yixue / Tongrenhui yixue zazhi

Toshi mondai

STATISTICAL GAZETTEERS

Kantō tōkei sho

Kensatsu tōkei nenpō

Mantetsu tōkei nenpō

Nihon teikoku tōkei nenkan / Dai Nihon teikoku tōkei nenkan

Taiwan tōkei sho

OTHER

Acker, Caroline Jean. *Creating the American Junkie: Addiction Research in the Classic Era of Narcotic Control.* Baltimore, MD: Johns Hopkins University Press, 2002.

Adas, Michael. *Machines as the Measure of Men: Science, Technology, and Ideologies of Western Dominance.* Ithaca, NY: Cornell University Press, 1989.

Aldous, Christopher. *The Police in Occupied Japan: Control, Corruption and Resistance to Reform.* New York: Routledge, 1997.

Alexander, Jeffrey W. "Japan's *Hiropon* Panic: Resident Non-Japanese and the 1950s Meth Crisis." *International Journal of Drug Policy* 24, no. 3 (2013): 238–43.

Ambaras, David. *Bad Youth: Juvenile Delinquency and the Politics of Everyday Life in Modern Japan.* Berkeley: University of California Press, 2006.

American Student Party's Visit to Manchoukuo. Dairen: South Manchuria Railway Company Information and Publicity Department, 1938.

Anderson, Benedict. *Imagined Communities: Reflections on the Origin and Spread of Nationalism.* New York: Verso, 2006.

Anderson, Warwick. *Colonial Pathologies: American Tropical Medicine, Race, and Hygiene in the Philippines.* Durham, NC: Duke University Press, 2006.

Andō Akimichi. *Kokusai ahen mondai kenkyū.* Dairen: Kantō-chō zaimubu, 1931.

Anzai Fuyue. "Gunkan Mari." In *Kitagawa Fuyuhiko, Anzai Fuyue, Kitasono Katsue, Haruyama Yukio, Takenaka Iku,* edited by Itō Shinkichi, 93–95. Tokyo: Chūo kōronsha, 1975.

Aoki kyozai zaidan, ed. *Shusei mondai kenkyū.* Tokyo: Aoki Shōzō, 1926.

Aoki Yoshiharu. "Kakuseizai chūdokushō no kankyō mondai." In *Hiropon chūdoku ni oite Sōbu Byōin de no kansatsu,* edited by Fukkōkai, 9–20. Funabashi: Fukkōkai, 1954.

Appadurai, Arjun. *Modernity at Large: Cultural Dimensions of Globalization.* Minneapolis: University of Minnesota Press, 1996.

Arendt, Hannah. *The Origins of Totalitarianism.* New York: Harcourt Brace Jovanovich, 1951.

Arnold, David. *Science, Technology, and Medicine in Colonial India.* New York: Cambridge University Press, 2000.

Asano Toyomi. *Teikoku Nihon no shokuminchi hōsei: Hōiki tōgō to teikoku chitsujo.* Nagoya: Nagoya Daigaku shuppankai, 2008.

Baba Shachi. *Ahen tōzenshi.* Shinkyō: Manshū jigyō annaisho, 1941.

Barkan, Elazar. *The Retreat of Scientific Racism: Changing Concepts of Race in Britain and the United States between the World Wars.* New York: Cambridge University Press, 1992.

Bartholomew, James. *The Formation of Science in Japan: Building a Research Tradition.* New Haven, CT: Yale University Press, 1989.

Baskett, Michael. *The Attractive Empire: Transnational Film Culture in Imperial Japan.* Honolulu: University of Hawai'i Press, 2008.

Baumler, Alan. *The Chinese and Opium under the Republic: Worse Than Floods and Wild Beasts.* Albany: State University of New York Press, 2007.

Becker, Howard. *Outsiders: Studies in the Sociology of Deviance.* New York: Free Press, 1963.

Bejerot, Nils. *Addiction and Society.* Springfield, IL: Charles C. Thomas, 1970.

Bello, David Anthony. *Opium and the Limits of Empire: Drug Prohibition in the Chinese Interior, 1729–1850.* Cambridge, MA: Harvard University Asia Center, 2005.

Benedict, Carol. *Golden-Silk Smoke: A History of Tobacco in China, 1550–2010.* Berkeley: University of California Press, 2011.

Berge, Jos Ten. "The Belle Epoque of Opium." In *Smoke: A Global History of Smoking,* edited by Sander L. Gilman and Xun Zhou, 108–17. London: Reaktion Books, 2004.

Berkov, Robert H. "The Press in Postwar Japan." *Far Eastern Survey* 16, no. 14 (1947): 162–66.

Berman, Marshall. *All That Is Solid Melts into Air: The Experience of Modernity.* New York: Simon and Schuster, 1982.

Berridge, Virginia. *Opium and the People: Opiate Use in Nineteenth-Century England.* New Haven, CT: Yale University Press, 1987.

———. "'The British System' and Its History: Myth and Reality." In *Heroin Addiction and the British System: Origins and Evolution,* vol. 1, *Origins and Evolution,* edited by John Strang and Michael Gossop, 7–16. New York: Routledge, 2005.

Best, Joel. *Damned Lies and Statistics: Untangling Numbers from the Media, Politicians, and Activists.* Berkeley: University of California Press, 2001.

Betta, Chiara. "Marginal Westerners in Shanghai: The Baghdadi Jewish Community, 1842–1945." In *New Frontiers: Imperialism's New Communities in East Asia, 1842–1953,* edited by Robert Bickers and Christian Henriot, 38–54. Manchester: Manchester University Press, 2000.

Bhabha, Homi. *The Location of Culture.* New York: Routledge, 1994.

Bickers, Robert. "Who Were the Shanghai Municipal Police, and Why Were They There? The British Recruits of 1919." In *New Frontiers: Imperialism's New Communities in East Asia, 1842–1953,* edited by Robert Bickers and Christian Henriot, 38–54. Manchester: Manchester University Press, 2000.

Block, Alan A. "European Drug Traffic and Traffickers between the Wars: The Policy of Suppression and Its Consequences." *Journal of Social History* 23, no. 2 (1989): 315–37.

Boon, Marcus. *The Road of Excess: A History of Writers on Drugs.* Cambridge, MA: Harvard University Press, 2002.

Borovoy, Amy. *The Too-Good Wife: Alcohol, Codependency, and the Politics of Nurturance in Postwar Japan.* Berkeley: University of California Press, 2005.

Bourdaghs, Michael. "The Disease of Nationalism, the Empire of Hygiene." *positions* 6, no. 3 (1998): 637–73.

Botsman, Daniel V. *Punishment and Power in the Making of Modern Japan.* Princeton, NJ: Princeton University Press, 2005.

———. "Freedom without Slavery? 'Coolies,' Prostitutes, and Outcastes in Meiji Japan's 'Emancipation Movement.'" *American Historical Review* 116, no. 5 (2011): 1323–47.

Bradburd, Daniel, and William Jankowiak. "Drugs, Desire, and European Expansion." In *Drugs, Labor, and Colonial Expansion,* edited by William Jankowiak and Daniel Bradburd, 3–30. Tucson: University of Arizona Press, 2003.

Braibanti, Ralph. "Neighborhood Associations in Japan and Their Democratic Potentialities." *Far Eastern Quarterly* 7, no. 2 (1948): 136–64.

Brill, Henry, and Tetsuya Hirose. "The Rise and Fall of a Methamphetamine Epidemic: Japan 1945–55." *Seminars in Psychiatry* 1 (1969): 4–6.

Brook, Timothy. "Opium and Collaboration in Central China, 1938–1940." In *Opium Regimes: China, Britain, and Japan, 1839–1952,* edited by Timothy Brook and Bob Tadashi Wakabayashi, 323–43. Berkeley: University of California Press, 2000.

———, and Bob Tadashi Wakabayashi. "Introduction: Opium's History in China." In *Opium Regimes: China, Britain, and Japan, 1839–1952,* edited by Timothy Brook and Bob Tadashi Wakabayashi, 1–28. Berkeley: University of California Press, 2000.

Brooks, Barbara J. "Peopling the Japanese Empire: The Koreans in Manchuria and the Rhetoric of Inclusion." In *Japan's Competing Modernities: Issues in Culture and Democracy 1900–1930,* edited by Sharon A. Minichiello, 25–44. Honolulu: University of Hawai'i Press, 1998.

Burns, Susan. "Contemplating Places: The Hospital as Modern Experience in Meiji Japan." In *New Directions in the Study of Meiji Japan,* edited by Helen Hardacre with Adam L. Kern, 702–18. New York: Brill, 1997.

Butcher, John. "Revenue Farming and the Changing State in Southeast Asia." In *The Rise and Fall of Revenue Farming: Business Elites and the Emergence of the State in Southeast Asia,* edited by John Butcher and Howard Dick, 19–44. New York: St. Martin's Press, 1993.

Cai Yuanpei and Wu Jingheng, eds. *Yapian zhanzheng shi.* Shanghai: Shangwu yinshuguan, 1931.

Campbell, Nancy D., J.P. Olsen, and Luke Walden. *The Narcotic Farm*. New York: Abrams, 2008.

Caprio, Mark E. *Japanese Assimilation Policies in Colonial Korea, 1910–1945*. Seattle: University of Washington Press, 2009.

Carstairs, Catherine. *Jailed for Possession: Illegal Drug Use, Regulation, and Power in Canada, 1920–1961*. Toronto: University of Toronto Press, 2006.

Chakrabarti, Pratik. *Western Science in Modern India: Metropolitan Models, Colonial Practices*. Delhi: Permanent Black, 2004.

Chan Airin. "'Man se ryū hō' hyō." In *Ri Kōran to Higashi Ajia*, edited by Yomota Inuhiko, 167–69. Tokyo: Tokyo Daigaku shuppankai, 2001.

Chang, Richard T. *The Justice of the Western Consular Courts in Nineteenth-Century Japan*. Westport, CT: Greenwood Press, 1984.

Chen, Edward I-te. "The Attempt to Integrate the Empire: Legal Perspectives." In *The Japanese Colonial Empire, 1895–1945*, edited by Ramon Myers and Mark Peattie, 240–74. Princeton, NJ: Princeton University Press, 1984.

Chen, Yung-fa. "The Blooming Poppy under the Red Sun: The Yan'an Way and the Opium Trade." In *New Perspectives on the Chinese Communist Revolution*, edited by Tony Saich and Hans van de Ven, 263–98. Armonk, NY: M.E. Sharpe, 1995.

Chen Zhimin. *Du Congming yu Taiwan yiliao shi yanjiu*. Taipei: Guoli Zhongguo yiyue yanjiusuo, 2005.

Chianbu keimushi. *Eisei keisatsu*. Shinkyō: Manshūkoku keisatsu kyōkai, 1938.

Cho Sei-ki. "Akuma wo kugurite." In *Mayaku chūdokusha to naku: Tō-A wo ahen kara kaikō seyo*, edited by Majima Kan, 101–2. Tokyo: Ajia seisaku kenkyūjo, 1935.

Chopra, R.N., and Khem Singh Grewal. "Opium Habit in India." In *Transactions of the Seventh Congress*, vol. 3, edited by the Far Eastern Association for Tropical Medicine, 568–75. Calcutta: Thacker's Press & Directories, 1927.

Chung, Yuehtsen Juliette. *Struggle for National Survival: Eugenics in Sino-Japanese Contexts, 1896–1945*. New York: Routledge, 2002.

Cochran, Sherman. "Marketing Medicine and Advertising Dreams in China, 1900–1950." In *Becoming Chinese: Passages to Modernity and Beyond*, edited by Wen-hsin Yeh, 62–97. Berkeley: University of California Press, 2000.

Cohen, Stanley. *Folk Devils and Moral Panics: The Creation of the Mods and Rockers*. New York: Routledge, 2002.

Collier, D.M.B., and Lt.-Col. L'E. Malone. *Manchoukuo: Jewel of Asia*. London: George Allen & Unwin, 1936.

Conklin, Alice. *A Mission to Civilize: The Republican Ideal of Empire in French West Africa, 1895–1930*. Stanford, CA: Stanford University Press, 1997.

Control of Opium in Japan: Report of the Japanese Delegates to the International Opium Commission. Shanghai, 1909.

Courtesans and Opium: Romantic Illusions by the Fool of Yangzhou. Translated by Patrick Hanan. New York: Columbia University Press, 2009.

Courtwright, David T. *Dark Paradise: Opiate Addiction in America before 1940*. Cambridge, MA: Harvard University Press, 1982.

———. *Forces of Habit: Drugs and the Making of the Modern World*. Cambridge, MA: Harvard University Press, 2001.

Crafts, Wilbur F. *Opium Cures: Opinions of American and European Physicians in China as to the Medical and Governmental Aid That Should Be Given to Those Compelled by Anti-Opium Legislation in Many Lands to Break Off the Opium Habit, and to Others Voluntarily Turning from It*. Washington, DC: International Reform Bureau, 1907.

———. *Intoxicants & Opium in All Lands and Times: A Twentieth-Century Survey of Temperance, Based on a Symposium of Testimony from One Hundred Missionaries and Travelers*. Washington, DC: International Reform Bureau, 1911.

Critcher, Chas. *Moral Panics and the Media*. Buckingham, PA: Open University Press, 2003.

Crossley, Pamela Kyle. *Orphan Warriors: Three Manchu Generations and the End of the Qing World*. Princeton, NJ: Princeton University Press, 1990.

Dairen chihō hōin. *Masuizai torishimari kisoku ihan nami sōshūwai hikoku jiken kokan sokki*. Dairen: Dairen chihō hōin, 1931.

Dairen Seiai Iin sanjūgo shūnen shi. Dairen: Seiai Iin, 1941.

Davenport-Hines, Richard. *The Pursuit of Oblivion: A Global History of Narcotics 1500–2000*. London: Weidenfield & Nicolson, 2001.

Davidann, Jon Thares. *A World of Crisis and Progress: The American YMCA in Japan, 1890–1930*. Bethlehem, PA: University of Lehigh Press, 1998.

Dazai, Osamu. *The Setting Sun*. Translated by Donald Keene. New York: New Directions Books, 1956.

———. *Self-Portraits: Tales from the Life of Japan's Great Decadent Romantic*. Translated by Ralph F. McCarthy. New York: Kodansha International, 1991.

De Kuinshii. *Ahen dekiaisha no kokuhaku*. Translated by Tsuji Jun. Tokyo: Shunjūsha, 1925.

De Quincey, Thomas. "*The Confessions of an English Opium-Eater" and "The English Mail-Coach*." Edited by E. Nagasawa. Tokyo: Kenkyūsha, 1923.

———. *The Confessions of an English Opium-Eater*. Edited by Y. Otagiri. Tokyo, 1928.

———. *The Confessions of an English Opium Eater*. Tokyo: Hokuseido Press, 1928.

Dei Kuinshii. *Ahen jōyōsha no kokuhaku.* Translated by Tanabe Jūji. Tokyo: Iwanami shoten, 1937.

Derks, Hans. *History of the Opium Problem: The Assault on the East, ca. 1600–1950.* Boston: Brill, 2012.

Deverall, Richard L.- G. *Mao Tse-Tung: Stop This Dirty Opium Business! How Red China Is Selling Opium and Heroin to Produce Revenue for China's War Machine.* Tokyo: Toyoh Printing and Book Binding, 1954.

———. *Red China's Dirty Drug War.* Tokyo: Toyoh Printing and Book Binding, 1954.

Dick, Howard. "A Fresh Approach to Southeast Asian History." In *The Rise and Fall of Revenue Farming: Business Elites and the Emergence of the State in Southeast Asia,* edited by John Butcher and Howard Dick, 3–18. New York: St. Martin's Press, 1993.

Dickinson, Frederick R. *War and National Reinvention: Japan in the Great War, 1914–1919.* Cambridge, MA: Harvard University Asia Center, 1999.

Dikötter, Frank. *Crime, Punishment, and the Prison in Modern China.* New York: Columbia University Press, 2002.

———. *Narcotic Culture: A History of Drugs in China.* London: Hurst, 2004.

———. *Exotic Commodities: Modern Objects and Everyday Life in China.* New York: Columbia University Press, 2006.

The Directory of Manchoukuo. Dairen: Oriental Publishing, 1936.

Do Kuinshi. *Ahenzuki na ichi Eijin no kokuhaku.* Translated by Suzuki Ken'ichirō. Tokyo: Tōhō shoin, 1934.

Do Kuinzui. *Ahen fukuyōsha no zange: Sono ta.* Translated by Isobe Ya'ichirō. Tokyo: Eibungakusha, 1929.

Dōjinkai. *Dōjinkai yonjū nen shi.* Tokyo: Dōjinkai zaidan hōjin, 1943.

Dormandy, Thomas. *Opium: Reality's Dark Dream.* New Haven, CT: Yale University Press, 2012.

Dorsey, James, and Douglas Slaymaker, eds. *Literary Mischief: Sakaguchi Ango, Culture, and the War.* Translated by James Dorsey. Lanham, MD: Lexington Books, 2010.

Dove, Michael R. *The Banana Tree at the Gate: A History of Marginal Peoples and Global Markets in Borneo.* New Haven, CT: Yale University Press, 2011.

Dower, John W. *Japan in War and Peace: Selected Essays.* New York: New Press, 1993.

———. *Embracing Defeat: Japan in the Wake of World War II.* New York: W. W. Norton, 1999.

Driscoll, Mark. *Absolute Erotic, Absolute Grotesque: The Living, Dead, and Undead in Japan's Imperialism, 1895–1945.* Durham, NC: Duke University Press, 2010.

Du Congming. *Du Congming yanlun ji.* Taipei: Du Congming boshi huanli jinian jiangxuejin guanli weiyuanhui, 1955.

———. *Huiyi lü*. Taipei: Du Congming boshi jiangxuejijinhui, 1982.

Duara, Prasenjit. "Transnationalism and the Predicament of Sovereignty: China, 1900–1945. *American Historical Review* 102, no. 4 (1997): 1030–51.

———. *Sovereignty and Authenticity: Manchukuo and the East Asian Modern*. Lanham, MD: Rowman & Littlefield, 2003.

DuBois, Thomas David. "Inauthentic Sovereignty: Law and Legal Matters in Manchukuo." *Journal of Asian Studies* 69, no. 3 (2010): 749–70.

Dudden, Alexis. *Japan's Colonization of Korea: Discourse and Power*. Honolulu: University of Hawai'i Press, 2005.

Dunn, Wie T. "The Opium Traffic in Its International Aspects." PhD dissertation, Columbia University, 1920.

Eda Izumi. "Seikatsu." In *Mantetsu rōdō shi no kenkyū*, edited by Matsumura Takao, Jie Xueshi, and Eda Kenji, 201–31. Tokyo: Nihon keizai hyōronsha, 2002.

Eguchi Keiichi. *Nit-Chū ahen sensō*. Tokyo: Iwanami shoten, 1988.

———. *Shōgon: Nit-Chū ahen sensō*. Tokyo: Iwanami shoten, 1991.

Elliott, Mark C. "The Limits of Tartary: Manchuria in Imperial and National Geographies." *Journal of Asian Studies* 59, no. 3 (2000): 603–46.

———. *The Manchu Way: The Eight Banners and Ethnic Identity in Late Imperial China*. Stanford, CA: Stanford University Press, 2001.

Ema Shū. *Ahen sensō*. Tokyo: Yumani shobō, 2004.

Endo, R. *Japan, China, and Manchukuo: The Kingly Way*. Tokyo: East Asiatic Society Press, 1933.

Endō, Shūsaku. *The Final Martyrs*. Translated by Van C. Gessel. New York: New Directions, 2009.

Epstein, Steven. *Inclusion: The Politics of Difference in Medical Research*. Chicago: University of Chicago Press, 2007.

Erbe, Annette. "Youth in Crisis: Public Perceptions and Discourse on Deviance and Juvenile Problem Behavior in Japan." In *Juvenile Delinquency in Japan: Reconsidering the "Crisis,"* edited by Gesine Foljanty-Jost, 51–73. Boston: Brill, 2003.

Esselstrom, Erik. *Crossing Empire's Edge: Foreign Ministry Police and Japanese Expansionism in Northeast Asia*. Honolulu: University of Hawai'i Press, 2009.

Eykholt, Mark. "Resistance to Opium as a Social Evil in Wartime China." In *Opium Regimes: China, Britain, and Japan, 1839–1952*, edited by Timothy Brook and Bob Tadashi Wakabayashi, 360–79. Berkeley: University of California Press, 2000.

Federal Bureau of Investigation. *Uniform Crime Reports for the United States*. Washington, DC: Government Printing Office, 1955.

Fogel, Joshua A. *Politics and Sinology: The Case of Naitō Konan (1866–1934)*. Cambridge, MA: Harvard University Council on East Asian Studies, 1984.

———. *The Literature of Travel in the Japanese Rediscovery of China, 1862–1945*. Stanford, CA: Stanford University Press, 1996.

———. "The Japanese and the Jews: A Comparative Analysis of Their Communities in Harbin, 1898–1930." In *New Frontiers: Imperialism's New Communities in East Asia, 1842–1953*, edited by Robert Bickers and Christian Henriot, 88–108. Manchester: Manchester University Press, 2000.

Foster, Anne L. "Opium, the United States, and the Civilizing Mission in Southeast Asia." *Social History of Alcohol and Drugs* 24, no. 1 (2010): 6–19.

Foucault, Michel. *The Birth of the Clinic: An Archaeology of Medical Perception*. Translated by A. M. Sheridan Smith. New York: Pantheon Books, 1973.

———. "Governmentality." Translated by Rosi Braidotti. In *Studies in Governmentality: The Foucault Effect*, edited by Graham Burchell, Colin Gordon, and Peter Miller, 87–104. Chicago: University of Chicago Press, 1991.

Foxcroft, Louise. *The Making of Addiction: The 'Use and Abuse' of Opium in Nineteenth-Century Britain*. Burlington, VT: Ashgate, 2007.

Friman, H. Richard. *NarcoDiplomacy: Exporting the U.S. War on Drugs*. Ithaca, NY: Cornell University Press, 1996.

Fu, Poshek. "The Ambiguity of Entertainment: Chinese Cinema in Japanese-Occupied Shanghai, 1941–1945." *Cinema Journal* 37, no. 1 (1997): 66–84.

Fukui, Susumu, Kiyoshi Wada, and Masaomi Iyo. "Epidemiology of Amphetamine Abuse in Japan and Its Social Implications." In *Amphetamine and Its Analogs: Psychopharmacology, Toxicology, and Abuse*, edited by Arthur K. Cho and David S. Segal, 459–78. New York: Academic Press, 1994.

Gaide, Laurent. *L'Assistance médicale et la protection de la santé publique*. Hanoi: Imprimerie d'Extrême Orient, 1931.

Gaimushō. *Ahen mondai*. Tokyo: Gaimushō tsūshō-kyoku, 1922.

Galloway, David J. "Opium Smoking." In *Transactions of the Fifth Congress*, edited by the Far Eastern Association for Tropical Medicine, 864–85. London: John Bale, Sons & Danielsson, 1923.

Gao Shaoyu. "Qianxi Riben diguo zhuyi dui Hua de yapian qinlüe." In *Dalian jindai shi yanjiu*, vol. 2, edited by Li Lilun, 82–89. Dalian: Dalian shi jindai shi yanjiusuo, 2005.

Garon, Sheldon. *Molding Japanese Minds: The State in Everyday Life*. Princeton, NJ: Princeton University Press, 1997.

Gavit, John Palmer. *"Opium."* New York: Brentano's, 1927.

———. *Ahen*. Translated by Andō Akimichi. Tokyo: Nihon hyōronsha, 1931.

Gayn, Mark. *Journey from the East: An Autobiography*. New York: A. A. Knopf, 1944.

Geison, Gerald L. "Divided We Stand: Physiologists and Clinicians in the American Context." In *The Therapeutic Revolution: Essays in the Social History of American Medicine*, edited by Morris J. Vogel and Charles E. Rosenberg, 67–90. Philadelphia: University of Pennsylvania Press, 1979.

Gerow, Aaron. "Narrating the Nation-ality of a Cinema: The Case of Prewar Japanese Film." In *The Culture of Japanese Fascism*, edited by Alan Tansman, 185–211. Durham, NC: Duke University Press, 2009.

Gluck, Carol. *Japan's Modern Myths: Ideology in the Late Meiji Period*. Princeton, NJ: Princeton University Press, 1985.

Goffman, Erving. *Asylums: Essays on the Social Situation of Mental Patients and Other Inmates*. New York: Anchor Books, 1961.

Goldberg, Ted. *Demystifying Drugs: A Psychosocial Perspective*. New York: St. Martin's Press, 1999.

Gong, Gerrit W. *The Standard of "Civilization" in International Society*. Oxford: Clarendon Press, 1984.

Goode, Erich, and Nachman Ben-Yehuda. *Moral Panics: The Social Construction of Deviance*. 2nd edition. Malden, MA: Wiley-Blackwell, 2009.

Gootenberg, Paul. *Andean Cocaine: The Making of a Global Drug*. Chapel Hill: University of North Carolina Press, 2008.

Gotō Asatarō. *Shina bunka no kaibō*. Osaka: Osaka yago shoten, 1921.

———. *Omoshiroi Shina no fūzoku*. Osaka: Osaka yago shoten, 1923.

———. *Shina shumi no hanashi*. Osaka: Osaka yago shoten, 1924.

———. *Shina kokuminsei kōwa*. Tokyo: Gansuidō shoten, 1927.

———. *Shina kidan: Ahen shitsu*. Tokyo: Marikaku shobō, 1928.

———. *Shina oyobi Manshū ryokō annai*. Tokyo: Shun'yōdō, 1932.

Gotō, Shimpei. "The Administration of Formosa (Taiwan)." In *Fifty Years of New Japan*, edited by Shigenobu Ōkuma and Marcus B. Huish, 530–53. New York: E. P. Dutton, 1909.

Gotō-Shibata, Harumi. "The International Opium Conference of 1924–1925 and Japan." *Modern Asian Studies* 36, no. 4 (2002): 969–91.

Gottschang, Thomas, and Diana Lary. *Swallows and Settlers: The Great Migration from North China to Manchuria*. Ann Arbor: University of Michigan Press, 2000.

Gray, Elizabeth Kelly. "The Trade-Off: Chinese Opium Traders and Antebellum Reform in the United States, 1815–1860." In *Drugs and Empires: Essays in Modern

Imperialism and Intoxication, c. 1500–c. 1930, edited by James H. Mills and Patricia Barton, 220–42. New York: Palgrave Macmillan, 2007.

Grinspoon, Lester, and Peter Hedblom. *The Speed Culture: Amphetamine Use and Abuse in America*. Cambridge, MA: Harvard University Press, 1975.

Han Suk-Jung. "The Problem of Sovereignty: Manchukuo, 1932–1937." *positions* 12, no. 2 (2004): 457–78.

Hanes, Jeffrey E. *The City as Subject: Seki Hajime and the Reinvention of Modern Osaka*. Berkeley: University of California Press, 2002.

Hara, Hiroko, and Mieko Minagawa. "From Productive Dependents to Precious Guests: Historical Changes in Japanese Children." In *Japanese Childrearing: Two Generations of Scholarship*, edited by David W. Schwalb and Barbara J. Schwalb, 9–30. New York: Guilford Press, 1996.

Harris, Sheldon H. *Factories of Death: Japanese Biological Warfare, 1932–1945, and the American Cover-Up*. New York: Routledge, 1994.

Harrison, Henrietta. "Narcotics, Nationalism and Class in China: The Transition from Opium to Morphine and Heroin in Early Twentieth-Century Shanxi." *East Asian History* 32/33 (2006/2007): 151–76.

Hashiya Hiroshi. *Teikoku Nihon to shokuminchi toshi*. Tokyo: Yoshikawa Kōbunkan, 2004.

Hastings, Sally Ann. *Neighborhood and Nation in Tokyo, 1905–1937*. Pittsburgh, PA: University of Pittsburgh Press, 1995.

Haynes, Douglas M. "The Persistence of Privilege: British Medical Qualifications and the Practice of Medicine in the Empire." In *Beyond Sovereignty: Britain, Empire and Transnationalism c. 1880–1950*, edited by Kevin Grant, Philippa Levine, and Frank Trentmann, 214–39. New York: Palgrave Macmillan, 2007.

Hayter, Alethea. *Opium and the Romantic Imagination: Addiction and Creativity in De Quincey, Coleridge, Baudelaire and Others*. Wellingborough, Northamptonshire: Crucible, 1988.

Hemmi Takemitsu. "How We Handled the Problem of Drug Abuse in Japan." In *Abuse of Central Stimulants: Symposium Arranged by the Swedish Committee on International Health Relations*, edited by Folke Sjökvist and Malcolm Tottie, 147–63. New York: Raven Press, 1969.

Hess, Christian A. "From Colonial Jewel to Socialist Metropolis: Dalian 1895–1955." PhD dissertation, University of California at San Diego, 2006.

Hickman, Timothy A. *The Secret Leprosy of Modern Days: Addiction and Cultural Crisis in the United States, 1870–1920*. Amherst: University of Massachusetts Press, 2007.

High, Peter B. *The Imperial Screen: Japanese Film Culture in the Fifteen Years' War, 1931–1945*. Madison: University of Wisconsin Press, 2004.

Hirano, Ken'ichirō. "The Japanese in Manchuria 1906–1931: A Study of the Historical Background of Manchukuo." PhD dissertation, Harvard University, 1983.

Honda Heisaburō. "Hanzai e hashiru kakuseizai jōyōsha no yokogao." In *Hiropon: Kakuseizai ka no higeki to sono taisaku*, edited by Shinkei eisei bunka kyōkai, 139–65. Tokyo: Shinkei eisei bunka kyōkai, 1955.

Hotta, Eri. *Pan-Asianism and Japan's War 1931–1945*. New York: Palgrave Macmillan, 2007.

Howard, Paul Wilson. "Opium Suppression in Qing China: Responses to a Social Problem, 1729–1906." PhD dissertation, University of Pennsylvania, 1998.

Hsu Hung Bin. "From Smokers to Addicts: A History of Opium and Its Uses in Taiwan." PhD dissertation, School of Oriental and African Studies, 2008.

Huffman, James L. *Creating a Public: People and Press in Meiji Japan*. Honolulu: University of Hawai'i Press, 1997.

Iijima Wataru. "Shokuminchi shugi to igaku," in *Manshū to wa nandatta no ka*, edited by Nakami Tatsuo, 134–39. Tokyo: Fujiwara shoin, 2004.

———. *Mararia to teikoku: Shokuminchi igaku to Higashi Ajia no kōiki chitsuryō*. Tokyo: Tokyo Daigaku shuppankai, 2005.

The Illicit Narcotics Trade of the Chinese Communists. Taipei: Asian Peoples' Anti-Communist League, 1957.

Imamura Yutaka. *Chōsen ni okeru jinkō ni kansuru sho tōkei*. Keijō: Chōsen kōsei kyōkai, 1943.

Inglehart, Charles W. *A Century of Protestant Christianity in Japan*. Rutland, VT: Charles E. Tuttle, 1959.

Inoue Hisashi. *Inoue Hisashi no Dairen: Shashin to chizu de miru Manshū*. Tokyo: Shōgakkan, 2002.

Inoue Kōbai. *Shina fūzoku*. Shanghai: Nihondō shoten, 1920.

———. *Sake, ahen, majan*. Tokyo: Marikaku shobō, 1930.

———. "Ahen to tabako." In *Ajia mondai kōza dai kyū moku: Shakai, shūzoku hen*, edited by Imai Toshiki and Ozaki Hotsumi, 263–76. Tokyo: Sōgensha, 1940.

———. *Chūka mangekyō*. Tokyo: Umiushisha, 1993.

Ishida Takeshi. *Kioku to bōkyaku no seijigaku: Dōka seisaku, sensō sekinin, shūgōteki kioku*. Tokyo: Akashi shoten, 2000.

Ishii, Akio, and Nobuo Motohashi. "Drug Abuse in Japan." *Addictive Diseases: An International Journal* 3, no. 1 (1977): 105–14.

Itō Kazuhiko. "Mantetsu rōdōsha to rōmu taisei." In *Mantetsu rōdō shi no kenkyū*, edited by Matsumura Takao, Jie Xueshi, and Eda Kenji, 123–76. Tokyo: Nihon keizai hyōronsha, 2002.

Itō Takeo. *Life along the South Manchuria Railway: The Memoirs of Itō Takeo.* Translated by Joshua A. Fogel. Armonk, NY: M. E. Sharpe, 1988.

Jankowiak, William, and Daniel Bradburd, eds. *Drugs, Labor, and Colonial Expansion.* Tucson: University of Arizona Press, 2003.

Jannetta, Ann Bowman. *The Vaccinators: Smallpox, Medical Knowledge, and the Opening of Japan.* Stanford, CA: Stanford University Press, 2007.

Japan-Manchoukuo Year Book. Tokyo: Asia Statistics, 1938.

Jennings, John M. "The Forgotten Plague: Opium and Narcotics in Korea under Japanese Rule, 1910–1945." *Modern Asian Studies* 29, no. 4 (1995): 795–815.

———. *The Opium Empire: Japanese Imperialism and Drug Trafficking in Asia, 1895–1945.* Westport, CT: Praeger, 1997.

Johnson, Clifford. *Pirate Junk: Five Months' Captivity with Manchurian Bandits.* New York: Charles Scribners' Sons, 1934.

Johnston, William. *The Modern Epidemic: A History of Tuberculosis in Japan.* Cambridge, MA: Harvard University Council on East Asian Studies, 1995.

Jones, F. C. *Manchuria since 1931.* London: Royal Institute of International Affairs, 1949.

Jones, Mark A. *Children as Treasures: Childhood and the Middle Class in Early Twentieth Century Japan.* Cambridge, MA: Harvard University Asia Center, 2010.

Jung, Moon-Ho. *Coolies and Cane: Race, Labor, and Sugar in the Age of Emancipation.* Baltimore, MD: Johns Hopkins University Press, 2006.

Kaku Sagatarō. *Opium Policy in Japan.* Geneva: Albert Kundig, 1924.

Kamachi, Noriko. "The Chinese in Meiji Japan: Their Interactions with the Japanese before the Sino-Japanese War." In *The Chinese and the Japanese: Essays in Political and Cultural Interactions,* edited by Akira Iriye, 58–73. Princeton, NJ: Princeton University Press, 1980.

Kaneko Junji. *Hanzai no shinri.* Tokyo: Kuresu shuppan, 2008.

Kaneko Mitsuzō. "Kakuseizai no mitsuzō no ru-to." In *Hiropon: Kakuseizai ka no higeki to sono taisaku,* edited by Shinkei eisei bunka kyōkai, 187–98. Tokyo: Shinkei eisei bunka kyōkai, 1955.

Kantō-chō. *Kantō-chō kannai shakai jigyō yōran.* Dairen: Kantō-chō naimu-kyoku chihōka, 1925.

———. *Shōwa go nen Kantō-chō kokusai chōsa kekka hyō.* Ryōjun: Kantō-chō chōkan kanbō chōsaka, 1933.

———. *Kantō-chō yōran.* Ryōjun: Kantō-chō, 1934.

Kantō-chō bunshoka. *Kantō-chō shisei nijū nenshi.* Dairen: Kantō-chō, 1926.

Kantō-chō keimu-kyoku eiseika. *Kokusai renmei Kyokutō ahen chōsa no shitsumon ni taisuru tōbensho.* Dairen: Kantō-chō keimu-kyoku eiseika, 1930.

Kantō-kyoku kanbō bunshoka. *Kantō-kyoku shisei sanjū nen gyōseki chōsa shiryō*. Dairen: Kantō-kyoku bunshoka, 1937.

———. *Kantō-kyoku yōran*. Dairen: Kantō-kyoku kanbō bunshoka, 1939.

Kantō-kyoku keimubu eiseika, ed. *Eisei gaikan*. Shinkyō: Kantō-kyoku keimubu eiseika, 1937.

Kaplan, David E., and Alex Dubro. *Yakuza: Japan's Criminal Underworld*. Berkeley: University of California Press, 2003.

Karatani Kōjin. *Origins of Modern Japanese Literature*. Edited and translated by Brett de Bary. Durham, NC: Duke University Press, 1993.

Karch, Steven B. "Japan and the Cocaine Industry of Southeast Asia, 1864–1944." In *Cocaine: Global Histories*, edited by Paul Gootenberg, 146–64. New York: Routledge, 1999.

Kashiwara Jun. "Shanhai ni okeru 'Kokusai ahen chōsa iinkai' to Nihon no ahen seisaku: Taiwan Sōtokufu no ahen senbai seido wo chūshin to shite." *Kindai Nihon kenkyū* 28 (2011): 3–50.

Katō Hisayuki. *Taiwan ni okeru ahen*. Taihoku, 1906.

Katō Kiyofumi. "Hara Kei to Mantetsu." In *Kindai Nihon to Mantetsu*, edited by Kobayashi Hideo, 31–63. Tokyo: Yoshikawa Kōbunkan, 2000.

Katō Masaaki. "An Epidemiological Analysis of the Fluctuation of Drug Dependence in Japan." *International Journal of the Addictions* 4, no. 4 (1969): 591–621.

———. "Epidemiology of Drug Dependence in Japan." In *Drug Abuse: Proceedings of the International Conference*, edited by Chris J. D. Zarafonetis, 67–70. Philadelphia: Lea & Febinger, 1972.

Katsuragawa Mitsumasa. "Gotō Asatarō, Chūgoku, ahen." *Ōsaka Sangyō Daigaku ronshū* 113 (1999): 57–65.

———. "Kantōshū ahen seido no seitai to Chūgoku shōnin: Kantōshū no tōchi wo meguru kōsatsu." *Shirin* 91, no. 2 (2008): 69–94.

Kawaji Toshiyoshi. "Kengi sōron." In *Nihon keisatsu shi*, edited by Yamamoto Kazuo, 132–34. Tokyo: Shōkadō shoten, 1934.

Kawashima, Ken C. *The Proletarian Gamble: Korean Workers in Interwar Japan*. Durham, NC: Duke University Press, 2009.

Kazama Hideto, ed. *"Kyōwa undō" bessatsu kaitei, sō mokuroku, sakuin*. Tokyo: Rokuin shobō, 1995.

Keishi-chō kakuseizai torishimari taisaku honbu. *Hiropon kakuseizai no gaiaku to sono taisaku*. Tokyo: Keishi-chō kakuseizai torishimari taisaku honbu, 1955.

Keizai chōsabu. *Manshū no kuri*. Dairen: Minami Manshū tetsudō kabushiki kaisha, 1934.

Keller, Richard C. *Colonial Madness: Psychiatry in French North Africa*. Chicago: University of Chicago Press, 2007.

Kikuchi Yūji. "Ahen haidoku undō ni kansuru iken." In *Ahen mondai no kenkyū*, edited by Kikuchi Yūji, 2–10. Tokyo: Kokusai renmei kyōkai, 1928.

———. "Shina ni okeru ahen no haidoku." In *Ahen mondai no kenkyū*, edited by Kikuchi Yūji, 12–24. Tokyo: Kokusai renmei kyōkai, 1928.

Kim X Joo. "Hanayaka na koshō kara suri no tsuma ni." In *Mayaku chūdokusha to naku: Tō-A wo ahen kara kaikō seyo*, edited by Majima Kan, 17–26. Tokyo: Ajia seisaku kenkyūjo, 1935.

Kim X Ki. "Kutsu wo shikkei suru no ga senmon." In *Mayaku chūdokusha to naku: Tō-A wo ahen kara kaikō seyo*, edited by Majima Kan, 6–9. Tokyo: Ajia seisaku kenkyūjo, 1935.

Kin Juhō. "Dairen to watashi wo tsunagu unmei no kei." In *Manshū to wa nandatta no ka*, edited by Nakami Tatsuo, 504–7. Tokyo: Fujiwara shoten, 2004.

Kinney, H. W. *Modern Manchuria*. Dairen: South Manchuria Railway Company, 1928.

Kinoshita Tetsuo. "Yakurigaku kyōshitsu." In *Manshū Ika Daigaku yonjū shūnen kinen shi*, edited by Hōjin Dōsōkai, 38–40. Tokyo: Hōjin Dōsōkai, 1952.

Kiyooka Takayuki. "Akashiya no Dairen." In *Kiyooka Takayuki Dairen shōsetsu zenshū*, 65–156. Tokyo: Bungeisha, 1992.

Kleinman, Arthur. *What Really Matters: Living a Moral Life amidst Uncertainty and Danger*. New York: Oxford University Press, 2006.

Kobayashi Hideo and Zhang Zhiqiang, eds. *Ken'etsu sareta tegami ga kataru: Manshūkoku no jittai*. Tokyo: Shōgakkan, 2006.

Kobayashi Michihiko. "Mantetsu to Gotō Shinpei." In *Mantetsu to wa nandatta no ka*, edited by Yoshida Yōji and Fujiwara Yoshio, 39–49. Tokyo: Fujiwara shoten, 2006.

Kobayashi Motohiro. "An Opium Tug-of-War: Japan versus the Wang Jingwei Regime." In *Opium Regimes: China, Britain, and Japan, 1839–1952*, edited by Timothy Brook and Bob Tadashi Wakabayashi, 344–59. Berkeley: University of California Press, 2000.

———. "Drug Operations by Resident Japanese in Tianjin." In *Opium Regimes: China, Britain, and Japan, 1839–1952*, edited by Timothy Brook and Bob Tadashi Wakabayashi, 152–66. Berkeley: University of California Press, 2004.

———. *Kindai Chūgoku no Nihon iryūmin to ahen*. Tokyo: Yoshikawa Kōbunkan, 2012.

Kohn, Marek. *Dope Girls: The Birth of the British Drug Underground*. London: Lawrence & Wishart, 1992.

Kokusai mondai kenkyū kyōkai. *Nihon wo mushibamu hiropon ka no jittai*. Tokyo: Kokusai mondai kenkyū kyōkai, 1954.

Komagome Takeshi. *Shokuminchi teikoku Nihon no bunka tōgō*. Tokyo: Iwanami shoten, 1996.

Kōseishō yakumu-kyoku. *Kokuren Ajia Kyokutō mayaku kyōgikai*. Tokyo: Kōseishō yakumu-kyoku, 1964.

Koshiro, Yukiko. *Trans-Pacific Racisms and the U.S. Occupation of Japan*. New York: Columbia University Press, 1999.

Koshizawa Akira. "Dairen no toshi keikaku shi." *Nit-Chū keizai kyōkai kaikoku* 134/135/136 (1984): 1–51.

Kotani Keisuke. *Kantōgun shūsai Manshū Ika Daigaku Nekka chihōbyō kenkyūdan kōdō no gaiyō*. Hōten: Manshū Ika Daigaku, 1934.

Kratoska, Paul H., ed. *Asian Labor in the Wartime Japanese Empire: Unknown Histories*. Armonk, NY: M. E. Sharpe, 2005.

Krueger, Hugo Martin. *Ahen arukaroido kagaku*. Translated by Takamoto Ryūji. Tokyo: Nankōdō, 1937.

———. *The Pharmacology of the Opium Alkaloids*. Washington, DC: Government Printing Office, 1943.

Kubota Seikō. "Ahen no hanashi." In *Manshū Ika Daigaku jutsu kōenkai kōenshū*, edited by Manshū Ika Daigaku, 11–32. Shinkyō: Manshū Ika Daigaku, 1934.

Kumar, Deepak. *Science and the Raj 1857–1905*. New York: Oxford University Press, 1995.

Kurahashi Masanao. "Chō Sakurin seiken no ahen kaikin seisaku (1927 nen)." *Aichi Kenritsu Daigaku bungaku ronshū* 44 (1995): 80–56.

———. *Nihon no ahen senryaku: Kakureta kokka hanzai*. Tokyo: Kyōei shobō, 1996.

———. *Ahen, teikoku, Nihon*. Tokyo: Kyōei shobō, 2008.

———. "Nazo no ahen tokkō yaku: Tōkōzai." *Kiyū: Chiiki kenkyū* 40 (2008): 63–85.

Kuratsuka Yoshio. "Ahen kara mita Nit-Chū kankei." *Kikan Chūgoku* 57 (1999): 2–15.

Kuroba Kiyotaka. *Jūgo nen sensō shi josetsu*. Tokyo: Sanshōtō, 1979.

Kuroshima Denji. *Kuroshima Denji shū*. Tokyo: Shin Nihon shuppansha, 1984.

———. *A Flock of Swirling Crows and Other Proletarian Writings*. Translated by Zeljko Cipris. Honolulu: University of Hawai'i Press, 2005.

Kwantung Government. *Outline of the Kwantung Government*. Dairen: Manchuria Daily News, 1926.

The Kwantung Government: Its Functions and Works. Ryōjun: Kwantung Government, 1929.

The Kwantung Government: Its Functions and Works. Dairen: Kwantung Government, 1934.

La Motte, Ellen N. *The Opium Monopoly*. New York: Macmillan, 1920.

Lederer, Susan E. *Subjected to Science: Human Experimentation in America before the Second World War*. Baltimore, MD: Johns Hopkins University Press, 1995.

Lee, Chulwoo. "Modernity, Legality, and Power in Korea under Japanese Rule." In *Colonial Modernity in Korea,* edited by Gi-Wook Shin and Michael Robinson, 21–51. Cambridge, MA: Harvard University Asia Center, 1999.

Lee, Helie. *Still Life with Rice: A Young American Woman Discovers the Life and Legacy of Her Korean Grandmother.* New York: Scribner, 1996.

Lei, Sean Hsiang-lin. "Sovereignty and the Microscope: Constituting Notifiable Infectious Disease and Containing the Manchurian Plague." In *Health and Hygiene in Chinese East Asia: Policies and Publics in the Long Twentieth Century,* edited by Angela Ki Che Leung and Charlotte Furth, 73–106. Durham, NC: Duke University Press, 2010.

Leung, Angela Ki Che. "The Evolution of the Idea of *Chuanran* Contagion in Imperial China." In *Health and Hygiene in Chinese East Asia: Policies and Publics in the Long Twentieth Century,* edited by Angela Ki Che Leung and Charlotte Furth, 25–50. Durham, NC: Duke University Press, 2010.

Li, Xiaoxing. *Poppies and Politics in China: Sichuan Province, 1840s to 1940s.* Newark: University of Delaware Press, 2009.

Lin, Man-houng. "The Power of Culture and Its Limits: Taiwanese Merchants and Asian Commodity Flows, 1895–1945." In *Chinese Circulations: Capital, Commodities, and Networks in Southeast Asia,* edited by Eric Tagliacozzo and Wen-Chin Chang, 305–35. Durham, NC: Duke University Press, 2011.

Lin Yutang. *Moment in Peking.* New York: John Day, 1939.

Lippit, Noriko. "Natsume Sōseki on Poe." *Comparative Literature* 14, no. 1 (1977): 30–37.

Liu Jianhui. "Demon Capital Shanghai: The 'Modern' Experience of Japanese Intellectuals: Taishō Writers Who Indulged in the Demon Capital." Translated by Joshua A. Fogel. *Sino-Japanese Studies* 16 (2009): 184–204.

———. *Demon Capital Shanghai: The "Modern" Experience of Japanese Intellectuals.* Translated by Joshua A. Fogel. Portland, ME: MerwinAsia, 2012.

Liu Jin-tan, Liu Jin-long, and Chow Shin-yi. *The Demand for Opium in Colonial Taiwan, 1914–1942.* Taipei: Academia Sinica Institute of Economics, 1996.

Liu, Peter, and Yingyi Situ. "Narcotics Control in China: A Growing Challenge." In *Crime and Social Control in a Changing China,* edited by Jianhong Lu, Lening Zhang, and Steven F. Messner, 37–53. Westport, CT: Greenview Press, 2001.

Liu Shi-yung. "Medical Reform in Colonial Taiwan." PhD dissertation, University of Pittsburgh, 2000.

Lo, Ming-cheng Miriam. *Doctors within Borders: Profession, Ethnicity, and Modernity in Colonial Taiwan.* Berkeley: University of California Press, 2002.

Lo, R. Y. *The Opium Problem in the Far East.* Shanghai: Commercial Press, 1933.

Lü Heruo. *Seishū.* Tokyo: Yumani shobō, 2001.

Lü Yonghua. *Wei-Man shiqi de Dongbei yandu*. Changchun: Jilin renmin chubanshe, 2004.

Lu, Hong, Terence D. Miethe, and Bin Liang. *China's Drug Practices and Policies: Regulating Controlled Substances in a Global Context*. Surrey: Ashgate, 2009.

Lyons, Phyllis. *The Saga of Dazai Osamu: A Critical Study with Translations*. Stanford, CA: Stanford University Press, 1985.

MacLeod, Roy. "On Visiting the 'Moving Metropolis': Reflections on the Architecture of Imperial Science." In *Scientific Colonialism: A Cross-Cultural Comparison*, edited by Nathan Reingold and Marc Rothenberg, 217–51. Washington, DC: Smithsonian Institution Press, 1987.

Madancy, Joyce. *The Troublesome Legacy of Commissioner Lin: The Opium Trade and Opium Suppression in Fujian Province, 1820s to 1920s*. Cambridge, MA: Harvard University Asia Center, 2003.

Majima Kan. *Mayaku chūdokusha to naku: Tō-A wo ahen kara kaikō seyo*. Tokyo: Ajia seisaku kenkyūjo, 1935.

Makuuchi Mitsuo. *Manshūkoku keisatsu gaishi*. Tokyo: San'ichi shobō, 1996.

The Manchoukuo Year Book. Tokyo: Tō-A keizai chōsa-kyoku, 1934.

The Manchoukuo Year Book. Tokyo: Tō-A keizai chōsa-kyoku, 1942.

Manela, Erez. *The Wilsonian Moment: Self-Determination and the International Origins of Anticolonial Nationalism*. New York: Oxford University Press, 2007.

Man-Mō tokushu ken'eki ron. Tokyo: Nihon hyōron shuppan, 1933.

Manshū Ika Daigaku. *Manshū Ika Daigaku gyōseki shū dai isshū*. Hōten: Manshū Ika Daigaku, 1940.

———. *Manshū Ika Daigaku gyōseki shū dai ni shū (Shōwa 14–16)*. Hōten: Manshū Ika Daigaku, 1942.

Mantetsu chōsabu. *Ahen sensō ni yoru dentōteki Shina kokka no hōkai to fukoku kyōhei undō*. Shinkyō: Mantetsu chōsabu, 1941.

Mantetsu keizai chōsakai dai go bu. *Chōsen ahen mayaku seido chōsa hōkoku*. Dairen: Minami Manshū tetsudō kabushiki kaisha, 1932.

Marez, Curtis. *Drug Wars: The Political Economy of Narcotics*. Minneapolis: University of Minnesota Press, 2004.

Marran, Christine L. *Poison Woman: Figuring Female Transgression in Modern Japanese Culture*. Minneapolis: University of Minnesota Press, 2007.

Martin, Brian G. *The Shanghai Green Gang: Politics and Organized Crime, 1919–1937*. Berkeley: University of California Press, 1996.

Masaki Akira. *Reminiscences of a Japanese Penologist*. Tokyo: Japanese Criminal Policy Association, 1964.

Materials on the Trial of Former Servicemen of the Japanese Army Charged with Manufacturing and Employing Bacteriological Weapons. Moscow: Foreign Languages Publishing House, 1950.

Matsubara Kazue. *Dairen dansu ho-ru no yoru.* Tokyo: Chūō kōronsha, 1998.

———. *Maboroshi no Dairen.* Tokyo: Shinchōsha, 2008.

Matsubara Nobuyuki. *Kantōshū ahen seido shi.* Dairen: Kantō-chō senbai-kyoku, 1932.

Matsui Kokichi. *Ei-Shin ahen sen shi.* Tokyo: Hakubunkan, 1895.

Matsui Yoshio. *Mayaku to bungaku.* Tokyo: Kōshinsha, 1938.

Matsumura, Janice. "Mental Health as Public Peace: Kaneko Junji and the Promotion of Psychiatry in Modern Japan." *Modern Asian Studies* 38, no. 4 (2004): 899–930.

Matsuo, M. *The Development of Science and Culture in Manchuria: Japan's Contributions.* Dairen: Research Committee of Pacific Relations in SMR, n.d.

Matsusaka, Yoshihisa Tak. *The Making of Japanese Manchuria, 1904–1932.* Cambridge, MA: Harvard University Asia Center, 2001.

Matsushige Mitsuhiro. "Shokuminchi Dairen ni okeru Kajin shakai no tenkai: 1920 nendai shotō Dairen Kashōdantai no katsudō wo chūshin ni." In *Kindai Chūgoku to Nihon—Teikei to tekitai no han seiki,* edited by Soda Saburō, 107–37. Tokyo: Ochanomizu shobō, 2001.

———. "Dai ichiji taisen sengo ni okeru Dairen no 'Santō hō.'" In *Nihon no Seitō senryō to Santō no shakai keizai,* edited by Honjō Hisako, 347–68. Tokyo: Tōyō Bunko, 2006.

Matsuzaki Keiji. *Ahen sensō: Sono shijitsu to monogatari.* Tokyo: Takayama shoin, 1942.

May, Herbert L. *Survey of Smoking Conditions in the Far East: A Report to the Executive Board of the Foreign Policy Association.* New York: Opium Research Committee of the Foreign Policy Association, 1927.

Mayaku chūdokusha kyūgokai. *Mayaku chūdokusha kyūgokai nenpō (Shōwa 14/15).* Tokyo: Mayaku chūdokusha kyūgokai, 1940.

———. *Mayaku chūdokusha kyūgokai nenpō (Shōwa 16).* Tokyo: Mayaku chūdokusha kyūgokai, 1941.

McAllister, William B. *Drug Diplomacy in the Twentieth Century: An International History.* New York: Routledge, 2000.

McCormack, Gavan. *Chang Tso-lin in Northeast China, 1911–1928: China, Japan, and the Manchurian Idea.* Stanford, CA: Stanford University Press, 1977.

McMahon, Keith. *The Fall of the God of Money: Opium Smoking in Nineteenth-Century China.* Lanham, MD: Rowman & Littlefield, 2002.

Mei Gongren. *Wangguo miezhong de yapian yanhuo.* Beijing: Beijing zhongxian tuofang keji fazhan youxian gongsi, 2007.

Merrill, Frederick. *Japan and the Opium Menace*. New York: International Secretariat, Institute for Pacific Relations, and the Foreign Policy Association, 1942.

Meyer, Kathryn, and Terry Parsinnen. *Webs of Smoke: Smugglers, Warlords, Spies, and the History of the International Drug Trade*. Lanham, MD: Rowman & Littlefield, 1998.

Middlemiss, Herbert Samuel, ed. *Narcotic Education: Edited Report of the Proceedings*. Washington, DC: World Conference on Narcotic Education, 1927.

Mill, James Stuart. *The History of British India*. Abridged by William Thomas. Chicago: University of Chicago Press, 1975.

Milligan, Barry. *Pleasures and Pains: Opium and the Orient in Nineteenth-Century British Culture*. Charlottesville: University Press of Virginia, 1995.

Mills, James H. "Drugs, Consumption, and Supply in Asia: The Case of Cocaine in Colonial India, 1900–1930." *Journal of Asian Studies* 66, no. 2 (2007): 345–62.

———, and Patricia Barton. "Introduction." In *Drugs and Empires: Essays in Modern Imperialism and Intoxication, c. 1500–c. 1930*, edited by James H. Mills and Patricia Barton, 1–16. New York: Palgrave Macmillan, 2007.

Mimura, Janis. *Planning for Empire: Reform Bureaucrats and the Japanese Wartime State*. Ithaca, NY: Cornell University Press, 2011.

Minami Manshū tetsudō kabushiki kaisha chōsabu. *Mantetsu tōkei nenpō*. Dairen: Minami Manshū tetsudō kabushiki kaisha, 1911.

Minami Manshū tetsudō kabushiki kaisha keizai chōsabu. *Manshū rōdō jigyō shūkan*. Dairen: Manshū bunka kyōkai, 1936.

Minami-Manshū tetsudō kabushiki kaisha Dairen Iin. *Dairen Iin shinchiku rakusei kinen igakkai shi*. Dairen: Minami-Manshū tetsudō kabushiki kaisha, 1927.

Mintz, Sidney W. *Sweetness and Power: The Place of Sugar in Modern History*. New York: Viking, 1985.

Mitchell, Richard. *Thought Control in Prewar Japan*. Ithaca, NY: Cornell University Press, 1976.

Mitter, Rana. *The Manchurian Myth: Nationalism, Resistance, and Collaboration in Modern China*. Berkeley: University of California Press, 2000.

Miyajima Mikinosuke. *Kokusai ahen mondai no keii*. Tokyo: Nihon kokusai kyōkai, 1935.

Miyauchi Isamu, ed. *Manshū kenkoku sokumenshi*. Tokyo: Shin keizaisha, 1942.

Mizobe Hideaki. "Gotō Shinpei ron: Tōsōteki sekai zō to 'risei no dokusai.'" *Hōgaku ronsō* 100, no. 2 (1976): 62–96.

Mizuno, Hiromi. *Science for the Empire: Scientific Nationalism in Modern Japan*. Stanford, CA: Stanford University Press, 2009.

Mizuno Jun. *Taiwan ahen shobun*. Tokyo: Mizuno Jun, 1898.

Mizuno Naoki. "Kokuseki wo meguru Higashi Ajia kankei: Shokuminchi ki Chōsenjin kokuseki mondai no isō." In *Kindai Nihon ni okeru Higashi Ajia mondai*, edited by Yamamuro Shin'ichi and Furuya Tetsuo, 211–37. Tokyo: Yoshikawa Kōbunkan, 2001.

Mold, Alex. *Heroin: The Treatment of Addiction in Twentieth-Century Britain*. DeKalb: Northern Illinois University Press, 2008.

Monnais, Laurence. "'Modern Medicine' in French Colonial Vietnam: From the Importation of a Model to Its Nativisation." In *The Development of Modern Medicine in Non-Western Countries: Historical Perspectives*, edited by Hormoz Ebrahimnejad, 127–59. New York: Routledge, 2009.

Montesquieu, Charles de Secondat, baron de. *The Spirit of the Laws*. Translated by Anne M. Cohler, Basia Carolyn Miller, and Samuel Harold Stone. New York: Cambridge University Press, 1989.

Mori Gōin. *Hoku-Man chihō no ahen*. Harbin: Harupin shohin chinritsu kan, 1925.

Morimoto Kiyoshi. "The Problem of the Abuse of Amphetamines in Japan." In *Bulletin on Narcotics*, vol. 9, edited by United Nations Bureau of Social Affairs, 8–12. Geneva: United Nations, 1957.

Morris-Suzuki, Tessa. *Borderline Japan: Foreigners and Frontier Controls in the Postwar Era*. New York: Cambridge University Press, 2011.

Motosada Zumoto. *Lytton Commission on China and Manchuria*. Tokyo: Herald Press, 1932.

Murakami Ryū. *Kagiri naku tomei ni chikai buru-*. Tokyo: Kōdansha, 1976.

———. *Almost Transparent Blue*. Translated by Nancy Andrews. Tokyo: Kodansha International, 1977.

Murayama Tomoyoshi. *Ahen sensō: Yonmaku hachiba*. Tokyo: Nitteishutsu, 1934.

Muroo Tadashi. *Kakuseizai*. Tokyo: San'ichi shobō, 1982.

Musto, David F. *The American Disease: Origins of Narcotic Control*. New York: Oxford University Press, 1999.

Nagahama Masamutsu. "A Review of Drug Abuse and Counter Measures in Japan since World War II." *Bulletin on Narcotics* 20, no. 3 (1968): 19–24.

Nakami Tatsuo. "Rekishi no naka no 'Manshū' zō. In *Manshū to wa nandatta no ka*, edited by Nakami Tatsuo, 13–26. Tokyo: Fujiwara shoten, 2004.

———. "Gaikokujin ni wa rikai shigatai: Nihon shi no kotoba 'tairiku rōnin' to sono shūben." *Nihon rekishi* 704 (2007): 126–31.

Nakamoto Shin'ichi. *Datsu 'aruko-ru izon shakai' wo mezashite: Nihon no aruko-ru seisaku e no teigen*. Tokyo: Akashi shoten, 2009.

Nakano Kaichi. "Oda Sakunosuke—Hiropon to 'bungaku no kanōsei' no chōsen." *Kokubungaku: Kaishaku to kanshō* 48, no. 7 (1983): 343–49.

Nakatani Yoshisaburō. "Nakatani Yoshisaburō wo kakonde." In *Zai-Sen Nihonjin yakugyō kaikō shi*, edited by Kubo Ken, 4–20. Tokyo, 1961.

Nakayama Shigeru. *Academic and Scientific Traditions in China, Japan and the West*. Translated by Jerry Dusenbury. Tokyo: University of Tokyo Press, 1984.

Namae Takayuki. *Waga kyūjū nen no shōgai*. Tokyo: Ōzorasha, 1988.

Nan-Man Igakudō. *Nan-Man Igakudō jū nen shi*. Hōten: Nan-Man Igakudō, 1923.

Nathan, Carl F. *Plague Prevention and Politics in Manchuria, 1910–1931*. Cambridge, MA: Harvard University East Asian Research Center, 1967.

Newman, R. K. "Opium Smoking in Late Imperial China: A Reconsideration," *Modern Asian Studies* 29, no. 4 (1995): 765–94.

Nieh, Christopher T. "Japan's Manchuria Policy from the Kwantung Leased Territory to the Formation of Manchukuo." PhD dissertation, Johns Hopkins University, 1993.

Nishihara Kazumi. "Shashin ni miru 'Manshū' ime-ji." In *Manshū to wa nandatta no ka*, edited by Nakami Tatsuo, 113–26. Tokyo: Fujiwara shoten, 2004.

Nishinomiya Kō. "Gotō Shinpei no Manshū keiryaku." In *Manshū to wa nandatta no ka*, edited by Nakami Tatsuo, 225–43. Tokyo: Fujiwara shoten, 2004.

Nishizawa Yasuhiko. *Zusetsu Dairen toshi monogatari*. Tokyo: Kawade shobō shinsha, 1999.

Nobiyuki Dairen. Dairen: Achō shuppan kyōkai, 1935.

Nolte, Sharon H., and Sally Ann Hastings. "The Meiji State's Policy toward Women, 1890–1910." In *Recreating Japanese Women, 1600–1945*, edited by Gail Lee Bernstein, 151–74. Berkeley: University of California Press, 1991.

Nonami Shizuo. *Kokusai ahen mondai*. Tokyo: Heibōsha, 1925.

O'Dwyer, Emer Sinead. "People's Empire: Democratic Imperialism in Japanese Manchuria." PhD dissertation, Harvard University, 2007.

Ogino Fujio. *Gaimushō keisatsu shi*. Tokyo: Azekura shobō, 2005.

Oguma Eiji. *Nihonjin no kyōkai: Okinawa, Ainu, Taiwan, Chōsen, shokuminchi shihai kara fukki undō made*. Tokyo: Shin'yōsha, 1998.

———. *A Genealogy of "Japanese" Self-Images*. Translated by David Askew. Melbourne: Trans Pacific Press, 2002.

Ōhara Masatoshi. *Ahen sensō*. Taihoku: Morioka shuppanbu, 1944.

Ōi Shizuo. *Ahen jiken no shinsō*. Tokyo: Ōi Shizuo, 1923.

Ōizumi Kokuseki. *'Bai gui lai': Ahen sensō wa kaku tatakarareta*. Tokyo: Daishinsha, 1942.

Oka Senjin. *Kankō kiyū*. Tokyo, 1886.

Okabe Makio, Yanagisawa Asobu, and Xing Bailin. "Kyōwakai to gozoku kyōwa." In *"Manshūkoku" to wa nandatta no ka,* edited by Shokuminchi bunka gakkai, 215–36. Tokyo: Shōgakkan, 2008.

Okauchi Hanzō, ed. *Sekai wo fubi seru ahen no ryūkō.* Dairen: Ryōtō shōtōsha, 1920.

Ōkawa Wataru. "Hiropon, adorumu, Tanaka Hidemitsu." *Chikuma* 348 (2004): 26–29.

The Opium War. Tokyo: Maruya and Kigyōsha, 1890.

Osaragi Jirō. *Ahen sensō.* Tokyo: Modan Nihon shahan, 1942.

Ōshita Udaru. *Ōshita Udaru shū.* Tokyo: Heibonsha, 1930.

Ota Naoki. *Tōjō Hideki: Ahen no yami, Manshū no yume.* Tokyo: Kadogawa gakugei shuppan, 2009.

Ōuchi Ushinosuke. *Shina ahen mondai kaiketsu iken.* Tokyo, 1917.

Padwa, Howard. *Social Poison: The Culture and Politics of Opiate Control in Britain and France, 1821–1926.* Baltimore, MD: Johns Hopkins University Press, 2012.

Park, Hyun Ok. *Two Dreams in One Bed: Empire, Social Life, and the Origins of the North Korean Revolution in Manchuria.* Durham, NC: Duke University Press, 2005.

Park Kang. *Zhong-Ri zhanzheng yu yapian.* Translated by You Juanhuan. Taipei: Guoshiguan, 1998.

Parssinen, Terry M. *Secret Passions, Secret Remedies: Narcotic Drugs in British Society, 1820–1930.* Philadelphia: Institute for the Study of Human Issues, 1983.

Paulès, Xavier. "Anti-Opium Visual Propaganda and the Deglamorisation of Opium in China, 1895–1937." *European Journal of East Asian Studies* 7, no. 2 (2008): 229–62.

———. "Drogue et transgressions socials: Les femmes et l'opium à Canton dans les années 1930." *Clio* 28 (2008): 225–44.

Peattie, Mark R. "Japanese Attitudes toward Colonialism, 1895–1945." In *The Japanese Colonial Empire, 1895–1945,* edited by Ramon H. Myers and Mark R. Peattie, 80–127. Princeton, NJ: Princeton University Press, 1984.

Pelling, Margaret. "The Meaning of Contagion: Reproduction, Medicine and Metaphor." In *Contagion: Historical and Cultural Studies,* edited by Alison Bashford and Claire Hooker, 15–38. New York: Routledge, 2001.

Perrins, Robert J. "Doctors, Disease, and Development: Engineering Colonial Public Health in Southern Manchuria, 1905–1926." In *Building a Modern Japan: Science, Technology, and Medicine in the Meiji Era and Beyond,* edited by Morris Low, 103–32. New York: Palgrave Macmillan, 2005.

Poe, Edgar Allan. *The Tell-Tale Heart.* New York: J. H. Eggers, 1916.

Polachek, James M. *The Inner Opium War.* Cambridge, MA: Harvard University Council on East Asian Studies, 1992.

Pomeranz, Kenneth, and Steven Topik. *The World That Trade Created: Society, Culture, and the World Economy, 1400 to the Present*. Armonk, NY: M. E. Sharpe, 2006.

Pooley, A. M. *Japan at the Cross Roads*. London: George Allen & Unwin, 1917.

Pyenson, Lewis. *Cultural Imperialism and Exact Sciences: German Expansion Overseas, 1900–1930*. New York: Peter Lang, 1984.

———. *Empire of Reason: Exact Sciences in Indonesia 1840–1940*. New York: Brill, 1989.

———. *Civilizing Mission: Exact Sciences and French Overseas Expansion, 1830–1940*. Baltimore, MD: Johns Hopkins University Press, 1993.

Rabson, Steve. *Righteous Cause or Tragic Folly: Changing Views of War in Modern Japanese Poetry*. Ann Arbor: University of Michigan Center for Japanese Studies, 1998.

Rangé, C. "L'intoxication par l'opium." In *Transactions of the Second Congress*, edited by the Far Eastern Association for Tropical Medicine, 219–28. Hong Kong: Noronha, 1912.

Rasmussen, Nicolas. *On Speed: The Many Lives of Amphetamines*. New York: New York University Press, 1998.

———. "Maurice Seevers, the Stimulants and the Political Economy of Addiction in American Biomedicine." *BioSocieties* 5, no. 1 (2010): 105–23.

Reardon-Anderson, James. *Reluctant Pioneers: China's Expansion Northward, 1644–1937*. Stanford, CA: Stanford University Press, 2005.

Reeves, Caroline. "From Red Crosses to Golden Arches: China, the Red Cross, and the Hague Peace Conference, 1899–1900." In *Interactions: Transregional Perspectives on World History*, edited by Jerry H. Bentley, Renate Bridenthal, and Anand A. Yang, 64–93. Honolulu: University of Hawai'i Press, 2005.

Reid, Roddey. *Globalizing Tobacco Control: Anti-Smoking Campaigns in California, France, and Japan*. Bloomington: Indiana University Press, 2005.

Reins, Thomas David. "China and the International Politics of Opium, 1909–1937: The Impact of Reform, Revenue, and the Unequal Treaties." PhD dissertation, Claremont Graduate University, 1981.

Reynolds, Douglas R. "Training Young China Hands: Tōa Dōbun Shoin and Its Precursors, 1886–1945." In *The Japanese Informal Empire in China, 1895–1945*, edited by Peter Duus, Ramon H. Myers, and Mark R. Peattie, 210–71. Princeton, NJ: Princeton University Press, 1989.

Rogaski, Ruth. *Hygienic Modernity: Meanings of Health and Disease in Treaty-Port China*. Berkeley: University of California Press, 2004.

———. "Vampires in Plagueland: The Multiple Meanings of *Weisheng* in Manchuria." In *Health and Hygiene in Chinese East Asia: Policies and Publics in the Long Twentieth

Century, edited by Angela Ki Che Leung and Charlotte Furth, 132–59. Durham, NC: Duke University Press, 2010.

Roman, Caterina Gouvis, Heather Ahn-Redding, and Rita J. Simon. *Illicit Drug Policies, Trafficking, and Use the World Over.* Lanham, MD: Lexington Books, 2005.

Rowntree, Joshua. *The Imperial Drug Trade: A Restatement of the Opium Question in Light of Recent Evidence and New Developments in the East.* London: Methuen, 1906.

Rush, James R. *Opium to Java: Revenue Farming and Chinese Enterprise in Colonial Indonesia, 1860–1910.* Ithaca, NY: Cornell University Press, 1990.

Ryū Meishū. *Taiwan tōchi to ahen mondai.* Tokyo: Yamakawa shuppansha, 1983.

Saenaga Keiko. *Senji igaku no jittai.* Tokyo: Seiunsha, 2005.

———. "Jūgo nen sensō ki no daigaku ni okeru igaku kenkyū—Kyū Manshū Ika Daigaku wo jirei to shite." *Nihon no kagakusha* 43, no. 2 (2008): 16–21.

Sakai Yoshio. *Kokka minzoku wo metsubō seshimuru ahen no maryoku.* Tokyo: Shintō kagaku kenkyūjo, 1938.

———. *Tō-A no reimei wa mayaku no genzetsu yori.* Tokyo: Shintō kagaku kenkyūjo, 1939.

———. *Ahen kyūin ni kansuru eiseiteki chōsa.* Kōain Kachū renrakubu, 1941.

Sams, Crawford F. *Medic: The Mission of an American Military Doctor in Occupied Japan.* Armonk, NY: M. E. Sharpe, 1998.

Sano, I. "Chronic Alerting Amine Addiction in Japan." *Fortschritte der Neurologie-Psychiatrie* 24, no. 7 (1956): 391–94.

Sano Shin'ichi. *Ahen Ō: Manshū no yoru to kiri.* Tokyo: Shinchōsha, 2008.

Sasaki Tōichirō. "Nit-Shi kyōgaku no shin'i tettei ni tsutomerareta Morinaka Kiyoshi gakuchō." In *Manshū Ika Daigaku yonjū shūnen kinen shi,* edited by Hōjin Dōsōkai, 924–25. Tokyo: Hōjin Dōsōkai, 1952.

Satō Akihiko. *Kakuseizai no shakai shi: Doraggu, disuko-su, tōchi gijutsu.* Tokyo: Tōshindo, 2006.

———. "Methamphetamine Use in Japan after the Second World War: Transformation of Narratives." *Contemporary Drug Problems* 35 (2008): 717–40.

Satō Haruo. "Shimon." In *Satō Haruo,* edited by Sunaga Asahiko, 9–70. Tokyo: Kokusho kankōkai, 1992.

Satō Saburō. *Kindai Nit-Chū kōshōshi no kenkyū.* Tokyo: Yoshikawa Kōbunkan, 1984.

Satō Shin'ichirō. *Daikan'en no kaibō: Kan minzoku shakai jittai chōsa.* Tokyo: Hara shobō, 2002.

Schmid, Andre. *Korea between Empires, 1895–1919.* New York: Columbia University Press, 2002.

Schorske, Carl. *Fin-de-Siècle Vienna: Politics and Culture.* New York: Alfred A. Knopf, 1980.

Scott, James C. *Weapons of the Weak: Everyday Forms of Peasant Resistance.* New Haven, CT: Yale University Press, 1985.

———. *Seeing Like a State: How Certain Schemes to Improve the Human Condition Have Failed.* New Haven, CT: Yale University Press, 1998.

Senda Kakō. *Kōgun "ahen bōryaku."* Tokyo: Sekibunsha, 1980.

Senga Motofumi. *Ahen Ō ichidai: Chūgoku ahen shijō no teiō Satomi Hajime no shōgai.* Tokyo: Kōjinsha, 2007.

Seymour, Christopher. *Yakuza Diary: Doing Time in the Japanese Underworld.* New York: Atlantic Monthly Press, 1996.

Shao Dan. *Remote Homeland, Recovered Borderland: Manchus, Manchoukuo, and Manchuria 1907–1985.* Honolulu: University of Hawai'i Press, 2011.

Sherratt, Andrew. "Introduction: Peculiar Substances." In *Consuming Habits: Global and Historical Perspectives on How Cultures Define Drugs,* edited by Jordan Goodman, Paul E. Lovejoy, and Andrew Sherratt, 1–10. New York: Routledge, 2007.

Shimada Hiroshi. *Mantetsu no isan Dairen Byōin.* Nijū seiki Dairen kaigi, 2004.

Shintō kagaku kenkyūjo, ed. *Ahen oyobi ruiji "arukaroido" mansei chūdokushō no kōkateki chiryō to sono hōsaku.* Tokyo: Shintō kagaku kenkyūjo, 1936.

Shōji Sōichi. *Chin fujin.* Tokyo: Tsūbunkaku, 1940.

Shōji Taichi. *Bindama tobaso.* Tokyo: Pareo, 1997.

Shorter, Edward. *A History of Psychiatry.* New York: John Wiley & Sons, 1997.

Slack, Edward, Jr. *Opium, State and Society: China's Narco-Economy and the Guomindang, 1924–1937.* Honolulu: University of Hawai'i Press, 2001.

Smith, Henry D., II. "Tokyo as an Idea: An Exploration of Japanese Urban Thought until 1945." *Journal of Japanese Studies* 4, no. 1 (1978): 45–80.

Smith, Norman H. "Opiate Addiction and the Entanglements of Imperialism and Patriarchy in Manchukuo, 1932–1945." *Social History of Alcohol and Drugs* 20 (2005): 66–104.

———. *Intoxicating Manchuria: Alcohol, Opium, and Culture in China's Northeast.* Vancouver: University of British Columbia Press, 2012.

Snow, Edgar. *Far Eastern Front.* New York: Harrison Smith & Robert Haas, 1933.

Sōmu-chō tōkei-kyoku. *Nihon chōki tōkei sōkan.* Tokyo: Nihon tōkei kyōkai, 1987.

South Manchuria Railway Company. *Report on Progress in Manchuria.* Dairen: South Manchuria Railway Company, 1929.

———. *Third Report on Progress in Manchuria to 1932.* Dairen: South Manchuria Railway Company, 1932.

———. *Sixth Report on Progress in Manchuria*. Dairen: South Manchuria Railway Company, 1939.

Spence, Jonathan. "Opium Smoking in Ch'ing China." In *Conflict and Control in Late Imperial China*, edited by Frederic E. Wakeman Jr. and Carolyn Grant, 143–73. Berkeley: University of California Press, 1975.

Stephens, Robert P. *Germans on Drugs: The Complications of Modernization in Hamburg*. Ann Arbor: University of Michigan Press, 2007.

Su Zhiliang. *Zhongguo dupin shi*. Shanghai: Shanghai renmin chubanshe, 1997.

Suleski, Ronald. *Civil Government in Warlord China: Tradition, Modernization and Manchuria*. New York: Peter Lang, 2002.

Summers, William C. *The Great Manchurian Plague of 1910–1911: The Geopolitics of an Epidemic Disease*. New Haven, CT: Yale University Press, 2012.

Sunaga Asahiko. "Dekadan no dōwa." In *Satō Haruo*, edited by Sunaga Asahiko, 255–70. Tokyo: Kokusho kankōkai, 1992.

Szasz, Thomas. *Ceremonial Chemistry: The Ritual Persecution of Drugs, Addicts and Pushers*. New York: Syracuse University Press, 2003.

T'ien Chün. *Village in August*. Cleveland, OH: World Publishing, 1944.

Taiwan no ahen seido. Taihoku: Taiwan Sōtokufu keimu-kyoku, 1939.

Takaki Mamoru. *Tsuji Jun: "Ko" ni ikiru*. Tokyo: Taimatsusha, 1979.

Takekoshi, Yosaburō. *Japanese Rule in Formosa*. Translated by George Braithwaite. Taipei: SMC, 1907.

Takenaka Ken'ichi. *Dairen rekishi sanpo*. Tokyo: Kōseisha, 2008.

Takeuchi Chūji. *Ahen sensō to Eikoku no tai-Shi shinryaku*. Tokyo: Takeuchi Chūji, 1939.

Takeuchi Yoshimi and Hashikawa Bunsō. *Kindai Nihon to Chūgoku (shita)*. Tokyo: Asahi Shinbunsha, 1974.

Tamanoi, Mariko Asano. "Knowledge, Power, and Racial Classifications: The 'Japanese' in 'Manchuria.'" *Journal of Asian Studies* 59, no. 2 (2000): 248–76.

Tamura, Masayuki. "The Yakuza and Amphetamine Abuse in Japan." In *Drugs, Law and the State*, edited by Harold H. Traver and Mark S. Gaylord, 99–117. Hong Kong: Hong Kong University Press, 1992.

Tan Romi. *Ahen no Chūgokushi*. Tokyo: Shinchōsha, 2005.

Tanaka, Stefan. *Japan's Orient: Rendering Pasts into History*. Berkeley: University of California Press, 1993.

Tanaka Tadao. *Ahen mondai to Shina nōson keizai*. Tokyo: Tō-A kenkyūkai, 1933.

Tanaka Tsunejirō. *"Manshūkoku" ni okeru han-Man kō-Nichi undō no kenkyū*. Tokyo: Rokuin shobō, 1997.

Taniyama Tsuneki. *Manshū no fūzoku to densetsu min'yū*. Tokyo: Matsuyama bō, 1938.

Tarumi Chie. "An Author Listening to Voices from the Netherworld: Lü Heruo and the *Kuso* Realism Debate." In *Taiwan under Japanese Colonial Rule, 1895–1945: History, Culture, Memory*, edited by Liao Ping-Hui and David Der-wei Wang, 262–78. New York: Columbia University Press, 2006.

Tatetsu Seijun, Gotō Akio, and Fujiwara Takeshi. *Kakuseizai chūdoku*. Tokyo: Igaku shoin, 1956.

Tawara Yutaka. *Man-Mō fūzoku taikan*. Tokyo: Otani Tokunosuke, 1939.

Tazawa Shingo, ed. *Ahen shiryō*. Taihoku: Tazawa kagaku kōgyō kenkyūjo, 1932.

Tengoku, jigoku. DVD. Directed by Kurosawa Akira. Tokyo: Tōhō Company, 1963.

Terry, Charles E., and Mildred Pellens. *The Opium Problem*. New York: Bureau of Social Hygiene, 1928.

Terry, T. Philip. *Terry's Guide to the Japanese Empire*. Boston: Houghton Mifflin, 1930.

Thomas, Julia Adeney. *Reconfiguring Modernity: Concepts of Nature in Japanese Political Ideology*. Berkeley: University of California Press, 2002.

Thompson, Kenneth. *Moral Panics*. New York: Routledge, 1998.

Thornber, Karen Laura. *Empire of Texts in Motion: Chinese, Korean, and Taiwanese Transculturations of Japanese Literature*. Cambridge, MA: Harvard University Asia Center, 2009.

Tipton, Elise K. *The Japanese Police State: The Tokkō in Interwar Japan*. Honolulu: University of Hawai'i Press, 1990.

Tominaga Toshiharu and Nurita Nobuyuki. "Nihon no Chūgoku senryaku ni okeru ahen seisaku." In *Chūgoku no daichi wa wasurenai: Shinryaku, katararenakatta sensō*, edited by Mori Masataka, 201–18. Tokyo: Shakai hyōronsha, 1995.

Tomita Shōji. "Yamato Hoteru to teikoku hoteru." In *Mantetsu to wa nandatta no ka*, edited by Yoshida Yōji and Fujiwara Yoshio, 206–7. Tokyo: Fujiwara shoten, 2006.

Totani, Yuma. *The Tokyo Trials: The Pursuit of Justice in the Wake of World War II*. Cambridge, MA: Harvard University Asia Center, 2008.

Tracy, Sarah W., and Caroline Jean Acker. "Psychoactive Drugs: An American Way of Life." In *Altering American Consciousness: The History of Alcohol and Drug Use in the United States, 1800–2000*, edited by Sarah W. Tracy and Caroline Jean Acker, 1–30. Amherst: University of Massachusetts Press, 2004.

Trentman, Frank. "The Modern Genealogy of the Consumer: Meanings, Identities and Political Synapses." In *Consuming Cultures, Global Perspectives: Historical Trajectories, Transnational Exchanges*, edited by John Brewer and Frank Trentmann, 19–69. New York: Berg, 2006.

Trocki, Carl. *Opium, Empire and the Global Political Economy: A Study of the Asian Opium Trade, 1750–1950.* New York: Routledge, 1999.

Tsai, Hui-yu Caroline. *Taiwan in Japan's Empire-Building: An Institutional Approach to Colonial Engineering.* New York: Routledge, 2009.

Tsukase Susumu. *Manshūkoku 'minzoku kyōwa' no jisshō.* Tokyo: Yoshikawa Kōbunkan, 1998.

———. *Manshū no Nihonjin.* Tokyo: Yoshikawa Kōbunkan, 2004.

Tsuneishi, Ken'ichi. "Unit 731 and the Human Skulls Discovered in 1989: Physicians Carrying out Organized Crimes." In *Dark Medicine: Rationalizing Unethical Medical Research,* edited by William La Fleur, Gernot Bihme, and Sususmu Shimazono, 73–84. Bloomington: Indiana University Press, 2007.

Tsurumi, M. *Public Hygiene in Manchuria and Mongolia.* Dairen: *Manshū Nichinichi Shinbun,* n.d.

Tsurumi Yūsuke. *Gotō Shinpei den.* Tokyo: Taiheiyō kyōkai shuppanbu, 1943.

Uchiyama Masao. "Minkoku shoki no Santō kara no tōhoku imin." In *Nihon no Seitō senryō to Santō no shakai keizai,* edited by Honjō Hisako, 325–46. Tokyo: Tōyō Bunko, 2006.

Uga Jirō. *Taiwan ahen shi.* Taihoku: Taiwan Sōtokufu senbai-kyoku, 1926.

United States Philippine Commission Opium Investigation Committee. *Use of Opium and Traffic Therein: Message from the President of the United States, Transmitting the Report of the Committee Appointed by the Philippine Commission to Investigate the Use of Opium and the Traffic Therein, and the Rules, Ordinances, and Laws Regulating Such Use and Traffic in Japan, Formosa, Shanghai, Hongkong, Saigon, Singapore, Burma, Java, and the Philippine Islands, and Inclosing a Letter from the Secretary of War Submitting the Report for Transmission.* Washington, DC: Government Printing Office, 1906.

Ushikubo Ainoshin. *Ahen ka: Eikoku Tōyō shinryaku shi.* Tokyo: Akatsuki shoin, 1933.

———. *Mayaku dokuhon: Ahen, moruhine, hiropon no seitai.* Tokyo: Rokushinsha, 1955.

Utena, H., T. Ezoe, N. Katō, and H. Hada. "Effects of Chronic Administration of Methamphetamine in Enzymic Patterns in Brain Tissue." *Journal of Neurochemistry* 4, no. 2 (1959): 161–69.

Vespa, Amleto. *Secret Agent of Japan.* Boston: Little, Brown, 1938.

Wagatsuma, Hiroshi, and George A. De Vos. *Heritage of Endurance: Family Patterns and Delinquency Formation in Urban Japan.* Berkeley: University of California Press, 1984.

Wakeman, Frederic E., Jr. *Policing Shanghai: 1927–1937.* Berkeley: University of California Press, 1995.

Walker, William O., III. *Opium and Foreign Policy: The Anglo-American Search for Order in Asia, 1912–1954*. Chapel Hill: University of North Carolina Press, 1991.

Wan shi liu fang. Directed by Bu Wancang. Shanghai: Tōhō and China United, 1943.

Wang Jinxiang. *Zhongguo jindu jianshi*. Beijing: Xuexi chubanshe, 1996.

Wang, Tay-Sheng. *Legal Reform in Taiwan under Japanese Colonial Rule, 1895–1945: The Reception of Western Law*. Seattle: University of Washington Press, 2000.

Washitani Hana. "The Opium War and the Cinema Wars: A Hollywood in the Greater East Asian Co-Prosperity Sphere." *Inter-Asia Cultural Studies* 4, no. 1 (2003): 63–76.

Watsuji Tetsurō. *Gendai dōtoku no jittai: Nihon ni okeru sengo no ijō*. Tokyo: Koshutsu shobō, 1954.

Watt, Lori. *When Empire Comes Home: Repatriation and Reintegration in Postwar Japan*. Cambridge, MA: Harvard University Asia Center, 2009.

Weber, Max. *The Theory of Social and Economic Organization*. Translated by A. M. Henderson and Talcott Parsons. New York: Oxford University Press, 1947.

Weiner, Michael A. *The Origins of the Korean Community in Japan, 1900–1923*. Atlantic Highlands, NJ: Humanities Press International, 1989.

———. "The Invention of Identity: 'Self' and 'Other' in Pre-War Japan." In *Japan's Minorities: The Illusion of Homogeneity*, edited by Michael Weiner, 1–16. New York: Routledge, 1997.

Weisheit, Ralph, and William L. White. *Methamphetamine: Its History, Pharmacology, and Treatment*. Center City, MN: Hazelden, 2009.

Whyte, Susan Reynolds, Sjaak van der Geest, and Anita Hardon. *Social Lives of Medicines*. New York: Cambridge University Press, 2002.

Wildes, Harry Emerson. *Typhoon in Tokyo: The Occupation and Its Aftermath*. New York: Macmillan, 1954.

Wong, J. Y. *Deadly Dreams: Opium, Imperialism, and the Arrow War (1856–1860)*. New York: Cambridge University Press, 1998.

Xu Jielin. "Gotō Shinpei to sono ahen mōryaku." *Shokuminchi bunka kenkyū* 4 (2005): 47–53.

Yakubutsu ran'yō taisaku shinpo honbu, ed. *Shiroi koma no kyōfu: Kakuseizai chūdokusha nado no koe*. Tokyo: Yakubutsu ran'yō taisaku shinpo honbu, 1977.

Yamada Gōichi. "Taiwan senbai shi josetsu: Mizuno Jun 'Taiwan ahen shobun' to Gotō Shinpei 'Taiwanjima ahen seido ni kansuru iken.'" *Shakai kagaku tōkyū* 38, no. 4 (1992): 31–68.

———. *O-rudo Shanhai no ahen jijō*. Tokyo: Aki shobō, 1995.

———. "Taiwan senbai sei no tenkai katei." *Shakai kagaku tōkyū* 44, no. 1 (1998): 1–37.

———. *Manshūkoku no ahen senbai: Waga Man-Mō no tokushu ken'eki ron*. Tokyo: Kyūko shoin, 2002.

Yamaguchi Takeshi. "Hō to iu kannen kara mita Man'ei no tokuisei to Amakasu Masahiko." In *Manshū to wa nandatta no ka,* edited by Nakami Tatsuo, 188–99. Tokyo: Iwanami shoten, 2004.

Yamaguchi Yoshiko and Fujiwara Sakuya. *Ri Kōran: Watashi no hansei*. Tokyo: Shinchōsha, 1990.

Yamamuro Shin'ichi. *Manchuria under Japanese Domination*. Translated by Joshua A. Fogel. Philadelphia: University of Pennsylvania Press, 2006.

Yamawaki Teijirō. *Kinsei Nihon no iyaku bunka*. Tokyo: Heibōsha, 1995.

Yanagisawa Asobu. *Nihonjin no shokuminchi keiken: Dairen Nihonjin shōkōgyōsha no rekishi*. Tokyo: Aoki shoten, 1999.

———. "Dairen kō no rōdō." In *Mantetsu rōdō shi no kenkyū,* edited by Matsumura Takao, Jie Xueshi, and Eda Kenji, 249–84. Tokyo: Nihon keizai hyōronsha, 2002.

Yano Jin'ichi. *Ahen sensō to Honkon*. Kyoto: Kōbundō shobō, 1939.

Yao Jin-to. "The Japanese Colonial State and Its Form of Knowledge in Taiwan." In *Taiwan under Japanese Colonial Rule 1895–1945: History, Culture, and Memory,* edited by Liao Ping-Hui and David Der-Wei Wang, 37–61. New York: Columbia University Press, 2006.

Yao Weiyuan. *Yapian zhanzheng shi shikao*. Guiyang: Wentong shuju, 1942.

Yokomitsu Riichi. *"Love" and Other Stories of Yokomitsu Riichi*. Translated by Dennis Keene. Tokyo: University of Tokyo Press, 1974.

———. *Yokomitsu Riichi zenshū dai ni ken*. Tokyo: Kawade shobō shinsha, 1981.

———. *Shanghai*. Translated by Dennis Washburn. Ann Arbor: University of Michigan Press, 2001.

Yosano Akiko. *Travels in Manchuria and Mongolia: A Feminist Poet Encounters Prewar China*. Translated by Joshua A. Fogel. New York: Columbia University Press, 2001.

Young, C. Walter. "Chinese Colonization and the Development of Manchuria." In *Problems of the Pacific: Proceedings of the Third Conference of the Institute of Pacific Relations,* edited by J. B. Condliffe, 423–65. Chicago: University of Chicago Press, 1930.

———. *Korean Problems in Manchuria as Factors in the Sino-Japanese Dispute: An Analytical and Interpretive Study*. Supplementary Documents to the Report of the Commission of Enquiry, 1933.

Young, John. *The Research Activities of the South Manchuria Railway, 1907–1945: A History and Bibliography*. New York: Columbia University East Asian Institute, 1966.

Young, Louise. *Japan's Total Empire: Manchuria and the Culture of Wartime Imperialism*. Berkeley: University of California Press, 1998.

Zhai Xin. *Tō-A Dōbunkai to Chūgoku: Kindai Nihon ni okeru taigai rinen to sono jissen.* Tokyo: Keiō Daigaku shuppankai, 2001.

Zheng, Yangwen. *The Social Life of Opium in China.* New York: Cambridge University Press, 2005.

Zhong Weimin. *Chaye yu yapian: Shijiu shiji jingji quanqiuhua zhong de Zhongguo.* Beijing: Sanlian shudian, 2010.

Zhou Jue. "'Manzhouguo' he yapian lingbaisuo." In *Yapian zhi jinxi,* edited by Tao Kangde, 9–13. Shanghai: Yuzhou feng she chuban, 1937.

Zhou Yongming. *Anti-Drug Crusades in Twentieth-Century China: Nationalism, History, and State-Building.* Lanham, MD: Rowman & Littlefield, 1999.

INDEX

Page numbers in italics refer to figures.